The Sybase IQ Survival Guide
First Edition
By Trevor Moore

Foreword

About the Author

Trevor Moore is an independent IT Consultant with 15 years industry experience (10 years working on IQ). He has also worked on Oracle, MS SQL Server, Sybase ASE and MySQL. He has written IQ based applications in Java, .NET, Perl and numerous Unix scripting languages and has also implemented IQ with Business Objects, Crystal Reports, Tibco Business Works and Sybase replication technologies connecting to SQL Server and Sybase ASE.

Having worked initially for Lehman Brothers for 18 years, Trevor has since worked as an independent Sybase IQ consultant for Sybase Inc, a technical lead on data warehousing projects for the UK government and as a database consultant/developer for numerous financial institutions.

From the Author

This book is a completely independent publication and has no affiliation with Sybase Inc .

Over the years I have worked with some great guys at Sybase, Dave Rittenhouse, Peter Stone, Darrell Gosden and Andrew Morris are a few names to mention. Another name worth mentioning is Andrew Harding who is the most knowledgeable IQ DBA I've worked with!

Thanks to my clients over the years for allowing me the opportunity to work on IQ and learn more and more on a daily basis about the quirks of this product.

Further Reading

There are thousands of pages of documentation on the Sybase website (commonly know as sybooks). There are also some good discussion forums at both Sybase and on the Google group's website. I would also suggest looking at the ASA documentation to see what you can do with the catalog store database component of IQ.

About the Book

We have attempted to produce a book that is both short enough that you can find what you need, but have enough content to cover 90% of IQ questions and issues. The problem with the is that there are tens of thousands of pages of documents out there, so hopefully this condensed survival guide will help you resolve issues quickly. Rather than concentrating on a specific version of IQ we have tried to encompass all versions and highlight where there may be differences between release versions. Depending on the demand for this book we may look at releasing specific versions in the future. This is not a "Learn SQL"type book and a basic knowledge of SQL is expected, e.g. you know a **SELECT**, **INSERT**, **DELETE** statements and are familiar with **RDBMs** concepts.

If you need further info or you have any comments ont he content then please email us at the address below stating the subject and/or page number.

contact@tdmcomputing.co.uk

The book uses several font types and box lines to determine what the subject is, in most cases these are self explanatory but below is a key for the diagrams anyway:-

```
THIS IS SQL
```

```
THIS IS ANOTHER LANGUAGE OR COMMAND PROMPT
```

```
THIS IS OTHER OUTPUT OR REMARKS
```

I have tested ALL the code in this book and it worked, however there may be typos that have appeared in translation or a newer release version of IQ which changed the behaviour etc so test everything yourself before using it in a production environment.

All in all, I believe this is a very useful book and you could certainly use it to pass the certification exam.

Apart from that everything else should be self explanatory.

Good Luck,
Trevor Moore
TDM Computing Ltd

Legal Disclaimer and Copyright

ISBN

This book has the following ISBN.

Contents

Foreword _____ **5**
    About the Author _____ 5
    From the Author _____ 5
    Further Reading _____ 5
    About the Book _____ 6
    Legal Disclaimer and Copyright_____ 7
    ISBN _____ 7

Contents _____ **9**

Introduction _____ **15**
    What's a column based database? _____ 16
    Why Sybase IQ? _____ 16
    Sybase IQ - not just one database but two!! _____ 17
    What's the downside?_____ 18
    T-SQL verses Watcom SQL_____ 18

*Creating, Running and Stopping a Database/Server*_____ **19**
    Database Storage_____ 20
    DB Spaces_____ 20
    IQ DBSpaces_____ 22
    Catalog Store DBSpaces_____ 23
    Dropping a DBSpace _____ 23
    Alter a DBSpace _____ 23
    Cache changes for version 15 and above _____ 27
    Creating a Database _____ 28
    Create a database using command_____ 28
    Create a database using Sybase Central _____ 29
    Starting a Server/Database _____ 29
    Stopping a Server/Database _____ 40

*Security and User Management*_____ **45**
    Security Tools and Considerations _____ 46
    Login Policies _____ 46
    Users and Groups _____ 49
    Changing a users assigned login policy_____ 54

Introduction

Welcome to the to the Sybase IQ survival guide!

Using this guide you will gain all the technical knowledge you require to administer, develop and performance tune Sybase IQ Databases.

This book is written for database administrators, developers and technical architects looking to gain an in depth knowledge of Sybase IQ. So whether you are upgrading from another database product or are building a brand new Greenfield data warehouse this is the book for you.

What's a column based database?

Sybase IQ is a column based database product marketed and sold by Sybase Inc across the globe. Its primary function is to hold large amounts of data in a low cost and high availability environment. Currently it can be deployed on Windows, Unix and Linux Operating Systems.
As a column-oriented DBMS, Sybase IQ stores data that the user sees as tables in columns of data rather than as rows of data. This has a number of advantages; if a search is being done for items matching a particular value in a column of data, only the storage objects corresponding to that data column within the table need to be accessed. Another advantage is that when indexed correctly a value that would have to be stored once in each row of data in a traditional database is stored only once and a bitwise index is used to access the data. Take Fig 1.1 for example:-

Fig 1.1

Shapes
Circle
Square
Circle
Triangle
Circle
Circle
Square
Circle

Shapes		
Circle	Square	Triangle
1	0	0
0	1	0
1	0	0
0	0	1
1	0	0
1	0	0
0	1	0
1	0	0

As per Fig 1.1 you can see that each value is only stored once using a bitmap to store the values. This means that data that is repeated many times can be stored in an efficient manner without the need to denormalise. The obvious benefits of this are that large data warehouses can store normalised data in fact tables allowing for fast data retrieval.
Because the column based approach means that as many columns are comprised of records of the same type and size, Sybase IQ can compress data on the fly with both speed and efficiency.

Why Sybase IQ?

Like any large software product there are competitors. Two that come to mind are Teradata and Vertica, but as at the time of writing neither offers the portability or range of features available for Sybase IQ.
Now you may also be thinking why not just use Oracle, SQL server or Sybase ASE to store my data. The main two reasons are cost and efficiency.
Cost, because Sybase IQ compresses data it uses less disk space, general consensus puts this at between 6-10 times less disk space is required.
Efficiency, because of the column based approach only the columns used in queries are searched. Consider our shapes example in Fig 1.2

Fig 1.2

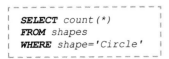

```
SELECT count(*)
FROM shapes
WHERE shape='Circle'
```

In a traditional RDBMS every row would need to search every row of the table (I'm excluding additional indexes for this example). Where as Sybase IQ can just search the values and then use the bit map to sum the count of the rows. This makes Sybase IQ extremely quick at searching and data retrieval on large amounts of data.

If the shapes table has 5 columns and ten rows a traditional database will have to perform a table scan that equals at least 50 I/O operations (it has to read whole pages of data) whereas Sybase IQ will only have to perform 10 at most (column scan).

Fig 1.3

Search in Traditional RDMS's

Search in Sybase IQ

The above example being a small table shows only a fraction of the performance gains column based data structures can give. Imagine a table of 255 columns wide and 1 million rows long, that is a minimum 255 Million I/O operations on a traditional database and a maximum of 1 million on Sybase IQ.

In the chapter on Indexing you will see how LF and HG indexes utilise the column based approach to increase query times.

Sybase IQ - not just one database but two!!

Sybase IQ is in fact two databases in one. The main part is of course a column based IQ database, but in order for IQ to handle connections and store metadata etc the IQ prodcust also encompasees a Sybase ASA database often referred to as the **SYSTEM** or **CATALOG** store. Throughout this book we will make references to the ASA/Catalog store for more documentation on ASA I suggest further reading of a good ASA book! But this book does go into some detail on the ASA features you will need to know to interact with Sybase IQ.

What's the downside?

As the data is stored in columns small multiple updates and deletes to data can be less efficient than on traditional RDBM's. That said many OLTP systems run batches on IQ with no issues.

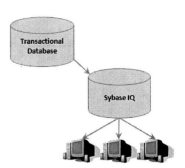

The recommended use is to have a transactional database running the batch updates and then data is transferred over the Sybase IQ for reporting.

In many cases there are multiple transactional databases each feeding data to Sybase IQ. An example of this is where a human resources system sends a list of sales people, an accounting system sends a list of sales figures and a customer relationship system sends customer details. This data is then consolidated and held in Sybase IQ for reporting.

T-SQL verses Watcom SQL

Sybase IQ uses a Sybase Adaptive Server Anywhere (ASA) database that is used internally to store database metadata, handle connections, security, CIS and most importantly query parsing. As such IQ can accept commands in either T-SQL or Watcom SQL (But not a combination of both in the same procedure).

All Sybase IQ system procedures are written in Watcom SQL, The examples in this book are mostly written in T-SQL, this is for the following reasons:-

- Developers of MS SQL Server and Sybase ASE are familiar with the language.

- It makes porting code from these others servers easier

- Most jobs on the market are for T-SQL developers, so I'd rather show examples in a way that will aid you in the real world.

Because T-SQL is a superset of ANSI standard SQL you may use ANSI syntax for your procedures and queries plus any additional Sybase T-SQL extensions that are compatible with Sybase ASA. Typically Sybase recommend using Watcom SQL for Sybase IQ and Sybase ASA as this was the native language of the original products (Before Sybase bought the products they were owned and developed by Watcom). In some cases (see the chapter on SQL) we will use Watcom SQL as some functionality only works in Watcom (Such as declaring waits for table locks).

Creating, Running and Stopping a Database/Server

In order to create a database in IQ you need first to log into another IQ database. At a first glance this may seem like a circular dependency where you cannot set up a database because you don't have a database to log into to do it. Luckily Sybase IQ comes with a "Utility" database that you can use to set up your database. You will also learn about DBSpaces in this section and how you can use logical names to reference them, Also Sybase IQ does not have tempdb, but it does make use of temporary DBSpace that for most purposes performs the same function.

We will look at the files that are automatically created when a new database is created and how to use some of these files to investigate issues. This chapter gives an overview of the transaction and message logs and how they are used.

Once the database creation section is complete we will look into database options and how they affect security, usage and performance.

Database Storage

Before you create your database there are some questions you need to ask.

- What architecture will I be running on, one host machine or many?
- Will you be running a single IQ server or multiple servers?
- Do I have RAW devices or will I use local storage?
- What RAID level is my storage?
- How is my storage configured?

All these questions (and probably some more) will determine the type of devices you use to set up your database. If you use RAW partitions for your data devices you will get a performance benefit, but you have the overhead of higher maintenance (but on Unix/Linux you will be able to use symbolic links). If you use the O/S file system you have the advantage of the devices being easier to manage, but the file system will not understand Sybase IQ data pages. Therefore there will be an overhead when Sybase IQ reads the data, as it has to be buffered into memory to be converted into a Sybase readable format.

From experience I have always found that raw devices on a Unix/Linux O/S offer a greater level of flexibility for both day to day usage and disaster recovery. As a DBFile (DBFiles in IQ are sometimes referred to as DBSpaces although in reality a DBSpace can hold many DBFiles) is just a logical name that points to a raw partition, you can point that logical name to a symbolic link that in turn points to storage on your SAN. The storage can then be replicated (via SRDF for example) and when there is a failure you can point the symbolic link to the replicated disk. Consideration must be given to not only the type of storage but how it is configured e.g. is it concatenated? What is the RAID level requirement? etc.

In general some design tips are:-

- Create many DBFiles (at least 2 per host CPU)
- Try to create one temporary DBSpace for every main DBSpace.
- Try to make the temporary DBSpaces at least 20% of the size of the main DBSpaces. (Unless you are building a multiplex read server).
- Try to add your space before you start loading data

If you are migrating from SQL server or Sybase ASE to Sybase IQ you are probably trying to analyse your size requirements, in the past I have seen IQ databases compressing the data to as much as 7 times compression, but on average when all indexes have been built this figure is closer to 20% (or 5 times compression).

DB Spaces

When you create your database, IQ is going to need somewhere to store metadata, you presumably will need to store application data and you will need some temporary space for IQ to process your requests. The catalog store will need somewhere to store system data and also some temporary space to process the catalog store data and finally you will want a database log. The solution in IQ is to use DBFiles to store the data and DBSpaces to logically split the DBFiles into there functional use.

In the world of IQ people often use the terms DBSpace and DBFile interchangeably (even by

Sybase themselves). To make a distinction you can think of DBSpaces as logical database containers that store pointers to physical file (DBFile) locations. DBFiles are used to store all data that is used within an IQ server and DBSpaces are used to segregate which type of data is held. The reason the names DBSpace and DBFile are used interchangeably is that prior to version IQ 15.x user DBSpaces could only have one DBFile. (I still prefer this approach for readability of the system).

There are differences in not only the types of DBSpaces that are used between version 15 and previous versions, but also in the way they are used. For example DBSpaces in 15 and above can have many DBFiles and cannot be set to **RELOCATE** mode (Seethe tips chapter for information on relocating DBSpace data to another DBSpace).

The types of DBSpace available in version 15.x are:-

Type	Name/Type of DBSpace	Usage	DBSpaces allowed	DBFiles allowed in each DBSpace
IQ	IQ_SYSTEM_MAIN	This DBSpace is used to point to the files used to store IQ database structures, rollbacks, check pointed transactions and database metadata relating to size. Users may store objects here but it is recommended that you create a separate user DBSpace for this purpose.	One or more	One or more
IQ	IQ_SYSTEM_TEMP	This DBSpace holds the files that are used by IQ to store temporary date (think of it being like tempdb in SQL Server or ASE).	One	One or more
IQ	IQ_SYSTEM_MSG	This DBSpace holds one DBFile, the file being the IQ message log.	One	One (if using multiplex then one per node)
ASA	The SYSTEM DBSpace	This DBSpace holds the file used to store ASA System (catalog) tables, views, stored procedures and function definitions. It is also used to store any tables that are created IN SYSTEM (in the catalog store)	One or more	One
ASA	Other catalog DBSpaces	SQL Anywhere tables	One or more	One

As you can see there are two main types of DBSpace, IQ or ASA. IQ DBSpaces are configurable can be **ONLINE** or **OFFLINE**, can be placed into different modes and allow for striping of data.

You can define which DBSpaces tables and indexes reside in, move them between different DBSpaces and even drop entire DBSpaces. From an administration perspective most work is carried out on user DBSpaces. User DBSpaces are added using the CREATE DBSPACE command as in the example in Fig 2.0, or you may opt to add the DBSpaces using Sybase Central. You may have up to 2,047 DBSpaces in IQ (If you are licensed to use that many).

Fig 2.0

```
CREATE DBSPACE user_DBSpace USING FILE user_DBFile
'user_DBSpaceSTRIPESIZEKB <size in KB>1' SIZE 10000
```

To view the current DBSpaces in a database you can execute the **SP_IQSTATUS** system procedure.

IQ DBSpaces

The syntax of the **CREATE DBSPACE** statement for creating DBSpaces for IQ (not for the ASA/Catalog store) is given in Fig 2.1

Fig 2.1

```
CREATE DBSPACE <DBSpace
USING <single file path>/ FILE <logical file name>  <single file path>
SIZE <file size> KB/MB/GB/TB  RESERVE
STRIPING ON/OFF
```

You can use this syntax to specify the name of the DBSpaces, and the DBFiles that are used in the DBSpaces to store data, the size of the files and whether data should be striped across the files. If you are not familiar with striping it basically means that if you for example had four DBFiles, then data will be distributed across all files in the size specified in the **STRIPSIZEKB** clause. The reason for doing this is that IQ allocates one CPU core for each DBFile it is accessing, meaning that each core can retrieve smaller amounts of data quicker rather than one core retrieving a large amount. If you do not specify the striping clause then IQ uses the value of the database option **DEFAULT_DISK_STRIPING** to determine what value to use (the default value for this option is ON)
Using the syntax given in Fig 2.1 we can look at an example.

If for example you wanted to create a DBSpace that had three DBFiles you could do this using the syntax from the example in Fig 2.2. (Note that if you do not specify a size type the default is MB)

Fig 2.2

```
CREATE DBSPACE user_space_1 USING
FILE
SIZE 20000 GB RESERVE
FILE
SIZE 50000 GB RESERVE
FILE
SIZE 25000 RESERVE
```

The example in Fig 2.2 is good for showing the syntax, but I would recommend trying to keep your DBFiles the same size and switching stripping ON. Another thing to remember when defining DBSpaces is that although DBSpace and DBFile names are case insensitive. If the database is **CASE RESPECT** then physical file paths have the case sensitivity of the operating system, but they are case insensitive if the database is **CASE IGNORE**. Also worth noting is that when adding, altering or deleting DBSpaces that an automatic **COMMIT** and **CHECKPOINT** are issued.

If you specify a raw device for a new DBSpace, IQ will obtain the raw device file size and allocate the whole device for use as an IQ store. When using a file device IQ is not too good at calculating the file size so you should specify the file size in the **CREATE DBSPACE** statement.

In order to make sure that user objects are automatically placed into this DBSpace you should set the database option **DEFAULT_DBSPACE** to the user space, **GRANT** the users access to the DBSpace by using a **GRANT CREATE** and as a final step **REVOKE** them access from the **IQ_SYSTEM_MAIN** DBSpaces, as in Fig 2.3

Fig 2.3

```
SET OPTION PUBLIC.DEFAULT_DBSPACE = 'user_DBSpace'
GRANT CREATE ON user_DBSpace TO PUBLIC
REVOKE CREATE ON IQ_SYSTEM_MAIN FROM PUBLIC
```

Catalog Store DBSpaces

Now if you want to create a DBSpaces on the ASA/catalog store then you would use the syntax given below in Fig 2.4

Fig 2.4

```
CREATE DBSPACE <DBSpaces name> AS
<file path>
CATALOG STORE
```

Dropping a DBSpace

You can drop a DBSpaces by issuing a **DROP DBSPACE** Statement. However there are some things to be aware of before you drop a DBSpace:-

- It must not contain any data i.e. it must me empty
- You can only drop user DBSpaces (not SYSTEM, IQ_SYSTEM_MAIN, IQ_SYSTEM_TEMP or IQ_SYSTEM_MSG)

To clear out a DBSpace you need to drop or relocate all objects within the space (see the tips chapter). If your tables are partitioned you can move partitions to different DBSpaces by using an ALTER TABLE statement as in the example in Fig 2.5

You can find out which DBSpace tables and indexes are located in by executing **SP_IQINDEXINFO**, **SP_IQSPACEINFO** and **SP_IQDBSPACEINFO**, all of which will show you the number of blocks used by objects in each DBSpace.

To find out whether you can drop a particular DBSpace first execute **SP_IQDBSPACE** and look at at the Block Types column. A DBSpace can be dropped if it contains only block types 'H,' 'F,' 'R', 'B,' 'X,' and 'C.' If it shows a Block type A,O or M then it cannot be dropped as 'A' mean active, O means an old version of the object is still in use and M is for multiplex objects!

Alter a DBSpace

To alter a DBSpace you need to execute the **ALTER DBSPACE** statement, the syntax of which is given below in Fig 2.5

Fig 2.5

```
ALTER DBSPACE <DBSpace name>
ADD      FILE <logical file name> 'file-path'
         SIZE                KB/MB/GB/TB
         RESERVE <reserve size> KB/MB/GB/TB
         [,FILE <logical file name> 'file-path'
         SIZE <                KB/MB/GB/TB
         RESERVE <reserve size> KB/MB/GB/TB

or
   READONLY/READWRITE
or
   ONLINE/OFFLINE
or
   STRIPING
   STRIPESIZEKB <size in KB>
or
   DROP FILE <logical file name> [, FILE <logical file name>, etc]
or
   ALTER FILE file-name
         READONLY/READWRITE
         SIZE <file size> KB/MB/GB/TB/PAGES
         ADD <file size>  KB/MB/GB/TB/PAGES
         RENAME PATH  <New file path>
or
RENAME TO <new DBSpace name>
```

By going through each of the alteration options we can give examples on how changes are achieved.

Adding files to a DBSpace

To add a file we use the syntax as in the example in Fig 2.6 below, this example adds 3 new DBFiles of 6GB to the DBSpace UserDBSpace1

Fig 2.6

```
ALTER DBSPACE UserDBSpace1
ADD
FILE UserFile2 '/data/file2' SIZE 6GB,
FILE UserFile3 '/data/file3' SIZE 6GB,
FILE UserFile4 '/data/file4' SIZE 6GB
```

As catalog DBSpaces can only have 1 file you cannot add files to them, also if you add files to a DBSpace defined as **READONLY** then the new file remains read-only until the DBSpace is altered to be **READWRITE**.

Dropping Files from a DBSpace

To drop a DBFile from a DBSpace we use the DROP FILE clause as in Fig 2.6, however if the DBSPACE contains only one file you must use the DROP DBSPACE statement instead. The example below drops the files we added in Fig 2.6, but before dropping files they MUST be empty.

Fig 2.7

```
ALTER DBSPACE UserDBSpace1
DROP
FILE UserFile2,
FILE UserFile3,
FILE UserFile4
```

Renaming DBSpaces

To rename a DBSpace we can use the syntax given in example Fig 2.8, you must ensure that the name is unique on the database and not one of the system names e.g. IQ_SYSTEM_MAIN.

Fig 2.8

```
ALTER DBSPACE UserDBSpace1
RENAME TO UserDBSpace100
```

Renaming File Paths

There two ways to rename a file path, one renames a file in a DBSpace that has only one file, the other is used to rename the pathname of a DBSpaces that have one or more files. When renaming a path you are only changing the pointer in the DBSpace to point at a new location, no changes are made to the physical file. Before renaming a file path the DBSpace must be offline and the new path will not be used until the database is restarted and the DBSpace is brought back online.

To rename a file pathname in a DBSpace that has only one file you may use the syntax given in Fig 2.9 or 2.10. To rename a file path in a DBSpaces with more than one file you must use the syntax in Fig 2.10.

Fig 2.9

```
ALTER DBSPACE UserDBSpace2
RENAME '/data/file22'
```

Fig 2.10

```
ALTER DBSPACE UserDBSpace2
ALTER FILE userFile2
RENAME PATH '/data/file22'
```

You cannot rename the path of a file in *IQ_SYSTEM_MAIN*, because if the new path were not accessible, the database would not be able to start up. To rename the path of a file in *IQ_SYSTEM_MAIN*, you should change the file to be read-only then empty the file then drop the file, and then finally add the file again with the new file path name.

Change DBSpaces to READONLY or READWRITE

When a DBSpace is in **READONLY** mode it does not allow any DML operations on any object held within the DBSpace, likewise in **READWRITE** mode a DBSpace allows DML operations. This option can only be used for DBSpaces in the IQ Main Store (Not ASA/Catalog Spaces, IQ Temp Spaces or the IQ Message Log Space). When the mode is changed to **READONLY**, IQ will immediately relocate all of the internal database structures on the DBSpace to one of the DBSpaces in

READWRITE mode.
Altering a DBSpace to read-only does not alter the status of is DBFiles to read-only, but does make the file(s) read-only at the O/S level. This means the DBFile's status in IQ remains the same, but data in the file cannot be modified.

To change the mode simply execute a statement as in the syntax in Fig 2.11 and 2.12

Fig 2.11
```
ALTER DBSPACE UserDBSpace1
READONLY
```

Fig 2.12
```
ALTER DBSPACE UserDBSpace1
READWRITE
```

Change DBSpaces to ONLINE or OFFLINE

If a DBSpace is offline then it cannot be used (even for reads). A DBSpace can only be put **OFFLINE** if it is already in **READONLY** mode and is in the IQ Main Store.

To change a DBSpace to **OFFLINE** or **ONLINE** you should execute a statement as in the examples Fig 2.13 and Fig 2.14

Fig 2.13
```
ALTER DBSPACE UserDBSpace1
ONLINE
```

Fig 2.14
```
ALTER DBSPACE UserDBSpace1
OFFLINE
```

Change the Striping of a DBSpace

To change the striping option of a DBSpace you may use the syntax from example Fig 2.15. The example below switches striping on and specifies the stripe size to use.

Fig 2.15
```
ALTER DBSPACE UserDBSpace1
STRIPING ON
STRIPSIZEKB 500
```

Change DBFiles to READONLY or READWRITE

You may change individual files within a DBSpace to **READONLY** or **READWRITE** modes. Only files in the IQ main store may be made **READONLY** and only files in the IQ main or temporary store can be specified as **READWRITE**.
A file is read-only when either the file status is read-only or the DBSpace in which the file resides status is read-only.

Fig 2.16

```
ALTER DBSPACE UserDBSpace1
ALTER FILE userFile2
READONLY
```

Fig 2.17

```
ALTER DBSPACE UserDBSpace1
ALTER FILE userFile2
READWRITE
```

Change a DBFiles size

You may increase a files size only if there is sufficient space within the DBSpace (including reserved space) and you can only decrease it if the portion to be truncated is empty. You may specify the change in KB/MB/GB or TB.

Fig 2.18

```
ALTER DBSPACE UserDBSpace1
ALTER FILE userFile2
SIZE 2 GB
```

Add space to a DBFile

You may add space to a DBFile only if there is sufficient space in the free list and if there is sufficient reserved space. You may specify the change in KB/MB/GB/TB or Pages. (If you don't specify the type it will default to pages).

Fig 2.19

```
ALTER DBSPACE UserDBSpace1
ALTER FILE userFile2
ADD 25 Pages
```

Rename a DBFiles logical name

This option will rename the logical name of a DBFile. Each DBFiles logical name must be unique in the database.

Fig 2.20

```
ALTER DBSPACE UserDBSpace1
ALTER FILE userFile2
RENAME TO userFile99
```

Cache changes for version 15 and above

Caching is important and you should be ware that if you are using Sybase 15 then the two database options **MAIN_CACHE_MEMORY_MB** and **TEMP_CACHE_MEMORY_MB** have been removed. These two options are only available as server level options in versions 15 and above and any changes to them require the database to be restarted in order for them to take effect. So instead of Fig 2.21 use Fig 2.22

Fig 2.21

```
SET OPTION "PUBLIC".MAIN_CACHE_MEMORY_MB = 200
```

Fig 2.22

```
EXEC                    (
```

If you set the server options the value will override the **-iqmc** or **-iqtc** switches.

Creating a Database

To create your Sybase IQ database you can either use a **CREATE DATABASE** command or use the Sybase Central Java GUI. Sybase recommend using Sybase Central but if you are particularly proficient at database creation scripting you can use DBISQL/ISQL to connect to the demo or utility database and run the script.

Create a database using command

If you wish to use a command to create you database using for example DBISQL, you will need to either start the ASIQ demo database or use the utility database. To use the utility database you need to run the start_asiq command as below (example is from windows). The -n option starts the server on the default port 2638.

```
C:\Program Files\Sybase\ASIQ-12_7\win32>start_asiq -n util_db
```

Depending on your operating system and installation options your directory may be different as will the server messages. On windows when you run this command in a prompt you will get the server message window (Fig 2.1).

Fig 2.23

When this window is minimized you will see an entry in your system tray. Once this database is running you can connect to it using DBISQL (Create an ODBC Connection), the default user is DBA and the default password is SQL.

Once in DBISQL and connected you can create a new database by running your create database command. For example Fig 2.2 is the create database command of the demo database.

Fig 2.24

```
CREATE DATABASE 'asiqdemo.db'
    BLANK PADDING ON
    CASE IGNORE
    IQ PATH 'asiqdemo.iq'
    IQ SIZE 50
    IQ PAGE SIZE 131072;


GRANT CONNECT TO "DBA" IDENTIFIED BY "SQL"
GRANT RESOURCE, DBA TO "DBA"
COMMIT
```

Once your database is created you can then use the various server and database level options, start up switches and configurations to alter your database behaviour.

Create a database using Sybase Central

Unless you have some aversion to doing things in a simple and easy manner I would suggest you use Sybase Central to set up your database. Why? Well it has a rather nifty wizard that will take all the pain out of setting up the server and database as well as letting you set up the initial options, DBSpaces and DBA user and password.

Starting a Server/Database

You can either use Sybase Central to start a database server or more conventionally use a command line to call the start_iq utility program. Most of the time I have found the command line to be a more flexible method as you can define where logs are written to, source control configuration files ,integrate with batch processing and pass server and database options to the utility. On Unix the utility program is a script called start_iq and on windows it is an executable called start_iq.exe. The utility program will perform some verification on the environment and start the server with some required switches at their default values. The utility will return a non zero value if it fails and if the **–o** switch was not used to specify a server output log then the errors are written to $IQDIR15/logfiles/ on Unix and Linux and to %ALLUSERSPROFILE%\SybaseIQ\IQ15_1\logfiles\ on windows.
The utility uses a default config file for server switches called default.cfg that is installed as part of the installation process to set initial options. This file is normally located in *$IQDIR/scripts* on Unix/Linux and in *%IQDIR%\scripts* on windows. The contents of this file on 15.1 are given below:

```
# default.cfg
# ------------------------------------------------------------------
# This file contains the default ASIQ startup parameters.  All servers
# started will default to these parameters, unless overriden by contents
# of parameter list.
# ------------------------------------------------------------------
# Must be in the format: One parameter [and value] per line
# ------------------------------------------------------------------

-c  48m
-gc 20
-gd all
-gl all
-gm 10
-gp 4096
-ti 4400
```

I suggest creating your own server properties file using the default.cfg as a template, you can then add new options or amend the defaults as required.

The syntax for calling the utility is given in Fig 2.25

Fig 2.25

```
start_iq -n db_name <server switches> <database file> <database options
```

In Fig 2.25 you see I have specified the –n switch, Sybase recommends you do this (as do I) as this switch names the server and stops you from connecting to the wrong server in error. However if you place a –n switch after the database file in the command line then it is used as a database option which has a different impact (see server and database options below in Fig 2.27 and 2.28).

You can add other server options (switches) to the command line; these are given in the table in Fig 2.27 (these can be placed into a file as you will see in the @filename switch).
The database file you specify is the name of the catalog database file, this will not be used to store IQ data (see the DBFile section), but it will contain your main catalog store data and will grow as you add data (It does not shrink when data is deleted). Be sure to set this file up in an area with sufficient space for your usage.
Finally after you define the database file you may optionally supply the database options, these are given in Fig 2.28.

An example of how to call start_iq with files is given in Fig 2.26; in this example I have added the database option **–m** to truncate the transaction log after each **CHECKPOINT**. I have also supplied the server configurations in a file (This file includes all the defaults from the default.cfg file plus an additional **–n** to name the database to mydb).

Fig 2.26

```
start_iq @/home/Sybase/MYDB/config/MYDB.cfg
/home/syabse/MYDB/catalog/MYDB.db -m
```

Server options/switches

Fig 2.27

Switch	Description
@filename	You may place a file name as an option and add switches to the contents of the file. For *example if you run:-* **start_iq** @/home/database_config/my_db.cfg /local/mydb/catalog.db The file /home/database_config/my_db.cfg can be used to hold a list of server switches.
@envvar	Like the @filename option you may instead place a list of switches inside an environment variable. E.g. set envvar= **-n** mydb c:\sybase\IQ-15_1\demo**start_iq** @envvar /local/mydb/catalog.db
-c <cache size> K or M or P	This is used to set the initial cache size for the catalog store. You can set the size to K (Kb), M (Mb) or P (Percentage of physical memory). For example "**-c 64M**" will start the server with 64Mb of catalog cache. "**-c30P**" will start the server with a cache size of 30% of the physical memory on the host" If you do not provide this switch then IQ calculates it to be the lesser of (The sum of the main db files specified at the command line) or (25% of physical memory on the host). **DO NOT USE IF SETTING THE -ch AND/OR -cl SWITCHES.**
-ca 0	By setting the **-ca** switch to 0 you effectively disable dynamic catalog store cache resizing by making it static.
-cc + or -	This is used to enable and disable the collection of information about database pages used for cache warming. By default this option is on. When the collection is on the server will keep track of every database page that is requested. It will only stop when the maximum (not definable) number of pages has been collected. The information is stored so that if you restart the database with the -cr switch then the cache can be warmed at start up. e.g. "**-cv+** "enables collection. "**-cv-**" disables collection.
-ch <size>K or M or P	This is used to provide an upper limit that the server can allocate when dynamically growing the catalog cache. You may specify the option using K (Kb), M (Mb) or P (Percentage). E.g. "**-ch** 32M" will limit it to 32Mb. "**-ch** 512K" will limit it to 512Kb. "**-ch** 15P" will limit the cache size of 15% of the physical memory on the host" You should use this in conjunction with the **-cl** option which sets the lower limit. **DO NOT USE IF THE -c SWITCH IS SET.**

Option	Description
-cl <size> K or M or P	This is used to provide a lower limit that the server can be set to when dynamically shrinking the catalog cache. You may specify the option using K (Kb), M (Mb) or P (Percentage). E.g. "-ch 4M" will limit it to 4Mb. "-ch 64K" will limit it to 64Kb. "-ch 5P" will limit the cache size of 5% of the physical memory on the host" You should use this in conjunction with the -ch option which sets the upper limit. **DO NOT USE IF THE -c SWITCH IS SET.**
-cm <size>h or m or g	This sets the windowing extension address space. You may set the size in k (Kb), m (Mb) or g (Gb). E.g. "-cm 512k" sets the size to 512Kb
-cp <path to directory of **JAR** files>	This is used to set a directory/jar files that is used to search for classes. It will add the value of this option to the classpath that the server uses when launching the Java Virtual Machine. E.g. "-cp /home/java/jars;/home/myjars/calc.jar"
-cr + or -	This switch warms (reloads) the cache with pages collected from last time the server was running. The pages are collected by the -cc option. E.g. "-cr+" warms the cache at start up "-cr-" Does not warm the cache at start up.
-cs	This is used to write information to the server log whenever the cache size changes.
-cv + or -	This is used to enable (+) or disable (-) messages about cache warming. (See **-cr** and **-cc**) options.
-cw	If this switch is used then IQ can take advantage of Windowing Extensions (AWE) or Windows XP, 2000 and Server 2003 when setting the size of the catalog cache. This enables IQ to use larger cache sizes on these platforms. For the exact performance gain for your platform and version of IQ refer to the Sybase server documentation.
-dt <dir>	This is used to specify the directory path where IQ will put temporary files. **THIS IS NOT TEMPORARY DATABASE** (Use DBFiles for temporary database space).
-ec <encryption options>	When the switch is specified then packet encryption is enabled on the network server.
-ep	This is used to display a dialog box where you can enter an encryption key. You must not use this switch in conjunction with the -ek switch. You cannot use this switch when starting the server as a windows service without the "interact desktop" option on.
-es	When this switch is defined then unencrypted shared memory connections are allowed.
-f	When this switch is used then the server is started without a transaction log.
-fc <file>	This is used to specify the file and path of a DLL containing the file system call-back function (The dll will be a shared object on Unix and Linux systems.
-fips	When specified this switch will force all strong encryption to use FIPS algorithms.

-ga	When their switch is specified then the database serer will automatically shut down when the last connection ends.
-gb \<level\>	This is used on windows host to set the priority class of the database. The \<level\> specified is the priority class.
-gc \<number of minutes\>	This sets the timeout period of checkpoints.
-gd ALL or NONE or DBA	This is used to set the permission level required to start and stop the database. The default is DBA. E.g. "-**gd** DBA" - This means only users with DBA authority can start and stop the database.
-ge \<size\>	This is a windows only switch and when defined will set the threads stack size that is used for executing external functions. The size specified is in bytes and the default if this switch is not specified is 16,384 bytes.
-gf	This is used to disable triggers from firing. This is interesting as you can see in the section on triggers that Sybase say they are not supported in IQ anyway. However I have found insert triggers do work with some limited functionality.
-gk ALL or NONE or DBA	This is used to set the permission level required to stop the server. The default is DBA. E.g. "-**gk** DBA" - This means only users with DBA authority can stop the server.
-gl ALL or NONE or DBA	ALL when started with start_iq (DBA for others).
-gm \<number of connections\>	This switch is used to specify the total connections (not queries or processes) that the server will allow at any one point in time (default is 10). You should set this to an expected number of users who will be connected at a single time. If using connection pools then you can use this option to set the connections the same as the pool (plus a couple extra for DBA/developer connections). If you set this option higher than your licensed number of connections then it has no effect.
-gn \<number of threads\>	This is used to specify the total execution threads that the catalog store can use for connectivity when multiple users are logging in. Sybase recommend the value of -gn is set to a minimum of the value of -gm times 2 with a minimum value of 25. However you must not set this to more threads than your platform can support, see the -iqmt switch for more details on this.
-gp \<page size in bytes\>	This is used to specify the maximum page size in bytes for the catalog store. The size must be 1024, 2048, 4096, 8192, 16384 or 32768. It is recommended you set this to at least 4096. (The minimum page size on Linux and Unix systems is 2048). The value you set this to will affect performance as if you are storing a lot of large data columns and this is set low then data will have to be spread across a larger number of pages meaning more page retrievals. However if you set this to high and you are brining back smaller amounts of data then you will be retrieving excess data in the pages that contain the data you require. Like most things in IQ the best set up will be dependant on your storage and use!!
-gr \<time in minutes\>	This is used to specify the maximum number of minutes that a server takes to recover after failure.

-gss <stack size> K/M	This sets the stack size of the catalog store. The default is 64K and the max is 4MB. You may set the size in either k (Kb) or M(Mb), be aware though that this switch has no effect on windows. E.g. "**-gss** 512k" sets the stack size to 512 Kb's.
-gt <number of processors>	This is used to set the maximum number of processors that IQ can use on a multi processor host (up to your licensed limit). However be aware that on version 15.1 and below that even with this switch set you cannot run IQ on a host with more processors than you are licensed for (unless you take the processors off the system, or restrict them in the **BIOS**).
-gtc <max processor concurrency>	This is used to set the max processor concurrency for the server, this includes hyperthreads and cores.
-gu ALL or NONE or DBA or UTILITY_DB	This is used to set the permission level for commands such as **DROP DATABASE**. If the **UTILITY_DB** value is used then only users who can connect to the utility database can perform the commands. Other wise it's **ALL, DBA** or **NONE** (None meaning absolutely no one).
-iqfrec <database name>	This is used to open the IQ database in forced recovery mode (it does not do this on the catalog store). The dbname is the physical name of the database you wish to open in forced recovery mode. Please note ONLY use this switch when doing a forced recovery not when using the database for other operations. I would suggest you never put this into a file and only set it on the command line.
-iqgovern <number of concurrent queries>	If there is any switch I have found to impact performance more than any other it is this. The iqgovern switch is used to set the maximum number of concurrent queries the server can execute at one time. The default value is 2 times the number of CPU's on your host machine plus 10. As a single connection can be executing sever queries at once (by IQ parallel processing the queries) it is advisable to spend some time optimizing this number. If this is et to high then a single connection may use all the threads available and leave other queries waiting for resource, on the flip side if this number is set to low then queries may not run efficiently as they may not use all the resources available. **Another Sybase recommended setting is 2 times CPU's +4.**
-iqmc <size in MB>	This is used to specify the size of the main IQ cache in Mb. The default value is 16MB if not specified. You may also set the option **MAIN_CACHE_MEMORY_MB** to set the value, but remember that the server switch -iqmc will override the value of the option. Even if you change the option you will need to restart the server in 15.x as they are server level, in 12.x it is a database level option.
-iqmsgnum <number of archives>	The switch only takes effect when the IQMsgMaxSize server property is set to a value other than zero. The value of the -iqmsgnum switch is then used to specify the number of message log archives. The default value is 0 which means messages will be wrapped in the message log file with no archiving. But the value can be 0-64 inclusive. This switch is only available in 15.x and above.
-iqmsgsz <size in MB>	This switch sets the maximum size of the IQ message log in MB. The default values of 0 means that there is no limit, allowable values are 0-2047. This switch is only available in 15.x and above.

-iqmt <number of threads>	This switch is used to specify the number of IQ threads to create. The default is 60 per CPU for the first four CPU's and 50 per CPU for the remainder, plus connection threads. e.g. On a server with 16 CPU's that has been set to have 20 connections the default will be, ((60 x 4) + 50 x 12) +(2 + (20+2) +1) The total number of threads (**-gn + -iqmt**) must be less than or equal to 4,096 on 64-bit platforms and 2,048 on 32-bit platforms. The default value of the switch -iqtss setting will normally be adequate to support the total thread but it is worth double checking.
-iqnotemp <size in MB>	This switch creates a temporary file that is <size in MB) in size that will be used instead of any temporary DBSpaces that have need defined on the server.
-iqnumbercpus <number of cpus>	This switch can override the number of CPU's available to the server (the default is all CPU's on the server). You should never set this value to a higher number than the physical number of CPU's on the host. Also you cannot use this option to stay within licensing (15.1 and below), e.g. you host has 16 CPU's and you are only licensed for 8, you cannot use this switch to stay within the licensed CPU boundaries.
-iqpartition <number of partitions>	This specifies the number of main and temp buffer cache partitions. The value must be a power of 2 from 0 to 64, the default is 0. IQ normally calculates the number of partitions using (**cpu's divded by 8**) rounder to the nearest power of 2. This switch will override the database option **CACHE_PARTITIONS**.
-iqsmem <size in MB>	This switch specified in MB the size to create a memory pool to increase the heap size.
-iqstart 1 or 2 or 4 or 8	This switch is used to specify the level of diagnostic information that is output to the console before database start up and to the IQ message log thereafter. The values correspond to:- 1 - Returns basic info on DBFiles. 2 - This stops diagnostics after the transaction log replay but before a recovery. 4 - This returns full diagnostic info. 8 - This allows the DBFile paths to be overwritten and will instead use the sysiqfile values. You may use this in conjunction with the -z switch to diagnose system problems.
-iqtc <size in MB>	This is used to specify the size of the temporary IQ cache in Mb. The default value is 8MB if not specified. You may also set the option **TEMP_CACHE_MEMORY_MB** to set the value, but remember that the server switch -iqtc will override the value of the option. Even if you change the option you will need to restart the server in 15.x as they are server level, in 12.x it is a database level option.
-iqtss <size in KB>	This is used for defining in Kb the stack size of internal execution threads for the server. The defaults are 512Kb on 64 bit systems and 200Kb on 32Bit systems and you should **NEVER** set the value less than these as it may effect system performance and stop queries from running as there are not enough threads. I would suggest increasing this value on 64 bit systems and leave alone on 32 bit, however the real constraints are on the system memory, CPU/cores and connections and how you are using your server.

-iqwmem <size in MB>	For Unix and Linux system only. This specifies the size in MB to create a wired memory pool. Remember that creating a wired memory pool on a host that does not have sufficient memory may impact performance.
-k	This switch specifies that the server should **NOT** collect performance statistics. If you don't require them then I would consider using this switch as collection performance stats can in itself impact performance. (Juts as running query plans can).
-kl <Kerberos file name>	This is used to specify the Kerberos GSS-API library on Windows or the Kerberos shared object on Unix and Linux systems.
-kr <realm of Kerberos server>	This is used to override the default Kerberos Server Principal realm and enable Kerberos connections. The normal realm is "server_name@default_realm_of_kerberos client".
-krb	This switch enables Kerberos security authentication on the system, but only if your system is licensed to use it.
-ks 0	This switch is used to disable the shared memory used by the performance statistics monitor.
-ksc <number of connections>	This is used to specify the number of connections that will be tracked by the performance monitor.
-ksd <number of databases>	Normally, this is used to specify the number of database that will be tracked by the performance monitor, but as you should only run one database on an IQ server is for all intensive purposes as redundant switch.
-m	When specified this switch will ensure that the transaction log is truncated each time a checkpoint is issued.
-n <database name>	This sets the name of the database server. Be carful though as if you set **-n** after the database file name in the start_iq command then it sets the database name which is something different.
-o <server messages filename>	This is used to specify the path and file used to store server messages i.e. The server message log (not the IQ message log). I would always suggest setting this as it is very useful in debugging and it is good practice to set up logs in sensible and consistent locations.
-oe <start up errors filename>	This specifies the file that should be used to log any errors that occurs on server start-up, any assertions or any fatal errors.
-on <file size>	This is used to specify how large the server log (specified with the -o switch) can grow to before it is renamed to <logname>.old and a new file is created.
-os <file size> k or m or g	This is used to specify the maximum size of the server message log (see the switch **-o** for the file location). The default is 0 which means no limit. You can specify the size in k(Kb), m (Mb) or g(Gb).
-ot <message windows copy filename>	This is used to truncate the server message log (specified with the -o switch) and copy its contents to the file specified in this -ot switch.
-p packet-size	This is used to define the maximum size of communication packets in bytes. The default is 1460 bytes but it can be any value between 300 and 16,000 bytes.
-pc	When this switch is specified then all communication packets with the exception of connections made from the server host machine (why compress when sending to the same machine!!) are compressed.
-pt <size in bytes>	This sets the threshold in bytes that is used for compression of packets. The default value is 120 bytes (Sybase recommends you should not set this to less than 80)
-qi	Windows Only. This switch is used to specify whether the database server window and tray icon are displayed.
-qp	If this switch is defined then performance messages are not displayed in the database server window.

-qs	Windows Only. This is used to disable start up error dialog boxes. This will only suppress errors if it is specified on the command line of start_iq, it will not work when used in a file or a variable.
-qw	This switch on Windows systems will suppress the database server window and on Linux and Unix it suppresses messages on the console.
-s <id>	Unix/Linux Only. This is used to specify the system user id that is used for messages in the syslog facility. You can specify a user id none to stop syslog messages and the default is the used id that runs the server.
-sb 0 or 1	This is used to specify how broadcasts on TCP/IP are handled. If set to 1 the server will not respond to broadcasts from dblocate but does not effect connection logic.
-sf <feature list>	This switch is used to enable and disable database server features. The feature list is a comma separated list of feature names or sets.
-sk <key>	This switch is used to specify a key that can be used to enable any features that are disabled.
-su <password>	This switch is used to specify the password for the DBA user in the utility_db, if you set t to none then the utility db is disabled.
-ti <minutes to disconnect>	This switch is used to specify in minutes how long the server will wait before disabling a connection that has not submitted a request. This is useful as a connection may be holding on to resources such as other versions or locks. However this switch will not disconnect connections using shared memory communications link of connections from the same host using shared memory. If you specify this value as zero then connections are never disconnected. I suggest always setting this to an appropriate non zero value as other versions can build quickly and will eventually use all free space and stop legitimate connections from being created. If you want to set this for individual connections then you can use the **IDLE** connection parameter.
-tl <interval in seconds>	This switch is used set the liveness timeout for client connections (not Unix non threaded client's or TDS connections). The default timeout if the switch is not specified is 120 seconds. The server sends a liveness packet using client/server TCP/IP to the client to ensure it the connection in live. If the server doesn't not detect a liveness packet within the specified timeout then the connection is dropped. Be aware that when there are more than 200 connections the server with calculate a higher timeout to handle the large number of liveness packets.
-tmf	This switch is used to force transaction manager recovery during recovery of distributed transaction when the distributed transaction co-ordinator is not available.
-tq <time in "YYYY/MM/DD HH:MM"> ot <time in HH:MM>	When this switch is specified then the server will shut down at a specified time **USING THE 24 HOUR CLOCK**. You may optionally provide a date; if you do then the date time must be enclosed in double quotes.
-u	This switch is used to specify that you wish to use the OS system disk cache when opening files rather than the database cache.
-ud	Unix/Linux Only. This switch makes the server run as a daemon in the root directory.

-uf <action to take>	Unix/Linux Only. This switch specifies which action should be taken upon a fatal error occurring. The default if the switch is not specified is the default action below. The available action values are:- **default** This action ensures that the server behaves the same as the abort action except when a device full fatal error occurs, and then is behaves the same as the defunct action. **defunct** This action caused the database to continue running but it will not accept any new connections. Any new connections who attempt to connect will receive the original fatal error message. **abort** This action will call the Unix/Linux abort function and generate a core file.
-ut <interval of minutes to touch>	Unix/Linux only. This switch is used to specify an interval that the server will use to touch temporary files. E.g. "-ut 10" will execute a touch on all temporary files every 10 minutes.
-v or -v2	When specified on windows this will display the IQ version in a message box, on Linux and Unix it will display the IQ version as a string.
-x list	This switch is used to specify either a TCP/IP or IPX comma separated list of communication links. The default behaviour will try a settings supported by The server on the O/S. You may also specify the parameters to the link as below:- -x "tcpip(PARAMETER1=VALUE1;PARAMETER2=VALUE2)" E.g. -x tcpip(HOST=my_server,my_other_server;PORT=2639;TO=20)
-xs all or none or <web-protocols>	This specifies the communication protocols for server side web services. The default is the server does not listen for web requests. You may specify all to listen for all supported protocols, none to only listen for shared memory protocols or web protocols ins the form:- http or https or hrrp_fips You may also specify protocol parameters. e.g. -xs "http(PARAMETER1=VALUE1;PARAMETER2=VALUE2; etc)
-z	This switch is used to specify that you wish to switch on information on communication links on start up. You should only use this when investigating communication issues.
-ze	This switch specifies that database server environment variables should be displayed in the database server message window.

-zl	This switch will capture the most recent prepared SQL statement for each connection. You can view these using the sa_conn_activity system procedure. You can also enable this using the option remember_last_statement in the sa_server_option system procedure. This will only show parent calls and not any child calls within the parent.
-zn <number of log files>	This switch is used to specify the number of request log files to keep. Also see the **-zs** switch.
-zo <file name and path>	This switch prevents request level logging from being displayed in the console and redirects request level logging (switched on using the **-zr** switch) to a separate log file (rather than the one specified using the **-o** switch).
-zoc <file path and name>	This switch outputs HTTP web client procedure debug messages to the specified log file.
-zr All or None or SQL	This is used to specify the level of server request level logging and prevent the logging from going to the console (It will go to the log specified in the -zo switch). All logs all requests to the server, None only logs non SQL statement requests and SQL logs the following SQL requests. **BACKUP** **BEGIN_TRANSACTION** **COMMIT** **CONNECT** **CONTROL_START_DATABASE** **CONTROL_STOP_DATABASE** **CONTROL_STOP_ENGINE** **CURSOR_CLOSE** **CURSOR_EXPLAIN** **CURSOR_OPEN** **CURSOR_RESUME** **DELETE_FILE** **DISCONNECT** **Errors** **PREPARE_TO_COMMIT** **ROLLBACK** **SQL_OPTION_SET** **STMT_DROP** **STMT_EXECUTE** **STMT_EXECUTE_ANY_IMM** **STMT_EXECUTE_IMM** **STMT_PREPARE**
-zs <integer> k or m or g	This switch is used to set the maximum file size of the request logging file (specified by the **-zo** switch). When the file reaches the size specified it is renamed to <filename>, old and a new file is created. The maximum size can be specified in k (Kb), m (Mb) or g (Gb), the default value is no limit.

Database options/switches

You may additionally add the following database options after declaring the location of the catalog database file.

Fig 2.28

Database switch	Description
-dh	This option is used to hide the database from dblocate -d.

-ds <dir>	This option is used to specify the directory path that contains all DBSpaces.
-ek <encryption key>	This is used to specify a database encryption key.
-m	This option will truncate the transaction log after checkpoint
-n <database name>	This option is used to name the database. If you use this as a database option then it is a database base switch, alternatively you can place this in the server config file (my preferred approach).
-sm <server name>	You may use this switch top provide an alternate server name for the database when it is acting as a read-only mirror.
-sn <server name>	This is used to provide and alternative server name for this database.
-r	This is used to stop database base modifications by placing the database into read-only mode.

Stopping a Server/Database

To stop a server/database you have several options.

- Use Sybase Central by selecting the server name and choosing Stop from the dropdown.

- On Unix/Linux systems you can use the **stop_iq** utility (much like **start_iq**), but this is not available on windows O/S systems.

- On Windows, you can quickly stop the database server by right-clicking the server icon in the taskbar and choosing Exit or by clicking Shutdown on the server window.

- Run the Interactive SQL (DBISQL) **STOP ENGINE** command

- Run the Stop utility, **dbstop**.

The sections below give examples of each of these options (except Sybase central as this is very simple).

stop_iq

The **stop_iq** utility is available for Unix and Linux Operating systems. You can pass a number of options to the utility to control what is shut down and when. The syntax for the utility is
When you execute **stop_iq** without any options it will list all of the servers owned by other users, and then list the servers you own. The utility will first prompt you for which server you wish to stop; it then asks if you want to stop the server you have chosen. When you answer Y (for Yes) then it will kill all connections and stops the server, you answer N (for No) if you just wanted to see what was running on the host. You may want to check if anyone is connected before doing this and you may lose any uncommitted transactions and the **stop_iq** utility will display a warning as such.
The syntax for the stop_iq utility is given in Fig 2.30

Fig 2.30

```
stop_iq <options>
```

The options available are

Option	Option Description
-agent <agent>	Stops the IQ Agent on Unix or Linux systems
-cleanup	Removes the orphan IQ process on Linux
-stop one or all	Removes user interaction with stop_iq. Assumes a yes response to all questions.
-user	Specify a user to stop server processes.
	If, due to truncation or substitution, **stop_iq** cannot find the server or agent owned by the current user, the system manager can specify the name and id found in the process table in the **-user** argument to shut down the server/agent with the **stop_iq** utility.
	A user with root privileges can shut down another user's server or agent without having to log in as that user. The **stop_iq** utility has no superuser (su) or root powers, so a nonprivileged user cannot shut down a server owned by another user.
-version	Specify the version of Sybase IQ the switch applies to.
-wait	Specify the time to wait for the server to shut down before timeout expires.

The example in Fig 2.31 will stop all IQ servers running on the host without asking if you want to (The -stop option assumes you know what you are doing).

Fig 2.31

```
stop_iq -all
```

If you do not specify any options then the utility will present you with a list of servers, each one numbered. You can then enter the number of the server you wish to stop. An example of the screen output for this is given in Fig 2.32

Fig 2.32

```
The following 1 server(s) are owned by 'sybase'

## Owner      PID  Started  CPU Time  Additional Information
-- --------- ------- -------- -------- -----------------------------------
1: sybase    20515   Dec21 12:47:35 SVR:MYDB DB:MYDB PORT:2638
        /home/sybase/MYDB/binaries/IQ-15_1/bin64/iqsrv15
@/home/sybase/MYDB/config_files/MYDB.cfg /home/sybase/MYDB_catalog/MYDB
--

    Please note that 'stop_iq' will shut down a server completely
    without regard for users, connections, or load process status.
    For more control, use the 'dbstop' utility, which has options
    that control stopping servers based on active connections.

Do you want to stop the server displayed above <Y/N>?
```

As the example in Fig 2.32 has only one server on the host the utility will ask if you want to stop it. If there is more than one server the utility will first ask for the number of the server you which to stop as in Fig 2.33

Fig 2.33

```
Checking system ...

The following 2 server(s) are owned by 'sybase'

## Owner      PID  Started  CPU Time  Additional Information
-- --------- ------- -------- -------- -------------------------------------
1: sybase    3371   Sep12 2-17:45:14 SVR:MYDB DB:MYDB PORT:2643
        /home/sybase/MYDB/binaries/IQ-15_1/bin64/iqsrv15
@/home/sybase/MYDB/config/MYDB.cfg /home/sybase/MYDB_catalog/MYDB
--
2: sybase    31323   07:03 00:00:09 SVR:MYDB2 DB:MYDB2 PORT:2643
        /home/sybase/MYDB2/binaries/IQ-15_1/bin64/iqsrv15
@/home/sybase/MYDB2/config/MYDB2.cfg /home/sybase/MYDB2_catalog/MYDB2
--

        Please note that 'stop_iq' will shut down a server completely
        without regard for users, connections, or load process status.
        For more control, use the 'dbstop' utility, which has options
        that control stopping servers based on active connections.

Enter the server to shutdown ('1'...'2') or 'Q' to Quit:.
```

STOP ENGINE

The **STOP ENGINE** statement can be run from dbisql to stop the database server, the syntax of

Fig 2.34

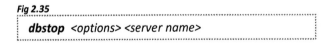

```
STOP ENGINE <server name> [UNCONDITIONALLY]
```

If the **UNCONDITIONALLY** option is used then the database will kill all connections to the server and stop. Otherwise if there are other connections and this is not specified then the server will not be stopped.

dbstop

The **dbstop** utility can be used on all platforms on the command line to stop a database cleanly. The syntax for dbstop is given in Fig 2.35.

Fig 2.35

dbstop *<options> <server name>*

You may read in the option from an environment variable of a file by preceding the file/variable name with an @ sign, as in the example in Fig 2.36.

Fig 2.35

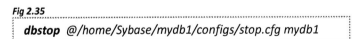

dbstop *@/home/Sybase/mydb1/configs/stop.cfg mydb1*

The following options are available to the **stopdb** utility.

Option	Option Description
-c <connection parameters>	Use this option if you do not provide a server name. In the connection parameters you provide you must include a User ID with permission to stop the server you are specifying to stop (normally set by the –gk server option in the server config file). The default is normally the DBA user (or a user with DBA authority). e.g. **dbstop** -c "uid=DBA;pwd=pa55word;eng=mydb1r;dbn=mydb1"
-d	This is normally used to only stop a database and not the server, however in most situations they are one and the same and I suggest not using this option1
-o <*filename*>	This is used to specify the path and filename of the output log file.
-q	This stops the server in quite mode (i.e. it does not output messages).
-x	This switch is used to tell the utility not to stop if there are other user connections.
-y	This forces the server to stop with no prompts even if there are user connections (to avoid confusion do not us in conjunction with –x).

Security and User Management

This chapter will take you through the basics of user security, for example how to set up groups, recommendations for object ownership, login policy's to control user's access.

Just because a user has rights to create objects and back up objects does not automatically grant them access to everyone's data. We shall also look at how to expire passwords, limit users connections, grant privileges on objects and some best practices when deciding on how users should be grouped. We shall also cover non-connecting users and how they are used for grouping and controlling object ownership.

Security Tools and Considerations

There are two main considerations in IQ when it comes to security.

- How does the user access the database and what actions can they perform on it?
- What can the user to data in the database and what objects can they do it on?

For example a user may be able to log in, create objects under their own name but not be able to see anyone else's data. Tools we shall use to do this are:-

- Creating login policy's to determine login characteristics such as password lifetime and maximum connections a user can have.
- Create non-connecting users to use as schema owners and to group users together.
- User authority parameters such as allowing user to create objects with the **RESOURCE** authority.
- Using the **GRANT** statement to implement object level security.
- System Procedures and options used for password management.

Login Policies

A login policy is used to set specific attributes that can be used across several login ids. For example you may want to create a different policy for general users than those used for developers. Every user must have a login policy, if you do not specify one or build any of your own then IQ comes with a policy called "root" that can/will be used as a default (the parameters for this are shown in the table in the Root Policy Defaults section). When you create a new policy and options that you do not specify will revert to the values in the "root" policy.

The syntax for the create login is given in Fig 3.1

Fig 3.1

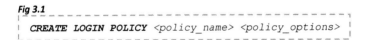

```
CREATE LOGIN POLICY <policy_name> <policy_options>
```

The <policy_name> can be any alphanumeric string up to 128 bytes and may include spaces but not control characters, double quotes or slashes. The policy options are listed in the table below:-

Policy Option	Description	Values
Locked	If the value for this option is ON, users are prohibited from establishing new connections. This is only settable for Non DBA users.	ON, OFF
max_connections	The maximum number of concurrent connections allowed for a user. This is only settable for Non DBA users.	0 - 2147483647
max_days_since_login	The maximum number of days that can elapse between two successive logins by the same user. This is only settable for Non DBA users.	0 - 2147483647
max_failed_login_attempts	The maximum number of failed attempts, since the last successful attempt, to login to	0 - 2147483647

	the user account before the account is locked. This is only settable for Non DBA users.	
max_non_dba_connections	The maximum number of concurrent connections that a user without DBA authority can make. This option is only supported in the root login policy.	0 - 2147483647
password_expiry_on_next_login	If the value for this option is ON, the user's password will expire in the next login.	ON, OFF
password_grace_time	The number of days before password expiration during which login is allowed but the default post_login procedure issues warnings.	0 - 2147483647
password_life_time	The maximum number of days before a password must be changed.	0 - 2147483647

Root Policy Defaults

For example the "root" policy has the following options by default

Policy Option	Value for "root" policy
locked	OFF
max_connections	Unlimited
max_days_since_login	Unlimited
max_failed_login_attempts	Unlimited
max_non_dba_connections	Unlimited
password_expiry_on_next_login	OFF
password_grace_time	0
password_life_time	Unlimited

Policy Creation

The example given below in Fig 3.2 gives the code required to create a new policy called sales_policy, this policy will set the max_connections and max_days_since_login values and use the values from the root policy to set all other policy options.

Fig 3.2

```
CREATE LOGIN POLICY sales_policy
 max_connections=8
 max_days_since_login=30
```

This means the values for the sales_policy are

Policy Option	Value for sales_policy
locked	OFF
max_connections	8
max_days_since_login	30
max_failed_login_attempts	Unlimited
max_non_dba_connections	Unlimited
password_expiry_on_next_login	OFF
password_grace_time	0
password_life_time	Unlimited

Policy removal

Before you drop your policy you must ensure there are no users with the policy assigned, you can check this in Sybase Central or by running the code in Fig 3.3:-

Fig 3.3
```
SELECT su.user_name, slp.login_policy_name
FROM sysuser su
JOIN sysloginpolicy slp ON
                    (su.login_policy_id = slp.login_policy_id)
WHERE login_policy_name = 'my_policy'
```

Once there are no users with your policy (see the user creation/alteration section below ion how to change the policy for a user), you may remove your policy by simply executing the code in Fig 3.4:-

Fig 3.4
```
DROP LOGIN POLICY <policy_name>
```

Changing a Policy

You may change a policy by running an ALTER LOGIN POLICY statement as the one in Fig 3.5.

Fig 3.5
```
ALTER LOGIN POLICY Test1
locked=ON
max_connections=5
```

The syntax for the alteration statement is given in Fig 3.6

Fig 3.6

```
ALTER LOGIN POLICY policy-name policy-options
[MULTIPLEX SERVER server-name]
```

Policy's in Multiplex

To use a policy in a multiplex you first **CREATE** a policy that prohibits access to all servers and then run an **ALTER** statement for each server you want to grant the policy access to.

For example:-
* Step 1 – create the policy

Fig 3.6

```
CREATE LOGIN POLICY sales_policy_for_IQNode1
LOCKED=ON
```

* Step 2 – Alter the policy to have access to the server IQNode1

Fig 3.7

```
ALTER LOGIN POLICY sales_policy_for_IQNode1
LOCKED=OFF
MULTIPLEX SERVER IQNode1
```

Any users that are assigned this policy will now be able to log into IQNode1, we can of course grant them access to multiple servers which depending on if you load balance your multiplex by user may be an option. For developers you will probably want to grant them access across all servers by creating the policy **LOCKED=OFF** for everything!

Users and Groups

This is probably the most important section of this entire book because you may have the best designed, highly optimised and technically correct data warehouse in the world, but without users....what's the point!!
Users in IQ in general are of two distinct types a user and a group (In IQ a group is actually a user).

Creating Groups

We shall first look at creating groups and sub groups as a well defined system should always group its users into functional areas. To create a group you just need to create a user and assign them group status as in Fig 3.8

Fig 3.8

```
CREATE USER sales_group

GRANT GROUP TO sales_group
```

A group is simply a user Id and any other users that are assigned to a group will inherit those users' permissions. For example when permissions on object (e.g. tables, views etc) are granted or revoked from a group, all members of the group inherit those changes. The exceptions to this are the **DBA**, **RESOURCE**, and **GROUP** permissions and they must be assigned individually to any user who requires them. You may also notice in the example above that no login policy or password was created for the user, this is deliberate as although it is possible you should really try to stop anyone login on as the group user id and use users in sub groups to perform your DDL and DML operations within the main groups schema.

In IQ a group may also be a member of another group allowing for a permission hierarchy to be created, a user may also be in many other groups. Because this can easily get confusing I recommend the following strategy when setting up a new database.

- Create a group that will hold all user objects and a single user assigned to this group who will in effect be the dbo for that schema. This functional dbo should be the only user with **RESOURCE** authority (The ability to create objects, and should be the only user able to **GRANT** privileges on them).

- Create two sub groups of the main group, one for read-only and one that has read-write permissions.

- Create functional groups in each of the read-only and read-write groups that can be used to hold users.

By following the advice above, if we created a simple sales database we could have group hierarchy as given in Fig 3.9.

Fig 3.9

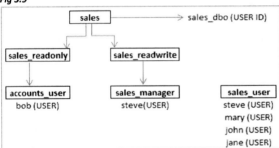

This is a very simple example but you can expand on the principals as required. For example you may also wish to create a batch user which your system will use to run jobs in an overnight batch scenario. You may want a system user id in a reporting sub group that you will use in a connection pool (e.g. a weblogic connection pool) or a reporting application (e.g. Business Objects). The point I am making is the options are almost infinite, but if you follow a simple hierarchy then it makes it a lot simpler when you try to trace permission issues.

In the next section we look how we create users, and remembering that a group is just a user id that can have members many of the options will also apply to groups.

Creating Users

In order to create a user we have different options on the commands we can execute, two of them are in Fig 3.9 and Fig 3.10

Fig 3.9

```
CREATE USER my_user
```

Fig 3.10
```
EXEC sp_iqlogin 'my_user'
```

However this user will not have a password and therefore cannot log into the database. To create a user who can connect we have several options, five of which are given in Fig 3.11, Fig 3.12, Fig 3.13, Fig 3.14 and Fig 3.15.

Fig 3.11
```
CREATE USER my_user IDENTIFIED BY 'pa55word'
```

Fig 3.12
```
EXEC sp_iqlogin 'my_user'
```

Fig 3.13
```
EXEC sp_iqaddlogin 'my_user','pa55word'
```

Fig 3.14
```
GRANT CONNECT TO my_user IDENTIFIED BY 'password'
```

Fig 3.15
```
CREATE USER my_user
EXEC sp_iqpassword 'DBA_PASSWORD','USERS_NEW_PASSWORD',my_user
```

To use any of the system procedures you must either have DBA authority or be granted execute permissions on the relevant system procedure. Options for creating users are not limited to just adding a user id and password. The syntax and options of the **CREATE USER** and **SP_IQADDLOGIN** procedures are given below:-

The CREATE USER statement requires DBA authority and has the syntax and options as in Fig 3.16.

Fig 3.16
```
CREATE USER <user_name> [IDENTIFIED BY <password>]
[ LOGIN POLICY <policy_name>]
[ FORCE PASSWORD CHANGE ON/OFF]
```

The **FORCE PASSWORD CHANGE** clause is used to control if the user must specify a new password when they log in. This clause overrides the password_expiry_on_next_login option setting in the user's policy.

You may want to verify the passwords against a set of rules, to do this you can use the **VERIFY_PASSWORD_FUNCTION** which holds as a value a function that is used to control the password. You can use this option to set a function to be called when a **GRANT CONNECT** to user **IDENTIFIED BY** password is executed. The option value is set to the form of owner.function_name and the function should take two parameters <user_name> and <new_pwd>. When you create your function it is recommended that you also run **ALTER FUNCTION** <function_name> **SET HIDDEN** to stop users from examining the code contained (if it is sensitive/security restricted). The function should return a string with a message if the password does not verify or **NULL** if it is ok. This option's default value is an empty string which means it has no function to run. Also because the input parameters are in Watcom format (no @ prefix), the function should be written in Watcom SQL.

The **SP_IQADDLOGIN** system procedure can also be used to add new users to the database and has the syntax and options as given in Fig 3.17

Fig 3.17

```
SP_IQADDLOGIN 'username_in', 'pwd', 'password_expiry_on_next_login '
[ , 'policy_name ']
```

- **username_in** is the user's login name.
- **pwd** is the user's password.
- **password_expiry_on_next_login** is an optional parameter and is used to specify if a user's password expires as soon as this user's login is created. The default setting is OFF (password does not expire).
- **policy_name** is also optional and is used to specify the user's login policy. the default is the 'root' policy.

When a user is created using the **SP_IQADDLOGIN** procedure and set to expire in one day it means it is valid for the next day but not after that. You can think of the expiration as in <days>+1 day's time.

Some general rules about user ids and passwords are.

- They cannot begin with white space, single quotes, or double quotes.
- They cannot end with white space.
- They cannot contain semicolons.
- Passwords are case sensitive
- A password must be either a valid identifier, or a string (maximum 255 bytes) placed in single quotes.
- Sybase recommend that the password be composed of 7-bit ASCII characters, as other characters may not work correctly if the database server cannot convert them from the client's character set to UTF-8.

You can add a comment to a user stating their full name or usage, for example by executing the code in Fig 3.18 we can add the comment to the user id tdmoore

Fig 3.18

```
COMMENT ON USER tdmoore IS 'TREVOR MOORE';
```

Once you have added comments to your users you can view them by executing the **SELECT** statement in Fig 3.19

Fig 3.19

```
SELECT user_name, remarks as 'Comment'
FROM sysuser su
    JOIN sysremark sr ON (su.object_id = sr.object_id)
```

Dropping and locking out users Users

A user id can only be dropped if it is not connected to the database, you can execute the **SP_IQCONNECTION** procedure to see who is logged in and then execute a **DROP CONNECTION** <connection_id> on each of the users connections before dropping them.

As with creating users there are a few of way to drop them (Fig 3.20, 4.21 and 4.22), however you must have DBA authority to do this or be granted execute permission on the sp_iqdroplogin procedure.

Fig 3.20
```
DROP USER my_user
```

Fig 3.21
```
SP_IQADDLOGIN 'my_user'
```

Fig 3.22
```
REVOKE CONNECT FROM my_user
```

You may also just want to stop a user from logging in, to do this you could change their password or a better way is to create a login policy where **LOCKED = ON** (Fig 3.23) and set the user to that policy (Fig 3.24).

Fig 3.23
```
CREATE LOGIN POLICY locked_user_ids locked=ON
```

Fig 3.24
```
ALTER USER my_user LOGIN POLICY locked_user_ids
```

I would always prefer locking out users as there may be data that relates to the user. If you want to see a list of all users and their associated policies then execute the code in Fig 3.25.

Fig 3.25
```
SELECT su.user_name,lp.login_policy_name
FROM SYSUSER su
   JOIN SYSLOGINPOLICY lp
         ON (lp.login_policy_id = su.login_policy_id)
```

Changing a password

In the above sections we have created, dropped and locked users. The following statements can be used to alter user properties such as passwords.

Fig 3.26
```
SP_IQPASSWORD '<caller password>','users new password','user_id'
```

The caller password is the password of the user executing the **sp_iqpassword** procedure as this may not always be the user whose password is being changed.

The users new password is exactly that, however if the executing user is for example a DBA and they do not add the user_id parameter then it will be the executing users new password.

The last parameter is user_id and this is the user id of the user whose password is to be changed. If this is omitted then the sp_iqpassword procedure will attempt to change the executing user's password.

In order to execute the sp_iqpassword procedure the executing users requires DBA authority.

Changing a users assigned login policy

To change a user's policy you may want to call the sp_iqmodifylogin procedure with the syntax in example Fig 3.27 or use the **ALTER USER** statement as in Fig 3.28.

Fig 3.27
```
SP_IQMODIFYLOGIN '<user_id>','<login policy name>'
```

Fig 3.28
```
ALTER USER <user_id> LOGIN POLICY <login policy name>
```

The user_id parameter is the <user_id> whose policy you want to change and the <login policy name> is the policy you want to assign to the user. If you do not pass the <login policy name> parameter to the **sp_iqmodifylogin** procedure then the user gets assigned the 'root' policy.

Changing other user properties

We have already used the **ALTER USER** statement for changing passwords and policies, but its worth looking at the entire syntax as in Fig 3.29

Fig 3.29
```
ALTER USER <user id>
[ IDENTIFIED BY <password> ]
[ LOGIN POLICY <policy name>]
[ FORCE PASSWORD CHANGE ON/OFF ]
```

As we have seen the **"IDENTIFIED BY"** clause is used to change a password, the **"LOGIN POLICY"** clause is used to change the login policy. There is also a **"FORCE PASSWORD CHANGE"** clause that if **ON** means that a user must specify a new password when they login (this option overrides the password_expiry_on_next_login option setting in the user's policy).

A less used syntax of the **ALTER USER** statement is to reset the login policy as in Fig 3.30. This syntax will change the user's login policy to the original values. This means that if the user's policy has been changed to lock them out etc then it will change the policy back to the original. This syntax will also clear the exceeding failed logins and maximum number of days since last login properties.

Fig 3.30
```
ALTER USER <user id>
RESET LOGIN POLICY;
```

Other User system procedures

Below is a list of other system procedures that effect user properties, more information on these procedures is given in the chapter on system procedures.

Procedure Name	Description
sa_get_user_status	Retrieve the current status of all existing users
sp_expireallpasswords	Cause all user passwords to expire immediately
sp_iqcopyloginpolicy	Create a new login policy by copying an existing one
sp_iqmodifyadmin	Set an option on a named login policy to a certain value

The permission hierarchy

It is worth noting that IQ operates a hierarchy when it comes to permissions, this is:-

- If the user has DBA authority they can do anything in the databases.

- If the user is not DBA then IQ first checks if the user has been granted permissions to perform the action they are attempting.

- If the user does not have permission then IQ checks to see if the user is a member of a group and checks if the group has permissions.

Object Inheritance

The basics

Every database object is an identifier, be it an identifier for a table or a view or a procedure. Every object also has an owner, be it a user owner, DBA, sys or dbo.

Most of the time an object only has one version and hence only one owner, but it is possible for many owners to have an object with the same name. For example you can create two tables named sales with different owners as in Fig 3.31.

Fig 3.31

```
CREATE TABLE sales.number_queue
(
        queue_number INT NOT NULL
)


CREATE TABLE accounts.number_queue
(
        queue_number INT NOT NULL
)
```

The example in Fig 3.31 will create two tables both called number_queue. Of course a normal user wouldn't be able to create a table for another user so assume Fig 3.31 was executed by a DBA (it was when I tested it).
Normally you would prefix an object before using it, as in Fig 3.32 where we are selecting from the number_queue table owned by user sales.

Fig 3.32

```
SELECT queue_number
FROM sales.number_queue
```

The only time you may not have to prefix the object with the owner is when you are the owner of an object or you are part of a group which owns the object (Of course you may be a member of both sales and accounts so you may still want to prefix).
In some circumstances you may be a member of a group and still not see all the objects owned by the group owner. An example may be that you work in accounts department but should not have access to see tables that contain payroll information.

We can do this as below. The first step is to create the accounts user and create its tables as in Fig 3.33

Fig 3.33

```
GRANT CONNECT TO accounts IDENTIFIED BY password


CREATE TABLE accounts.bought_ledger (<columns>)
CREATE TABLE accounts.sales_ledger ( <columns> )
CREATE TABLE accounts.payroll ( <columns> )
```

Now say we have a user called Susan who needs to see the bought_ledger table but not the sales_ledger or payroll tables. To do this we could create a group called bought_ledger, grant is privileges on the accounts.bought_ledger table and grant Susan membership to that group as in Fig 3.34.

Fig 3.34

```
GRANT CONNECT TO bought_ledger_user IDENTIFIED BY password

GRANT GROUP TO bought_ledger_user

GRANT ALL ON accounts.bought_ledger TO bought_ledger_user

GRANT MEMBERSHIP IN GROUP bought_ledger_user TO Susan
```

Lucky Susan now has permission on the accounts.bought_ledger table but she will have to qualify it with the owner to use it. To get round this we simply grant group access to the user accounts and add the bought_ledger group to the accounts group as in Fig 3.35.

Fig 3.35

```
GRANT GROUP TO accounts
GRANT MEMBERSHIP IN GROUP accounts TO bought_ledger_user
```

Now Susan can see the data in the accounts.bought_ledger table without qualifying the table but she still won't be able to see the data in the other tables owned by accounts because the accounts user has not been granted permissions. However the accounts user will still be able to see the data as they created the tables but any member of the accounts group or its sub groups will be required to have explicit **GRANT**s to see data in the tables.

Views and Stored Procedures

You may wish to use views or stored procedures to enforce your security. There are some good reasons why.

- A user can be granted select permission on a view without having permissions on the underlying tables.
- A user can be granted execute permissions on a stored procedure without having any permission on the underlying objects.

When creating stored procedures as long as you qualify the procedure name in the **CREATE PROCEDURE** statement then IQ will assume that all objects referenced by the procedure will be for the same owner. You may of course not qualify the procedure name, and then the procedure will be created with the user name you are logged in as (and IQ will assume all unqualified objects in the procedure are owned by the user).

Of course things in life would be easy if they were consistent, and in this case IQ is not!! When you create a view you still need to qualify the tables you are using even if the **CREATE VIEW** statement is qualified and/or the user you are logged in as owns the tables/procs/views used in the view.

Granting DBA functionality to non-DBA users

There may be occasions where you want a user to have certain DBA functionality but do not want to grant them DBA Authority. To do this we get a DBA user to create a procedure that contains the code we wish the non DBA to execute and **GRANT** the non DBA Permissions.

For example if we wanted the user "bob" to be able to change user's passwords, we can do this by creating the procedure below (Fig 3.36) as DBA.

Fig 3.6.

```
CREATE PROCEDURE DBA.change_password
(        @userid         VARCHAR(30)  = NULL,
         @new_password  VARCHAR(30)  = NULL
)
AS
BEGIN
     DECLARE @SQL_ALTER VARCHAR(255)


     SELECT @SQL_ALTER = 'ALTER USER' + @userid
                       + ' IDENTIFIED BY  ' + @change_value


     EXECUTE (@SQL_ALTER)
END
go
GRANT EXECUTE ON DBA.change_password To BOB
go
```

Because the procedure is owned by DBA the code executed within it will be executed with DBA permissions. As "bob" is granted execute permissions on the change_password procedure he will be able to change passwords when the procedure executes the **ALTER USER**. However "bob" still cannot directly execute an **ALTER USER** statement.

This workaround can be used in other scenarios where you want one user to be able to have permissions for specific functionality. You can even pass a parameter as a string containing SQL and have it dynamically executed with the permissions of the procedure owner!

SQL

A chapter called SQL can open a big can of worms as 90% of this book contains SQL. This chapter covers all the most commonly used SQL functions in IQ, common programming functionality and how best to structure your queries. It also covers some examples where you will want to use Watcom SQL over T-SQL. 90% of this book covers SQL in one way or another but

We will cover how to use data functions and also how to use IQ advanced SQL techniques such as the analytical functions **ROLLUP**, **CUBE** and **PARTITION BY**.

This chapter shows how to get round various errors such as allowing result sets when running dynamic SQL, using **GOTO** and **LEAVE** statements.

There are examples showing the effects of the numerous **DATE** functions and the way they can be used to alter, calculate and display date data.

WATCOM SQL versus T-SQL

If it wasn't confusing enough having two data databases in an IQ server (ASA and IQ) there are also two different dialects of SQL. IQ will run ANSI compliant SQL the wrapper around this and the extensions you can use can be in either Watcom or T-SQL.

Watcom SQL offers a different syntax to T-SQL, but there are some cross over's. If you want to convert a stored procedure from one syntax to the other you can open the stored procedure (or function) in Sybase Central right click on the procedure and there is a "**Convert to Watcom**" and "**Convert to T-SQL**" option. Otherwise you can use the functions in the section below on converting between syntax's.

Be aware that this is only 80-90% accurate. For example it will convert the overall structure but may allow some keywords to slip through. For example the **BEGIN TRANSACTION** statement only works in T-SQL but the conversion in Sybase Central does not convert it!!
Some general differences between the languages are given below:-

Stored Procedure/Function Creation/Structure

The examples below show a Watcom Stored Procedure creation script (Fig 4.1) and a T-SQL equivalent (Fig 4.2).

Fig 4.1
```
CREATE PROCEDURE my_test_proc
( in      @input_variable VARCHAR(20) DEFAULT 1,
  inout @outut_variable VARCHAR(20))
ON EXECPTION RESUME
BEGIN
        SELECT  'HELLO WORLD';
END
```

Fig 4.2
```
CREATE PROCEDURE my_test_proc
(@input_variable VARCHAR(20)= 1,
@outut_variable VARCHAR(20) OUTPUT)
AS
BEGIN
        SELECT 'HELLO WORLD'
END
```

As you can see there are differences in the parameter (variable) decelerations and in Watcom the clause "**ON EXCEPTION RESUME**" is used. This clause is used to mimic T-SQL behaviour to allow the procedure to continue when an error occurs. There are several differences in the **CREATE PROCEDURE** syntax between the two SQL languages, below are the basic structure and clauses that can be used when creating a procedure in each:-

Watcom SQL CREATE PROCEDURE statement

Fig 4.3

```
CREATE PROCEDURE [ owner.]procedure-name ( [ parameter, ...] )
{
[ RESULT ( <result column name>, ...)  | NO RESULT SET ]
[ ON EXCEPTION RESUME ] compound statement
| AT <location string> |
| [  DYNAMIC RESULT SETS <integer expression> ]
[ EXTERNAL NAME <java call> LANGUAGE JAVA ]
}
<procedure code>
```

T-SQL CREATE PROCEDURE statement

Fig 4.4

```
CREATE PROCEDURE [ owner.]procedure_name
[ ( ] @parameter_name data-type [ = default ] [ OUTPUT ] [ , ... ]
[ WITH RECOMPILE ]
AS
<procedure code>
```

To execute a procedure in Watcom you use the **CALL** <stored procedure> syntax and in T-SQL you use the **EXECUTE** (or **EXEC**) <stored procedure> syntax.

Differences and options

Parameters in Watcom are declared as **IN**, **OUT** or **INOUT**, in T-SQL they are **INPUT** (default) or **OUTPUT** (which is actually an **INPUT/OUTPUT** parameter).

The **RESULT** clause in the Watcom **CREATE PROCEDURE** statement allows you to specify the result-set that will be returned from the procedure. This result set is then stored in the meta-data allowing calling applications and programming languages to use this information. For a T-SQL procedure this meta-data will be the first result-set returned. Obviously some procedures return more than one result-set, for these the meta data returned depends on the connection method ODBC/Open Client/JDBC. Each connection method is dependant on the behaviour indicated by the drivers, I therefore recommend reading the Sybase documentation on the driver you are using.

ON EXCEPTION RESUME invokes behaviour that is akin to the option **ON_TSQL_ERROR='CONTINUE'** for a Watcom procedure. If it is omitted then the Watcom procedure will error immediately.

The "**AT** <location string>" clause in Watcom SQL is used to create a local procedure as a proxy to a procedure stored on a remote server.

DYNAMIC RESULT SETS in Watcom is used in procedures that are in fact wrappers of Java/C# methods that return result sets, if the clause is not used then IQ assumes there is no result set returned from the Java program. If it is declared then the **EXTERNAL NAME** <java call>**LANGUAGE JAVA** will also be used to declare the Java method called. If the number of parameters passed to the Java method is less than the number in the method signature then the difference needs to be the
If the number of parameters is less than the number indicated in the

method signature, the difference must equal the number specified in <integer expression> of the
DYNAMIC RESULT SETS CLAUSE.

The final clause is a T-SQL one called "**WITH RECOMPILE**", this is used in ASE/SQL Server to
recompile the procedure each time it runs. In IQ this does absolutely nothing and is only included
so it doesn't cause syntax errors when converting procedures. Procedures on IQ are not actually
ever compiled as the query plans are generated one statement at a time based on the current
statistics, indexes and cardinality of the data.

Some other differences are that T-SQL variables/parameters must always start with an @ sign, T-
SQL Procedures prefix their procedure code with an AT keyword and to invoke a Watcom
procedure you use the **CALL** statement and in T-SQL you use **EXECUTE**.
In Watcom procedures the variable **DECLARE** statements must always be the first statements in
the procedure and the values of them are set with a **SET** statement rather than **SELECT**.

Command Delimiters

Commands in Watcom are delimited by semi-colons as in the examples given below (note the
differences in variable identifiers, and value setting statements.

Watcom Statements

Fig 4.5
```
DECLARE my_variable    INT;
DECLARE my_variable_2 CHAR(4);


SET my_variable = 10;
SET my_variable_2 = 'TEST';


SELECT col_1
FROM my_table
WHERE col_1 = my_variable
AND col_2 = my_variable_2;
```

T-SQL Statements

Fig 4.6
```
DECLARE @my_variable INTEGER
DECLARE @my_variable_2 CHAR(4)


SELECT @my_variable = 10,
       @my_variable_2 = 'TEST'


SELECT col_1
FROM my_table
WHERE col_1 = @my_variable_1
AND col_2 = @my_variable_2
```

IF Statements

An IF statement has a completely different syntax in Watcom versus T-SQL.

Fig 4.7 – A Watcom IF Statement

```
IF @variable_1 = 0 THEN
        SET @variable_2 = @variable_1;
ELSE
        SET @variable_2 = 100/@variable_1;
END IF;
```

Fig 4.8 – T-SQL IF Statement

```
IF ( @variable_1 = 0)
BEGIN
        SELECT @variable_2 = @variable_1
END
ELSE
BEGIN
        SELECT @variable_2 = 100/@variable_1
END
```

You do not have to use the **BEGIN** and **END** statements in the T-SQL block if there is only one statement; however I like to do this to keep code consistent and improve readability. You will also notice that in Watcom there is a more programming language like syntax using the **END IF** to signify the end of the **IF** statement.

The WHILE Loop Statement

Watcom Loop Statement

Fig 4.9 – A Watcom Loop Statement

```
WHILE @i < 100 LOOP
        INSERT INTO my_table( counter_val) VALUES ( @i ) ;
        SET @i = @i + 1 ;
END LOOP ;
```

Fig 4.10 – A T-SQL Loop Statement

```
WHILE (@i < 100)
BEGIN
        INSERT my_table (counter_val) VALUES ( @i )
        SELECT @i = @i +1
END
```

Now this is all well and fine, but say we want to break out of the loop early. To do this we use the **LEAVE** statement in Watcom and the **BREAK** statement in T-SQL, as per the examples below:-

Fig 4.11 – LEAVE A Watcom Loop Statement early

```
WHILE @i < 100 LOOP
        INSERT INTO my_table( counter_val) VALUES ( @i ) ;
        SET @i = @i + 1 ;
        IF @i = 50 THEN
                        LEAVE;
        END IF;
END LOOP ;
```

Fig 4.12 – BREAK from A T-SQL Loop Statement early

```
WHILE (@i) < 100
BEGIN
        INSERT my_table (counter_vale) VALUES ( @i)
        SELECT @i = @i +1

        IF (@i = 50)
        BEGIN
                BREAK
        END
END
```

In T-SQL you can also use the **CONTINUE** statement, were-as a **BREAK** statement terminates the loop immediately and goes to the **END** statement of the **LOOP**. The **CONTINUE** statement will instead cause the **LOOP** to return immediately to the **BEGIN** and skip any statements in the loop after the **CONTINUE**.

Variable Deceleration

There are few differences in variable declarations

- In Watcom SQL the **DECLARE** statements must be at the beginning of a batch/stored procedure.
- Watcom variables are generally assigned using the **SET** statement, in T-SQL the **SET** statement is used to assign values to a sub set of database options.
- To assign a variable value from an SQL statement in Watcom SQL you use the **SELECT INTO** syntax.
- Variables in T-SQL must have an @preceding the variable name

Fig 4.13 – A Watcom Batch

```
BEGIN
    DECLARE @my_name varchar(10);
    DECLARE @my_obj_count integer;
    SET  @my_name='Trevor';
    SELECT count(1) INTO @my_obj_count FROM sysobjects
END
```

Fig 4.14 – A T-SQL Batch

```
BEGIN
        DECLARE @my_name varchar(10),
                @my_obj_count integer


        SELECT @my_name='Trevor'
        SELECT @my_obj_count = count(1) FROM sysobjects
END
```

Converting between T-SQL and Watcom SQL

There are three useful functions that you can use to convert from one SQL dialect to another and also tell you which dialect your SQL is in. The functions are:-

Function Syntax	Description
WatcomSQL('<SQL Statements>')	This returns a result set containing <SQL Statements> converted to Watcom SQL (If <SQL Statements> are valid).
TransactSQL('<SQL Statements>')	This returns a result set containing <SQL Statements> converted to Watcom SQL (If <SQL Statements> are valid).
SQLDialect('<SQL Statements>')	Returns a result set containing the Strings "Watcom-SQL" or "**TransactSQL**" depending on which SQL Dialect <SQL Statements> is in. The default is Watcom-SQL.

For example the code in Fig 4.15 converts the SQL provided (in T-SQL) to the function into Watcom SQL.

Fig 4.15 – Convert to Watcom

```
SELECT WatcomSQL('IF EXISTS (SELECT 1 FROM SYSOBJECTS)
BEGIN SELECT ''ITS ALIVE''
END')
```

This returns the result set in Fig 4.16.

Fig 4.16 – The converted result-set

```
if exists(select 1 from SYSOBJECTS) then select 'ITS ALIVE' end if
```

Like wise the example given in Fig 4.17 translates a SQL statement in Watcom into T-SQL.

Fig 4.17 – Convert to T-SQL

```
SELECT TransactSQL('IF  1 = (SELECT COUNT(1) FROM SYSOBJECTS WHERE
name like ''%Bob%'')
then
       SELECT ''BOB has more than one object'';
       message ''ok''
end if')
```

this (Fig 4.17) produces the result-set given in Fig 4.18

Fig 4.18 – The converted result-set

```
if 1 = (select COUNT(1) from SYSOBJECTS where name like '%Bob%')
begin
    select 'BOB has more than one object'
    message 'ok' to console
end
```

To check which SQL dialect a statement is in you can execute the **SQLDialect** statement as in Fig 4.19 producing the result in Fig 4.20.

Fig 4.19 – Check the SQL dialect

```
SELECT SQLDialect('IF EXISTS (SELECT 1 FROM SYSOBJECTS) BEGIN SELECT
''ITS ALIVE''  END')
```

Fig 4.20 – Result of SQLDialect

```
TransactSQL
```

The default result from SQLDialect is "Watcom-SQL", for example if you parse the function an ambiguous (can be either dialect) statement it will assume it is Watcom. An example of this is given in Fig 4.21 with the result in Fig 4.22.

Fig 4.21 – Check the SQL dialect of an ambiguous statement

```
SELECT
```

Fig 4.22 – Result of SQLDialect

```
Watcom-SQL
```

If when converting from one dialect to another a statement is detected that cannot be translated then the statement is commented out with a message. An example is given in Fig 4.23 with the resulting translation in Fig 4.24.

Fig 4.23 – Attempt to convert Watcom only statement (LOCK TABLE) to T-SQL

```
SELECT TransactSQL ('SELECT * FROM products; LOCK TABLE
sales IN WRITE MODE WAIT ''00:10:00''; UPDATE sales SET
region=1 WHERE sales_id =23;')
```

Fig 4.24 – Result of Fig 4.23

```
select * from products
/* Watcom only
lock table gen_lg_account_basic in write mode
wait '00:10:00'
*/
update sales set region=1 where sales_id=23
```

As we can see from Fig 4.24 the statement that could not be translated/converted were simply commented out with the comment "Watcom only".

However the above situation does not always work the other way. It appears that when converting T-SQL to Watcom no errors are reported. For example in Fig 4.25 the raiserror statement should be converted to Watcom and the **SQLDialect** statement should return "Watcom-SQL" however no conversion occurs and it is reported still as T-SQL. In this situation there are no errors reported and the user (I.e. you) are unaware that the conversion has not worked.

Fig 4.25 – Attempt T-SQL to Watcom Translation

```
SELECT SQLDialect (WatcomSQL ('raiserror 62001'))
```

Fig 4.26 – Result of Fig 4.25

```
TransactSQL
```

BEGIN -END

Firstly the **BEGIN-END** statement should not be confused with **BEGIN TRANSACTION** as doing so may produce unexpected results. For more on Transactional processing see the chapter on Transaction Management.

When used in T-SQL the **BEGIN_END** statement is used to group a set of statements into a single compound statement, that can be used in batches or control structures such as **WHILE** loops or **IF-ELSE** statements as in the example in Fig 4.27

Fig 4.27

```
IF (@my_variable = 1)
THEN
BEGIN
        SELECT 'My variable is equal to 1'
        SELECT @my_variable = 10
        SELECT 'My variable is now equal to 10'
END
ELSE
BEGIN
        SELECT 'My variable is not equal to 1'
        SELECT @my_variable = 1
        SELECT 'My variable is now equal to 1'
END
```

Also in T-SQL if any one of your statements fails then it is only that statement that has the failure, and depending on your error trapping options further processing may not take place. Watcom SQL offers a way of declaring that if any statement in your **BEGIN-END** compound statement fails then every statement within the **BEGIN-END** is rolled back. To do this we use the **ATOMIC** option as in Fig 4.28

Fig 4.28

```
BEGIN ATOMIC
        INSERT sales
        (sales_id, sales_person)
        SELECT 12,'fred'

        INSERT sales
        (sales_id, sales_person)
        SELECT 'I WILL FAIL'
END
```

In the example in Fig 4.28 the second **INSERT** causes a failure and thus the first statement is also rolled back.

Another big difference in the **BEGIN-END** statement is that in Watcom variable **DECLARE** statements must be place immediately after the **BEGIN**. For example Fig 4.29 will produce a compilation error but Fig 4.30 will execute.

Fig 4.29

```
BEGIN
        SELECT 'This will not compile ';
        DECLARE @my_var INT;

        SET @my_var=1;
        SELECT 'Complete', @my_var;
END
```

Fig 4.30

```
BEGIN
        DECLARE @my_var INT;
        SELECT 'This will compile ';
        SET @my_var=1;
        SELECT 'Complete', @my_var;
END
```

Statement Labels

Statement Labels can be a usefully way of commenting your code and showing what statements are for, controlling the process flow and providing a readable way to analyse your code. Below are some examples. Any procedure or batch can be labelled and the label name is a valid identifier followed by a colon. When used in the control part of the label is identified without the colon.

The GOTO statement – TSQL Only

This is only applicable in TSQL and is used to send the procedure execution path to the label as in Fig 4.31

Fig 4.31

```
DECLARE @counter INT

    SELECT @counter = 10

    CREATE TABLE #my_count_table (counter INT NOT NULL)

    loop_control:
        IF @counter < 110
        BEGIN

            INSERT #my_count_table
            SELECT @counter

            SELECT @counter = @counter + 10

            GOTO loop_control
        END

  SELECT * FROM #my_count_table
```

This produces the result set in Fig 4.32

Fig 4.32

Counter
10
20
30
40
50
60
70
80
90
100

Loop Control in Watcom

The example in Fig 4.33 produces the same results as in Fig 4.32, but uses a label to exit the loop in a Watcom Batch. This code uses the **LEAVE** statement to exit the loop when the variable reaches a value over 100.

Fig 4.33

```
BEGIN

    DECLARE @counter INT;

    SET @counter = 10;

    CREATE TABLE #my_count_table (counter INT NOT NULL);

    loop_control:
    LOOP
        IF @counter > 100 THEN
            LEAVE loop_control;
        ENDIF;

        INSERT #my_count_table
        SELECT @counter;

        SET @counter = @counter + 10;

    END LOOP loop_control;

    SELECT * FROM #my_count_table;
```

Common SQL Functions

One thing to remember when executing code with functions in them is that if you do not include a **FROM** clause then they will run on the ASA/Catalog store database. IQ and the catalog store may return different results, especially for numerical functions. I recommend always including a table in the **FROM** clause. If you are setting variables you can always include the IQ_DUMMY table and set the where clause to "**WHERE 1=0**".

Date Functions

The following date functions are available for use in IQ. Many of these functions use a <Date Component> input. The available date components are:-

Date Part

Date Part	Description
yy	Year
qq	Quarter
mm	Month
wk	Week
dd	Day
dy	Day Of Year
dw	Weekday
hh	Hour
mi	Minute
ss	Seconds

ms	Milliseconds

When formatting dates you may use the date parts above or use longer versions to improve data. For example the month may be supplied as MM, MMM or MMMM to the **DATEFORMAT** Function. The M will return the number of the month (e.g. 6 for June), a 'MM' will return the short name of the month (e.g. JUN for JUNE) or you may supply 'MMMM' which will return for example JUNE.

Date format strings/parts you may use are

Format string	Description
d	The Day
dd	This forces a two digit day by prefixing single digits with a zero.
ddd	The three digit day abbreviations e.g. SAT for Saturday
dddd	The full weekday name. But I have noticed that IQ truncates this so I tend not to use it.
h	The one- or two-digit hour in 12-hour format.
hh	This forces a two digit hout by prefixing single digit hours with a zero.
H	The one- or two-digit hour in 24-hour format.
HH	The two-digit hour in 24-hour format. This prefixes single digit hours with a zero.
m	The one- or two-digit minute.
mm	The two-digit minute, this prefixes single digit minutes with a zero
M	The one- or two-digit month.
MM	The two-digit month, this prefixes single digit months with a zero.
MMM	The 3 character month abbreviation, e.g. MAR for March.
MMMM	The full month name.
s	The one- or two-digit second.
ss	The two-digit second, this prefixes the single digit seconds with a zero.
y	The one-digit year (the last digit of the year)
yy	The two-digit year.
yyy or yyyy	The full year.

Date Functions

The <Date> that is supplied to these functions may be a **DATE**, **DATETIME** or **TIMESTAMP** data type where it is relevant to do so.

Function	Description	Example	Example Result
DATE(<String>)	Returns a String as a Date data type	DATE('JUN 16 2010')	16/06/10

DATEADD (<Date Part>, <Number to add or subtract by), <Date>)	Returns a Date that has been added or subtracted by the supplied date part to a date, for example minus some minutes or add a month.	**DATEADD**(mm,1,'JUN 16 2010') or **DATEADD**(mm,-1,'JUN 16 2010')	16/07/10 00:00 and 16/05/10 00:00
DATEDIFF(<Date Part>, <Date>, <Date>)	Returns the differences in two dates as an integer, the integer represents the different in the data component supplied.	**DATEDIFF**(dd,'JUN 16 2010','JUL 20 2010')	34
DATEFORMAT(<Date>, <Date Format>)	Returns a string of a date in the format supplied to the function. The format can be any comprised of any date format parts.	**DATEFORMAT**('JUN 16 2010','MMM-DD-YY')	JUN-16-10
DATENAME(<Date Part>, <Date>)	Returns a string containing the name of the date part supplied.	**DATENAME**(mm,'JUN 16 2010')	June
DATEPART(<Date Part>, <Date>	Returns a number of the date part supplied.	**DATEPART**(dd,'JUN 16 2010')	16
DATETIME(<String>)	Returns a DATETIME from a supplied string.	**DATETIME**('JUN 16 2010')	16/06/10 00:00
DAY(<Date>)	Returns the DAY date part of a date as an small int.	**DAY**('JUN 16 2010')	16
DAYNAME(<Date>)	Returns the DAY date part as a string containing the day.	**DAYNAME**('JUN 16 2010')	Wednesday
DAYS(<Date>)	Returns the DAYS of the date supplied since Feb 29th 0000.	**DAYS**('JUN 16 2010')	734245
DAYS(<Date>, <Date>)	Returns the number of days between two dates	**DAYS**('JUN 16 2010','DEC 16 2010')	183
DOW(<Date>)	Returns the day of the week date part as a number	**DOW**('JUN 16 2010')	4
HOUR(<Date>)	Returns the hour date part	**HOUR**('JUN 16 2010 02:30:20PM')	14
HOURS(<Date>)	Returns the number of hours of the given date since Midnight on 29th February 0000.	**HOURS**('JUN 16 2010 02:30:20PM')	17621894
HOURS(<Date>)	Returns the number of hours between two supplied date times.	**HOURS**('JUN 16 2010 02:30:20PM','JUN 17 2010 01:30:20PM')	23
MONTH(<Date>)	Returns the month date part as a number	**MONTH**('JUN 16 2010')	6
MONTHNAME(<Date>)	Returns the Month name of the supplied date.	**MONTHNAME**('JUN 16 2010')	June
MONTHS(<Date>)	Returns the number of months between February 0000 and the supplied date.	**MONTHS**('JUN 16 2010')	24124
MONTHS(<Date>,<Date>)	Returns the number of months	**MONTHS**('JUN 16	4

	between the two supplied dates.	2010','OCT 16 2010')	
QUARTER(<Date>)	Returns the number of the quarter JAN,FEB,MAR =1 APR,MAY,JUN =2 JUL,AUG,SEP=3 OCT,NOV,DEC=4	QUARTER('JUN 16 2010')	2
SECOND(<Date>)	Returns the seconds component from the supplied date time.	SECOND('JUN 16 2010 02:30:20PM')	20
SECONDS(<Date>, <Date>)	Returns the seconds between two supplied date times.	SECONDS('JUN 16 2010 02:30:20PM','JUN 16 2010 02:31:20PM')	60
WEEKS(<Date>)	Returns the number of weeks between 29th February 0000 and the supplied date.	WEEKS('JUN 16 2010')	104892
WEEKS(<Date>, <Date>)	Returns the number of weeks between two supplied dates.	WEEKS('JUN 16 2010','OCT 16 2010')	17
YEAR(<Date>)	Returns as a number the year of the supplied date.	YEAR('JUN 16 2010')	2010
YEARS(<Date>, <Date>)	Returns the years between two dates.	YEARS('JUN 16 2010','OCT 16 2015')	5
YMD(YYYY,MM,DD)	Returns a DATE from the supplied components.	YMD(2010,6,16)	16/06/10
GETDATE()	Returns as a TIMESTAMP the current date time.	GETDATE()	11/06/10 17:00
NOW()	Returns as a TIMESTAMP the current date time.	NOW()	11/06/10 17:00
TODAY()	Returns today's date as a date data type	TODAY()	11/06/10

You may wish to stack the above functions, for example if you wanted to convert a supplied date to the first day in the supplied date's month you could do so as in Fig 4.34.

Fig 4.34 – Stacked date functions

```
DECLARE @my_date DATE
SELECT @my_date = '15 JUN 2009'
SELECT CONVERT(DATE,DATEADD(dd,- ((DAY(@my_date)-1) ),@my_date))
```

Fig 4.35 – The result of 4.34

```
2009-06-01
```

String Functions

Sybase IQ provides all of the most common string functions (plus a few extras). As with most forms of programming you may use different functions to achieve the same goal, for example if you wanted the first 4 characters of a string/char column you could use the **LEFT** function or a **SUBSTRING**.

You can also nest functions, when nesting the inner most function is called first. For example in Fig 4.36 the string is first trimmed of any spaces on the left hand side and then it gets the first three characters 'abc'.

Fig 4.36

```
SELECT LEFT(LTRIM('     abcdef'),3)
```

Below is a table of string functions and examples on how they can be used.

String function	Description	Example	Example Result
ASCII (<string>)	This returns the ASCII value of the first character in a string.	ASCII('a') ASCII('z') ASCII('az')	97 122 97
BIT_LENGTH (<column name>)	This returns the length in bits of data held in the supplied column. This function only works on a supplied column and cannot be used on a string literal or variable. (The returned values will normally be a multiple of 8 , i.e. A string of 9 characters would normally return 72)	SELECT BIT_LENGTH(sales_id) FROM sales	72
BYTE_LENGTH (<string>)	This returns the length in bytes of a given string or column.	BYTE_LENGTH('BLAH')	4
CHAR (<ASCII value>)	This returns a converted supplied ASCII value as its corresponding string value, this will return **NULL** if the supplied code is more than 255 or less than 0.	CHAR(97)	'a'
CHAR_LENGTH (<string>)	This returns as a number the length in characters of a supplied string	CHAR_LENGTH('BLAH BLAH')	9
CHARINDEX (<search string>, <string>)	This returns the index location as a number of the search string within a string	CHARINDEX('A','BLAH BLAH')	3
DIFFERENCE (<string 1>, <string 2>)	This compare two supplied strings and returns a number between 0 and 4 which indicates the similarity of the two strings. 4 means the strings are very similar and 0 indicates they are completely different. (see also the **SIMILAR** function)	DIFFERENCE ('sales','sails') DIFFERENCE ('sales','miles') DIFFERENCE('sales','shoes') DIFFERENCE ('sales','smiles') DIFFERENCE ('sales','DATABASE')	4 3 2 1 0

GRAPHICAL_PLAN (<string>)	This is used in ISQL to generate and return a graphical query plan in XML format. Note this will not work for stored procedures. To create the plan in correct xml format that can be read by a browser user the **HEXADECIMAL ASIS QUOTE** " options should be used in any output statement. The **HEXADECIMAL ASIS** will write values as they actually are without any escaping, even if the value contains control characters. The **QUOTE** option specifies how quotes are written.	**SELECT GRAPHICAL_PLAN** ('SELECT * FROM sysobjects'); OUTPUT to 'c:\graphical_plan.xml' HEXADECIMAL ASIS quote '';	Check the file C:\graphical_plan.xml
HTML_PLAN (<string>)	This is used generate and return a query plan in HTML format. Note this will not work for stored procedures. To create the plan in correct html format that can be read by a browser user the **HEXADECIMAL ASIS** quote " options should be used in any output statement. The **HEXADECIMAL ASIS** will write values as they actually are without any escaping, even if the value contains control characters. The **QUOTE** option specifies how quotes are written.	**SELECT HTML_PLAN** ('SELECT * FROM sysobjects'); **OUTPUT TO** 'C:\html_plan.html' **HEXADECIMAL** ASIS **QUOTE** '';	Check the file C:\html_plan.html
INSERTSTR (<location to insert>, <original string>, <insert string>)	This returns a string inserted into another string at the location specified.	**INSERTSTR** (4,'abcdhijk','efg')	'abcdefghijk'
LCASE (<string>)	This returns a supplied string in lowercase (Also see **LOWER**)	LCASE('BLAH')	'blah'
LEFT (<string>, <length to return>)	This returns a string from the left of the supplied string for the number of characters specified.	LEFT('abcdefg',4)	'abcd'
LEN (<string>)	This returns a number specifying the length of the string. (This is an alias of the **LENGTH** function)	LEN('abcdefg')	7
LENGTH (<string>)	This returns a number specifying the length of the string. (see also **LEN**)	LENTH('abcdefg')	7
LOCATE (<string to serach>, <find string> [, <offset>])	This returns a number of the location of a search string within a string; you may optionally add a search start offset number. If the search offset number is negative then it returns the last matching	LOCATE ('abcdefgabcdefg','a') LOCATE ('abcdefgabcdefg','a',-1) LOCATE ('abcdefgabcdefg','a',-8) LOCATE	1 8 1 8

	string. Also A negative offset will be used to specify how many characters from an end of a string to exclude from the search.	('abcdefgabcdefg','a',-7) **LOCATE** ('abcdefgabcdefg','a',1) **LOCATE** ('abcdefgabcdefg','a',2)	1 8
LOWER (<string>)	This returns a supplied string in lowercase (Also see **LCASE**)	LOWER('BLAH')	'blah'
LTRIM (<string>)	This returns a string that has spaces from the left side of the string trimmed. Note: The result data type is a LONG VARCHAR. Therefore you must have a Large Objects Manage-ment option license to use in a select into, or you can **CON-VERT/CAST to** the correct data type and size.	LTRIM(' BLAH')	'BLAH'
PATINDEX ('%<pattern>%', <string to search>)	This returns the first occur-rence of the supplied pattern in the supplied string. You must use the wildcards either side to find a string in the mid-dle of another string.	**PATINDEX** ('%efg%','abcdefghij') **PATINDEX** ('efg','abcdefghij') **PATINDEX** ('abc%','abcdefghij') **PATINDEX** ('abc','abcdefghij') **PATINDEX** ('%hij','abcdefghij') **PATINDEX** ('hij','abcdefghij')	5 0 1 0 8 0
REPEAT (<string>, <number of repeats>)	This returns a string repeated the number of supplied times. Also see **REPLICATE**	REPEAT('x',10)	XXXXXXXXXX
REPLACE (<string>, <string to replace>, <replacement string>)	This returns a string that re-places a substring within a string with a new string. Also the **STR_REPLACE**	REPLACE('BLAH','LA','LOX')	'BLOXH'
REVERSE (<string> or <unicode>)	This returns a string in reverse order from a supplied string or binary	REVERSE('1234567890')	'0987654321'
REPLICATE (<string>, < times to replicate>)	This returns a string repeated the number of supplied times. Also see **REPLACE**	REPLICATE('x',10)	XXXXXXXXXX
RIGHT (<string>, <numeric expression>)	This returns a String containing the number of characters from the right of the string a speci-fied.	RIGHT('BLAH',2)	'AH'
RTRIM (<string>)	This returns a string that has spaces trimmed from the right side of a supplied string. Note: The result data type is a LONG VARCHAR. Therefore you must have a Large Objects Manage-ment option license to use in a select into, or you can **CON-VERT/CAST to** the correct data	RTRIM('BLAH ')	'BLAH'

	type and size.		
SIMILAR (<string 1>, <string 2>)	This will return an integer between 0 and 100 (a percentage) saying how similar the two strings are. The greater the number the more similar the strings, for example 100 means they are identical. See also the **DIFFERENCE** function; although the two are not always compatible e.g. The **SIMILAR** function says 'smiles' is more similar to sales than shoes, whereas the **DIFFERENCE** function has it the other way round!	**SIMILAR**('sales','sails') **SIMILAR**('sales','miles') **SIMILAR**('sales','smiles') **SIMILAR**('sales','shoes') **SIMILAR** ('sales','DATABASE')	80 45 27 15 0
SORTKEY (<string> , <collation id> or <collation name> [<collation tailoring string>] }])	This function generates values based on the supplied collation that can be used to sort values. A list of collations is available in the spt_collation_map table.	**SELECT** name, **SORTKEY**(name, '1252LATIN1') **FROM** sysobjects **WHERE** name in ('SYSCOLUMNS', 'SYSOBJECT')	'SYSCOL- UMNS','0xa8 b4a888a09aa c9c9ea800' 'SYSOB- JECT','0xa8b4 a8a086968c8 8aa00'
SOUNDEX (<string>)	This returns a number that represents the sound of a string, it will normally return the same number for words that start with the same character and sound the same.	**SOUNDEX**('sales') **SOUNDEX**('sails') **SOUNDEX**('sayles') **SOUNDEX**('shoes')	2675 2675 2675 371
SPACE (<number of spaces>)	This returns a string containing the supplied number of spaces.	**SPACE**(10)	' '
STR (<number> [, <length> [, <decimal>]])	This returns a string representation of a number. If <length> is supplied then it the number of character to return (the default is 10 and the max is 255) and <decimal> is used to supply the number of digits to the right of the decimal point to be included in the returned string.	**STR** (1234567890), **STR** (1234567890123456789), **STR** (1234567890123456789,2 5), **STR** (1.12345678,10,2)	'1234567890' '**********' "1234567890 12345678' '1.12'
STR_REPLACE (<string>, <string to replace>, <replacement string>)	This returns a string that replaces a substring within a string with a new string. It is better than the **REPLACE** function as you can supply it with a **NULL** to cut values from a string. Also see **REPLACE**	**STR_REPLACE** ('BLAH','LA','LOX') **STR_REPLACE** ('BLAH','LA',NULL)	'BLOXH' 'BH'
STRING (<first string>, <second string>, ..., <last string>)	This concatenates all the supplied strings into one string ignoring any nulls supplied.	**STRING** ('abc','def',null,'ghi')	'abcdefghi'

STUFF (<original string>, <start position>, <length to replace>, <replacement string>)	This returns a String where a substring is replaced by a different substring from within a string.	**STUFF** ('abcxxxjk',4,3,'defghi')	'abcdefghijk'
SUBSTRING (<original string>, <start pos> [, <length to obtain>])	This returns a sub string from a string starting at the supplied length for the supplied length. If no length is supplied then a substring from the start position to the end of the string is returned.	**SUBSTRING** ('abcdefghijk',4) **SUBSTRING** ('abcdefghijk',4,2)	'defghijk' 'de'
TRIM (<string>)	This returns a string that has the spaces trimmed from the beginning and end of a string. Note: The result data type is a **LONG VARCHAR**. Therefore you must have a Large Objects Management option license to use in a select into, or you can **CONVERT/CAST** to the correct data type and size.	**TRIM**(' BLAH ')	'BLAH'
UCASE (<string>)	This returns a string in upper case, see also **UPPER**	**UCASE**('Blah')	'BLAH'
UPPER (<string>)	This returns a string in upper case, see also **UCASE**	**UPPER**('Blah')	'BLAH'

Numeric Functions

Numerical functions are used to execute mathematical operations and return the result via the function call. Sybase state that IQ and the ASA catalog store can produce different results you need to know which store the function is running in (I have never encountered an issue with results though). You may want to ensure that functions execute in IQ by always using an IQ store table in the **FROM** clause (the iq_dummy table is fine, or if your install does not have this then just create an empty IQ table you can use). If you do not use a **FROM** clause then the function will run in the ASA/Catalog store (Which may be slower!!).

Numeric function	Description	Example	Example Result
ABS(<numeric expression>)	This returns the supplied numeric expression as a positive number. For expressions that evaluate to a negative this equate to multiplying the expression by -1.	ABS(-1.2345678)	1.2345678
ACOS (<numeric expression>)	This returns the arc-cosine (in radians) of the supplied numeric expression.	ACOS(1)	0
ASIN (<numeric expression>)	This returns the arc-sine (in radians) of the supplied numeric expression.	ASIN(1)	1.570796327
ATAN (<numeric expression>)	This returns the arc-tangent (in radians) of the supplied numeric expression.	ATAN(1)	0.785398163

ATAN2 (<numeric expression 1>, <numeric expression 2>)	This returns the arc-tangent (in radians) of the ration of the two supplied numeric expressions.	**ATAN2**(10,1)	1.471127674
CEIL (<numeric expression>)	This returns the next highest integer above the supplied numeric expression. Also see **CEILING**	**CEIL**(1.2345678) **CEIL**(-1.2)	2 -1
CEILING (<numeric expression>)	This returns the next highest integer above the supplied numeric expression. Also see **CEIL**	**CEILING**(1.2345678) **CEILING**(-1.6)	2 -1
COS (<numeric expression>)	This returns the cosine of the supplied numeric expression.	**COS**(1.2345678)	0.329929155
COT (<numeric expression>)	This returns the cotangent of the supplied numeric expression.	**COT**(1.2345678)	0.349499115
DEGREES (<numeric expression>)	This returns a number representing the degrees of a supplied numeric expression representing radians. (Converts radians to degrees).	**DEGREES**(1.2345678)	70.73552446
EXP (<numeric expression>)	The returns the exponential function of the supplied numeric expression that represents the exponent. (e to the power of a number).	**EXP**(1.2345678)	3.436892775
FLOOR (<numeric expression>)	Returns the next integer below the supplied numeric expression.	**FLOOR**(1.2345678) **FLOOR**(-22.44)	1 -23
LN(<numeric expression>)	This returns the natural logarithm of the supplied numeric expression. Also see **LOG**	**LN**(1.2345678)	0.210720949
LOG (<numeric expression>)	This returns the natural logarithm of the supplied numeric expression. Also see **LN**	**LOG**(1.2345678)	0.210720949
LOG10 (<numeric expression>)	This returns the base 10 logarithm of the supplied numeric expression.	**LOG10**(1.2345678)	0.091514946
MOD (<dividend>, <divisor>)	This returns the remainder when performing modular arithmetic on the dividend by the divisor.	**MOD**(20, 3)	2
PI(*)	This returns the value of PI	**PI**(*)	3.141592654
POWER (<numeric expression 1>, <numeric expression 2>)	The returns the result of calculating the supplied numeric expression 1 to the power of the supplied numeric expression 2.	**POWER**(3,2)	9
RADIANS (<numeric expression>)	This converts a supplied numeric expression that represents degrees into radians.	**RADIANS**(45)	0.785398163 397448

RAND(<integer>)	This returns a double precision random number less than 1 but greater then or equal to 0. This may be called with **RAND()** to obtain a random number but if a number is supplied it will return the same value (repeatable value)	RAND(5)	0.24255482
REMAINDER (<numeric expression 1>, <numeric expression 2>)	This returns the remainder when dividing numeric expression 1 by the numeric expression 2 value.	REMAINDER(10,3)	1
ROUND (<numeric expression>, <integer>)	This returns the supplied numeric expression rounded after the decimal point by the supplied integer. Be aware that there will be the same number of digits after the decimal point but the result is rounded. Also see **TRUNCATE** and **TRUNCNUM**	ROUND(1.236,2)	1.240
SIGN (<numeric expression>)	This returns -1 when the supplied numeric is negative, 1 when it is positive, 0 if the supplied value is 0 and **NULL** if the supplied value is **NULL**.	SIGN(1.2345678) SIGN(-22) SIGN(0) SIGN(NULL)	1 -1 0 NULL
SIN(<numeric expression>)	This returns the sine of the supplied numeric expression.	SIN(1.2345678)	0.944005695
SQRT (<numeric expression>)	This returns the square root of the supplied numeric expression.	SQRT(64)	8
SQUARE (<numeric expression>)	This returns the square of the supplied numeric expression.	SQUARE(5)	25
TAN (<numeric expression>)	This returns the tangent of the supplied numeric expression.	TAN(1.2345678)	2.861237576
[TRUNCATE] (<numeric expression>, <integer>)	This returns the supplied numeric expression truncated after the decimal point by the supplied integer. Be aware that there will be the same number of digits after the decimal point but the result is truncated. You need to put this function name in quotes if using quoted identifiers or in block brackets. Also see **ROUND** and **TRUNCNUM**	[TRUNCATE](1.236,2)	1.23

TRUNCNUM (<numeric expression>, <integer>)	This returns the supplied numeric expression truncated after the decimal point by the supplied integer. Be aware that there will be the same number of digits after the decimal point but the result is truncated. Also see **ROUND** and **TRUNCATE**	TRUNCNUM(1.2345678, 4)	1.2345
WIDTH_BUCKET (<numeric expression>, <minimun value>, <maximum value>, <number of buckets>)	This is used to create a the supplied number of buckets between the min and max numbers. In our example we say to create 3 buckets between 20k and 50k. The number returned from this function will be determined which bucket the supplied numeric expression falls into. For our example these are:- =< 20000 = bucket 0 (not in range) 20000-29999 = bucket 1 30000-39999 = bucket 2 40000-49999 = bucket 3 >=50000 = bucket 4	**WIDTH_BUCKET** (10000,20000,50000,3) **WIDTH_BUCKET** (20000,20000,50000,3) **WIDTH_BUCKET** (30000,20000,50000,3) **WIDTH_BUCKET** (40000,20000,50000,3) **WIDTH_BUCKET** (50000,20000,50000,3) **WIDTH_BUCKET** (60000,20000,50000,3)	0 1 2 3 4 4

Aggregate Functions

There are several types of aggregate functions (basic, mathematical and regression). Each of these has its own tables below.

Basic Aggregate Functions

Aggregate function	Description	Example	Example Result
AVG([DISTINCT] --optional <column_name> or <numeric expression>)	This returns the average of the supplied <column_name> or <numeric_expression> ignoring any **NULL** values. If the optional **DISTINCT** is specified then it will return the average of the distinct values.	**SELECT** **AVG**(DISTINCT length), AVG(length - colno) **FROM** sys.syscolumns	1252.9152 343.2093
COUNT([DISTINCT] --optional <column_name> or <numeric expression>)	This returns the count of the supplied <column_name> or <numeric_expression> ignoring any **NULL** values. If the optional **DISTINCT** is specified then it will return a count of the distinct values.	**SELECT** **COUNT**(DISTINCT cname), **COUNT**(DISTINCT length - 1), **COUNT**(tname), **COUNT**(*) **FROM** sys.syscolumns	5689 59 17709 17709

MAX([DISTINCT] --optional <column_name> or <numeric expression>)	This returns the maximum value of the supplied <column_name> or <numeric_expression> ignoring any NULL values. If the optional DISTINCT is specified then it will return the maximum value of the distinct values.	SELECT MAX(DISTINCT cname), MAX(DISTINCT length - 1), MAX(tname) FROM sys.syscolumns	write_cost 32766 user_test
MEDIAN(<numeric_column> or <numeric_expression>)	This returns the median of the supplied <column_name> or <numeric_expression> ignoring any NULL values. **THIS DOES NOT WORK AGAINST SYSTEM TABLES AS IT PRODUCES AND ERROR ASKING FOR AN OLAP EXTENSION.**	SELECT MEDIAN(principal) FROM my_iq_table	2865.93
MIN([DISTINCT] --optional <column_name> or <numeric expression>)	This returns the minimum value of the supplied <column_name> or <numeric_expression> ignoring any NULL values. If the optional DISTINCT is specified then it will return the minimun value of the distinct values.	SELECT MIN(DISTINCT cname), MIN(DISTINCT length), MIN(tname) FROM sys.syscolumns	ASC_OR_DES C 1 DUMMY
SUM([DISTINCT] --optional <column_name> or <numeric expression>)	This returns the sum of the supplied <column_name> or <numeric_expression> values ignoring any NULL values. If the optional DISTINCT is specified then it will return the sum of the distinct values.	SELECT SUM(length), SUM(DISTINCT length) FROM sys.syscolumns	8206848 73943

Mathematical Aggregate Functions

The functions below are designed to work on large sets of data, hence it is more appropriate to show the calculations they use rather than an example that won't mean anything to you! Also note that some mathematical aggregate functions are used only with OLAP and windowing, these are given in the OLAP section of this chapter.

Aggregate Function	Description	Calculation
CORR (<dependent expression> <independent-expression>)	This function returns the correlation coefficient of a set of number pairs. The function first converts its arguments to the DOUBLE datatype and then calculates the result in double-precision floating-point and finally returns the result as a DOUBLE datatype. If the set supplied is empty the function will return NULL.	$$\frac{COVAR\_POP(y, x)}{STDDEV\_POP(x) * STDDEV\_POP(y)}$$

COVAR_POP(<dependent expression>, <independent expression>)	This function returns the population covariance of a set of number pairs. This function first converts its arguments to **DOUBLE** data types, then calculates the result double-precision floating-point, and finally returns the result as a **DOUBLE** datatype. If applied to an empty set, then **COVAR_POP** returns NULL.	$$\left(\dfrac{\dfrac{SUM(x*y)-(SUM(x)*SUM(y))}{n}}{n}\right)$$
COVAR_SAMP(<dependent expression>, <independent expression>)	This function returns the sample covariance of a set of number pairs. This function first converts its arguments to **DOUBLE** data types, then calculates the result double-precision floating-point, and finally returns the result as a **DOUBLE** datatype. If applied to an empty set, then **COVAR_SAMP** returns **NULL**.	$$\left(\dfrac{\dfrac{SUM(x*y)-(SUM(x)*SUM(y))}{n}}{n-1}\right)$$
CUME_DIST( )	This function returns the relative position of a value in a group of rows. It returns a decimal value between 0 and 1.	The number of values in a SET that come before the value in the specified order divided by the total number of values in the set.
STDDEV([ALL] <numeric expression>)	This function returns the standard deviation of a set of number pairs. If applied to an empty set, then **STDDEV** returns **NULL**.	$$\sqrt{Variance}$$
STDDEV_POP([ALL] <numeric expression>))	This function calculates the population standard deviation of the supplied numeric expression, evaluated for each row of the group or partition as the square root of the population variance. If you use with a **DISTINCT** clause then is will only calculate the deviation for rows after the duplicates have been eliminated from the results.	$$\sqrt{\dfrac{\sum(x_i-\bar{x})^2}{n}}$$
STDDEV_SAMP([ALL] <numeric expression>))	Computes the standard deviation of a sample consisting of a numeric-expression, as a **DOUBLE**.	$$\sqrt{\dfrac{\sum(x_i-\bar{x})^2}{(n-1)}}$$
VARIANCE([ALL] --optional <numeric expression>)	This function returns the variance of a set of supplied numeric values. For example if col1 in our table vartest has the values 10,20,30 and 40. The variance is 166.6666.	$$\dfrac{n\sum x^2-\left(\sum x\right)^2}{n(n-1)}$$

Datatype validation and conversion functions

Function	Description	Example	Example Result
BIGINTTOHEX (<big integer>)	This converts a supplied big integer to it hexadecimal value. If the value supplied cannot be converted then an error is returned unless the database option **CON-VERSION_ERROR** is set to OFF, then the returned value is **NULL**.	BIGINTTOHEX(000000) BIGINTTOHEX(111111)	0000000000000000 000000000001b207

CAST (<expression> AS <data type>)	This returns a value of one datatype converted to another datatype. You should always specify a length for char and varchars and precision/scale for numeric's as IQ will try to this implicitly if not supplied and MAY get it wrong!!	CAST('JUL 19 2010' AS DATE) CAST (10 * 2 AS CHAR(2))	2010-07-19 20
CONVERT (<data type>, <expression> [,<format>])	Like cast this returns a value of one datatype returned as another datatype. You may optionally provide it with a format style to format dates and times in styles.	CONVERT(VARCHAR(30),GETDATE(),101) CONVERT(VARCHAR(30),GETDATE(),102) CONVERT(VARCHAR(30),GETDATE(),103) CONVERT(VARCHAR(30),GETDATE(),104) CONVERT(VARCHAR(30),GETDATE(),105) CONVERT(VARCHAR(30),GETDATE(),106) CONVERT(VARCHAR(30),GETDATE(),107) CONVERT(VARCHAR(30),GETDATE(),108) CONVERT(VARCHAR(30),GETDATE(),109) CONVERT(VARCHAR(30),GETDATE(),110) CONVERT(VARCHAR(30),GETDATE(),111) CONVERT(VARCHAR(30),GETDATE(),112) CONVERT(VARCHAR(30),GETDATE(),113) CONVERT(VARCHAR(30),GETDATE(),114) CONVERT(VARCHAR(30),GETDATE(),120) CONVERT(VARCHAR(30),GETDATE(),121)	09/25/2010 2010.09.25 25/09/2010 25.09.2010 25-09-2010 25 Sep 2010 Sep 25, 2010 17:12:06 Sep 25 2010 05:12:06:444PM 09-25-2010 2010/09/25 20100925 25 Sep 2010 17:12:06:444 17:12:06:444 2010-09-25 17:12:06 2010-09-25 17:12:06.444
HEXTOBIGINT (<hex string>)	This converts a supplied string of a hexadecimal value into is equivalent BIGINT value. If the string supplied cannot be converted then an error is returned unless the database option **CONVERSION_ERROR** is set to OFF, then a **NULL** is returned.	HEXTOBIGINT ('0x00000007') HEXTOBIGINT ('0X9999990') HEXTOBIGINT ('cccccccc3')	7 161,061,264 3,435,973,827
HEXTOINT (<hex string>))	This converts a supplied string of a hexadecimal value into is equivalent INT value. If the string supplied cannot be converted then a error is returned unless the database option **CONVERSION_ERROR** is set to OFF, then a **NULL** is returned.	HEXTOINT ('0x000007') HEXTOINT ('0X999999') HEXTOINT ('00000001')	7 10,066,329 1
INTTOHEX (<integer>)	This converts a supplied integer to it hexadecimal value. If the value supplied cannot be converted then an error is returned unless the database option **CONVERSION_ERROR** is set to OFF, then the returned value is **NULL**.	INTTOHEX(000000) INTTOHEX(111111)	00000000 0001b207
ISDATE (<string>)	This function returns a 1 if the supplied string can be converted to a **DATE**, a 0 if it cannot (including if a **NULL** is supplied).	ISDATE('JUN 10 2015') ISDATE('BLAH') ISDATE(NULL)	1 0 0

ISNUMERIC (<string>)	This function returns a 1 if the supplied string can be converted to a NUMERIC datatype, a 0 if it cannot (including if a **NULL** is supplied).	ISNUMERIC('100'), ISNUMERIC('BLAH'), ISNUMERIC(NULL)	1 0 0

System Functions

Below is a sample of the most commonly used System functions.

Function	Description	Example	Example Result
COL_LENGTH (<table name, <column_name>)	This returns the length of the column in the table supplied.	COL_LENGTH('sales','sales_id')	9
COL_NAME (<table id>, <column id>)	This returns the name of a column name for the supplied table and column ids.	COL_NAME(1182,1)	sales_account
CONNEC-TION_PROPERTY (<property id> or <property name> [,<connection id>])	This returns the values of a supplied property id or property name. You can add the optional connection id parameter to get the value for another connection (the default is the value of the connection executing the **CONNEC-TION_PROPERTY** function.	CONNEC-TION_PROPERTY('Language') CONNECTION_PROPERTY(526) CONNECTION_PROPERTY(189) CONNECTION_PROPERTY(189,1012)	us_english dbo.sa_post_login_proce dure DBA a_user
DATALENGTH (<exepression>)	This returns the length of the supplied expression in bytes.	DATALENGTH(10*10) DATALENGTH('BLAH BLAH BLAH')	4 14
DB_ID (<database name>)	This returns the database **ID** number for the supplied database name.	DB_ID('MY_DB")	0
DB_NAME (<database id>	This returns the database name of the supplied database id.	DB_NAME(0)	MY_DB
DB_PROPERTY (<property id> or <property name>, [<database id> or <database name>])	This returns the value of the supplied database property id or name; you can optionally use the database id/name parameters.	DB_PROPERTY('CatalogCollation')	ISO_BINENG
GROUP_MEMBER (<group name>, [<user name>])	This will return 1 if the supplied group exists or the supplied user is in the group supplied. If the group does not exist or the user is not in the group it returns 0.	GROUP_MEMBER('sales_group')	1
INDEX_COL(<table name>, <index id>, <key number>, [<user id>])	This returns the name of an indexed column. The key number can be a 0 for a single column index and for multicolumn's 0 is the first column, 1 is the second etc.	INDEX_COL('sales',2,0)	sales_id

NEXT_CONNECTION(<connection id>)	This returns the next connection number available. You can use **NULL** to return the first connection.	**NEXT_CONNECTION**(9083) **NEXT_CONNECTION**(NULL)	8985 10,150
OBJECT_ID (<object name>)	This returns the object id of the supplied object name.	**OBJECT_ID**('accounts')	1523
OBJECT_NAME(<object id>)	This returns the object name of the supplied object id.	**OBJECT_NAME**(1523)	accounts
PROPERTY(<property id> or <property name>)	This returns the value of the supplied server property id or name	**PROPERTY**('PageSize')	4096
PROP- ERTY_DESCRIPTION(<property id> or <property name>)	This returns the description of the supplied server property id or name	**PROP- ERTY_DESCRIPTION**('PageSize')	Database Page Size
PROPERTY_NAME(<property id>)	This returns the property_name of the supplied server property id.	**PROPERTY_NAME**(184)	PageSize
PROPERTY_NUMBER(<property name>)	This returns the property_id of the supplied server property name.	**PROPERTY_NUMBER**('PageSize')	184
SUSER_ID ([<user name])	This returns the integer value of the optionally supplied user's id number.	**SUSER_ID**() **SUSER_ID**('sales')	102 110
SUSER_NAME([<user id])	This returns the user name of the optionally supplied user id.	**SUSER_NAME**() **SUSER_NAME**(110)	super_user sales
USER_ID([<user name])	This returns the integer value of the optionally supplied user's id number.	**USER_ID**() **USER_ID**('sales')	102 110
USER_NAME[<user id])	This returns the user name of the optionally supplied user id.	**USER_NAME**() **USER_NAME**(110)	super_user sales

Dynamic SQL and Code Execution

When running Dynamic SQL you should be aware of some differences in the T-SQL and Watcom Syntax.

For example the **EXECUTE IMMEDIATE** statement in Watcom can only be used in procedures and functions where as you can execute Dynamic SQL anywhere using TSQL.

A T-SQL example is given in Fig 4.36 and a Watcom example in Fig 4.37

Fig 4.37

```
DECLARE @my_sql VARCHAR(100)
SELECT @my_sql = 'TRUNCATE TABLE my_table'
EXECUTE (@my_sql)
```

Fig 4.38

```
DECLARE @my_sql VARCHAR(100);
SET @my_sql = 'TRUNCATE TABLE my_table';
EXECUTE IMMEDIATE(@my_sql);
```

There as issues when executing Dynamic SQL, For example the code in Fig 4.38 will return the sqlcode -946, result set not permitted.

Fig 4.38

```
DECLARE @my_sql VARCHAR(100)
SELECT @my_sql = 'SELECT TOP 10 *'
SELECT @my_sql = @my_sql + ' FROM SYSOBJECTS'
EXECUTE (@my_sql)
```

To get round this you need to declare that your statement returns results. The best way to do this is to use Watcom SQL and declare the statement as returning a resultset as in Fig 4.39

Fig 4.39

```
DECLARE @my_sql VARCHAR(100);
SET @my_sql = 'SELECT TOP 10 *';
SET@my_sql = @my_sql + ' FROM SYSOBJECTS';
EXECUTE IMMEDIATE WITH RESULT SET ON @my_sql;
```

Advanced OLAP Queries

Group by Rollup

The **ROLLUP** functionality first calculates aggregate values as per the **GROUP BY** clause. It then moves from right to left through the columns in the **GROUPING** creating progressively higher levels of totalling until it creates a grand total at the end. You can think of the **ROLLUP** as a operating like a **UNION** on a set of selects with **GROUP BY**'s.
The syntax is given in Fig 4.40

Fig 4.40

```
SELECT <column name> , GROUPING (<column name>, (<column name>, ..etc)
GROUP BY ROLLUP ( <expression>, <expression>, ..etc)
```

The **ROLLUP** will create a **NULL** value in place of the actual value to indicate the row is a sub total as in Fig 4.41

Fig 4.41

```
SELECT   day(creation_time) AS day, month(creation_time) AS month, COUNT(*)
FROM     sysobject
GROUP BY rollup (month, day)
ORDER BY month desc , day DESC
```

Fig 4.41 will produce the results below. As you can see the first **NULL** value in the day column is a sub total of all the values in the **COUNT**(*) column for month 3, and like wise this continues for other columns. Also at the end of the table is a row with a **NULL** in day and **MONTH** and this provides a grand total for all days and months.

day	month	count()
23	7	111
22	7	4
15	7	38
14	7	5
13	7	29
9	7	246
8	7	141
7	7	48
6	7	401
5	7	4959
2	7	4
NULL	7	5986
30	6	10769
22	6	345
8	6	808
NULL	6	11922
28	5	1
12	5	1
7	5	3493
NULL	5	3495
NULL	NULL	21403

Now, what would happen if there were **NULL**s in the day column? For example if the day 6 in the month 7 was **NULL** then we may see a result like the one below for month

day	month	count()
23	7	111
22	7	4
15	7	38
14	7	5
13	7	29
9	7	246
8	7	141
7	7	48
5	7	4959
2	7	4
NULL	7	401
NULL	7	5986
30	6	10769
22	6	345
8	6	808
NULL	6	11922
28	5	1
12	5	1
7	5	3493
NULL	5	3495
NULL	NULL	21403

Now we have two rows where day is **NULL** and month is 7, so which one is the sub total??? This is where we can use the **GROUPING** functionality.

For example we change our query to the one in Fig 4.42

Fig 4.42

```
SELECT  day(creation_time) AS day, month(creation_time) AS month,
count(*), GROUPING (day(creation_time) ) AS day_g, GROUPING
(month(creation_time) ) AS month_g
FROM     sysobject
GROUP BY ROLLUP (month, day)
ORDER BY month desc , day desc
```

We now get the result below.

day	month	count()	day_g	Month_g
23	7	111	0	0
22	7	4	0	0
15	7	38	0	0
14	7	5	0	0
13	7	29	0	0
9	7	246	0	0
8	7	141	0	0
7	7	48	0	0
5	7	4959	0	0
2	7	4	0	0
NULL	7	401	1	0
NULL	7	5986	0	0
30	6	10769	0	0
22	6	345	0	0
8	6	808	0	0
NULL	6	11922	1	0
28	5	1	0	0
12	5	1	0	0
7	5	3493	0	0
NULL	5	3495	1	0
NULL	NULL	21403	1	1

You can now use the values produces by the grouping column to determine the level of totalling. So where the day column has a value one you know that the day columns are totalled, and if the month column and day column both have a value 1 we know that it is the grant total.

You may use any of the standard aggregate functions in a **ROLLUP** that you would normally use in **GROUP BY** queries. However here are some restrictions when using the **ROLLUP** functionality, these are:-

* You cannot combine multiple **ROLLUP**, **CUBE** and **GROUP BY** columns in the same **GROUP BY**

* You cannot use **ROLLUP** functionality in sub queries.

* You cannot use a constant expression in the **GROUP BY**

Group by CUBE

Much like the **ROLLUP** examples above the **CUBE** funtionality is used to produce subtotals, if we change the code from Fig 4.42 in the **ROLLUP** examples to the code in Fig 4.43 you will see we produce subtotals for every possible permitation of month and day. In our code this adds day subtotals (for all months) to the bottom of the resulset, we can see this be looking at the

Month_g column.

Fig 4.43

```
SELECT  day(creation_time) AS day, month(creation_time) AS month,
count(*), GROUPING (day(creation_time) ) AS day_g, GROUPING
(month(creation_time) ) AS month_g
FROM     sysobject
GROUP BY CUBE (month, day)
ORDER BY month desc , day desc
```

This returns the result below.

day	month	count()	day_g	Month_g
23	7	111	0	0
22	7	4	0	0
15	7	38	0	0
14	7	5	0	0
13	7	29	0	0
9	7	246	0	0
8	7	141	0	0
7	7	48	0	0
5	7	4959	0	0
2	7	4	0	0
NULL	7	401	1	0
NULL	7	5986	0	0
30	6	10769	0	0
22	6	345	0	0
8	6	808	0	0
NULL	6	11922	1	0
28	5	1	0	0
12	5	1	0	0
7	5	3493	0	0
NULL	5	3495	1	0
2	NULL	4	0	1
5	NULL	4959	0	1
7	NULL	3541	0	1
8	NULL	949	0	1
9	NULL	246	0	1
12	NULL	1	0	1
13	NULL	29	0	1
14	NULL	5	0	1
15	NULL	38	0	1
22	NULL	349	0	1
23	NULL	111	0	1
28	NULL	1	0	1
30	NULL	10769	0	1
NULL	NULL	21403	1	1

Partition By

To demonstrate the partition by functionality we will use the dataset below:-

sales_person	region	year	total_sales
bob	AMERICAS	2006	1000
fred	AMERICAS	2006	2000
susan	EUROPE	2006	1500
jo	EUROPE	2006	500
chris	EUROPE	2006	5000
billy	ASIA	2006	4500
bob	AMERICAS	2007	1500
fred	AMERICAS	2007	5000
susan	EUROPE	2007	7000
jo	EUROPE	2007	1500
chris	EUROPE	2007	2000
billy	ASIA	2007	1500
bob	AMERICAS	2008	2500
fred	AMERICAS	2008	5000
susan	EUROPE	2008	3000
jo	EUROPE	2008	9500
chris	EUROPE	2008	500
billy	ASIA	2008	2000

If we wanted to know the total sales per year we could write a simple query as in Fig 4.44

Fig 4.44

```
SELECT   YEAR, SUM(total_sales) AS total_sales
FROM sales
GROUP BY year
```

This will return the results

year	total_sales
2006	14500
2008	22500
2007	18500

Now say we want to include the sales_person column but still show the total sales for the year for all sales people. We can do this by using the **PARTITION BY** logic in Fig 4.45. This example says to sum up the values of year but also partition by it so the sum appears in all rows for that year. Notice we do not have to use a group by when doing this.

Fig 4.45

```
SELECT   sales_person,
         year,
         SUM(total_sales) OVER (PARTITION BY  year) AS total_sales_for_year
FROM sales
```

Fig 4.45 produces the results below.

sales_person	year	total_sales_for_year

bob	2006	14500
fred	2006	14500
susan	2006	14500
jo	2006	14500
chris	2006	14500
billy	2006	14500
bob	2007	18500
fred	2007	18500
susan	2007	18500
jo	2007	18500
chris	2007	18500
billy	2007	18500
bob	2008	22500
fred	2008	22500
susan	2008	22500
jo	2008	22500
chris	2008	22500
billy	2008	22500

We are not restricted to using a **SUM** function, in fact most aggregate functions can be used, and some are exclusive to the **PARTITION BY** statement. The example in Fig 4.46 uses an **AVG** (average) function instead of a **SUM** to give the average for all sales people in a year but repeated for every sales person.

Fig 4.46

```
SELECT  sales_person,
        year,
        AVG(total_sales) OVER (PARTITION BY  year) AS total_sales_for_year
FROM sales
```

sales_person	year	average_sales_for_year
bob	2006	2416.666667
fred	2006	2416.666667
susan	2006	2416.666667
jo	2006	2416.666667
chris	2006	2416.666667
billy	2006	2416.666667
bob	2007	3083.333333
fred	2007	3083.333333
susan	2007	3083.333333
jo	2007	3083.333333
chris	2007	3083.333333
billy	2007	3083.333333
bob	2008	3750
fred	2008	3750
susan	2008	3750
jo	2008	3750
chris	2008	3750
billy	2008	3750

We can use this syntax to introduce another column but still keep the same averages, the example in Fig 4.47 adds in the region column.

Fig 4.47

```
SELECT  sales_person,
        region,
        year,
        AVG(total_sales) OVER (PARTITION BY  year) AS total_sales_for_year
FROM sales
```

sales_person	region	year	average_sales_for_year
Bob	AMERICAS	2006	2416.6667
Fred	AMERICAS	2006	2416.6667
Susan	EUROPE	2006	2416.6667
Jo	EUROPE	2006	2416.6667
Chris	EUROPE	2006	2416.6667
Billy	ASIA	2006	2416.6667
Bob	AMERICAS	2007	3083.3333
Fred	AMERICAS	2007	3083.3333
Susan	EUROPE	2007	3083.3333
Jo	EUROPE	2007	3083.3333
Chris	EUROPE	2007	3083.3333
Billy	ASIA	2007	3083.3333
Bob	AMERICAS	2008	3750
Fred	AMERICAS	2008	3750
Susan	EUROPE	2008	3750
Jo	EUROPE	2008	3750
Chris	EUROPE	2008	3750
Billy	ASIA	2008	3750

Now we can start to get a bit more complicated. If we wanted to show the average sales for each region in a year on every row for that region and year. We can do this by changing our example to be partitioned by year and region as in Fig 4.48.

Fig 4.48

```
SELECT  sales_person,
        region,
        year,
        total_sales,
        AVG(total_sales) OVER (PARTITION BY year,region) AS
                        average_sales_for_year_per_region
FROM sales
```

sales_person	region	year	total_sales	average_sales_for_year_per_region
bob	AMERICAS	2006	1000	1500
fred	AMERICAS	2006	2000	1500
billy	ASIA	2006	4500	4500
susan	EUROPE	2006	1500	2333.3333
chris	EUROPE	2006	5000	2333.3333
jo	EUROPE	2006	500	2333.3333
bob	AMERICAS	2007	1500	3250
fred	AMERICAS	2007	5000	3250
billy	ASIA	2007	1500	1500
susan	EUROPE	2007	7000	3500
chris	EUROPE	2007	2000	3500

jo	EUROPE	2007	1500		3500
bob	AMERICAS	2008	2500		3750
fred	AMERICAS	2008	5000		3750
billy	ASIA	2008	2000		2000
susan	EUROPE	2008	3000	4333.3333	
chris	EUROPE	2008	500	4333.333333	
jo	EUROPE	2008	9500	4333.333333	

RANK OVER AND PARTITION BY

Ranking is a useful OLAP feature that enables you to rank results by there values within a result set, this is not the same as ordering as we will see (You don't have to order a rank). For this we will assume the same data as we used in the previous part of the **PARTITION BY** section.
We will start with a simple query to sum up the total sales per year.

Fig 4.49

```
SELECT   year, SUM(total_sales)
FROM     sales
GROUP BY year
ORDER BY year
```

This produces the results

year	SUM(sales.total_sales)
2006	14500
2007	18500
2008	22500

Now if we want to **RANK** the results we can use the **RANK OVER** statement as in Fig 4.50

Fig 4.50

```
SELECT   year,
         SUM(total_sales),
         RANK() OVER (ORDER BY year DESC)
AS average_sales_for_year
FROM sales
```

Now we also have a rank column.

year	SUM(sales.total_sales)	average_sales_for_year
2008	22500	1
2007	18500	2
2006	14500	3

We can now take this to the next level by ranking each sales person within a year based on their sales. To do this we re-introduce the **PARTITION BY** statement as in Fig 4.51

Fig 4.51

```
SELECT sales_person,
       year,
       total_sales,
       RANK() OVER (PARTITION BY  year order by total_sales desc)
            AS sales_person_rank
FROM     sales
```

sales_person	year	total sales	sales_person_rank
chris	2006	5000	1
billy	2006	4500	2
fred	2006	2000	3
susan	2006	1500	4
bob	2006	1000	5
jo	2006	500	6
susan	2007	7000	1
fred	2007	5000	2
chris	2007	2000	3
billy	2007	1500	4
bob	2007	1500	4
jo	2007	1500	4
jo	2008	9500	1
fred	2008	5000	2
susan	2008	3000	3
bob	2008	2500	4
billy	2008	2000	5
chris	2008	500	6

Now things are getting more interesting, let's rank each sales person by there total sales, but we will still order by the sales person name as in Fig 4.52

Fig 4.52

```
SELECT          sales_person,
                SUM(total_sales) AS sum_of_sales,
                RANK() OVER (ORDER BY sum_of_sales)
                        AS rank_of_sales_person
FROM    sales
GROUP BY sales_person
ORDER BY sales_person
```

sales_person	sum_of_sales	rank_of_sales_person
billy	8000	3
bob	5000	1
chris	7500	2
Fred	12000	6
Jo	11500	4
Susan	11500	4

In the example above both jo and susan are in joint 4th in the ranking and fred is in 6th. Now say we wanted to show fred as being 5th and count the joint 4th as 1 rank. We can do this using the **DENSE_RANK** function as in example 4.53

Fig 4.53

```
SELECT          sales_person,
                SUM(total_sales) AS sum_of_sales,
                DENSE_RANK() OVER (ORDER BY sum_of_sales)
                        AS rank_of_sales_person
FROM      sales
GROUP BY sales_person
ORDER BY sales person
```

sales_person	sum_of_sales	rank_of_sales_person
Billy	8000	3
Bob	5000	1
Chris	7500	2
Fred	12000	5
Jo	11500	4
Susan	11500	4

We can also display rankings as percentages using the **PERCENT_RANK** function as in Fig 4.54.

Fig 4.54

```
SELECT          sales_person,
                SUM(total_sales) AS sum_of_sales,
                PERCENT_RANK() OVER (ORDER BY sum_of_sales)
                        AS rank_of_sales_person
FROM      sales
GROUP BY sales person
```

sales_person	sum_of_sales	rank_of_sales_person
Bob	5000	0
Chris	7500	0.2
Billy	8000	0.4
Susan	11500	0.6
Jo	11500	0.6
Fred	12000	1

We can use other functions to obtain other types of **RANK**s. For example the **CUME_DIST** function can be used to calculate the relative position of a value in a group, returned as a number between 0 and 1. As in Fig 4.55

Fig 4.55

```
SELECT          sales_person,
                SUM(total_sales) AS sum_of_sales,
                CUME_DIST() OVER (ORDER BY sum_of_sales)
                        AS rank_of_sales_person
FROM      sales
GROUP BY sales person
```

sales_person	sum_of_sales	rank_of_sales_person
bob	5000	0.166666667
chris	7500	0.333333333
billy	8000	0.5
susan	11500	0.833333333
jo	11500	0.833333333
fred	12000	1

XML

At some point you may either want to output results as XML query some XML data or load XML into your database. IQ provides some in build functionality that allows you to do both. Although not as flexible as many ETL tools, it does provide some useful statements and options. There is also a useful data type that variables can be declared as named XML. The sections below give tested examples using system table to explain the most common functionality of the XML statements.

Extracting XML

In order to extract data in simple XML you need to add the "**FOR XML RAW**" statement after your **SELECT** statement as in Fig 4.56 which produces the results in Fig 4.57. You can also use the **OUTPUT_FORMAT XML** as in the chapter on Loading and Extracting Data if all you require is a simple XML format and you don't want to manipulate it in any way.

Fig 4.56

```
SELECT    cname, coltype
FROM sys.syscolumns
WHERE tname = 'sysusers'
FOR XML RAW
```

Fig 4.57

```
<row cname="suid" coltype="unsigned int"/>
<row cname="uid" coltype="unsigned int"/>
<row cname="gid" coltype="unsigned int"/>
<row cname="name" coltype="varchar"/>
<row cname="environ" coltype="varchar"/>
```

To wrap the xml into a node you can use the **XMLELEMENT** statement as in Fig 5.58 which produces the results as in Fig 4.59.

Fig 4.58

```
SELECT XMLELEMENT(
   NAME sysusers,
      (SELECT    cname, coltype
      FROM sys.syscolumns
      WHERE          'sysusers'
      FOR XML RAW));
```

Fig 4.59

```
<sysusers>
   <row cname="suid" coltype="unsigned int"/>
   <row cname="uid" coltype="unsigned int"/>
   <row cname="gid" coltype="unsigned int"/>
   <row cname="name" coltype="varchar"/>
   <row cname="environ" coltype="varchar"/>
</sysusers>
```

If however you want to include the table name as a node you can use the **XML AUTO** statement as in Fig 4.60 producing the results in Fig 4.61.

Fig 4.60

```
SELECT    cname, coltype
FROM sys.syscolumns
WHERE tname = 'sysusers'
FOR XML AUTO
```

Fig 4.61

```
<syscolumns cname="suid" coltype="unsigned int"/>
<syscolumns cname="uid" coltype="unsigned int"/>
<syscolumns cname="gid" coltype="unsigned int"/>
<syscolumns cname="name" coltype="varchar"/>
<
```

You can also use the **ELEMENTS** statement with the **XML AUTO** statement which has the effect of producing individual elements for every row selected. The example in Fig 4.62 yields the results in Fig 4.63.

Fig 4.62

```
SELECT    cname, coltype
FROM sys.syscolumns
WHERE tname = 'sysusers'
FOR XML AUTO, ELEMENTS
```

Fig 4.63

```
<syscolumns>
    <cname>suid</cname>
    <coltype>unsigned int</coltype>
</syscolumns>
<syscolumns>
    <cname>uid</cname>
    <coltype>unsigned int</coltype>
</syscolumns>
<syscolumns>
    <cname>gid</cname>
    <coltype>unsigned int</coltype>
</syscolumns>
<syscolumns>
    <cname>name</cname>
    <coltype>varchar</coltype>
</syscolumns>
<syscolumns>
    <cname>environ</cname>
    <coltype>varchar</coltype>
</syscolumns>
```

You can also add **ORDER BY** statements to your **SELECT** that will affect the order in which the elements are produced (just as results sets rows are affected when using a normal **SELECT**). The example in Fig 4.64 yields the results in Fig 4.65

Fig 4.64

```
SELECT    sc.tname, sc.cname
FROM sys.syscolumns sc
WHERE UPPER(sc.tname) IN ('SYSUSER','SYSUSERAUTH')
ORDER BY sc.tname
FOR XML AUTO
```

Fig 4.65

```
<sc tname="SYSUSER" cname="user_id"/>
<sc tname="SYSUSER" cname="object_id"/>
<sc tname="SYSUSER" cname="user_name"/>
<sc tname="SYSUSER" cname="password"/>
<sc tname="SYSUSER" cname="login_policy_id"/>
<sc tname="SYSUSER" cname="expire_password_on_login"/>
<sc tname="SYSUSER" cname="password_creation_time"/>
<sc tname="SYSUSER" cname="failed_login_attempts"/>
<sc tname="SYSUSER" cname="last_login_time"/>
<sc tname="SYSUSERAUTH" cname="name"/>
<sc tname="SYSUSERAUTH" cname="password"/>
<sc tname="SYSUSERAUTH" cname="resourceauth"/>
<sc tname="SYSUSERAUTH" cname="dbaauth"/>
<sc tname="SYSUSERAUTH" cname="scheduleauth"/>
<sc tname="SYSUSERAUTH" cname="user_group"/>
```

When you **JOIN** tables in the **SELECT** statement then the XML produced will create a root element for each tname as in the statement Fig 4.66 and results Fig 4.67.

Fig 4.66

```
SELECT    sc.tname, sc.cname, *
FROM sys.syscolumns sc
JOIN      sys.syscolumns sc2 ON (sc.tname = sc2.tname
                                 AND sc.cname = sc2.cname)
WHERE UPPER(sc.tname) IN ('SYSUSER','SYSUSERAUTH')
ORDER BY sc.tname
FOR XML AUTO
```

Fig 4.67

```
<sc tname="SYSUSER">
    <sc cname="user_id"/>
    <sc cname="object_id"/>
    <sc cname="user_name"/>
    <sc cname="password"/>
    <sc cname="login_policy_id"/>
    <sc cname="expire_password_on_login"/>
    <sc cname="password_creation_time"/>
    <sc cname="failed_login_attempts"/>
    <sc cname="last_login_time"/>
</so>
<sc tname="SYSUSERAUTH">
    <sc cname="name"/>
    <sc cname="password"/>
    <sc cname="resourceauth"/>
    <sc cname="dbaauth"/>
    <sc cname="scheduleauth"/>
    <sc cname="user_group"/>
</so>
```

We can also use the statement **XMLGEN** to produce well formed XML and even add a header to our XML output. We need to name our **SELECT** statement when using this functionality, in our example we name it xml_results using the **AS** statement. The example in Fig 4.68 and results in Fig 4.69 show how to achieve this.

Fig 4.68

```
SELECT XMLGEN( '<?xml version="1.0" encoding="ISO-8859-1"?>
<r>{$xml_results}</r>',
                (       SELECT tname, cname
                        FROM sys.syscolumns
                        WHERE tname = 'SYSOPTION' FOR XML RAW
                )       AS xml_results
)
```

Fig 4.69

```
<?xml version="1.0" encoding="ISO-8859-1" ?>
<r>
        <row tname="SYSOPTION" cname="user_id"/>
        <row tname="SYSOPTION" cname="option"/>
        <row tname="SYSOPTION" cname="setting"/>
</r>
```

Finally you can use the **XMLELEMENT** statement to produce some columns with normal results and other containing XML as in Fig 4.70 and results Fig 4.71. This example also shows how to join columns and values into one node and how to add hardcoded text into the values.

Fig 4.70

```
SELECT sc.tname,
XMLELEMENT( NAME column_data,
            XMLELEMENT( NAME column_name, sc.cname ),
            XMLELEMENT( NAME column_type_and_is_nullable, sc.coltype
||
' allows nulls = ' || sc.nulls  )
        ) AS results
FROM sys.syscolumns sc
WHERE
```

Fig 4.71

tname	Results
SYSUSER	<column_data> <column_name>user_id</column_name> <column_type_and_is_nullable>unsigned int allows nulls = N</column_type_and_is_nullable> </column_data>
SYSUSER	<column_data> <column_name>object_id</column_name> <column_type_and_is_nullable>unsigned bigint allows nulls = N</column_type_and_is_nullable> </column_data>

SYSUSER	`<column_data>`
	`<column_name>user_name</column_name>`
	`<column_type_and_is_nullable>char allows nulls = N</column_type_and_is_nullable>`
	`</column_data>`

SYSUSER	`<column_data>`
	`<column_name>password</column_name>`
	`<column_type_and_is_nullable>binary allows nulls = Y</column_type_and_is_nullable>`
	`</column_data>`

SYSUSER	`<column_data>`
	`<column_name>login_policy_id</column_name>`
	`<column_type_and_is_nullable>unsigned bigint allows nulls =`
	`N</column_type_and_is_nullable>`
	`</column_data>`

SYSUSER	`<column_data>`
	`<column_name>expire_password_on_login</column_name>`
	`<column_type_and_is_nullable>tinyint allows nulls = N</column_type_and_is_nullable>`
	`</column_data>`

SYSUSER	`<column_data>`
	`<column_name>password_creation_time</column_name>`
	`<column_type_and_is_nullable>timestamp allows nulls = Y</column_type_and_is_nullable>`
	`</column_data>`

SYSUSER	`<column_data>`
	`<column_name>failed_login_attempts</column_name>`
	`<column_type_and_is_nullable>unsigned int allows nulls = N</column_type_and_is_nullable>`
	`</column_data>`

SYSUSER	`<column_data>`
	`<column_name>last_login_time</column_name>`
	`<column_type_and_is_nullable>timestamp allows nulls = Y</column_type_and_is_nullable>`
	`</column_data>'`

Querying and Loading XML

First we shall look at declaring a variable to be of type **XML**, assigning a value to it and displaying the variable value.

Fig 4.72

```
DECLARE @my_xml XML

SELECT @my_xml=(SELECT XMLELEMENT( NAME rootxml,
        (    SELECT tname, cname, coltype
             FROM sys.syscolumns
             WHERE tname = 'SYSUSER'
             FOR XML AUTO, ELEMENTS)))

SELECT @my_xml
```

Fig 4.73

```
<rootxml>
        <syscolumns>
                <tname>SYSUSER</tname>
                <cname>user_id</cname>
                <coltype>unsigned int</coltype>
        </syscolumns>
        <syscolumns>
                <tname>SYSUSER</tname>
                <cname>object_id</cname>
                <coltype>unsigned bigint</coltype>
        </syscolumns>
        <syscolumns>
                <tname>SYSUSER</tname>
                <cname>user_name</cname>
                <coltype>char</coltype>
        </syscolumns>
        <syscolumns>
                <tname>SYSUSER</tname>
                <cname>password</cname>
                <coltype>binary</coltype>
        </syscolumns>
        <syscolumns>
                <tname>SYSUSER</tname>
                <cname>login_policy_id</cname>
                <coltype>unsigned bigint</coltype>
        </syscolumns>
        <syscolumns>
                <tname>SYSUSER</tname>
                <cname>expire_password_on_login</cname>
                <coltype>tinyint</coltype>
        </syscolumns>
        <syscolumns>
                <tname>SYSUSER</tname>
                <cname>password_creation_time</cname>
                <coltype>timestamp</coltype>
        </syscolumns>
        <syscolumns>
                <tname>SYSUSER</tname>
                <cname>failed_login_attempts</cname>
                <coltype>unsigned int</coltype>
        </syscolumns>
        <syscolumns>
                <tname>SYSUSER</tname>
                <cname>last_login_time</cname>
                <coltype>timestamp</coltype>
        </syscolumns>
</rootxml>
```

Of course this example does nothing we can't do in SQL alone. But now we can assign an XML variable we can use it to produce a standard result set from an XML input by using the **OPENXML** function.

The example below uses the same @my_xml variable we declared but selects the data out in a tabular format by declaring the elements as columns with corresponding data types. One thing to note is that IQ produces some null results, to get round this we add the 'tname is not null' clause. You may need to tweak this for your own results particularly if the column or columns can have **NULL** values you want to display.

Fig 4.74

```
DECLARE @my_xml XML

SELECT @my_xml=(SELECT XMLELEMENT( NAME rootxml,
          (      SELECT tname, cname, coltype
                 FROM sys.syscolumns
                 WHERE tname = 'SYSUSER'
                 FOR XML AUTO, ELEMENTS)))

SELECT *
FROM OPENXML( @my_xml , '//*' ) WITH (tname VARCHAR(100)
'tname',cname VARCHAR(100) 'cname', coltype VARCHAR (50) 'coltype')
WHERE tname IS NOT NULL
```

Fig 4.75

tname	cname	coltype
SYSUSER	user_id	unsigned int
SYSUSER	object_id	unsigned bigint
SYSUSER	user_name	char
SYSUSER	password	binary
SYSUSER	login_policy_id	unsigned bigint
SYSUSER	expire_password_on_login	tinyint
SYSUSER	password_creation_time	timestamp
SYSUSER	failed_login_attempts	unsigned int
SYSUSER	last_login_time	timestamp

Now we can query xml we have generated lets look at loading XML from a file into a variable and then running a query against it. This example is almost identical to the previous one except we are loading the XML from a file!

First let's assume we have a file called test.xml in the C: drive on the machine our Sybase IQ server is running. This file has the contents as in Fig 4.76

Fig 4.76 – c:\test.xml

```
<rootxml>
        <syscolumns>
                <tname>SYSUSER</tname>
                <cname>user_id</cname>
                <coltype>unsigned int</coltype>
        </syscolumns>
        <syscolumns>
                <tname>SYSUSER</tname>
                <cname>object_id</cname>
                <coltype>unsigned bigint</coltype>
        </syscolumns>
        <syscolumns>
                <tname>SYSUSER</tname>
                <cname>user_name</cname>
                <coltype>char</coltype>
        </syscolumns>
        <syscolumns>
                <tname>SYSUSER</tname>
                <cname>password</cname>
                <coltype>binary</coltype>
        </syscolumns>
        <syscolumns>
                <tname>SYSUSER</tname>
                <cname>login_policy_id</cname>
                <coltype>unsigned bigint</coltype>
        </syscolumns>
        <syscolumns>
                <tname>SYSUSER</tname>
                <cname>expire_password_on_login</cname>
                <coltype>tinyint</coltype>
        </syscolumns>
        <syscolumns>
                <tname>SYSUSER</tname>
                <cname>password_creation_time</cname>
                <coltype>timestamp</coltype>
        </syscolumns>
        <syscolumns>
                <tname>SYSUSER</tname>
                <cname>failed_login_attempts</cname>
                <coltype>unsigned int</coltype>
        </syscolumns>
        <syscolumns>
                <tname>SYSUSER</tname>
                <cname>last_login_time</cname>
                <coltype>timestamp</coltype>
        </syscolumns>
</rootxml>
```

We can read in the file from Fig 4.77 and select data from it by using the xp_read_file command to read the file contents into an **XML** variable as in Fig 4.77 which produces the results in Fig 4.78

Fig 4.77

```
DECLARE @file_xml XML

SELECT xp_read_file( 'c:\\test.xml' )
 INTO @file_xml

SELECT *
FROM OPENXML( @file_xml , '//*' ) WITH (tname VARCHAR(100)
'tname',cname VARCHAR(100) 'cname', coltype VARCHAR (50) 'coltype')
WHERE tname IS NOT NULL
```

Fig 4.78

tname	Cname	coltype
SYSUSER	user_id	unsigned int
SYSUSER	object_id	unsigned bigint
SYSUSER	user_name	char
SYSUSER	Password	binary
SYSUSER	login_policy_id	unsigned bigint
SYSUSER	expire_password_on_login	tinyint
SYSUSER	password_creation_time	timestamp
SYSUSER	failed_login_attempts	unsigned int
SYSUSER	last_login_time	timestamp

Query Plans

There are are a wealth of options related to query plans (see the chapter on Options) below is an example on how to output a query plan in HTML.

Fig 4.79

```
SET TEMPORARY OPTION QUERY_PLAN_AS_HTML_DIRECTORY ='/home/myarea
/query_plans/';\
SET TEMPORARY OPTION QUERY_PLAN_AS_HTML ='ON';
SET TEMPORARY OPTION QUERY_TIMING ='ON';
SET TEMPORARY OPTION QUERY_DETAIL ='ON';\
SET TEMPORARY OPTION QUERY_PLAN_AFTER_RUN = 'ON'

EXEC my_proc;
```

A separate html file will be generated for each statement in the procedure my_proc, using the options above it will include the query time and detail. You can also use the options to include index advice or you may choose to output the query plan into the message log.

I have found that HTML query plans are a very useful way to see where time is being spent on a query. The example in Fig 4.80 and its associated query plan is given in Fig 4.81.

Fig 4.80

```
SET TEMPORARY OPTION QUERY_PLAN_AS_HTML_DIRECTORY ='/home/myarea
/query_plans/';
SET TEMPORARY OPTION QUERY_PLAN_AS_HTML ='ON';
SET TEMPORARY OPTION QUERY_TIMING ='ON';
SET TEMPORARY OPTION QUERY_DETAIL ='ON';
SET TEMPORARY OPTION QUERY_PLAN_AFTER_RUN = 'ON'

SELECT COUNT(*)
FROM    table_1 a
JOIN    table_2 b  ON (a.col_1 = b.col_1)
```

Fig 4.81

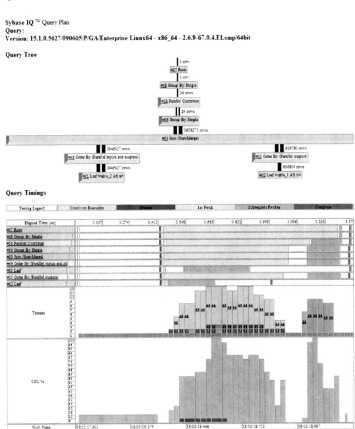

Applogies if the text is to small in the above diagram (it isn't even the whole plan), but basically it shows the tables that were used, elapsed time of the query is the types of joining it is doing, the SQL executed, the parallelism of the query, the trheading, the CPU usage and IO data). There is also much more listed sucg as
It is worth experimenting with the options to obtain your optimal output and also to include further detail on the query.

Loading , Extracting and Moving Data

Whatever your requirements are for Sybase IQ, one thing that is almost for certain is that you want to either load or extract data at some stage.

IQ provides the **LOAD TABLE** statement for loading data from files, the **INSERT LOCATION** statement for inserting directly from other databases and various extraction utility statements and options for getting data out into files.

This chapter covers the various options available to you in getting data in and out of the database quickly. It also points out differences in IQ versions and how a simple option can mean the difference between a load parallel processing and loading in single threaded mode.

The LOAD Table

Overview

Permissions

In order to execute the **LOAD TABLE** statement the server switch **–gl** must be set to **ALL** for the table owner (or DBA) with **ALTER** permission on the tables or set to DBA for DBA's to Load Tables. If the **–gl** switch is not set then no one can execute a **LOAD TABLE**!!!

The input file – delimiters vs separators

The first thing you need to understand before we get on to syntax and examples is the difference between a delimiter and a separator. IQ uses the **LOAD TABLE** statement to load delimited files and will not work with separated file (Unless you use the **FORMAT BCP** option in IQ version 15). If you look at the two files below you will see one has a **|**(pipe) at the end of the last column of data, this is a delimiter!!

A Separated file

```
Column_1|Column_2|Column_3|Column_4
1|2|3|4
a|b|c|d
9|8|7|6
```

A Delimited file

```
Column_1|Column_2|Column_3|Column_4|
1|2|3|4|
a|b|c|d|
9|8|7|6|
```

Unfortunately one of the most common file types out there is a csv and as this is separated not delimited a csv file will require some manipulation before attempting to load via a **LOAD TABLE** statement (unless you use the 15.x **FORMAT BCP** clause).

The bcp utility (Sybase and Microsoft versions) extract files with a separator so you need to add an extractor one in your "bcp out" as a row terminator as in Fig 5.1.

Fig 5.1

```
bcp sysobjects out c:\test.txt -c –STEST_IQ  -Udbo_user  -Ppa55word  -
t"|" -r"|\n"
```

The **–t** option will append a **|** between each column and the **–r** will add a **|** to the end of the last column (along with a line end).
This means your file is now nicely delimited. Of course this is ok when your system handles the data extracts but if you have files sent to your system you may not be able to add the delimiter at the end. To get round this you can use programs like "sed" to add the delimiter or write a simple Perl script to do this for you!!

* The FORMAT BCP clause in IQ 15.x can be used to circumvent this, please see the section below "LOAD TABLE clauses and options".

Load Table Basics

Ok, time for a quick and easy example, for the file given below and a table called my_table which has four columns of **CHAR**(1) (called col1,col2,col3 and col4) data type, we can write a **LOAD TABLE** statement as the one given in Fig 5.2.

File C:\test.txt

```
Column_1|Column_2|Column_3|Column_4|
1|2|3|4|
a|b|c|d|
9|8|7|6|
```

Fig 5.2

```
LOAD TABLE my_table
(col1,
col2,
col3,
col4)
FROM 'c:\test.txt'
DELIMITED BY '|'
ROW DELIMITED BY '\n'
QUOTES OFF
ESCAPES OFF;
```

This can also be executed as in Fig 5.3, but if you are using version IQ 12.x then specifying a delimiter after a column means the file will not be parallel loaded and hence will be slower!! The unfortunate part about this is that when using the "**DELIMITED BY**" clause your delimiter can only be one character (But it will load a hex that relates to a single character such as **\X0A** and also escape references such as **\t** and **\n**)

Fig 5.3

```
LOAD TABLE my_table
(col1 '|',
col2 '|',
col3 '|',
col4 '|')
FROM 'c:\test.txt'
ROW DELIMITED BY '\n'
QUOTES OFF
ESCAPES OFF;
```

LOAD TABLE statement

First there are a couple of differences between 12. And 15.x, these are:-

* The **LOAD TABLE** syntax now includes a **STRIP** clause keyword **RTRIM**. The keyword **RTRIM** replaces the keyword **ON**.

* There is a **FORMAT BCP** option in 15.x that can be used to load files without a column delimited after the last column (i.e. the default for files that are bcp's out from ASE/SQL

Server)

* When bulk loading large objects, the **USING CLIENT FILE** clause applies to both primary and secondary files.

LOAD TABLE Statement Syntax

Fig 5.4

```
LOAD [ INTO ] TABLE [ owner.]table_name
( <load specification> )
{ FROM/USING [ CLIENT ] FILE }
{ '<filename_string>' or filename_variable } [, …]
ESCAPES OFF
  [ CHECK CONSTRAINTS { ON/OFF } ]
  [ DEFAULTS { ON/OFF } ]
  [ QUOTES ON/OFF ]
  [ FORMAT { ASCII/BINARY/BCP } ]
  [ DELIMITED BY '<field delimiter>' ]
  [ STRIP { ON (IQ 12.x) or RTRIM (IQ 15.x)/OFF | RTRIM } ]
  [ WITH CHECKPOINT { ON/OFF } ]
  [ { BLOCK FACTOR number or BLOCK SIZE number } ]
  [ BYTE ORDER { NATIVE/HIGH/LOW } ]
  [ LIMIT <number of rows> ]
  [ NOTIFY <number of rows> ]
  [ ON FILE ERROR { ROLLBACK/FINISH/CONTINUE } ]
  [ PREVIEW { ON/OFF } ]
  [ ROW DELIMITED BY '<row delimiter>' ]
  [ SKIP <number of rows> ]
  [ WORD SKIP integer ]
  [ START ROW ID integer ]
  [ UNLOAD FORMAT ]
  [ ON PARTIAL INPUT ROW { ROLLBACK/CONTINUE } ]
  [ IGNORE CONSTRAINT constraint type]
  [ MESSAGE LOG '<string>' ROW LOG '<string>' [ ONLY LOG logwhat]
  [ LOG DELIMITED BY '<string>' ]
```

Now let's analyse what the syntax means

<load specification>

The load specification can be thought of as the list of columns you are loading into, how the columns are delimited in the file, if the field in the file should be loaded into any columns (Your file may have more columns than you want to load)
Each column in the load specification takes the form given in Fig 5.5

Fig 5.5

```
<destination column_name>  <column specification> or <filler type>
(optional <delimiter>)
```

So for example the load specification in Fig 5.6 will load column_1 with data and any **BLANKS** in the field from the file will be loaded as **NULL** values and for column_2 we are loading a **DATETIME** field and the data in the source file is in the date format 'MM-DD-YYYY hh:mm:ss' no delimiter is required. The first **FILLER** is used because when specifying the date format for column_2 the format also implicitly declares the column to be the fixed width of the format. The second filler specifies that the third field in the file will not be loaded and column_3 will now be loaded with the files 4 field of data.

Fig 5.6

```
CREATE TABLE my_destination_table(
        column_1        CHAR(1)         NULL,
        column_2        DATETIME        NULL,
        column_3        VARCHAR(50)     NULL
);


LOAD TABLE my_destination_table
(
        /* THIS IS THE LOAD SPECIFICATION */
        column_1        '|'     NULL(BLANKS)                    ,
        column_2        DATETIME('MM-DD-YYYY hh:nn:ss')         ,
        FILLER('|')                                             ,
        FILLER('|')                                             ,
        column_3        '|'
)
FROM '/home/my_area/test_2.txt'
ROW DELIMITED BY '\n'
QUOTES OFF
ESCAPES OFF;
```

If the file test_2.txt contained the data in as below then the table (if empty before the load) would contain the data in Fig 5.7

File test_2.txt

```
A|03-02-2002 11:12:47|Test String|I am Field 4|
 |02-07-2005 13:32:47|Test String 2|I am Field 4|
 |12-29-2008 19:07:47|Test String 2|I am Field 4|
A|04-22-2013 02:45:47|Test String 2|I am Field 4|
```

Fig 5.7 (Table of data loaded)

column_1	column_2	column_3
A	MAR-02-2002 11:12:47	I am Field 4
<NULL>	FEB-07-2005 13:32:47	I am Field 4
<NULL>	DEC-29-2008 19:07:47	I am Field 4
A	APR-22-2013 02:45:47	I am Field 4

Now is a good point to give you a little trick. If you only wanted the **DATE** portion of the file, simply change the column specification to the one below in Fig 5.8.

Fig 5.8

```
column_1        '|'     NULL(BLANKS),
column_2        DATETIME('MM-DD-YYYY'),
FILLER('|'),
FILLER('|'),
column_3        '|'
```

And the data loaded will be as in Fig 5.9

Fig 5.9 (new data loaded)

column_1	column_2	column_3
A	MAR-02-2002 00:00:00	I am Field 4
<NULL>	FEB-07-2005 00:00:00	I am Field 4
<NULL>	DEC-29-2008 00:00:00	I am Field 4
A	APR-22-2013 00:00:00	I am Field 4

Because the **DATETIME**(<format>) option also uses the length of the format string to implicitly declare the column length it will now ignore everything after the date in the field and the **FILLER** will not load anything from the end of the **DATETIME** until the delimiter specified in the **FILLER**. This trick only works if the date part you want is at the beginning of the field i.e. '12:45:59 12-31-2010' will just return an error saying it could not convert '12:45:59 12' to a **TIMESTAMP** (**DATETIME** and **TIMESTAMP** is the same thing in IQ).

Anyway back to the column specifications........

The column specification syntax tells the load how long the data is or how it is separated and optionally the type of data being loaded and/or how the data is formatted and/or what to do with data in certain formats.

The syntax is given in Fig 5.10

Fig 5.10

```
ASCII  ( <input width> )
or   BINARY [ WITH NULL BYTE ]
or   PREFIX { 1/2/4 }
or   '<delimiter>'
and/or
DATE /DATETIME ( <format> )
and/or
ENCRYPTED (<data type> '<encryption key>' [, '<algorithm>' ] )
or
DEFAULT <default value >
and then optionally  at the end
NULL ( BLANKS/ZEROS/ 'literal' )
and
finally a comma (if there are more columns to follow)!
```

Not all combinations of options make sense or work with each other. For example if you specify the field as an **ASCII** fixed width field then you would not also put a field delimiter.
There are quite a lot of options for the column specification so I have listed these below with a description of each:-

Column Specification Option	Description
ASCII (<*input width*>)	This indicates the field is an **ASCII** field with a fixed length. The value of <*input width*> is an integer specifying the length of the field in bytes. Every record in your file for the specified field must be the same length for this to work.
BINARY	If the data you are loading was unloaded from IQ with the **TEMP_EXTRACT_BINARY** option set ON, you must use the **BINARY WITH NULL** option for every column when loading binary data.
PREFIX 1/2/4	This indicates this is a **BINARY** field, the **PREFIX** value of 1, 2 or 4 is used to specify the length of the binary field.

'<delimiter>'	When a delimiter is specified in the column specification as opposed to using the 'DELIMITED BY' clause of the LOAD TABLE statement then a delimiter may be a combination of a maximum of 4 printable characters. You may also use hex ASCII codes to represent non printable character for example '\x0a' to represent a newline. The 'DELIMITED BY' clause only allows one character. The downside of using delimiters in the column specification is that in IQ 12.x the load will not spawn threads to run in parallel and hence the data is serially loaded and will therefore take longer to load.
DATE/DATETIME (<format>)	This option is used to specify the format of a fields datetime, the format specified will also be used to calculate the length of the field for example the format 'MMDDYY' implicitly marks the field as a fixed width 6 character field. This means that if you specify the format in a delimited file then you must use the FILLER (<delimiter> as the column specification of the next column. It also means you can strip trailing times off of DATETIME fields.
ENCRYPTED (<datatype> '<encryption key>' [, '<algorithom>'])	This enables you to load a columns data as encrypted, the algorithm option is a not relevant at the moment as only AES is supported and is also the default!! Remember to save your encryption keys somewhere safe as you cannot access the data without it!!
DEFAULT '<default value >'	Used to load a default value into a column rather than use data from the file, if you also want to skip a field's data and load a default you will still need to use a FILLER option to move to the skip over the field in the file!!
NULLS (BLANKS/ZEROS /'literal')	This is used to specify that blanks, data containing only zeros or a specified 'literal' should be loaded as NULLS into the specified column. E.g. NULLS(BLANKS) would load any blank fields (or fields with a list of spaces) as a NULL value into the column.

LOAD TABLE clauses and options

Apart from the column specification there are also clauses and options that can be used to effect the whole LOAD TABLE statement. As we have seen in the basics section we can declare delimiters in either the column specification or by using the 'DELIMITED BY' clause to affect the whole file being loaded.

You MUST always specify the following:-

Versions 12.x and 15.x

* ESCAPES OFF –"OFF" is the only allowable value in IQ.
For versions prior to IQ 12.7 you must also set

* QUOTES OFF

The list of available clauses and their values is given below, there are 24 different clauses and in conjunction with column specifications should cover almost everything you could want to do when loading files.

Clause	Values	Description
FROM/USING CLIENT] FILE	'<filename_string>' or <filename_variable> or '<filename_string>', '<filename_string>', etc or <filename_variable>,	The USING FILE clauses is used to load one or more files from the server file area, where are the USING CLIENT FILE bulk loads one or more files from a client file area. When specifying the file location on windows the backslash character must be represented as two backslashes e.g. 'c:\\my_data\\my_file.txt' . When using the 'USING CLIENT FILE' clause the character

	\<filename_variable\>, etc or '\<filename_string\>', \<filename_variable\> , etc	set of the client file must be the same as the one used by the IQ server. This clause is a welcome addition to IQ as it means you may not have to ftp files to the server!! However client side loading can only be used with ODBC or JDBC connections that use the Command Sequence network protocol. TDS connections such as Open Client and (JDBC) JConnnect cannot use the client side loader. If more than one file is specified then the files are processed serially and each file is locked until it is processed. When using the '**USING FILE**' clause the server **MUST** have access to the file location, if the file does not exist or the IQ server does not have permissions then IQ believes it should be checking in the root directory of the IQ server and will give an error indicating the root path followed by the path of the file entered in the '**USING FILE**' clause.
CHECK CONSTRAINTS	ON or OFF	When this clause value is ON (default), then check constraints are evaluated and you are can either log or ignore them. When **CHECK CONSTRAINTS** are OFF then IQ ignores all check constraint violation. You may wish to do this if reloading several tables or rebuilding a database from files. Also when a table has check constraints that call UDF's (User Functions) that are not created, the rebuild fails unless this option is set to OFF. This option is mutually exclusive with the four options below. If any of these options are specified in the same load, you will get an error:- 1) **LOG ALL** 2) **LOG CHECK** 3) **IGNORE CONSTRAINT ALL** 4) **IGNORE CONSTRAINT CHECK**
DEFAULTS	ON or OFF	When the **DEFAULTS** are ON (the default) and a column has a default value, then that default value is used if the column is not in the **LOAD TABLE** column specifications. If the **DEFAULTS** option is OFF, and the column is not in the **LOAD TABLE** column specifications then it is assigned **NULL**. This setting applies to all column **DEFAULT** values, including **AUTOINCREMENT/IDENTITY** columns

QUOTES	ON or OFF	This parameter is optional for versions 12.7 onwards and must be set to OFF for versions prior to that (The default setting is ON). When this clause is ON the **LOAD TABLE** statement expects strings in the input file to be enclosed in quote characters (single or double). The first such character encountered in a string is treated as the quote character for the string and the string data must also be terminated with a matching quote. You would use this option if you wanted to include the delimiters within the data. For example in a csv file you may want to include commas in address data. However there are some restrictions for this clause. • With **QUOTES** ON, the first character of a column delimiter or row terminator cannot be a single or double quote mark. • The **QUOTES** ON option applies only to column-delimited **ASCII** fields. and doe4s not apply to **BLOBS** or **CLOBS** • If **LOAD TABLE** encounters any non-white characters after the terminating quote character an error is reported.
ESCAPES OFF	OFF	This option must be set to OFF in Sybase IQ. For some strange reason the default is ON and IQ reports a man error if it is left that way. The documentation says that is a column specification is omitted and **ESCAPES** is ON , characters following the backslash character are interpreted as special characters by the database server. But it's a mute point as every **LOAD TABLE** statement from 12.x through to 15.2 must set **ESCAPES**=OFF.
FORMAT ascii/binary/bcp	ASCII, BINARY OR BCP	This clause is used to provide a default format for data where a column specification has not specified if the data is **ASCII** or **BINARY**. The default format is ASCII, and the following options are allowed:- **BINARY** – The default load format for a column is binary data delimited by the **DELIMITED BY** clause. **ASCII**– The default load format for a column is ascii data delimited by the **DELIMITED BY** clause. **BCP** – The default format is a bcp file. When the format is BCP the column specifications can only have column names, **NULL**, and **ENCRYPTED** and the default **DELMITED** BY delimiter is a <tab> (but you can override this) and the default **ROW DELMITED BY** is a <newline>. To load a file with the **BCP** option is must have the following characteristics • The data was bcp's out using the –c (cross-platform option). • The last column **MUST NOT HAVE** a column delimiter as BCP files are separated. If the column delimiter is after the last column of data and before the row terminator, then the column delimiter is treated as a part of the data.

DELIMITED BY \<delimiter\>'	'\<delimiter\>'	The **DELIMITED BY** option is used if a delimiter does not form part of the column specification, the default delimiter is a comma. Delimiters can be hex representations such as '\x0a' or escaped characters such as '\n', and of course they can also be ACII characters. when using the **DELIMITED BY** clause you can only specify a single character (4 characters are allowed in the column specification), but the upside is that for versions 12.x using the **DELIMITED BY** clause will mean you load can be run in parallel and thus will be faster. I have found on 15.x all loads appear to be parallelised
STRIP	ON (IQ 12.x) or RTRIM (IQ 15.x) or OFF	When the **STRIP** clause is set to ON (12.x) or **RTRIM** (IQ 15.x) (defaults) then any trailing blanks are stripped from non quoted strings, and also for leading blanks and tabs if the **QUOTES** clause is also set to ON. The **STRIP OFF** option provides for a faster **LOAD** and ensures the load adheres to **ASNI** standards where **STRIP** affects **VARCHAR** columns but not **CHAR** columns as a **CHAR** is always padded as such **STRIP** applies only to variable-length non-binary data and does not apply to **ASCII** fixed-width inserts. The effect of the **TRIM** option is also affected by the column specification as below:- **STRIP RTRIM** on a delimited or **BINARY** field or will trim the blanks **STRIP RTRIM** on a fixed width **ASCII** field that is loading into a **VARCHAR** column of the same length will not trim the blanks **STRIP OFF** on a delimited or **BINARY** field or will not trim the blanks **STRIP OFF** on a fixed width **ASCII** field that is loading into a **VARCHAR** column of the same length will trim the blanks
WITH CHECKPOINT	ON or OFF	If the is not specified or set to OFF (The default) then a checkpoint is not issued when the **LOAD TABLE** completes. This means it is advisable to store the file/files you used for loading in case you need to restore the data. When this is set to ON a checkpoint it issued after the successful completion and logging of the **LOAD TABLE**. For more information on checkpoints see the chapter on Back-up and recovery.
BLOCK FACTOR or BLOCK SIZE	Number	The **BLOCK FACTOR** clause is used to specify the blocking factor (number of records per block used when a tape was created), the default value is 10,000. It is used when loading into column specifications of fixed-width and can be used for performance tuning. The **BLOCK SIZE** clause is used to specify the default block size (in bytes) that input data should be read. It is used when loading into column specifications of variable-length, the default value is 500,000.

BYTE ORDER	NATIVE or HIGH or LOW	This option is used when loading data into binary columns, if your **LOAD TABLE** statement does not load into any binary columns and you specify this clause then it is ignored! When loading data specified as binary in the column specification IQ will always read the binary data in the format native to the host machine. Therefore IQ allows you to use the **BYTE ORDER** clause to specify the data as one of the following options. • **NATIVE** (The default) used to use the format native to the host. • **HIGH** used on Unix based platforms (SUN, AIX, HP etc) when multi byte quantities have the high order byte. • **LOW** used on systems (e.g. windows) where the multi byte quantities have a low byte order.
LIMIT	Number of rows to limit	This is used to specify a limit on the number of rows that can be loaded in the **LOAD TABLE** statement, the default is 0 which means no limit.
NOTIFY	Number of rows to notify on	The **NOTIFY** clause is used to specify of a message is produced each time a specific number of rows (default 100,000) are successfully loaded. The value of this clause overrides the value of the **NOTIFY_MODULUS** database option.
ON FILE ERROR	ROLLBACK or FINISH or CONTINUE	This clause is used to specify what happens when a file error occurs. A file error can occur when a file cannot be opened (due to incorrect permissions or if it does not exist at the location specified). The values of the **ON FILE ERROR** clause are • **ROLLBACK** which will abort the entire LOAD table transaction (the default). • **FINISH** will finish any data inserts already completed and then end the load. • **CONTINUE** will skip the bad file, produce and error message but then continue the load. This clause cannot be used if you are running a partial width load.
PREVIEW	ON or OFF	This clause is used to display the layout of the input data in relation to the destination table, the information is also written in the server log. The information displayed includes the data type of each column and the starting position in the file of the data. The information is displayed at the beginning of the load.
ROW DELIMITED BY	'<row delimiter>'	This clause is used to specify the character that delimits a row (normally a '**/n**' or '**/x0a**'). This clause can only be used it all fields in your load are delimited with column terminators or defined by the **DATE** or **DATETIME** column specification options or **ASCII** fixed length fields. All rows must have the same row delimiter and the row delimiter cannot be contained in a column delimiter and vice versa. One of the most common causes of errors is when row delimiters have not been specified correctly or if there is not a column delimiter after the last column (and the **FORMAT BCP** option is not used).
SKIP	Number of rows to skip	The value of the **SKIP** clause specifies how many rows at a beginning of a file the Load should skip. This is useful for

		skipping header rows in a file.
WORD SKIP	Number of words to skip	This clause is used when loading data into columns with a **WD** index on them. It is used to allow a load to continue when the load attempts to load data longer than the limit specified when the word index was created. For any rows of data that cannot be loaded because a word exceeds the limit a waning message is placed in the IQ message log file. These errors can be optionally logged to the message log file and any rejected rows logged to a row log file that is specified in the **LOAD TABLE** statement. When this option is not used and an error occurs then IQ rolls back when encountering the first occurrence of loading a word longer than the limit. The value of the **WORD SKIP** clause is used to specify the number of times (The default is 0 meaning no limit) the error is ignored.
START ROW ID	Row Number to start at	This clause is used to specify the row number in the table being loaded where IQ should begin loading. This clause is used with partial width inserts where you are loading some columns from one file and other columns from a different file. The default for IQ is to append to a table but in the case or partial width loads you need a way to specify the row that you want to begin loading at. The default value for this option is 0, but partial width inserts need to begin at an existing row. You must also remember that when doing partial width inserts the columns for the rows being inserted into cannot have any data in them. You cannot use this clause in a partitioned table.
UNLOAD FORMAT		**UNLOAD FORMAT** Is used to specify that a file has internal IQ formats created by versions of IQ pre 12.X , The **UNLOAD FORMAT** option has the restrictions listed below:- The only column specification you can use is **BINARY** (You can't even use **PREFIX**), you cannot use the **NULL()** options either. When loading null values you must specify the **WITH NULL BYTE** keyword. You cannot use the **DELIMITED BY** or **ROW DELIMITED BY** clauses in the **LOADT TABLE** statement.
ON PARTIAL INPUT ROW	ROLLBACK or CONTINUE	This clause specifies what IQ should do then a partial row is encountered in the load. The options are **CONTINUE** (the default) where IQ will issue a warning message and continue with the load, or **ROLLBACK** where the entire load operation is aborted, rolled back and IQ will issue and error message.
IGNORE CONSTRAINT	constraint type or constraint type, constraint type, etc	When loading data this clause gives you the option of ignoring constraints and setting a limit on the number to ignore. You may specify the following constraints to ignore where <limit> is the maximum number of constraint errors to ignore; if this number is zero then there is no limit. Please remember that by logging violations the load time may be impaired.

• **NULL** <limit>
If the **NULL** <limit> is not specified, then the first occurrence of any **NULL** constraint violation causes the **LOAD** statement to roll back otherwise it will rollback when it encounter (<limit> +1) **NULL** constraint violations.

• **UNIQUE** <limit>
If the **UNIQUE** <limit> is not specified, then the first occurrence of any **UNIQUE** constraint violation causes the **LOAD** statement to roll back otherwise it will rollback when it encounter (<limit> +1) **UNIQUE** constraint violations.

• **CHECK** <limit>
If the **CHECK**<limit> is not specified, then the first occurrence of any **CHECK** constraint violation causes the **LOAD** statement to roll back otherwise it will rollback when it encounter (<limit> +1) **CHECK** constraint violations.

• **FOREIGN KEY** <limit>
If the **FOREIGN KEY** <limit> is not specified, then the first occurrence of any **FOREIGN KEY** constraint violation causes the **LOAD** statement to roll back otherwise it will rollback when it encounter (<limit> +1) **NULL** constraint violations.

• **DATA VALUE** <limit>
When the database option **CONVERSION_ERROR = ON** then an error is reported and the statement rolls back otherwise if the **DATA VALUE** <limit> is not specified, then the first occurrence of any **DATA VALUE** constraint violation causes the **LOAD** statement to roll back otherwise it will rollback when it encounter (<limit> +1) **DATA VALUE** constraint violations.

• **ALL** <limit>
If the database option **CONVERSION_ERROR = ON**, an error is reported and the statement rolls back. Otherwise if the **ALL** <limit> option is used then the load only rolls back when (<limit> +1) total constraint violations of all types (**NULL, DATA VALUE, FOREIGN KEY** & **UNIQUE**) is reached. If you set <limit> to 0 then all constraints all ignored. If you specify another constraint option along with the ALL option then either may cause a rollback e.g. "FOREIGN KEY 25, ALL 100" then in this case a roll back will occur on 25 **FOREIGN KEY** violations or 100 violations of **DATA VALUE, NULL** and **UNIQUE** constraints.

MESSAGE LOG, ROW LOG and optional ONLY LOG	[MESSAGE LOG 'string' ROW LOG 'string' [ONLY LOG <log option> [<log option> , ...]]	Firstly you must declare **BOTH** a **MESSAGE LOG** and **ROW LOG** together you cannot use one clause without the other. Both clauses take the option of a file location and name that cannot be named pipes or raw partitions and the **ROW** and **MESSAGE LOG**s cannot be the same file name. You may also optionally use the ONLY LOG clause which will allow the logs to capture integrity constraint violations; otherwise the logs just record the start and end times of the load. The **ROW LOG** will record the integrity violations for each row (And add one row in the log for each violation) and the **MESSAGE LOG** has information about the entire **LOAD TABLE** process. The messages that are captured are also affected by the **IGNORE CONSTRAINT** clause.
		The syntax of the clause is
		MESSAGE LOG <message log file name>, **ROW LOG** <row log file name> [**ONLY LOG (CHECK | ALL | NULL | UNIQUE | DATA VALUE | FOREIGN KEY | WORD**)]
		The options of the **ONLY LOG** clause indicate which type of integrity violations should be recorded (see the **IGNORE CONSTRAINT** clause for details on the constraints) in the **ROW LOG**.
		The types of messages sent to the **MESSAGE LOG** are affected by the **IGNORE CONSTRAINT** clause. Where the **IGNORE CONSTRAINT** clause is specified then all integrity constraint violations are logged along with their limits up to the point of a rollback. If the **IGNORE CONSTRAINT** clause is not specified then only the first violation is recorded prior to a rollback.
LOG DELIMITED BY	'<log delimiter>'	This clause specifies how data values in the row log are separated (not delimited as the name suggests) in the file specified in the **ROW LOG**. The default is a comma.

Examples

Example 1 – Multiple loading options and logging load messages

If for example you declare the table test1 as in Fig 5.11 below
Fig 5.11

```
CREATE TABLE test1
(
        col1    INT NULL,
        col2    VARCHAR(20) NULL
)
```

And you have a file called /tmp/test.txt with the contents as in Fig 5.12 below

Fig 5.12 - /tmp/test.txt

```
1|Test Row 1
2|Test Row 2
3|Test Row 3
4|Test Row 4
```

We have two choices to load this, one as a **FORMAT BCP** (Fig 5.13) and the other as an **ASCII** fixed width (Fig 5.14).
Fig 5.13

```
LOAD TABLE test1
(col1,
col2
)
FROM '/tmp/test.txt'
ESCAPES OFF
QUOTES OFF
FORMAT BCP
DELIMITED BY '|'
MESSAGE LOG '/tmp/test1_load.log'
        ROW LOG '/tmp/test1_load_row_log.log'
        ONLY LOG ALL
```

Fig 5.14

```
LOAD TABLE test1
(
        col1 ASCII(1),
        FILLER('|'),
        col2 ASCII(10),
        FILLER('\n')
)
FROM '/tmp/test.txt'
ESCAPES OFF
QUOTES OFF
MESSAGE LOG '/tmp/test1_load.log'
        ROW LOG '/tmp/test1_load_row_log.log'
        ONLY LOG ALL
```

The **MESSAGE LOG** (Fig 5.15) and **ROW LOG** (Fig 5.16) for both of these produce the same results:-

Fig 5.15 – MESSAGE LOG

```
2010-07-07 10:37:24 Load Table test1: Integrity Constraint Violations
2010-07-07 10:37:24 Load Table test1: Completed
```

Fig 5.16 – ROW LOG

```
2010-07-07 10:37:24 Load Table test1: Integrity Constraint Violations
Date Format: YYYY-MM-DD
Time Format: HH:NN:SS.SSS
Datetime Format: YYYY-MM-DD HH:NN:SS.SSS
2010-07-07 10:37:24 Load Table test1: Completed
```

If we also include the **PREVIEW ON** clause we could see in the server log the output in Fig 5.17.

Fig 5.17 - SERVER LOG using the PREVIEW ON clause

```
I. 07/04 10:43:04. Length 1,          0 nulls,    A->integer col1
I. 07/04 10:43:04. Delimiter |                    FILLER
I. 07/04 10:43:04. Length 10,         0 nulls,    A->varchar col2
I. 07/04 10:43:04. Delimiter \x0a                 FILLER
I. 07/04 10:43:04. *** Record size: variable, Block size:  500000
I. 07/04 10:43:04.
In table 'test1', the full width insert of 2 columns will begin at record 9.
I. 07/04 10:43:04. Portions of the insert/load will be single threaded.
I. 07/04 10:43:04. Insert Pass 1 completed in 0 seconds.
I. 07/04 10:43:04. Insert Pass 2 completed in 0 seconds.
I. 07/04 10:43:04.
        4 records were inserted into 'test1'.
I. 07/04 10:43:04. Insert for 'test1' completed in 0 seconds.  4 rows
inserted.
```

If we did not specify the **PREVIEW** clause or set it to OFF (The default) then the server log will only show the out put in Fig 5.17.

Fig 5.17 - SERVER LOG using the PREVIEW OFF (or not set) clause

```
I. 07/04 10:43:54.
In table 'test1', the full width insert of 2 columns will begin at record 13.
I. 07/04 10:43:54. Portions of the insert/load will be single threaded.
I. 07/04 10:43:54. Insert Pass 1 completed in 0 seconds.
I. 07/04 10:43:54. Insert Pass 2 completed in 0 seconds.
I. 07/04 10:43:54.
        4 records were inserted into 'test1'.
I. 07/04 10:43:54. Insert for 'test1' completed in 0 seconds.  4 rows
inserted.
```

Example 2 – Skipping rows and delimiters

If the file /tmp/test.txt contained the data in Fig 5.18

Fig 5.18 - /tmp/test.txt

```
column_1|column_2|
1|Test Row 1|
2|Test Row 2|
3|Test Row 3|
4|Test Row 4|
```

To load this file (Fig 5.18) we execute the **LOAD TABLE** in Fig 5.19

Fig 5.19

```
LOAD TABLE test1
(col1,
col2
)
FROM '/tmp/test.txt'
ESCAPES OFF
QUOTES OFF
SKIP 1
DELIMITED BY '|'
```

We have used the **SKIP** 1 clause to skip the first row of the file as it now contains a header row. If we did not use the **SKIP** clause we would get an error message "Cannot convert column_1 to a int(4) (column col1)" SQLCODE=-157, ODBC 3 State="07006".
Now suppose the delimiter in the file /tmp/test.txt was a double pipe as in Fig 5.20

Fig 5.20

```
column_1||column 2||
1||Test Row 1||
2||Test Row 2||
3||Test Row 3||
4||Test Row 4||
```

We will now have to specify the delimiter in every column definition. This is because the **DELMITED BY** clause can only contain a single character (for **ASCII** Files).
If tried the **LOAD TABLE** statement in Fig 5.21 we would get the error "An invalid size (too large) was specified for a **LOAD** option. " SQLCODE=-1013028, ODBC 3 State="HY000"

Fig 5.21

```
LOAD TABLE test1
( col1,
  col2
)
FROM '/tmp/test.txt'
SKIP 1
ESCAPES OFF
QUOTES OFF
DELIMITED BY '||'
```

However you may load the table with the **LOAD TABLE** statement in Fig 5.22.

Fig 5.22

```
LOAD TABLE test1
(col1 '||',
col2 '||'
)
FROM '/tmp/test.txt'
SKIP 1
ESCAPES OFF
QUOTES OFF
```

 * Remember that in IQ 12.x using a delimiter in the column specification instead of the **DELIMITED BY** Clause will mean the load will not parallel process (Contrary to Sybase docs I have read it does parallel process in 15.x in tests I have conducted).

Example 3 – Loading from Local Files (A bit like a BCP in)

Consider the file c:\test.txt on your local pc with the contents

Fig 5.23 – Local file c:\test.txt

```
1|Test Client Row 1|
2|Test Client Row 2|
3|Test Client Row 3|
4|Test Client Row 4|
```

We can load this local client file into a table on the database server (running on a different host/file system to the client file) by executing the code below in Fig 5.24 (IQ 15.x only).

Fig 5.23 – Local file c:\test.txt

```
LOAD TABLE test1
(
        col1,
        col2
)
USING CLIENT FILE 'c:\\test.txt'
DELIMITED BY '|'
ESCAPES OFF
QUOTES OFF
```

Load Table Failures

If you load table fails due to space issues on your MAIN IQ DBSpaces then the load will suspend until you add more DBFiles to accommodate the space. Once the space has been added then your load can proceed.

The Insert Location Statement

Overview

This is probably one of my favourite and most useful IQ commands; it enables you to select data from a table held in a different database on a different server directly into a table on your IQ database. It is also the recommended method for transferring data from the catalog store into IQ tables (but it doesn't work the other way).

If for example we have a local table called accounts in our IQ database and there is a table called source_accounts with the same definition as our table in an ASE database called FINANCE on a server called FIN_SERVER.

If the relevant external logins, interface/sql.ini entries etc have been set up we can simply execute

INSERT accounts **LOCATION** 'FIN_SERVER.FINANCE' {**SELECT** * **FROM** source_accounts}

This command will suck the data from the source_accounts table on the FINANCE database into our local IQ table.

Similarly if we create a table in the IQ store called IQ_objects with the same definition as the system table sysobjects. Then the recommended way to populate our IQ table from the table in the catalog/system store is to execute the code below:-

INSERT IQ_objects **LOCATION** 'this_IQ_server.this_IQ_server' {select * from sysobjects}

Setting up an external login

In order for Insert location to work from any server (including from the catalog store of the server the command is executing on) there needs to be an entry in the interfaces file (Unix/Linux) or the SQL.ini file on Windows. At very least this should always contain information about the IQ servers actually running on a host.

If you are executing your **INSERT LOCATION** statement with a user id that has a corresponding user id on the remote server with the same password then all you need to do is set up the remote server by running a **CREATE SERVER** command as in Fig 5.24

Fig 5.24

```
CREATE SERVER MY_REMOTE_DATABASE
CLASS 'sajdbc'
USING 'my_remote_host:2638'
```

You can set up a remote server based on a number of different server classes passed into the **CLASS** clause. For ASE and IQ you can use JDBC and ODBC connections and for others you can only use ODBC.

The Server class options are given in the table below.

Class Option	Type	Description
CLASS 'asajdbc'	JDBC	Used to connect to IQ and ASA databases via JDBC. The **USING** clause must specify to host, port (<remote database name> is not require/optional). e.g. USING '<remote host name>: <port of remote database server>/ <remote database name>'
CLASS 'asejdbc'	JDBC	Used to connect to IQ and ASA databases via JDBC. The **USING** clause must specify to host, port and database. e.g. **USING** '<remote host

		name>: <port of remote database server>/ <remote database name>'
CLASS 'asaodbc'	ODBC	Used to connect to ASA and IQ databases via ODBC, the **USING** clause must specify an ODBC data source name e.g. **USING** '<data source name>'
CLASS 'aseodbc'	ODBC	Used to connect to Sybase ASE databases via ODBC, the **USING** clause must specify an ODBC data source name e.g. **USING** '<data source name>'
CLASS 'db2odbc'	ODBC	Used to connect to OBM DB2 databases via ODBC, the **USING** clause must specify an ODBC data source name e.g. **USING** '<data source name>'
CLASS 'mssodbc'	ODBC	Used to connect to Microsoft SQL Server databases via ODBC, the USING clause must specify an ODBC data source name e.g. **USING** '<data source name>'
CLASS 'oraodbc'	ODBC	Used to connect to Oracle databases via ODBC, the USING clause must specify an ODBC data source name e.g. **USING** '<data source name>'
CLASS 'odbc'	ODBC	Used to connect to generic ODBC databases via ODBC, the USING clause must specify an ODBC data source name e.g. **USING** '<data source name>'

If we want to connect to the remote host with a different ID then for each user executing an **INSERT LOCATION** we need to set up as remote login as in the example in Fig 5.25

Fig 5.25

```
CREATE EXTERNLOGIN DBA
TO MY_REMOTE_DATABASE
REMOTE LOGIN DBA
IDENTIFIED BY pa55word
```

The **IDENTIFIED BY** clause in the **CREATE EXTERNLOGIN** statement is optional and will default to **NULL** if not specified.

INSERT LOCATION Syntax

Syntax overview

The syntax of the insert location statement is given in fig 5.26

Fig 5.26

```
INSERT <table owner>.<table name>

( <column name>,<column name>, etc ) -- Optional - columns to insert into.

<insert load options> -- Optional

<insert select load options> --Optional

LOCATION '<remote server name>.<remote database name>'

<location options> --Optional

{ <select statement to execute on remote server> }
```

Syntax breakdown

INSERT

INSERT can be specified as below, the use of **INTO** keyword is optional and the <table owner> may be omitted if the user executing the **INSERT LOCATION** table owns the local table being inserted into.

INSERT <table *owner*>.<*table name*>
or
INSERT INTO <table *owner*>.<*table name*>
or
INSERT <table name>
or
INSERT INTO <*table name*>

Column Listing

(<column name>,<column name>, etc)
You may specify only a subset of columns to insert into, of course any columns not specified must be nullable or have a default

insert load options

You may provide options that effect the loading operation of the **INSERT LOCATION** statement, these are.

insert load option	Description
LIMIT <number of rows>	This is used to limit the number of rows inserted. The default is zero meaning there is no limit the maximum limit is (2Gb -1). This means that regardless of the **SELECT** statement run on the remote server <number of rows> rows will be inserted into the local table.
NOTIFY <number of rows>	This enables you to specify that a message is written to the message log each time <number of rows> is reached. For example if this was set to 1000 and the remote select returned 20,000 rows then a message will be written 20 times (once for each <number of rows> inserted).
SKIP <number of rows>	You can use this to specify how many rows from the

	beginning of the returned results should be skipped. For example if this was set to 10 then the first 10 rows of the result set returned from the remote host would not be inserted.
START ROW ID <row number to start insert>	Just like to option in the **LOAD TABLE**, this enables you to specify the row in the local table that you want to start inserting data at. The default is 0. This is only used for partial width loading and the columns being loaded cannot already have data in them. You cannot use this option on a portioned table.

Example

The example **INSERT LOCATION** statement in Fig 5.27 will only load up to 150 rows from the remote table and will output a message to the message log every 50 rows. This example is loading from another IQ database so the '<SOURCE_SERVER>.<SOURCE_DATABASE>' has the same name (SALESIQ) for both the server and the database.

Fig 5.27

```
INSERT sales  LIMIT 150 NOTIFY 50 LOCATION 'SALESIQ.SALESIQ ' {select * from
remote_sales_table}
```

The output to the IQ message log is:-

```
In table 'sales', the full width insert of 115 columns will begin at record
1.
I. 07/12 12:50:39.      50 Rows, 0 Seconds
I. 07/12 12:50:39.     100 Rows, 0 Seconds
I. 07/12 12:50:39.     150 Rows, 0 Seconds
I. 07/12 12:50:39. Insert Pass 1 completed in 0 seconds.
I. 07/12 12:50:39. Insert Pass 2 completed in 0 seconds.
I. 07/12 12:50:39.
        150 records were inserted into 'sales'.
I. 07/12 12:50:39. Insert for 'sales' completed in 0 seconds.   150 rows
inserted.
```

If we wanted to change the notification to output a messages every 10 rows loaded we could change our statement to the one in Fig 5.28.

Fig 5.28

```
INSERT sales  LIMIT 150 NOTIFY 10 LOCATION 'SALESIQ.SALESIQ ' {select * from
remote_sales_table}
```

insert select load options

Apart from the "insert load options" you may also use any of the "insert select load options" given below. These options have the same functionality as when they are used in a **LOAD TABLE** statement.

Insert Select Load Option	Values	Description
IGNORE CONSTRAINT	constraint type or constraint type, constraint type, etc	When inserting data this clause gives you the option of ignoring constraints and setting a limit on the number to ignore. You may specify the following constraints to ignore where <limit> is the maximum number of constraint errors to ignore; if this number is zero then there is no limit. Please remember that by logging violations the insert time may be impaired. • **NULL** <limit> If the **NULL** <limit> is not specified, then the first occurrence of any **NULL** constraint violation causes the **INSERT** statement to rollback otherwise it will rollback when it encounter (<limit> +1) **NULL** constraint violations. • **UNIQUE** <limit> If the **UNIQUE** <limit> is not specified, then the first occurrence of any **UNIQUE** constraint violation causes the **INSERT** statement to roll back otherwise it will rollback when it encounter (<limit> +1) **UNIQUE** constraint violations. • **CHECK** <limit> If the **CHECK**<limit> is not specified, then the first occurrence of any **CHECK** constraint violation causes the **INSERT** statement to roll back otherwise it will rollback when it encounter (<limit> +1) **CHECK** constraint violations. • **FOREIGN KEY** <limit> If the **FOREIGN KEY** <limit> is not specified, then the first occurrence of any **FOREIGN KEY** constraint violation causes the INSERT statement to roll back otherwise it will rollback when it encounter (<limit> +1) **NULL** constraint violations. • **DATA VALUE** <limit> When the database option **CONVERSION_ERROR = ON** then an error is reported and the statement rolls back otherwise if the **DATA VALUE** <limit> is not specified, then the first occurrence of any **DATA VALUE** constraint violation causes the **INSERT** statement to roll back otherwise it will rollback when it encounter (<limit> +1) **DATA VALUE** constraint violations. • **ALL** <limit> If the database option **CONVERSION_ERROR = ON**, an error is reported and the **INSERT** statement rolls back. Otherwise if the ALL <limit> option is used then the insert only rolls back when (<limit> +1) total constraint violations of all types (**NULL, DATA VALUE, FOREIGN KEY & UNIQUE**) is reached. If you set <limit> to 0 then all constraints all ignored. If you specify another constraint option along with the ALL option then either may cause a rollback e.g. "FOREIGN KEY 25, ALL 100" then in this case a roll back will occur on 25 **FOREIGN** KEY violations or 100 violations of **DATA VALUE, NULL** and **UNIQUE** constraints.

WORD SKIP	Number of words to skip	This clause is used when inserting data into columns with a WD index on them. It is used to allow an insert to continue when the **INSERT** statement attempts to insert data longer than the limit specified when the word index was created. For any rows of data that cannot be inserted because a word exceeds the limit a waning message is placed in the IQ message log file. These errors can be optionally logged to the message log file and any rejected rows logged to a row log file that is specified in the **ROW LOG** option statement. When this option is not used and an error occurs then IQ rolls back when encountering the first occurrence of inserting a word longer than the limit. The value of the **WORD SKIP** clause is used to specify the number of times (The default is 0 meaning no limit) the error is ignored.
MESSAGE LOG, ROW LOG and optional **ONLY LOG**	[MESSAGE LOG 'string' ROW LOG <file path > [ONLY LOG <log option>[<log option>[, , …]]	Firstly you must declare **BOTH** a **MESSAGE LOG and ROW LOG** together you cannot use one clause without the other. Both clauses take the option of a file location and name that cannot be named pipes or raw partitions and the **ROW** and **MESSAGE LOGS** cannot be the same file name. You may also optionally use the **ONLY LOG** clause which will allow the logs to capture integrity constraint violations; otherwise the logs just record the start and end times of the insert. The **ROW LOG** will record the integrity violations for each row (And add one row in the log for each violation) and the **MESSAGE LOG** has information about the entire **INSERT** process. The messages that are captured are also affected by the **IGNORE CONSTRAINT** clause. The syntax of the clause is **MESSAGE LOG** <message log file name>, **ROW LOG** <row log file name> [**ONLY LOG (CHECK | ALL | NULL | UNIQUE | DATA VALUE | FOREIGN KEY | WORD)**] The options of the **ONLY LOG** clause indicate which type of integrity violations should be recorded (see the IGNIRE **CONSTRAINT** clause for details on the constraints) in the **ROW LOG**. The types of messages sent to the **MESSAGE LOG** are affected by the **IGNORE CONSTRAINT** clause. Where the **IGNORE CONSTRAINT** clause is specified then all integrity constraint violations are logged along with their limits up to the point of a rollback. If the **IGNORE CONSTRAINT** clause is not specified then only the first violation is recorded prior to a rollback.
LOG DELIMITED BY	'<log delimiter>'	This clause specifies how data values in the row log are separated (not delimited as the name suggests) in the file specified in the **ROW LOG**. The default is a comma.

Example

The example below will collect information about the **INSERT LOCATION** statement in a message and row log.

Fig 5.29

```
INSERT my_test_table  LIMIT 150
MESSAGE LOG '/tmp/insert_msg.log'
ROW LOG '/tmp/insert_row.log'
LOCATION 'source_server.source_db '
{SELECT * from source_table}
```

The **MESSAGE LOG** output for the example in Fig 5.29 is given below (* note it calls it a **LOAD TABLE** in the output messages).

```
10-07-20 09:58:57 Load Table my_test_journals: Integrity Constraint
Violations
2010-07-20 09:59:07 Load Table my_test_journals: Completed
```

The **ROW LOG** output for the example for the example in Fig 5.29 is given below

```
2010-07-20 09:58:57 Load Table my_test_journals: Integrity Constraint Violations
Date Format: YYYY-MM-DD
Time Format: HH:NN:SS.SSS
Datetime Format: YYYY-MM-DD HH:NN:SS.SSS
2010-07-20 09:59:07 Load Table my_test_journals: Completed
```

location options

These options are placed after the **LOCATION** '<remote *server name>.<remote database name>*' statement and like the other options these are optional. These options are used to affect the way the statement you want to execute and the way you want to connect on the remote server are performed.
You may use the following options

Location option	Values	Description
ENCRYPTED PASSWORD		When this option is specified then the Open Client Library default password encryption is used when connecting to the remote server. This feature is only supported in Open Client 15.0 and above. If the remote server does not support the encryption (IQ does not support it) then an error is returned stating an invalid login was used.
PACKETSIZE	<packet size>	This option specifies the TDS packet size (in bytes), the specified size must be a multiple of 512 and the maximum is 524,288 (or the network maximum). Most platforms have a default of 512 bytes but if you are transferring a large amount of data across the network then a larger packet size may improve the performance. When using **INSERT LOCATION** from an IQ or ASE database the packet size will be 512 regardless if you specify a different value using this option.
QUOTED_IDENTIFIER	ON or OFF	This specifies that your SQL can use quoted identifiers in the select.

ISOLATION LEVEL	READ UNCOMMITTED Or READ COMMITTTED Or SERIALIZABLE	This allows you to specify the isolation level that your select will use when reading data from the remote database. (IQ will ignore this for queries from the main store as IQ is always in Level3). <ul><li>**READ UNCOMITTED** – Isolation Level 0</li><li>**READ COMITTED** – Isolation Level 1</li><li>**SERIALIZABLE** – Isolation Level 3</li></ul>

Other considerations for Insert Location

There are other options and restrictions that may affect the performance and usage of the **INSERT LOCATION** statement. Apart from the requirement to have interfaces/sql.ini entries, set up a server and external login (see the section above about **INSERT LOCATION** basics) there are further considerations.

- You must have permissions to read from the remote database tables you are selecting from and insert permissions on the table being inserted into.

- You cannot use local variables in the **SELECT** statement, you may use global server variable e.g. @@servername but the value of the server variables on the remote server.

- When connecting to ASE you must have the Sybase connectivity libraries installed and the environment variable for the load library path must be pointed to them

- You cannot insert (in a **INSERT LOCATION** statement) as column of more than 2Gb (and will truncate at 2gb).

- When inserting into a View the view can only be defined on a single table with no union or group by operations used in the view definition.

- IQ does not support **UNITEXT, UNICHAR** or **UNIVARCHAR** types.

- Char and Varchar data inserted will always be in the Character Case of the source data regardless on whether your local database is case sensitive.

- IQ does not support **TEXT** or **IMAGE** datatypes but can insert data from them into other datatypes.

- When selecting from **VARBINARY** columns set the **LOAD_MEMORY_MB** database option to limit the memory used by the **INSERT LOCATION** statement. If selecting fro an IQ remote database then also set the option **ASE_BINARY_DISPLAY** to OFF on the remote server.

- **MOST IMPORTANT – EXECUTE A COMMIT AFTER THE INSERT LOCATION STATEMENT TO COMMIT THE DATA!!!!!!**

Moving data from system/catalog to IQ

When moving data from a SYSTEM table into an IQ Table it is recommended you use the **INSERT LOCATION** statement command. This is because creating statements across stores can cause contention issues. So instead of the syntax in Fig 5.30 you should us the one in Fig 5.31

Fig 5.30

```
INSERT <IQ TABLE>
SELECT * FROM <SYSTEM TABLE>
```

Fig 5.31

```
INSERT <IQ TABLE> LOCATION ('<SERVER_NAME>.<SERVERNAME>')
{SELECT * FROM <SYSTEM TABLE>
```

The local **INSERT LOCATION** statement causes IQ to pass the command through the connection and return the data through the recommended connection data transfer methods.

You may (depends on the system config options) also have to create an external login and server entry for the id you are using even though it is on the same server.

Extracting to a Server Side File

If you want to output a resultset to a directory relative to the IQ server (As opposed to file relative to the client executing the SQL) you have several options depending on the type of output and the type of resultset you wish to extract.

Temp Extract Options

IQ provides a set of options that can be used to extract data; these can be set for **PUBLIC** or for an individual connection. Some of them require DBA authority to set them, a basic list of them and a description of what they are used for is given below, however for a more detailed description see the Extract and Load Options section in the Options chapter.
Files produced using the **TEMP_EXTRACT** options will be owned by the O/S user running the IQ server.

* YOU CANNOT USE THE TEMP_EXTRACT OPTION'S TO SELECT RESULTS FROM CATALOG STORE TABLES ONLY IQ STORE (MAIN AND TEMP).

Option	Description	Allowed Values
TEMP_EXTRACT_APPEND	Specifies that any rows extracted by the data extraction facility are added to the end of an output file.	ON or OFF
TEMP_EXTRACT_BINARY	In combination with the **TEMP_EXTRACT_SWAP** option, specifies the type of extraction performed by the data extraction facility.	ON or OFF
TEMP_EXTRACT_COLUMN_DELIMITER	Specifies the delimiter between columns in the output of the data extraction facility for an **ASCII** extraction.	STRING
TEMP_EXTRACT_DIRECTORY	Controls whether a user is allowed to use the data extraction facility. Also controls the directory into which temp extract files are placed and overrides a directory path specified in the **TEMP_EXTRACT_NAMEn** options.	String
TEMP_EXTRACT_ESCAPE_QUOTES	Specifies whether all quotes in fields containing quotes are escaped in the output of the data extraction facility for an **ASCII**	ON or OFF

	extraction.	
TEMP_EXTRACT_NAMEn	Specifies the names of the output files or named pipes used by the data extraction facility. There are eight options: *TEMP_EXTRACT_NAME1* through *TEMP_EXTRACT_NAME8*.	String
TEMP_EXTRACT_NULL_AS_EMPTY	Controls the representation of null values in the output of the data extraction facility for an **ASCII** extraction.	ON or OFF
TEMP_EXTRACT_NULL_AS_ZERO	Controls the representation of null values in the output of the data extraction facility for an **ASCII** extraction.	ON or OFF
TEMP_EXTRACT_QUOTE	Specifies the string to be used as the quote to enclose fields in the output of the data extraction facility for an ASCII extraction, when either the *TEMP_EXTRACT_QUOTES* option or the *TEMP_EXTRACT_QUOTES_ALL* option is set ON.	String
TEMP_EXTRACT_QUOTES	Specifies that string fields are enclosed in quotes in the output of the data extraction facility for an **ASCII** extraction.	ON or OFF
TEMP_EXTRACT_QUOTES_ALL	Specifies that all fields are enclosed in quotes in the output of the data extraction facility for an **ASCII** extraction.	ON or OFF
TEMP_EXTRACT_ROW_DELIMITER	Specifies the delimiter between rows in the output of the data extraction facility for an **ASCII** extraction.	String
TEMP_EXTRACT_SIZEn	Specifies the maximum sizes of the corresponding output files used by the data extraction facility. There are eight options: *TEMP_EXTRACT_SIZE1* through *TEMP_EXTRACT_SIZE8*.	Disk file AIX and HP-UX: 0 – 64GB Sun Solaris & Linux: 0 – 512GB Windows: 0 – 128GB Tape* 524288KB (0.5GB) Other 9007199254740992KB (8192 Petabytes "unlimited")
TEMP_EXTRACT_SWAP	In combination with the *TEMP_EXTRACT_BINARY* option, specifies the type of extraction performed by the data extraction facility.	ON or OFF
TEMP_RESERVED_DBSPACE_MB	Controls the amount of space Sybase IQ reserves in the temporary IQ store.	Integer greater than or equal to 200 in megabytes

To see your current settings run the code in Fig 5.34

Fig 5.34

```
SELECT *
FROM sysoptions
WHERE UPPER([option]) LIKE 'TEMP_EXTRACT%'
```

Let's look at a basic example, if we want to output to a file called test_results.txt in the directory /tmp we can specify this as in Fig 5.33. (In this example I am using an IQ server running on Unix, you can also use this functionality on other O/S).

Fig 5.35

```
CREATE TABLE #results (col1 VARCHAR(100) NULL);

INSERT INTO #results
SELECT 'TEST FILE OUTPUT';

SET  TEMPORARY OPTION TEMP_EXTRACT_NAME1 = '/tmp/test_results.txt';

SELECT *
FROM #results
```

The example in Fig 5.35 will produce the file /tmp/test_results.txt with one row of content as in Fig 5.36. Notice the field is delimited by a comma.

Fig 5.36

```
TEST FILE OUTPUT,
```

Let's expand on our example a little bit more by outputting a couple of rows and changing the file to be pipe delimited.

Fig 5.37

```
CREATE TABLE #results (col1 VARCHAR(100) NULL, col2 VARCHAR(100) NULL);

INSERT INTO #results
SELECT 'ROW 1 COL 1','ROW 1 COL2';

INSERT INTO #results
SELECT 'ROW 2 COL 1','ROW 2 COL2';

SET  TEMPORARY OPTION TEMP_EXTRACT_NAME1 = '/tmp/test_results.txt';
SET  TEMPORARY OPTION TEMP_EXTRACT_COLUMN_DELIMITER = '|';

SELECT *
FROM #results
```

The results in the output file are:-

Fig 5.38

```
ROW 1 COL 1|ROW 1 COL2|
ROW 2 COL 1|ROW 2 COL2|
```

Fig 5.39

```
CREATE TABLE #results (col1 VARCHAR(100) NULL, col2 VARCHAR(100) NULL);

INSERT INTO #results
SELECT 'ROW 1 COL 1','ROW 1 COL2';

INSERT INTO #results
SELECT 'ROW 2 COL 1','ROW 2 COL2';

SET  TEMPORARY OPTION TEMP_EXTRACT_NAME1 = '/tmp/test_results.txt';
SET  TEMPORARY OPTION TEMP_EXTRACT_COLUMN_DELIMITER = '|';
SET  TEMPORARY OPTION TEMP_EXTRACT_BINARY = 'OFF';
SET  TEMPORARY OPTION TEMP_EXTRACT_QUOTE = '"';
SET  TEMPORARY OPTION TEMP_EXTRACT_QUOTES = 'ON';

SELECT *
FROM #results
```

The results in the output file are now quoted.

Fig 5.40

```
"ROW 1 COL 1"|"ROW 1 COL2"|
"ROW 2 COL 1"|"ROW 2 COL2"|
```

Fig 5.41

```
TRUNCATE TABLE #results;

INSERT INTO #results
SELECT 'NEW RESULTS','NEW RESULTS';

SET  TEMPORARY OPTION TEMP_EXTRACT_NAME1 = '/tmp/test_results.txt';
SET  TEMPORARY OPTION TEMP_EXTRACT_COLUMN_DELIMITER = '|';
SET  TEMPORARY OPTION TEMP_EXTRACT_BINARY = 'OFF';
SET  TEMPORARY OPTION TEMP_EXTRACT_QUOTE = '"';
SET  TEMPORARY OPTION TEMP_EXTRACT_QUOTES = 'ON';
SET  TEMPORARY OPTION TEMP_EXTRACT_APPEND = 'ON';

SELECT *
FROM #results
```

The latest execution in Fig 5.41 has appended the results to the output file.

Fig 5.42

```
"ROW 1 COL 1"|"ROW 1 COL2"|
"ROW 2 COL 1"|"ROW 2 COL2"|
"NEW RESULTS"|"NEW RESULTS"|
```

Extracting to a Local File

When outputting to a local file you can use the explicit **OUTPUT TO** statement or output redirection. Each is slightly different and can be altered using the dbisql **FORMAT** keyword.

The OUTPUT statement

For example the code in Fig 5.43 outputs to a file called c:\objects.txt on the local file system where the client is being executed from.

Fig 5.43
```
SELECT *
FROM sysobjects
WHERE name IN ('SYSCOLUMNS','SYSOPTIONS';
OUTPUT TO c:\objects.txt;
```

You can also specify the format you wish to output your data as in Fig 5.44 producing the results in Fig 5.45.

Fig 5.44
```
SELECT name
FROM sysobjects
WHERE name IN ('SYSCOLUMNS','SYSOPTIONS';
OUTPUT TO c:\objects.txt FORMAT ASCII;
```

Fig 5.45
```
'SYSCOLUMNS'
'SYSOPTIONS'
```

You may also specify other formats, below are examples of output if we used another value instead of **ASCII**.

XML

Fig 5.46
```
<?xml version="1.0" encoding="UTF-8"?>
<!DOCTYPE resultset [
    <!ELEMENT resultset (resultsetdata) >
    <!ELEMENT resultsetdata (row)* >
    <!ELEMENT row (column)+ >
    <!ELEMENT column (#PCDATA)>
    <!ATTLIST column
        null (true | false) "false"
        name CDATA #IMPLIED
    >
]>
<resultset>
    <row>
        <column name="name">SYSCOLUMNS</column>
    </row>
    <row>
        <column name="name">SYSOPTIONS</column>
    </row>
</resultset>
```

HTML

Fig 5.47

```
<html>
<head>
<META content="text/html;charset=Cp1252">
</head>
<body>
<table border>
<tr><th>name</th></tr>
<tr><td>SYSCOLUMNS</td></tr>

<tr><td>SYSOPTIONS</td></tr>

</table>
</body>
</html>
```

FIXED

Fig 5.48

```
SYSCOLUMNS
SYSOPTIONS
```

SQL

Fig 5.49

```
SELECT name
FROM sysobjects
WHERE name IN ('SYSCOLUMNS','SYSOPTIONS');
input format sql;
'SYSCOLUMNS'
'SYSOPTIONS'
END
```

TEXT

Fig 5.50

```
'SYSCOLUMNS'
'SYSOPTIONS'
```

Output Redirection

You may decide you wish instead to use the output redirection syntax, using the same output at in the OUTPUT statement section above we can us the code in Fig 5.51 to output to the c:\objects.txt file.

Fig 5.51

```
SELECT *
FROM sysobjects
WHERE name IN ('SYSCOLUMNS','SYSOPTIONS'
># c:\objects.txt
```

This will produce the c:\objects.txt file with the contents in Fig 5.52

Fig 5.52

```
'SYSCOLUMNS'
'SYSOPTIONS'
```

The syntax above used ># to specify the output file, but we can use other syntax's given below:-

Syntax	Descriptions	Sample Output
>#	Output results to a file, creating the file if it does not exist or overwriting the contents if it does.	'SYSCOLUMNS' 'SYSOPTIONS'
>&	Output results and all output including stats and error messages to the file. This creates a new file if it does not exist or overwrites the contents if it does.	-- Executing command: -- SELECT name -- FROM sysobjects -- WHERE name IN ('SYSCOLUMNS','SYSOPTIONS') -- Execution time: 0.047 seconds 'SYSCOLUMNS' 'SYSOPTIONS' -- 2 rows written to "H:\objects.txt"
>>#	The outputs the results to a file appending the results to the contents f the file already exists and creates a new file if not.	'SYSCOLUMNS' 'SYSOPTIONS' 'SYSTABLE' 'SYSUSER'
>>&	Output results and all output including stats and error messages to the file. This appends the results to the file if it already exists and creates a new file if not.	-- Executing command: -- SELECT name -- FROM sysobjects -- WHERE name IN ('SYSCOLUMNS','SYSOPTIONS') -- Execution time: 0.047 seconds 'SYSCOLUMNS' 'SYSOPTIONS' -- 2 rows written to "H:\objects.txt" -- -- Executing command: -- SELECT name -- FROM sysobjects -- WHERE name IN ('SYSTABLE', 'SYSUSER') -- Executing command: -- SELECT name -- FROM sysobjects -- WHERE name IN ('SYSTABLE', 'SYSUSER') -- Execution time: 0.031 seconds 'SYSTABLE' 'SYSUSER' -- 2 rows written to "H:\objects.txt"

You can also specify the format of the output as when using the **OUTPUT** statement. You can do this by selecting the format from the output menu in dbisql if using interactively or by setting the **OUTPUT_FORMAT** options at the command line as in Fig 5.53 which sets the **OUTPUT_FORMAT** to **XML** using the **OUTPUT_FORMAT** dbisql option.

Fig 5.53

```
dbisql -NOGUI -C "UID=DBA;PWD=sql;DBN:MY_DB" -host myhostmachine -port 2643
"SET OPTION OUTPUT_FORMAT = 'XML'; SELECT name FROM sysobjects WHERE name in
('SYSCOLUMNS','SYSOPTIONS') ># c:\objects.txt"
```

Using UNLOAD TABLE to extract ASA/Catalog Tables Only

If you wish to **UNLOAD** the entire contents of a catalog store table you can do this using the
UNLOAD TABLE command. This statement will unload the file to the server file system on which
the database is running. If you do not specify a path then the file will by default go to the
directory where the database is running. The file will output one line per row and by default will
be delimited with a comma. The data is Unloaded in the order of the primary key (although you
can switch this off using the **ORDER OFF** clause
The code in Fig 5.54 will output the contents of the isysobject table to the file test.txt

Fig 5.54

```
UNLOAD TABLE isysobject
TO 'test_unload.txt'
```

Let's change our example to unload the data using a pipe as a delimiter, turning quotes off and
specifying the **ORDER** as OFF to not bother ordering the output.

Fig 5.54

```
UNLOAD TABLE isysobject
TO 'test_unload.txt'
DELIMITED BY '|'
QUOTES OFF
ORDER OFF
```

Using INPUT INTO to Load data.

The input **INTO** can be used instead of a **LOAD TABLE** to insert into tables from a **LOCAL FILE**,
although it is not has fast it does allow some file formats not available in the **LOAD TABLE**
statement. The syntax is given in Fig 5.55.

Fig 5.55

```
INPUT INTO [ owner.]table-name
FROM filename
--options
BY ORDER or BY NAME
COLUMN WIDTHS ( <integer>, ...)
DELIMITED BY <string>
ESCAPE CHARACTER character ]
ESCAPES ON or OFF
FORMAT ASCII or DBASE or DBASEII or DBASEIII
or EXCEL or FIXED or FOXPRO or LOTUS
NOSTRIP (<column name>, ... )
ENCODING <encoding>
```

If for example we have a table declared as in Fig 5.56

Fig 5.56

```
CREATE TABLE test
(
    col_1 VARCHAR(10) NULL,
    col_2 VARCHAR(10) NULL
)
```

And we have a file called c:\test.txt with the contents in Fig 5.57

Fig 5.57

```
Hello1|World1
Hello2|World2
Hello3|World3
```

We can use the code in Fig 5.58 to load the file into the table.

Fig 5.57

```
INPUT INTO test
FROM c:\test.txt
DELIMITED BY '|'
FORMAT ASCII
```

This is a very easy way to load local files, but I would normally prefer using **LOAD TABLE** as it can be used to load files local to the client or the database.

Tables, Data Types and Views

This chapter groups together the three interrelated subjects of Tables, Views and data types.

The four different table types are covered as is the importance of using correct data types not only for storage but also to ensure that joins and **SARGs** (Search Arguments) are optimized correctly. There is an overview of global temporary tables and how to use them to optimise your database queries. How to use primary keys and unique constraints to optimise your database. How to ensure referential integrity via the use of foreign keys.

There are tips on how to use primary keys to index your temporary table in stored procedures. How local temporary table can be used to aid your queries and how to create tables on the system store (Sybase ASA).

We shall look at aggregation in views and how incorrect data types can cause views used in Joins not to operate as you would expect.

Table's are the most important part of any relational database and time spent understanding there use early on can avoid issues, problems and expensive (time and cost) re-factoring in the future. We will also look at Large Objects (LOBS) and there guises as **BLOBS** (Binary Large Objects) and **CLOBS** (Character Large Objects). These are specific data types used to hold data typically Megabytes and Gigabytes in size (Up to Terabytes).

Tables

Table Types

In most RDBMS you normally have two types of table, Base and Temporary. In Sybase IQ there are four. Although in everyday use you will only use three of them it is useful to know how they differ from each other and how they can be used to optimise your storage space and query times. The four main types of tables are:-

Base Tables

These are what most developers would consider as normal tables, these are stored in the IQ database and when insert, updates or deletes to the data are committed (or a truncate is run) the changes are made permanent in the database. Base tables are the backbone of any database system and Sybase IQ is no different.

Local Temporary Tables

These are tables that are used to temporarily store data, they only exist until a connection ends or within the space of a compound statement, transaction or stored procedure. These tables are most often used in stored procedures and as indexes cannot be created in Sybase IQ stored procedures they can cause query optimisation issues. A way round this constraint is to use Global Temporary Tables.

Global Temporary Tables

The definition of a global temporary table exists for all connections but each connection can only see rows that it has inserted, updated and deleted. Options can be used to keep data after commit statements are run, but in all cases all rows are deleted when the connection ends. These tables can only be dropped or altered when any connection that is using the table has disconnected.

Tables on the Catalog Store

Sometimes it is unavoidable that you need to perform multiple writes to a table. As a write once ready many database IQ does not allow two transactions to write to the same table without one of them being committed. By utilising the ASA/Catalog store we can by pass this constraint, but extreme care must be taken.

Base Tables

What can be written about base tables that have not been said thousands of times before for just about every RDBM's ever produced.
Well Sybase IQ does add a few extra features that are not found in other databases and the storage of them is also slightly different.
The IQ base table definitions are stored in the catalog store whereas the data is stored in indexes in the IQ Store. Also because storage of data is held in a column not row based structure the row of a table is not constrained to page sizes (or multiples there of). Therefore a table can hold many more columns of data and is not constrained in the same way. Current information from Sybase indicates that the maximum number of columns per table in Sybase IQ is approximately 45,000. The standard syntax of a create statement is the same as ANSI standard:

Fig 6.1

```
CREATE TABLE customers
(
  customer_id               int             NOT NULL,
  customer_name             varchar(255)    NOT NULL,
  customer_region           char(3)         NULL,
  customer_telephone_no     int             NULL
)
```

You may drop tables by using the **DROP TABLE** <table name> command.
The current ASNI standard for column definitions for a table is:-

* Column Name

* Column Data type

* Column Property **NULL** or **NOT NULL** (This is optional)

Column Properties - NULLS

Although the column property is optional, if this is left empty then a default of either **NULL** or **NOT NULL** will be assigned depending on which type of connection is used to run the create table statement. When using ODBC or JDBC to run the create table statement then **NULL** is the default, this is also ANSI standard. If however your client connects via open client then **NOT NULL** is the default. Caution is recommended when writing re-runnable table creation scripts as you can never 100% guarantee that the same client will also be used so it is always best to specify the **NULL/NOT NULL** property in the create table statement.

Column nullability has no bearing on storage or performance as each cell uses a bit that is set when a value is **NULL** in a cell. A count of **NULL** values in a column is recalculated after every data modification statement on a column has been committed.

ANSI Constraints

You may use the following ANSI standard constraints in the create table statement:-

* **PRIMARY KEY** Constraints

* **UNIQUE** Constraints

* **CHECK** Constraints

PRIMARY KEY Constraints

A primary key constraint may be built into the create table statement (Fig 6.2).

Fig 6.2

```
CREATE TABLE customers
(
customer_id               int             NOT NULL,
customer_name             varchar(255)    NOT NULL,
customer_region           char(3)         NULL,
customer_telephone_no     int             NULL,
CONSTRAINT myPrimaryKey PRIMARY KEY (customer_id)
)
```

The syntax when adding a primary key in as create table statement is to code the key as if it were a column (using a comma after the column before) and then use the syntax in Fig 6.3.

Fig 6.3
```
CONSTRAINT <primary_key_name>
PRIMARY KEY (Column 1, Column 2, Column 3 ....)
```

If only one column is used in the primary key then a **UNIQUE HG** Index is implicitly built on that column. If multiple columns a built then a **UNIQUE HG** index is built on the entire key but not on each individual column. If each column or a sub set of the primary key columns are used in searches or joins then you should consider building individual **HG** indexes on each column after the table is built (but for speed, before data is loaded).
It should also be noted that if your primary key is only on one column then you can use the syntax in Fig 6.4.

Fig 6.4
```
CREATE TABLE customers
(
customer_id            int           PRIMARY KEY,
customer_name          varchar(255)  NOT NULL,
customer_region        char(3)       NULL,
customer_telephone_no  int           NULL
)
```

You may also want to create your primary key after the initial table creation to do this you can issue an alter table command (Fig 6.5).

Fig 6.5
```
ALTER TABLE <TABLE NAME> ADD PRIMARY KEY (column 1, column2 ...)
```

A primary key and its associated indexes may be dropped by using the **ALTER TABLE** statement (Fig 6.6), running a drop Index on Primary Keys will not work.

Fig 6.6
```
ALTER TABLE <TABLE NAME> DROP PRIMARY KEY
```

When building primary keys it is important to remember that no column used in the primary key can be nullable.

UNIQUE Constraints

The unique constraint as an almost identical syntax to the primary key constraint one of the main differences is that you can have multiple unique indexes on the same table. A typical unique key constraint is seen in Fig 6.7

Fig 6.7

```
CREATE TABLE sales
(
        sales_person_id         int       NOT NULL,
        customer_id             int       NOT NULL,
        order_id                int       NOT NULL,
        product_id              int       NOT NULL,
        quantity                int       NOT NULL,
        UNIQUE (order_id, product_id)
)
```

Like the primary key index if the unique constraint is only on one column then you can declare it in the column declaration as part of the column property (Fig 6.8).

Fig 6.8

```
CREATE TABLE orders
(
        order_id        int     NOT NULL,
        customer_id     int     NOT NULL,
        sales_id        int     UNIQUE
)
```

Like primary keys if one column is used in the unique constraint then it has a Unique **HG** index built on that column if the unique constraint if multiple column then the unique **HG** index is built on the whole key. So if you want to use columns individually in searches and joins then you will need to add HG indexes to them.

You can also add unique indexes after table creation by using the alter table statement (Fig 6.9).

Fig 6.9

```
ALTER TABLE <TABLE NAME> ADD UNIQUE (column 1, column2 ...)
```

In order to drop indexes associated with unique constraints you will need to run an alter table statement.

Fig 6.10

```
ALTER TABLE <TABLE NAME> DROP UNIQUE (Column 1, Column2 ...)
```

UNIQUE indexes are used by the query optimiser when analysing table joins. Although there are no restrictions on the number or type of columns (except they cannot be nullable) in a unique index, the maximum key length is 5300 bytes (and 1 byte is used for each column as an additional overhead regardless of data type).

CHECK Constraints

Although Sybase IQ enforces check constraints it does not allow the creation of a check constraint that it cannot evaluate, such as check constraints comprised of user-defined functions, proxy tables, or non-IQ tables. Constraints that cannot be evaluated are detected the first time the table has a data added, deleted or updated after the check constraint is added.

This obviously is not ideal as you run a create table statement with a check constraint that my not work.

Sybase IQ does not allow check constraints containing:

- Sub-queries

* Expressions specifying a host language parameter, an SQL parameter, or a column as the target for a data value
* Set functions
* Invocations of non-deterministic functions or functions that modify data

The syntax for creating a column in-line check constraint is given in Fig 6.11 and at a table level in Fig 6.12

Fig 6.11

```
CREATE TABLE orders
(
        order_id        int     NOT NULL
                CONSTRAINT order_id_constraint
                CHECK ( order_id > 1000 ),
        sales_id        int     NOT NULL
)
```

Fig 6.12

```
CREATE TABLE orders
(
        order_id        int     NOT NULL ,
        sales_id        int     NOT NULL,
        CONSTRAINT constraint_name
        CHECK ( order_id > 1000 )
)
```

A table level check constraint may also be added after a table creation using and **ALTER TABLE** (Fig 6.13)

Fig 6.13

```
ALTER TABLE orders
ADD CONSTRAINT sales_id_constraint
                        CHECK ( sales_id between 0 and 999 )
```

IQ Unique Constraint

The **IQ UNIQUE** constraint is an ANSI SQL extension. **IQ UNIQUE** is used to give the storage optimizer a hint at how many distinct values will be stored in a column.
For columns with an **IQ UNIQUE** values under 256 the storage optimizer will create a single byte **FP** index, for values between 255 and 65,537 it will build a two byte **FP** Index. For **IQ UNIQUE** values over 65,537 it will create a flat FP index. If you are unsure about the use of an **FP** index please see the chapter on indexes.
The syntax for the **IQ UNIQUE** constraint is given after the data type in a column declaration of a create table statement (Fig 6.14).

Fig 6.14

```
CREATE TABLE products
(
        product_id      int IQ UNIQUE (100)         NOT NULL,
        product_name    varchar(255)                NULL,
        product_type    char(2) IQ UNIQUE (20)      NULL
)
```

You may also set the database option **MINIMIZE_STORAGE** ON, this has the same effect as adding an **IQ UNIQUE (255)** after every column declaration you make (from the point you switch the option on). If you specify **IQ UNIQUE** in a table creation statement while this option is on the **IQ UNIQUE** value in the creation statement will take precedence.

Please note that if you specify a value that is to small then the index optimizer will change the index type during the loading of a table and will have to rebuild the index. As this will only happen the first time you load the table you may want to accept this as an acceptable overhead. If you specify a value to large in IQ unique the storage optimizer will use a large index type, this means that queries may take longer and storage will not be as efficiently optimised.

Given the advice above if you have an column where you think there will be between 250 and 260 unique values then it is best to go with an **IQ UNIQUE (255)** as storage optimisation and query performance should normally take precedence over a one time index rebuild.

Putting it all together

As you would expect you can combine any of these constraints into your table definition as in Fig 6.15.

Fig 6.15

```
CREATE TABLE orders
(
        order_id                int                 NOT NULL,
        customer_id             int                 NOT NULL
                        CONSTRAINT customer_id_constraint
                        CHECK ( customer_id between 1 and 999
),
        sales_id                int                 UNIQUE,
        product_id      int                 NULL,
        sales_person_id         int IQ UNIQUE(150)  NOT NULL,
        CONSTRAINT orders_PK PRIMARY KEY (order_id)
)
```

This example shows the orders table with a primary key on order_id, a check constraint on customer_id, a unique constraint on sales_id and an IQ UNIQUE hint on sales_person_id.

Of course column can have multiple constraints such as both a **UNIQUE** and a **CHECK** as in Fig 6.16 where we have added a check to the sales_id and order_id columns

Fig 6.16

```
CREATE TABLE orders
(
        order_id              int                    NOT NULL
                    CONSTRAINT order_id_constraint
                    CHECK ( order_id between 1000 and 99999 ),
        customer_id           int                    NOT NULL
                    CONSTRAINT customer_id_constraint
                    CHECK ( customer_id between 1 and 999 ),
        sales_id              int                    UNIQUE
                    CONSTRAINT sales_id_constraint
                    CHECK ( sales_id > 0 ),
            product_id        int                    NULL,
        sales_person_id       int IQ UNIQUE (150)    NOT NULL,
                    CONSTRAINT orders_PK PRIMARY KEY (order_id)
)
```

Identity Columns

Often you will need a way of uniquely identifying a row in a table. You should always try to maintain a key yourself in the data by using a primary key on physical data. If this is not possible you may consider using an identity column (Fig 6.17).

Fig 6.17

```
CREATE TABLE orders
(
        order_id      int      IDENTITY,
        customer_id   int      NOT NULL,
        sales_id      int      NOT NULL,
        product_id    int      NOT NULL
)
```

In the above example the order_id field is set as an identity. This means that you cannot normally insert into the order_id field as this field will be auto incremented with each row inserted.
You may insert into all the other columns and the value of order_id will be incremented from the previous value as per the example in Fig 6.18.

Fig 6.18

```
INSERT  orders(customer_id, sales_id, product_id)
SELECT 22,44,55
```

If the insert statement in Fig 6.18 was the first insert into the order table it would insert the following values.

order_id	customer_id	sales_id	product_id
1	22	44	55

There may be times when you wish to insert your own values into the identity field. You may do this by setting the database option identity insert on for the table you wish to insert into. For example, if you wish to insert into every field the orders table you should run the code in Fig 6.19.

Fig 6.19

```
SET OPTION IDENTITY_INSERT = 'orders'


INSERT  orders(order_id,customer_id, sales_id, product_id)
SELECT 2, 22,44,55


INSERT  orders(order_id,customer_id, sales_id, product_id)
SELECT 1, 22,44,55


SET OPTION IDENTITY_INSERT = ''
```

By running the code from Fig 6.18 and then running Fig 6.19 the table will contain the following.

order_id	customer_id	sales_id	product_id
1	22	44	55
2	22	44	55
1	22	44	55

It is important to note that setting the identity_insert option for the table is a different syntax to other T-SQL databases. It is also important to set the table to '' (empty string) when you have finished else when you revert back to inserting in other columns then no identity number will be entered.
You cannot alter or drop a table while the identity_insert is set to on for a table.
It is also useful to either a primary key to the column that has an identity set on it to ensure uniqueness. An alternative to adding a unique index or primary key is to set the database option **IDENTITY_ENFORCE_UNIQUENESS** to ON which will create a **UNIQUE HG** index on all identity columns. It is worth noting that you must set the option on before creating tables with identity columns if you want unique **HG** indexes to be automatically built.

Create a Base Table with "Select Into "

You may also create tables with a select into statement (Fig 6.20).

Fig 6.20

```
SELECT order_id,
       sales_id
INTO  new_orders
FROM orders
```

This example will create a table with two columns called order_id and sales_id that will have the same data types as the table orders and be populated with the data from the orders table.
A table created with a **SELECT INTO** does not inherit any constraints, defaults or indexes from the table selected from.
You can use the **SELECT INTO** statement to create an empty table by using a simple 1=0 where clause (Fig 6.21).

Fig 6.21

```
SELECT   *
INTO new_products
FROM products
WHERE 1=0
```

You may also want to create a copy of a table with a sub-set of data, you can do this by using the where clause as you would with any select. You can also use joins in the **FROM** clause. In fact you can create your table using any IQ compatible **SELECT** statement.

Foreign Keys

Sybase IQ supports foreign keys to enforce referential integrity by restricting the values of a column or set of columns to the values of a primary key or unique constraint of another table. You may have several foreign keys on a table and a role name is assigned to distinguish them. In Fig 6.22 the role names fk_sales and fk_product are used for foreign keys that reference the sales table and the products table respectively.

Fig 6.22

```
CREATE TABLE orders
(
        order_id        int      NOT NULL,
        customer_id     int      NOT NULL,
        sales_id        int      NOT NULL,
        product_id      int      NOT NULL,
        FOREIGN KEY fk_sales  (sales_id)
                        REFERENCES sales(sales_id),
        FOREIGN KEY fk_product (product_id)
                        REFERENCES
products(product_id),
)
```

When a foreign key is created on a single column then a **HG** index is created on that column. If a foreign key is created on a group of columns then a **HG** index is created on the whole key (not on each individual column). These indexes can only be dropped using the **ALTER TABLE** command to remove the foreign key(Fig 6.23).

Fig 6.23

```
ALTER TABLE orders DROP FOREIGN KEY fk_sales
```

When data manipulation (DML) commands (insert and updates) and data loads are performed on the table the new values are checked against the reference key. If any value fails then the entire transaction will rollback. There are options to stop this happening at a database level and also in the load table statement to skip loading rows where the foreign key fails.

Foreign Key checks are made after **ALL** data has been read or prepared to be updated, hence you may not get an error until the very end of a transaction or load. It is therefore best to ensure you know the source of your data when inserting or updating into tables with foreign keys.

Foreign Key enforcement during loads has a maximum 5% performance hit but because they can provide the query optimizer with joins they will also aid in query performance.

Partitioning

Partioning is a scheme of dividing logical or physical (or both) storage into chunks. We already have techniques in IQ to logically partition data (See Fig 6.53). However in Version15 Sybase introduced physical partitioning by allowing storage space to be partitioned into table spaces and it increases logical partitioning of tables in the table partitions (If you have used Oracle you may already be familiar with these concepts).

Range Partitions

In Sybase IQ a table range partition is a group of rows within a table that are split into a subset of that data. A row cannot be in more than one partition and each partition is allocated its own DBSpace and therefore can be managed in silo. As a partition is a subset of rows it shares all of its parent table's constraints and definitions. Tables are partitioned in the **CREATE TABLE** statement (or in an **ALTER TABLE**) as in Fig 6.24

Fig 6.24

```
CREATE TABLE my_partitioned_table
  (
        column1 int NOT NULL,
        column2 char(3) NOT NULL,
        column3 char(10) NOT NULL
) (
PARTITION BY RANGE(column1),
  (     partition_1 VALUES <= (0),
        partition_2 VALUES <= (99),
        partition_3 VALUES <= (999)
  )
)
```

In Fig 6.24 the example creates 3 partitions as these do not specify any DB Spaces the partitions will be created in the default DB Space. Sybase IQ supports a maximum of 1024 partitions for range partitioning.

There are certain operations you can perform on partitions. You may drop a partition as long as it is not the last remaining partition in a table. You may also merge two partitions as long as they reside in the same DB Space. You may also move a partition into a new DB Space or split a partition further as long as the split partition is on the same DB Space as the original partition..

Range Partitions split into DB Spaces

You may specify the DB Space that pertains to a partition data at a column level. This is especially useful when you want to separate off large data chunks such as **BLOBs** and **CLOBs**. You may also specify where the table will save by default. In Fig 6.25 below the default DB Space is DBSpace1, the primary key data is held in DBSpace2 with other data held in DB Spaces depending on the partition. As in Fig 6.25 the most common range to partition by is date, this is because you can move historical data on to cheaper/slower storage while keeping recent (and therefore more active) data on faster more expensive storage. It also allows you to decide on back up strategies for the host file system or SAN, for example you may only want to back up older data once a month but recent data daily. Partitioning should be investigated for any enterprise warehouse system.

Fig 6.25

```
CREATE TABLE my_partitioned_table
(
   column_1 BIGINT,
   column_2 VARCHAR(20),
   column_3 CLOB
              PARTITION (     Partition1 IN DBSpace11,
                              Partition2 IN DBSpace12),
   column_4 DATE,
   column_6 VARCHAR(1000)
              PARTITION (     Partition1 IN Dbspace_21,
                              Partition2 IN DBSpace22),
   PRIMARY KEY (column_1) IN DBSpace2
) IN DBSpace1
PARTITION BY RANGE (column_4)
(
       Partition1 VALUES <= ('2009/06/30') IN DBSpace31,
       Partition2 VALUES <= ('2011/09/30') IN DBSpace33
)
```

On partitions you can perform DML operations including delete, insert, truncate & load, and truncate table partition. Update is supported except updating the partition key column.
IQ will return an error when operations are performed on a read-only table partition or read-only table. Load, insert or insert by update cursor operations will generate an error and roll back, if the given row does not fit into the specified range of partitions.

Temporary Tables

Temporary tables are used to temporarily store data, they only exist until a connection ends or within the space of a compound statement, transaction or stored procedure.
You may not explicitly build indexes on temporary tables in stored procedures (you may in other code).However to get round this restriction you may use table constraints such as **PRIMARY KEYS** which will build a HG Indexes. Also you may not use **ALTER TABLE** commands on temporary tables. There are three ways of creating temporary tables

Creation Option 1 Declaring a Local Temporary Table

Fig 6.26

```
DECLARE LOCAL TEMPORARY TABLE mytemptable
(
       column_name_1  int      NULL,
       column_name_2  int      NULL,
       column_name_3  int      NULL,
       column_name_4  int      NULL
)
```

This is the only way of creating a local temporary table and avoiding the naming convention of starting a local temporary table name with a #. For consistency it is worth remembering to use the # when creating the table. You may also add table constraints when declaring the table as above. And also by using this creation deceleration you can also add the options **ON COMMIT PRESERVE ROWS** and **NOT TRANSACTIONAL**.

The **ON COMMIT PRESERVE ROWS** clause means that when a commit statement is run it will only commit the changes instead of deleting all the data. It also means that a rollback will just undo any changes made since the previous commit statement was run.

Also the **ON COMMIT PRESERVE ROWS** clause doesn't mean the data is permanent. All the data will still be deleted when the table is dropped at the end of the block containing the table declaration.

The **NOT TRANSACTIONAL** clause means that commit and rollback statements will have no effect on the data. There is no automatic deletion on commit; in fact, there is no concept of commit or rollback, and the data persists until explicitly deleted or the table is dropped. Sybase suggest using **NOT TRANSACTIONAL** if possible to optimize performance. Temporary table changes are not recorded in the transaction log, but they are recorded in the rollback log unless you specify **NOT TRANSACTIONAL**. However in practice **NOT TRANSACTIONAL** does not appear to have any material impact. It may be a case of trying your code both ways.

In order to declare a table using these clauses you just add them to then of the declaration as in Fig 6.27

Fig 6.27

```
DECLARE LOCAL TEMPORARY TABLE mytemptable
(
        column_name_1  int     NULL,
        column_name_2  int     NULL,
        column_name_3  int     NULL,
        column_name_4  int     NULL
)
ON COMMIT PRESERVE ROWS
```

Creation Option 2 Creating a # Table

This option is almost identical to declaring a local temporary table in option 1. The only difference is that if you name the table #<table name> (as in Fig 6.28) then Sybase IQ knows you are referring to a local temporary table. You may still use the table constraints but not the **ON COMMT PRESERVE ROWS** or **NOT TRANSACTIONAL** options. You also cannot name your primary key or unique key indexes. Fig 6.28 shows a temporary table created with a primary key index.

Fig 6.28

```
CREATE TABLE #mytemptable2
(
        column_name_1  int     NULL,
        column_name_2  int     NULL,
        column_name_3  int     NULL,
        column_name_4  int     NULL,
        PRIMARY KEY    (column_name_1)
)
```

Creation Option 3 Creating a selecting into a #table

As with standard tables this option just creates an unindexed table based on a **SELECT** statement. The syntax is also the same as when creating a standard table via **SELECT INTO**. Using this method do additional indexes (apart from **FP** indexes) will be built and no table constraints will be ported. The syntax is given in Fig 6.29

Fig 6.29

```
SELECT  order_id,
        sales_id
INTO    #temp_orders
FROM orders
```

Global Temporary Tables

Global temporary tables are am important feature of Sybase IQ and one that can prove very powerful if used correctly. Basically the definition of a global temporary table exists permanently but the data can only be accessed by the connection that created it.

A global temporary table is created in a similar way to standard temporary tables (Fig 6.30).

Fig 6.30

```
CREATE GLOBAL TEMPORARY TABLE myGlobalTempTable
(
        column_name_1  int      NULL,
        column_name_2  int      NULL,
        column_name_3  int      NULL,
        column_name_4  int      NULL,
  PRIMARY KEY    (column_name_1)
)
ON COMMIT PRESERVE ROWS
```

As per this example you can see you can use the **ON COMMIT** clause, the default is **ON COMMIT DELETE** rows. You can also use the **NOT TRANSACTIONAL** clause.
A global temporary table can be used by many connections simultaneously with each connection only seeing the rows they have inserted. Because of this a global temporary table can only be dropped when there are no other connections using the table apart from the one that issues the drop table command.

A global temporary table will exists permanently until it is explicitly dropped.
Global temporary tables can have indexes created on them meaning that if you are required to **INSERT** temporary data in a stored procedure that requires indexing then a global temporary table is ideal. They are also used where several procedures or scripts require the same temporary table; a global temporary table ensures that the data is indexed correctly and that primary and unique keys are maintained across all uses of the table.

Tables on the Catalog Store/System

You have the option when creating a table to specify which store you want the table's data to be held on. When you issue a create table without specifying the db space then the data is held in the IQ data store. This means the data is write once-read many, meaning only one transaction can insert, update or delete the data at one time. Any other transactions attempting to change the data will have an error returned informing them the table is locked by another transaction. However you can specify a table to have its data stored in the catalog (ASA) store declared in the table creation clause as **ON SYSTEM** (Fig 6.31)

Fig 6.31

```
CREATE TABLE ProcRunList
(
        procedure_name          varchar(20)     NULL,
        run_date                datetime        NULL
)
ON SYSTEM
```

When a table is held in the catalog store (ASA) it behaves more like a traditional RDBM's table meaning that several transactions can be writing to the same table and the database locking mechanism keeps transactions waiting until pages are free to write and update.

Tables created on the catalog are useful if for example you wish to have an auditing table that every procedure writes to throughout the batch. You should be aware however that the catalog store is nowhere near as performant as IQ and your system performance may be impacted when using system tables. Also the catalog store (.db file) can only grow and not shrink, this means the file will stay at whatever its largest ever size is. You should also make sure that there is enough space in the file location of the .db file to cope with the data you are inserting into the catalog store.

IMPORTANT: *As you are running Sybase IQ and not directly running ASA there is not the monitoring facilities provided to keep an eye on the catalog (ASA) store. Therefore you should keep any table created on ASA very small and either move or delete data from them on a regular basis.*

Data Types

Standard Data Types

Sybase IQ offers several standard data types as well as allowing you to create domains to standardise your own types throughout the database.

The Sybase IQ standard data types that you can use in columns, variables and parameters are:-

Fig 6.30

Sybase IQ data type	Range	Max Precision	Storage (bytes)
CHAR (n)	1 to (32k-1)	N/A	Column width
VARCHAR (n)	1 to (32k-1)	N/A	Data width
INT/INTEGER	-2,147,483,648 to 2,147,483,647	10	4
UNSIGINED INT/INTEGER	0 to 4,294,967,294	10	4
BIGINT	-9.2(^18) to (9.2(^18))-1	20	8
UNSIGNED BIGINT	0 to (1.8(^19))-1	20	8
SMALLINT	-32,768 to 32,767	5	2
TINYINT	0 to 255	3	1
FLOAT	OS/Platform dependant	16	4 or 8
REAL	OS/Platform dependant	7	4
DECIMAL	-10^38 to (10^38)-1	126	2 to 69
NUMERIC	-10^38 to (10^38)-1	126	2 to 69

DOUBLE	2.2250738585072014e-308 to 1.797693134862315708e+308	DOUBLE	8
MONEY	NUMERIC(19,4) for compatibility with other RDBM's	19	16
SMALLMONEY	NUMERIC(10,4) for compatibility with other RDBM's	10	8
DATE	January 1st 0001 to Dec 31st 9999	N/A	4
DATETIME	January 1st 0001 00:00:00.000000 to Dec 31st 9999 23:59:59.999999	N/A	8
SMALLDATETIME	January 1st 0001 00:00:00.000000 to Dec 31st 9999 23:59:59.999999	N/A	8
TIMESTAMP	January 1st 0001 00:00:00.000000 to Dec 31st 9999 23:59:59.999999	N/A	8
TIME	00:00:00.000000 to 23:59:59.999999	N/A	8
BIT	0 or 1	N/A	1 BIT
BINARY		N/A	1 to 255
VARBINARY		N/A	1 to (32K-1)
UNIQUEIDENTIFIERSTR	CHAR(36) for MSSQL Server compatibility	N/A	36

When deciding on which data types to use the general rule is to use the smallest type you can. For example if you only require a field to hold a date then use a **DATE** rather than a **DATETIME** type. There are a couple of reasons for this, firstly data compression is better as there is no redundancy of space, and secondly query times are faster.

Another very important tip is to use the same types on columns that will be joined. This can be done via the use of domains (we will come to them in a minute). This also counts when creating temp tables and especially views (we will come to that later too).
Let's say for example you declare a column to be a **NUMERIC(20,5)** and only populate it with integers. You then have another table and declare a column as an integer and create a **SELECT** statement joining the two tables. When checking the **NUMERIC(20,10)** the optimizer must first check the precision and even though it is not used it will also have to check the scale for each number. When joining across tables this kind of inefficiency can add time to your queries all that is required to fix this is a simple data type change.

CHAR/CHARACTER(n) Data Types

Although character data types can be up to (32k-1) in when they are greater than 255 bytes they are stored in 255 byte chunks. Also when they are larger than 255 bytes only **FP, CMP** and **WORD** indexes can be used, also the only functions that can be used are **LIKE, CONTAINS** and **SUBSTR**. If data is under 255 bytes then all index types, except **DATE, TIME**, and **DTTM** are supported.

VARCHAR/CHARACTER VARYING(n) Data Types

There is no difference in storage for **CHAR** and **VARCHAR** types, but **CHAR** types are generally faster. However if the data is to be concatenated in queries then you should use **VARCHAR**'s because **CHAR** types will be padded. All other behaviours are the same as the **CHAR** data type.

INTEGERS and UNSIGNED INTEGERS

First let's get the bad news out of the way; you cannot use unsigned integers with open client/ISQL. Due to the Open Client restriction this means you may have issues when moving the data between servers. For ISQL it is more basic in that it just can interpret an integer that is greater than 2,147,483,648 (max positive value of a signed integer).

With the bad news out of the way there is still a lot to be said for using unsigned integers as keys on tables. This is because the query optimizer does not have to check for sign when processing joins

BIGINT and UNSIGNED BIGINT

Both these data types suffer from the same issues as the unsigned integer and thus cannot be used with Open Client. On the plus side they are extremely useful for keys and when unsigned can hold values from zero to 18,446,744,073,709,551,615.

SMALLINT and TINYINT

Both **SMALLINT** and **TINYINT** offer a very small storage option for lower integers, this has an obvious benefit on storage cost but will also improve query times.

FLOAT

If *precision* is not supplied, the **FLOAT** data type is the same as the **REAL** data type. If *precision* supplied, then the **FLOAT** data type is the same as the **REAL** or **DOUBLE** data type, depending on the value of the precision. The difference between **REAL** and **DOUBLE** is dependent on the Operating System/Platform. It is the number of bits used in the storage of single-precision floating point number on the platform. The **FLOAT** data type is an approximate numeric data type in that it may have rounding errors after arithmetic operations.

You can tune the behaviour of the **FLOAT** data type to be compatible with Sybase ASE and MS SQL server using the **FLOAT_AS_DOUBLE** database option.

REAL

A **REAL** data type holds a signed single precision floating-point number with a range of 1.175494351e-38 to 3.402823466e+38. The REAL data type is accurate to 6 significant digits, but may have rounding errors beyond this. It may also have rounding errors after arithmetic operations.

DECIMAL and NUMERIC

In Sybase IQ the **NUMERIC** and **DECIMAL** data types are identical.

They are both a signed decimal number with *precision* total digits and with *scale* of the digits after the decimal point.

Precision can be between 1 to 126, and the scale can be between 0 and 126.

Obviously the precision and scale values used will affect the storage space required to hold each value. For data types declared with a precision less than 18 the values are:-

Fig 6.33

Precision	Storage in Bytes
1 to 4	2 bytes
5 to 9	4 bytes
10 to 18	8 bytes

For precision over 18 the total storage in bytes can be calculated (Fig 6.32) using a formula.

Fig 6.34

```
4 + 2 * (int(((prec - scale) + 3) / 4) + int((scale + 3) / 4) + 1)
```

The storage required by a column is based upon the precision and scale of the column. Each cell in the column has enough space to hold the largest value of that precision and scale.
Both the **NUMERIC** and **DECIMAL** data types are exact numeric data types and their accuracy is preserved during and after arithmetic operations.
Although you should always set the precision and scale the defaults are 38 for scale and 126 for precision. These are large numbers and as such will take up more space than you would probably require. The default value for scale can be changed by setting the database option (Fig 6.33). For further information read the chapter on database options.

Fig 6.35

```
SET OPTION scale=15
```

The maximum value of both a **NUMERIC** and **DECIMAL** is the number of nines defined by [*precision - scale*], followed by the decimal point, and then followed by the number of nines defined by *scale*.
The minimum absolute non-zero value is the decimal point, followed by the number of zeros defined by [*scale* - 1], then followed by a single one. An example is given in Fig 6.36

Fig 6.36

```
NUMERIC/DECIMAL (5,2)
Max positive = 999.99
Min non-zero = 0.0001
Max negative = -999.99
```

DOUBLE

The **DOUBLE** data type holds a signed double precision floating-point number stored in 8 bytes. The range of absolute, non-zero values is between 2.2250738585072014e-308 and 1.797693134862315708e+308. Values held as **DOUBLE** are accurate to 15 significant digits, but may be subject to rounding errors after the fifteenth digit. They can also have rounding errors after arithmetic operations.

MONEY and SMALLMONEY

Sybase IQ includes two user-defined data types, **MONEY** and **SMALLMONEY**. They are implemented as **NUMERIC(19,4)** and **NUMERIC(10,4)** and are provided for compatibility with Sybase ASE and MS SQL Server.

DATE and DATETIME

Dates can have the following operations on them. These operations work using implicit conversions:-

Fig 6.37

Operation	Effect	Example
date + integer	Add the specified (by the integer) number of days to the date.	Select datefield + 1
date - integer	Subtract the specified (by the integer) number of days to the date.	Select datefield -1
date - date	Returns the number of days between two dates.	Select datefield_1 - datefield_2
date + time	Creates a timestamp (Datetime)	Select "13 Jun 2009" + "20:15.000000"

You may also use the normal T-SQL functions such as dateadd, datediff etc. The data types **TIMESTAMP** and **SMALLDATETIME** are in fact held in the database as a **DATETIME** so there is no storage difference between them.

A quick tip is if you want to remove the time component from a **TIMESTAMP/DATETIME/SMALLDATETIME** is just to run **CONVERT(DATE**, <datetime field), this will remove the time component.

Large Objects

*Note: Existing **LONG BINARY** columns created on Version 12.5 (ESD 8) or before are not supported on versions after that. All existing **LONG BINARY** columns created before 12.5 (ESD8) have to be explicitly dropped before installing onto later versions, then recreated after installing the later version.*
*Also please note that the **ALTER DATABASE UPGRADE** command does not upgrade LONG BINARY columns created prior to 12.5 (ESD8). I would always recommend referring to the latest Sybase documentation and advice before attempting to upgrade Large Object columns as the old adage says its better to be safe than sorry.*

With the warning out of the way we can now concentrate on functionality

Overview

An additional license is required to use large objects so you will need to contact Sybase about upgrading your licence prior to using large objects.

The Large Objects Management options extend the functionality of Sybase IQ to allow storage and retrieval of Binary Large Objects (**BLOB**s) and Character Large Objects (**CLOB**s) within the Sybase IQ.

Users must be specifically licensed to use the Large Objects Management functionality described in this product documentation.

As data volumes increase and data types change (video, images etc) there is an increasing need to store and retrieve large object data.

Typical types of large object data are XML, images, video, pdf, spreadsheets etc. Large objects can be in either a structured format such as XML or text or unstructured, for structured data IQ provides functions to operate on the data but for unstructured it is used simply as a data store.

The size of all Large objects depends on the size of the IQ store page size. If the page size is 128kb (the minimum for **BLOB** storage) then the data can be 0-512TB, however if the page size is 512Kb then the Blob can be up to 2PB(Petabytes). The maximum size is equal to 4GB multiplied by the size of the IQ store Page Size.
It is probably advisable to discuss with Sybase your requirements when purchasing the additional license for Large Object storage to ensure that the functionality you require is included.

The Large Objects data types (**BLOB** and **CLOB**) stored in columns much like any other datatype, you can still have **NULL** values, zero length values, the only constraint is you cannot index the column explicitly and have to rely on IQ's **FP** indexes.
An example of a **CREATE** and a **ALTER** statement for **BLOB**'s are given in Figure 6.38

Fig 6.38

```
CREATE TABLE myBlobTable
(
            blob_name      varchar(20)     NULL,
            blob_data      BLOB            NULL
);
CREATE TABLE myClobTable
(
            clob_name      varchar(20)     NULL,
            clob_data      CLOB            NOT NULL
);
ALTER TABLE myBlobTable ADD more_blob_data BLOB;
ALTER TABLE myClobTable ADD more_clob_data CLOB;
```

Functions on BLOB's

You may use **UPDATE, INSERT, LOAD TABLE, DELETE, TRUNCATE, SELECT...INTO** and **INSERT...LOCATION** SQL statements on **BLOB**s and the ASE **IMAGE** data type can be inserted into a **LONG BINARY.**

There are no implicit data type conversions from **BLOB**'s any other data type, with the exception of **BINARY/VARBINARY** when data is being inserted or updated. There are implicit conversions to **LONG BINARY** data type from **INTEGER** and **CHAR/VARCHAR** data types but not for **BIT, REAL, DOUBLE,** or **NUMERIC.**

You may not use *CAST* or *CONVERT* on **BLOB**'s.

When using **BLOB**s in where clauses you may use the functions in Fig 6.39.

Fig 6.39

BLOB_COLUMN **IS NULL**	**OCTET_LENGTH** (BLOB_COLUMN)
BLOB_COLUMN **IS NOT NULL**	**BIT_LENGTH** (BLOB_COLUMN)
BYTE_LENGTH (BLOB)	**BYTE_SUBSTR** (BLOB_COLUMN, start, length)
SUBSTRING64 (BLOB_COLUMN, start [, length]))	**BYTE_SUBSTR64** (BLOB_COLUMN, start, length

	)

Functions on CLOB's

You may use **UPDATE, *INSERT*, *LOAD TABLE*, *DELETE*, *TRUNCATE*, *SELECT*...*INTO*** and ***INSERT*...*LOCATION*** SQL statements on **BLOBs** and the ASE ***TEXT*** datatype can be inserted into a ***LONG BINARY***.

There are no implicit data type conversions from *CLOBS* any *other* data type, with the exception of **BLOBs**, **CHAR/VARCHAR** when data is being inserted or updated. There are implicit conversions to ***LONG VARCHAR*** data type from ***CHAR/VARCHAR*** data types but not for ***BIT***, ***REAL***, ***DOUBLE***, ***NUMERIC***, ***TINYINT***, ***SMALLINT***, ***INT***, ***UNSIGNED INT***, ***BIGINT***, ***UNSIGNED BIGINT***, ***BINARY***, ***VARBINARY***, or ***LONG BINARY*** data types to ***LONG VARCHAR*** data type.

You may not use ***CAST*** or ***CONVERT*** on *CLOB*'s.

When using **CLOBS** in where clauses you may use the functions in Fig 6.30.

Fig 6.40

CLOB_COLUMN **IS NULL**	**OCTET_LENGTH**(*CLOB_COLUMN*)
CLOB_COLUMN **IS NOT NULL**	**BIT_LENGTH** (*CLOB_COLUMN*)
SUBSTRING(*CLOB_COLUMN, start [, length]*)	**CHAR_LENGTH**(*CLOB_COLUMN*)
SUBSTRING64(*CLOB_COLUMN, start [, length]*))	**CHAR_LENGTH64**(*CLOB_COLUMN*)

You may not return **CLOBs** in **SELECTs**, or use them in **GROUP BY**, **HAVING** or **ORDER BY** clauses.

You may want to declare a variable of type **CLOB** and use it in a procedure. You may do this but there are limits on size. An Inbound variable is limited to 32767 bytes in length and an outbound variable is limited to 2GB in length.

Exporting BLOBs and CLOBS

The IQ extraction functionality includes a **BFILE** function which facilitates the extraction of single **BLOB** and **CLOB** values (I.e. one value) to a single file.

An example using the **BFILE** function to extract Large Object Data is given in Fig 6.41

Fig 6.41

```
SELECT
BFILE("C:\temo\mylobfile.dat",, large_object_column)
FROM my_large_object_table
WHERE large_object_column IS NOT NULL
```

Views

Views can be used to substitute sub selects, in-line SQL queries and tables in you SQL. A View can be based on any valid SQL **SELECT** statement. They are also particularly useful when you wish to use a layer between a table's implementation and the data it provides. A View is created by using a create view statement followed by a select for example (Fig 6.42)

Fig 6.42

```
CREATE VIEW vtotal_orders
AS
SELECT order_id,
       SUM(quantity) as total_order_quantity
FROM orders
GROUP BY order_id
```

The view can then be used in the same way as a table (Fig 6.43)

Fig 6.43

```
SELECT s.sales_person, o.total_order_quantity
FROM sales s join vtotal_orders o on (o.order_id = s.order_Id)
WHERE s.sales_person = 'ntaylor'
```

Data Type Mismatches in Views

Data type mismatches can have adverse effects on views, for example take the following tables and views.

Fig 6.44

```
CREATE TABLE sales
(
     sales_id           int          not null,
     sales_person_id    int          not null,
     sales_amount    NUMERIC(20,4)  not null
)
```

Fig 6.45

```
CREATE TABLE orders
(
     order_id     NUMERIC(20,0)  not null,
     sales_id     NUMERIC(20,0)  not null
)
```

Fig 6.46

```
CREATE VIEW vtotal_sales
AS
SELECT sales_id,
       SUM(sales_amount) as total_sales_amount
FROM sales
GROUP BY sales_id
```

Using the objects above, we have a query that runs SQL against the view (Fig 6.47):-

Fig 6.47

```
SELECT  o.order_id,
         SUM(ts.total_sales_amount) as total_sales_by_order
FROM    orders o
             join vtotal_sales vts on (vts.sales_id = o.sales_id)
WHERE   o.sales_id = 7
GROUP BY o.order_id
```

As you can see there is a data type mismatch because sales_id in the sales table is an int and in the sales table it is a **NUMERIC(20,0).**

When the view **vtotal_sales** is used in the query (Fig 6.47) the optimiser detects the data type mismatch and proceeds to run the entire view for all sales_id's before returning it for use in the **SELECT** statement. The **SELECT** statement will then perform the join and obtain the total_sales_amount for sales_id number 7.

To put this into context, if the sales table has 200 Million rows, the optimiser will do the following (Fig 6.48).

- First it will have to group all 200 Million rows in the sales table.
- It then performs a join on the orders table to return the total for sales_id number 7.

Fig 6.48

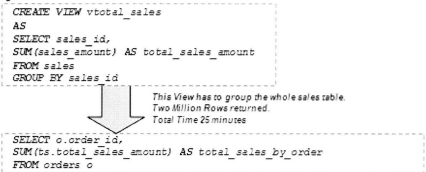

```
CREATE VIEW vtotal_sales
AS
SELECT sales_id,
SUM(sales_amount) AS total_sales_amount
FROM sales
GROUP BY sales_id
```

This View has to group the whole sales table.
Two Million Rows returned.
Total Time 25 minutes

```
SELECT o.order_id,
SUM(ts.total_sales_amount) AS total_sales_by_order
FROM orders o
```

If the data types were the same (preferably both int), it will do the following (Fig 6.49)

- First it will group all rows in sales with the sales_id number 7
- It then performs the join

Fig 6.49

```
CREATE VIEW vtotal_sales
AS
SELECT sales_id,
SUM(sales_amount) as total_sales_amount
FROM sales
WHERE sales_id = 7
GROUP BY sales_id
```

This View only groups the sales table for sales_id 7.
1 Row returned.
Total Time 5 seconds

```
SELECT o.order_id,
SUM(ts.total_sales_amount) as total_sales_by_order
FROM orders o
join vtotal_sales vts on (vts.sales_id = o.sales_id)
WHERE
o.sales_id = 7
GROUP BY
o.order_id
```

As per the example in Fig 6.49 the performance benefit can be dramatic as instead of grouping 200 million rows it may only have to group 1.

It is in cases like this that domains are preferable when defining id columns as they can help to ensure that all join columns have the same data type.

Using Views to optimise your queries

Views can be used to optimise your data queries by utilising parallel processing through the use of UNION ALL. If for example we have a database that uses a sales_by_region table with 500 million rows and 3 columns sales_person, customer_region, order_amount.

If the data in the table is split by customer_region as in Fig 6.51.

Fig 6.51

customer_region	Row count for region
AMERICAS	200 Million
EUROPE	150 Million
ASIA	150 Million

When queries are used to select from the sales_by_region table they often use the customer_region column along with sales_person.

Rather than running the SQL in Fig 6.52 in which the optimizer will have to group all values in the sales_by_region table in one query.

Fig 6.52

```
SELECT customer_region,
       SUM(order_amount)
FROM sales_by_region
WHERE sales_person = 'ntaylor'
GROUP BY order_amount
```

If you instead create the view as defined in Fig 6.53.

Fig 6.53

```
CREATE VIEW vOrderAmountByRegion
AS
SELECT customer_region,
       SUM(order_amount)
FROM sales_by_region
WHERE customer_region = 'AMERICAS'
GROUP BY order_amount
UNION ALL
SELECT customer_region,
       SUM(order_amount)
FROM sales_by_region
WHERE customer_region = 'EUROPE''
GROUP BY order_amount
UNION ALL
SELECT customer_region,
       SUM(order_amount)
FROM sales_by_region
WHERE customer_region = 'ASIA'
GROUP BY order_amount
```

Once this view is built you can run the same SQL as in Fig 6.2 but instead of the table using the view instead.

Fig 6.54

```
SELECT customer_region,
       SUM(order_amount)
FROM vOrderAmountByRegion
WHERE sales_person = 'ntaylor'
GROUP BY order_amount
```

When you run this query the query optimiser will run the three component selects used in the view simultaneously (Fig 6.55).

Fig 6.55

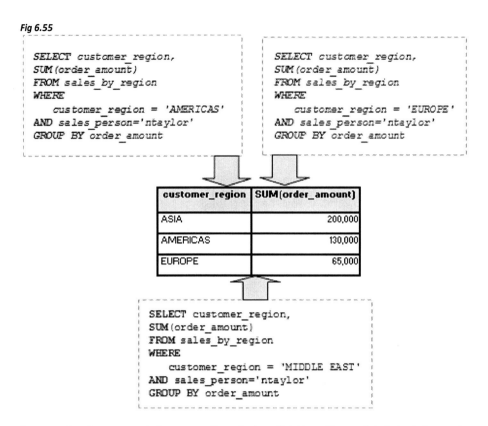

So as per the above example it can sometimes be beneficial to split your data but a judgement should be made based on the cardinality, data type, query use and query frequency.

Another problem that can occur is when joining to a view that has a select distinct statement. The query optimizer seems to get confused as it tries to select the distinct values before taking into consideration any search arguments that may be passed to the view via the join. It is therefore best to try and avoid using **SELECT DISTINCT** in views, it is far better to try and use some other method such as grouping data , using a sub select in the where clause or joining to an in-line view to obtain distinct values.

Overall the use of joins can greatly enhance your queries multi-threading capabilities but using distinct or having data type mismatches can not only negate the optimisation but can actually make things worse.

Indexes

This chapter goes in-depth about the various indexes used in Sybase IQ. If you're used to other transact SQL databases then get ready to throw away everything you know. Sybase IQ does not use non clustered or clustered indexes; in fact there are a lot more indexing options available depending on the data type and the cardinality of the column being indexed.

Sybase IQ also has some great tools for analysing your queries and telling you about Indexes (and data type) mismatches in your queries. It will generate information on joins, search arguments and groupings used in your queries and tell you how to optimise them,

It is worth remembering that every column in Sybase IQ has a (fast projection) index built on it for free I.e. you do not have to create it explicitly.

Index Overview

Most Sybase IQ indexes use a bitmap to store data, bit maps can be built very fast compared to other index types and use less disk space. Bit Maps also mean that queries (data extraction) and data loading can be processed very fast. Other advantages are that as the data used is less then more can be cached in memory meaning less I/O. They also mean that when data is added, deleted or updated the indexes do not need to be rebuilt like traditional b-tree indexes used in many other RDBM's.

Because each value uses a bit map only a zero or a one has to be retrieved rather than searching each char value held in the shape column.

Fig 7.1

Shapes		Shapes		
		Circle	Square	Triangle
Circle		1	0	0
Square		0	1	0
Circle		1	0	0
Triangle		0	0	1
Circle		1	0	0
Circle		1	0	0
Square		0	1	0
Circle		1	0	0

SELECT * FROM shapes where shape='Circle'

Only one column needs to be searched.

Traditional Database Table — Sybase IQ Storage

In Sybase IQ the indexes are used as data access methods (in fact this is what they are), and they are not stored in any sorted order. This means that if you want data back in a particular order you should include an order by clause in your query.

A traditional RDBM's will only use one index per table per query. Sybase IQ uses every available index it can for all column used in query. It uses indexes for table joins, group by clauses, search arguments and some functions (datepart, count and count distinct). As such it is best to try to use every available index possible (depending on cardinality, the data type and the use of the data) so that the query optimizer can choose the best possible options when returning your query. Sybase IQ is built for large data loads and as such its indexes are built for this use, a table with many indexes will not like being loaded every 5 seconds with a one row update and this type of use will hit performance. Also to aid performance you should create your indexes prior to loading a table so the data storage optimizer is ware of the data it is loading during the load.

There are nine type of index in Sybase IQ, these shown in Fig 7.2

Fig 7.2

Index Name	Index Abbreviation	Index Purpose
Fast Projection	FP	Built by IQ for free, however you can tell IQ the cardinality of a column which will help it decide if a 1 byte or 2 byte (or in IQ Version 15

		upwards a 3 byte) index is used.
Low Fast	LF	Used in columns that have a low cardinality, normally less than 1500 distinct values (but it holds up to 50k)
High Group	HG	Used in columns with high cardinality data normally over 1500 distinct values. This is also recommended for all columns used in table joins
High Non-Group	HNG	Used in columns that is involved in ranges, betweens, min, max etc. Although generally a HG, DATE or DTTM indexes are better.
Word	WD	Used to index columns with lists of words.
Compare	CMP	Used to compare 2 columns in the same table.
Date	DATE	As the name suggests use this on data columns (where time is not required).
Datetime	DTTM	Again very simple, this should be used on column of data type datetime.
Time	TIME	And finally if your column holds time data then this is the index to use.

Fast Projection Indexes

Fast projection indexes are sometimes referred to as default indexes; this is because they are generated for free. In other words these indexes are how Sybase IQ physically stores data, as such they can only be dropped by using an alter table statement to drop the column indexed. This means that every column has and is a Fast projection index. **FP** indexes are stored with a standard index name generated by the system, this is ASIQ_IDX_T<tn>_C<cn>_FP, where <tn> is the table id and <cn> is the column number.

If you run a select from the system table sys.syscolumns for a specific table you can see all indexes used on the specified table. In Fig 7.3 and Fig 7.4 there is a select for the orders table.

Fig 7.3

```
SELECT *
FROM sys.sysindexes
WHERE tname = 'orders'
```

Fig 7.4

icreator	iname	fname	creator	tname	indextype	colnames	interval	levelnum
DBA	ASIQ_IDX_T818_C1_FP	asiqdemo.iq	DBA	orders	Non-unique	order_id ASC	0	0
DBA	ASIQ_IDX_T818_C2_FP	asiqdemo.iq	DBA	orders	Non-unique	customer_id ASC	0	0
DBA	ASIQ_IDX_T818_C3_FP	asiqdemo.iq	DBA	orders	Non-unique	sales_id ASC	0	0
DBA	ASIQ_IDX_T818_C4_FP	asiqdemo.iq	DBA	orders	Non-unique	product_id ASC	0	0
DBA	ASIQ_IDX_T818_C1_	asiqdemo	DBA	order	Unique	order_id ASC	0	0

HG	.iq		s				

In this case the first four rows show the FP indexes generated and the firth row is the **PRIMARY KEY**. As you can see the FP indexes have this tagged at the end of the name where as the **PRIMARY KEY** is generated as a unique HG index.

There are three (four in IQ version 15+) types of Fast Projection index, 1 byte, 2 byte (3 byte in version 15+) or flat, the difference depends on two factors.

- The cardinality of the data

- The value of IQ Unique given in the table creation statement, or if the MINIMIZE_STORAGE database option is set to on (This is like declaring **IQ UNIQUE** (255) on every column).

The space used to store the index is dependant on the type of fast projection index used and the datatype being stored.

A flat index stores the data as it is loaded with no storage optimization and the space used to store a value is dependant on the data type. For example a **CHAR**(20) will use 20 bytes of space per value.

The 1 and 2 byte indexes are known as optimized FP indexes because they read faster from disk, use less disk space and are used by the query optimizer to obtain information about the data stored in a column.

The 3 byte index in IQ version 15 upwards is structurally the same as a 1 & 2 byte but can hold between 65,537 and 16,777,216 unique values (inclusive)

In order to create an optimized index you **MUST** either specify a value for **IQ UNIQUE** in a create table statement (Fig 7.3) or set the **MINIMIZE_STORAGE** database option on(Fig 7.4). If you intend on setting the database option then you must do this prior to creating tables where you want the **IQ UNIQUE** value to be defaulted.

Fig 7.5

```
CREATE TABLE orders
(
        order_id        int                          IDENTITY,
        customer_id     int     IQ UNIQUE (255)      NOT NULL,
        sales_id        int     IQ UNIQUE (10000)    NOT NULL,
        product_id      int     IQ UNIQUE (5000)     NOT NULL
)
```

Fig 7.6

```
SET OPTION MINIMIZE_STORAGE='on'
```

In a flat fast projection index a columns raw data is compressed but there is no storage optimization used. In 1, 2 and 3 byte indexes the data is converted via the use of look up tables to 1 , 2 or 3 bytes values. If we has a shapes column that has multiple rows containing the values 'CIRCLE','SQUARE','TRIANGLE' or 'RECTANGLE' then the three indexes would store the data differently (Flat **FP** Fig 7.7, One Byte **FP** Fig 7.8, Two Byte **FP** Fig 7.9 and Three byte FP Fig 7.10).

Fig 7.7 (Flat FP)

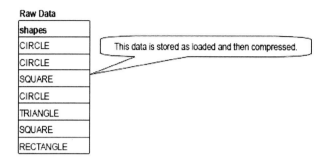

Fig 7.8 (1 Byte FP)

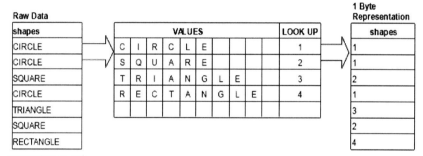

Fig 7.9 (2 Byte FP)

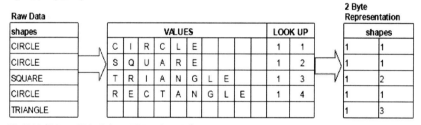

Fig 7.10 (3 Byte FP in Sybase IQ Version15+)

Optimized **FP** indexes are used in the absence of **HG** and **LF** indexes to determine the cardinality of the data in a column. They are also used by the query optimizer to search and locate data values. If a value of 255 or less is used in an **IQ UNIQUE** hint in a create table statement then a 1 byte FP index is created any value over 255 and a 2 Byte **FP** index is created. Inversions before 15 if the value is over 65,536 then a flat **FP** index is created. In version 15+ a 3 byte FP is created before progressing onto a flat **FP** when there are more than 16,777,216 unique values.

However the **IQ UNIQUE** value is just a hint to the optimizer and the correct type of FP index will still be created regardless of value when data is loaded. There can be a performance hit if for example you hint that every column has a **IQ UNIQUE** value of 255 or less (or **MINIMIZE_STORAGE** is set to 'on') and a large file is loaded that has to reformat all the 1 byte FP indexes as 2 byte or flat indexes. This performance hit is due to memory thrashing during the formatting,. You can avoid this by setting any **IQ UNIQUE** values in the create table statements to more appropriate ones, For example if you expect high cardinality then set **IQ UNIQUE** to 70,000. However this performance overhead will only happen once when the data is first loaded into a table so in most cases is an allowable one given the advantages of using optimized FP indexes over flat FP indexes.

High Group (HG) Indexes

High Group (HG) indexes are by far the most common, useful and powerful indexes that Sybase IQ has to offer. These indexes should be created in Columns with cardinality of over 1500 distinct values or on any columns used in a join, regardless of their cardinality.
HG Indexes can be used on any datatype except bit and any varbinary, varchar or char over 255 characters in length. They are automatically created on primary and foreign keys and on unique constraints. They may be created on a single column or on a composite (in composite key constraints). While they are being created the system utilises the Sybase IQ temporary cache (memory) and the Sybase IQ temporary store (Disk) for sorting the data while the index is created. The **HG** Index does take the longest time of any index to load and it also uses the most storage space, but the advantages of using them far out weigh these disadvantages.
Non unique **HG** indexes consist of both a B-Tree and a G-Array to store the index. The B-Tree is used to store the distinct values held in a column and then each leaf of the B-Tree has a reference in a G-Array that stores the rows ids for all the rows that store the value in the leaf. The G-Array may or may not contain rows from different leafs of the B-Tree.
Of course if the HG index is unique there is no need for the G-Array as each value is used in only one row so only a B-Tree is required.
If for example a column is used to store surnames in a non unique HG index it may be held as in Fig 7.11.

Fig 7.11

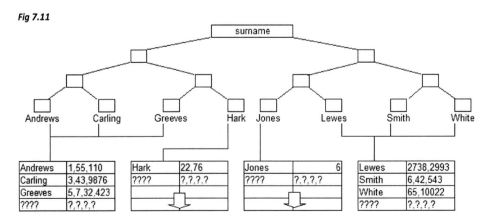

In this example (Fig 7.11) you can see that the value "Andrews" Can be found in rows 1, 55 and 110 while the value Carling is in rows 3,43 and 9876 etc etc.

A unique **HG** index would just have a B-Tree index that held the row id and value in the leaf node making a unique index a much simpler and quicker index. Therefore it is always best to use a unique index whenever possible.

Low Fast (LF) Indexes

Low Fast Indexes are used on columns with a low cardinality, they can be used on columns of up to 10,000 distinct values but the recommended cardinality is 1500. If you try to insert more than 9,999 distinct values then you will receive an error, the only way to solve the problem is to drop the LF index or change the data to fit.

A Non Unique **LF** index is comprised of a B-Tree that holds the distinct values and then each distinct value has a bitmap, this is faster than the **HG** index that has to use a G-Array. A unique **LF** index just uses the B-Tree as per a HG Unique index. Therefore you may as well use a **HG** unique and then you never have to worry about cardinality issues. Other similarities with **HG** indexes are the data types that an **LF** index can be created on, Like **HG** Indexes, **LF's** can be used on any data type except Bit and any Varbinary, Varchar or Char over 255 characters in length.

A non unique **LF** index based on a column called shapes could be stored as in Fig 7.12

Fig 7.12

ROW ID	CIRCLE	SQUARE	TRIANGLE	RECTANGLE
1	1	0	0	0
2	0	0	1	0
3	0	1	0	0
4	0	1	0	0
5	0	0	0	1
6	0	0	1	0
7	0	0	0	1
8	0	1	0	0
9	0	1	0	0
10	1	0	0	0
11	1	0	0	0
12	1	0	0	0
13	0	0	1	0
14	0	1	0	0
15	0	0	0	1

Given Fig 7.12 if a **SELECT** statement was run as in Fig 7.13 then the query planner would just use the B-Tree to obtain the correct bitmap for the value SQUARE and then select all the rows where the bitmap value is 1.

Fig 7.13

```
SELECT shapes
FROM mytable
WHERE shapes = 'SQUARE'
```

A similar process will be followed when an update is run,

If for example the value "SQUARE" is updated to "OCTAGON" then there is no need to re-build a bitmap. However if the value "SQUARE" is updated to "TRIANGLE" then the bitmap associated with TRIANGLE is rebuilt and the one for SQUARE can be dropped. It is for this reason that LF's are used for low cardinality data as the overhead of storing and searching a bitmap for each distinct value on high cardinality data could be potentially huge.

High Non Group (HNG) Indexes

First and foremost, do not use this index. Why? Well **HNG** indexes are a patented Sybase IQ index used for high cardinality data used in aggregation and ranges. But in everyday use I have never seen any benefit from them over normal **HG** indexes; in fact they cannot be used on some of the data types where they would be most useful. You cannot use a **HNG** index on real, float, binary, varbinary, double, bit, char and varchar's over 255 characters in length. As the main function of a HNG index for columns that are in **SUM,MAX,MIN** and **AVG** functions and also in ranges (**BETWEENS**) then the restriction on double, real and float types precludes them from regular use.

Sybase themselves also state that since the introduction of **DATE** and **DTTM** indexes and the fact that **FP** indexes can now be optimised that the use of **HNG** indexes are no longer given high importance. That said it is still worth knowing how to use them, even if only because you may have to support them on a legacy system.

For numerical values the **HNG** index converts the value to binary and then each binary bit is stored vertically, for characters each byte is converted to binary and stored. As a zero but compresses to almost nothing the **HNG** index can be very fast to load and use minimal storage.

For example if you place a **HNG** index on a column called account_balance it may be stored as in Fig 7.14

Fig 7.14

account_balance	256	128	64	32	16	8	4	2	1
				Binary Representation					
435	0	0	0	0	0	0	0	0	0
60	0	0	0	1	1	1	1	0	0
2	0	0	0	0	0	0	0	1	0
55	0	0	0	1	1	0	1	1	1
243	0	1	1	1	1	0	0	1	1
87	0	0	1	0	1	0	1	1	1
176	0	1	0	1	1	0	0	0	0
345	1	0	1	0	1	1	0	0	1
344	1	0	1	0	1	1	0	0	0
110	0	0	1	1	0	1	1	1	0

Now if for example the query in Fig 7.19 was run the query optimizer would perform the following:-

* Check for the highest binary column, in this case 256

* Look for values in this column, in this case 345 and 344

* Repeat the process I.e. find the next highest and check for a value

Fig 7.19

```
SELECT max (account_balance)
FROM bank_accounts
```

Word (WD) Indexes

WD indexes are used access columns containing a list of words, as such they are restricted to char and varchar data types. These indexes are useful for searching for specific words in a string and example would be searching in a website for a product description. The minimum length of the char or varchar is 3 characters, but it is impossible to get a list of characters in anything less anyway. A **WD** index is stored in a similar way to a **HG** index and as such will also require more disk space than an **FP** or **LF** index. Of course the performance gains can be very large when using a **WD** as only a few G-Arrays are searched rather than am entire **FP** Index.

An **WD** index will separate all words in a varchar/char column into words based on a delimiter between the words. The default delimiters are all non alpha-numeric's excluding the hyphen and single quote. For example the string in Fig 7.19 will be split into the words in Fig 7.21.

Fig 7.20

Number 10 Downing Street, London, WC1

Fig 7.21

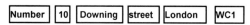

So the data is physically split in the index meaning that if a query like Fig 7.22 is run then the optimizer knows that it just has to search the G-Array associated with the value WC1.. As you can see this kind of search can be useful when trying to pick certain values from columns.

Fig 7.22

```
SELECT *
FROM contacts
WHERE address LIKE 'WC1'
```

The two main operators for accessing data in a WD index are the LIKE operator and the **CONTAINS** verb, If you have never used the **CONTAINS** verb it can be used as in examples Fig 7.23 and Fig 7.24.

Fig 7.23

```
SELECT *
FROM contacts
WHERE address CONTAINS ('London','WC1')
```

This will return any varchar that has BOTH LONDON and WC1 in them, it is important to remember this is not an OR but an AND, so both values must be present. The values in the CONTAINS list can be in any order as long as all words are present in the varchar.

Fig 7.24

```
SELECT*
FROM contacts
WHERE address NOT CONTAINS ('WC1')
```

This variation uses a **NOT**, this means that any row that does not contain the values in the **CONTAINS** list is used. All words in the WD index are obtained from the varchar column the index is based on, by the use of the delimiter. In the example given in Fig 7.21 the default delimiter (non-alphas) are 1 used, however you can specify this when creating the index (Fig 7.25).

Fig 7.25

```
CREATE WD INDEX my_wd ON  WORD_TABLE(words) DELIMITED BY '|'
```

In Fig 7.25 the word index will create a **WD** index using pipe as the delimiter. This means that if the column value was the same as Fig 7.26 then it will be split as in Fig 7.27.

Fig 7.26

This is my|pipe|delimiter, and|it|works

Fig 7.27

This is my	pipe	delimiter, and	it	works

Because of this split Fig 7.28 will return a result but Fig 7.29 would not.

Fig 7.28

```
SELECT *
FROM  WORD_TABLE
WHERE words CONTAINS ('delimiter, and')
```

Fig 7.29

```
SELECT *
FROM  WORD_TABLE
WHERE words CONTAINS ('delimiter')
```

Another option when creating a **WD** index is that you can specify the maximum length of any words in the column (by word I mean any characters between delimiters). To add this limit you can declare it when creating the index as in Fig 7.30, which limits the length of a word to 25 characters. Any insert into the table (or existing data) will throw an error and either the data will not be inserted or the index will not be created (depending on if you are creating the index on an empty table).

Fig 7.30

```
CREATE WD INDEX my_wd ON WORD_TABLE(words) LIMIT 25
```

Compare (CMP) Index

This index is used to compare data in two columns of the same data type (and length/precision/scale) in the same table.
An example of this index could be where you want to check that an employee is also manager of there own department (Fig 7..31).

Fig 7.31

```
SELECT employee_name
FROM   employees
WHERE  employee_id = manager_id
```

In this case we would create a CMP index on the employee_id and manager_id columns as in Fig 7.32

Fig 7.32

```
CREATE CMP INDEX employee_cmp
ON employees(employee_id, manager_id)
```

When a CMP index is created a series of bitmaps are used to store a binary relationship (Fig 7.33) on the two columns to say if one is greater than, less than or equal to the other.

Fig 7.33

employee_id	less than	equal	greater than	manager_id
7	1	0	0	23
23	0	1	0	23
64	0	0	1	23
78	0	0	1	54
33	0	0	1	1
854	1	0	0	1543
8	0	1	0	8
3	1	0	0	8
2	1	0	0	4
9	0	0	1	3

However there are some constraints around using a CMP index.

- They cannot be a unique index

- Both column become mandatory on insert and load operations, although you can still insert **NULL** into them.

- They cannot be created on bit, float, real or double data types.

Date, Datetime (DTTM) and Time(TIME) Indexes

We finish this chapter with the simplest of indexes, they behave exactly as you see them and act on the data types that there names correspond to. Hence **DATE** indexes can only be created on columns of the **DATE** data type, **DTTM** on columns of type **DATETIME** or **TIMESTAMP** and **TIME** indexes on data type TIME.

None of these indexes can be declared as unique and can only be created on a single column. It should be noted that in many cases a **HG/LF** or even the standard FP index may work better than these indexes. This is because the query optimizer does not search these indexes in parallel.

However if you are performing a lot of range searches then these indexes may help as they may if you are using the DATEPART function to perform comparisons.

Which Indexes To Use and Why

In order to decide which indexes to use we first need to know if the table has already been created and in use, why?
Well Sybase IQ has a rather useful index advisor. You can set the amount of index advice it should hold, flush it out, or just read and use it. It will also give you advice about data type mismatches used in joins. However in most cases if you are preparing a table, optimising a query or data modelling then you can use the diagram in Fig 7.35 to help you decide.

Fig 7.35

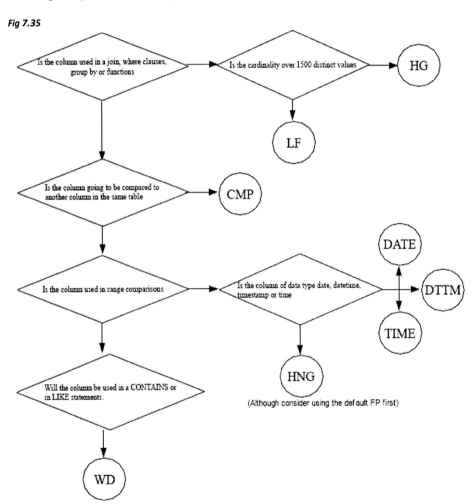

Fig 7.35 is fine if you have a clean environment but to really find out how a column is used you can use the Index advisor. To do this you first need to set the index advisor on Fig 7.36. You next specify how much advice you want it to hold (Fig 7.37), as the advice is held in a table and only

one entry is required for each individual piece of advice I would suggest setting this at a couple of thousand. For more information of setting options see the chapter on Options.

Fig 7.36

```
SET OPTION Index_Advisor=ON
```

Fig 7.37

```
SET OPTION Index_Advisor_Max_Rows=1000
```

If you ran these two statements the index advisor would hold 1,000 rows of index advice. You can now run one query, a thousand or stored procedures. In fact run anything you like and the index_advisor will store the advice until it is retrieved. To retrieve the advice you should use the system procedure in Fig 7.38, which will return the results in Fig 7.39

Fig 7.38

```
sp_iqindexadvice
```

Fig 7.39

Advice	NInst	LastDT
Add a LF index to grouping column ORDERS.order_date	115	18/02/2008
Add a LF index to grouping column SALES.sales_region	119	18/02/2008
Add a unique HG index to join key column ORDERS.order_id	119	18/02/2008
Add a unique HG index to join key column	148	18/02/2008
Add a HG index to join key column ORDERS.sales_id	116	18/02/2008
Join Key Columns ORDER.product_id (bigint) and PRODUCT.product_id (integer) have mismatched data types Predicate: (O.product_id = P.product_id)	116	18/02/2008 10:06

The first column advice is self explanatory, you will normally be told the type of index you should add or if there is a datatype mismatch and also the column effected. The NInst is the instance number of the advice and LastDT is the time that this advice was last detected (You don't get duplicate advice). It is always best to check the advice before you use it though. For example if you get advised to add LF indexes to a column in a global temp table,. It may be that on a particular run there was less than 1500 rows inserted into the global temp table. If you add the indexes and then on a later run of code an attempt to insert 10k rows is made, then an error will occur and the data will not be able to be inserted.

If you want to clear out all the advice then you can just pass a number into the proc, any number will do but I tend to use the number 1 to keep it looking clean (Fig 7.40).

Fig 7.40

```
sp_iqindexadvice 1
```

You will get the same advice from using a query plan but the index advisor is much quicker and easier to use.

Join Indexes

Join indexes are more or less useless since at least version 12.5 of Sybase IQ, it is for this reason I didn't include them in the main index types. The main reason is that they require too much administration to be used in frequently changing tables and no longer provide any benefits over **HG** indexes. Still, as with **HNG** indexes it is worth giving an overview of them as you may come across them in legacy systems.

Join indexes are used to index a join between two tables where the relationship is one to many, Join indexes require more space than other indexes and both tables used in a join index must be loaded before a join index can be created and loaded. There is a heft reading section on the Sybase website relating to these indexes. But some important things to remember are:-

* When a user is updating a join index all tables in that index are locked for writing.

* If you need to add columns to a table in a join index you first need to drop the index.

In order to create a Join Index you can use the syntax given in Fig 7.41

Fig 7.41

```
CREATE JOIN INDEX order_to_sales_join
FOR orders FULL OUTER JOIN sales
ON order_id=sales.order_id
```

In Fig 7.41 the index will create a full outer join on the orders and sales tables on the column order_id from each table. There are many options such as using primary keys, foreign keys, natural joins etc and each used to have their merits. But as we have already covered the basics I would suggest that if you see any join indexes that your time is better spent replacing them with HG indexes than reading any further on Join indexes.

Index Maintenance

Although Sybase IQ does not require the maintenance overhead of most RDBMs there are still occasions when index maintenance should be performed.

* Rows have been deleted from a table and then new ones were inserted when the option Append_Load was set to ON. (This option means that when rows are deleted the newly inserted rows backfill the empty rows before appending to the end of a table).

* Table were created when the Minimize_Storage option was set to **OFF** and the IQ UNIQUE option was not used on some/any columns.

* The cardinality of columns has changed so that a flat **FP** index can now be optimized. I.e. The distinct values have changed from over 65,536 to under 65,536. This means a 2-byte **FP** index can be used instead of a flat FP (or 3 byte FP in versions 15+).

To rebuild an index you may use the procedure sp_indexrebuild 'tablename','index_clause'. The index_clause option can be used to re-build a specific named index or be used to update the FP index.

If you wish to rebuild a specific index then you can use the procedure as in Fig 7.42 which will rebuild the index called order_id_hg on the orders table.

Fig 7.42

```
sp_iqrebuildindex 'orders','index order_id_hg'
```

Alternatively you can rebuild the **FP** index by giving the column name and a hint at the number of distinct values, as you would when using an **IQ UNIQUE** in a table declaration. In Fig 7.43 the **FP** index on the sales_id column of the orders table is rebuilt with an **IQ UNIQUE** hint of 10000 distinct columns.

Fig 7.43

```
sp_iqrebuildindex 'orders','column sales_id 10000'
```

As you can see from the above examples you could quite easily script something to run these rebuilds automatically. When you rebuild indexes the time and number of records rebuilt is recorded in the IQ server log and the IQ message file. In order to rebuild the indexes you **MUST** have insert permission on the table.
In databases where data changes frequently you may want to run these rebuilds more frequently. In order to check the health of your indexes you can use the two system procedures sp_iqindexfragmentation and sp_iqrowdensity.

sp_iqindexfragmentation

This procedure is will tell you the index type, and the number of pages used in any b-tree, g-array or bitmaps used to hold the index. It will also tell you hows full the pages are. If you require regular reporting using this procedure it may be worth checking the online Sybase guide for the version of IQ you are using to ensure that you can obtain the information you require. To run the procedure you may use a syntax as in Fig 7.44 which gives the fragmentation for the order table.

Fig 7.44

```
sp_iqindexfragmentation 'table orders'
```

sp_iqrowdensity

This procedure checks the index fragmentation of **FP** indexes in either an entire table or a specific column. It will report the row density which is a number between 0 and 1. This number is a ratio of the minimum number of index pages required to the actual number of pages used. The closer this number is to 1 the better. The code in Fig 7.45 gives the ratio for all columns in the orders table.

Fig 7.45

```
sp_iqrowdensity 'table orders'
```

Creating Indexes in Parallel

There is a very useful transaction in Sybase IQ called **PARALLEL IQ**, in fact why this only works on index creation is a failing because this would be useful in lots of other contexts.
Anyway if you have multiple indexes you want to create you can place them in a parallel transaction as in Fig 7.46 and all the statement will be run in parallel (resources and options permitting).

Fig 7.46

```
BEGIN PARALLEL IQ
        CREATE HG INDEX myidx1_HG ON my_table (col_1);
        CREATE HG INDEX myidx2_HG ON my_table (col_2);
        CREATE LF INDEX myidx3_LF ON my_table (col_3);
        CREATE HNG INDEX myidx4_HNG ON my_table (col_4);
END PARALLEL IQ
```

User Create Stored Procedures, Functions and Triggers

This chapter concentrates on user stored procedures and functions how to create them, passing variables in and out, return codes, output messages and best practises.

Stored Procedures in Sybase IQ operate in much the same way as they do on other transact SQL databases. There are of course differences in the code, syntax and differences in features, but the basic premise of executing a stored procedure to either return results or change data is the same.

One thing to remember is that stored procedures on IQ are not compiled in a traditional way, they are stored as a set of commands, and as such they do not pre-compile a query plan. The only advantage they have over scripts is they can be called easier and are stored in the database.

In the last few years I have written hundreds of stored procedures (sprocs) on IQ, these include procedures to report data, procedures to perform data transformations in a batch environment, check system properties and ensure the database is healthy.

As IQ can handle stored procedures in either T-SQL or Watcom SQL you should be aware that certain functions will only work in one or the other. As the rest of this book is written in T-SQL we shall continue the trend here, but will also show Watcom equivalents were specified and will use Watcom were it is relevant. You should also check the chapter on SQL to obtain functions and syntax you can use within your procedures.

Stored Procedure Basics

The example below is a simple procedure to return a list of sales people.

Fig 8.1

```
CREATE PROCEDURE sp_sales_people
AS
BEGIN
        SELECT DISTINCT sales_person
        FROM sales
END
```

To execute this procedure you simply run the code in Fig 8.2

Fig 8.2

```
EXEC sp_sales_people
```

Now if you want to change this procedure to include the sales region you would use an ALTER command as in Fig 8.2

Fig 8.3

```
ALTER PROCEDURE sp_sales_people
AS
BEGIN
        SELECT DISTINCT sales_person, sales_region
        FROM sales
END
```

The next step is to pass in a parameter, say for example we only wanted to display sales people from a specific sales region, we could do this by passing a parameter into the procedure as in Fig 8.4

Fig8.4

```
ALTER PROCEDURE sp_sales_people @sales_region VARCHAR(20) = 'EUROPE'
AS
BEGIN
        SELECT DISTINCT sales_person, sales_region
        FROM sales
        WHERE sales_region = @sales_region
END
```

You may now call this procedure with parameters as in one of the ways specified in Fig 8.5. You may also call the procedure without any parameters and the @sales_region will default to 'EUROPE' and specified in the procedure DDL.

Fig 8.5

```
EXEC sp_sales_people @sales_region = 'USA'
or
EXEC sp_sales_people 'USA'
```

Parameters in IQ procedures can be declared as **IN** meaning the parameters is passed into the procedure or as an OUT which means the procedure will pass out the value. In fact **OUT** parameters in Sybase IQ are in fact **INOUT** parameters so you can pass in a value and return the changed value in one call.

Now let's assume we want to add an entry to an auditing table to so we can check when the procedure was executed. We can do this as in Fig 8.6

Fig 8.6

```
ALTER PROCEDURE sp_sales_people @sales_region VARCHAR(20) = 'EUROPE'
AS
BEGIN


        INSERT  my_auditing_table
        (       procedure_name,
                execution_time
        )
        SELECT 'sp_sales_people', GETDATE()


        SELECT DISTINCT sales_person, sales_region
        FROM sales
        WHERE sales_region = @sales_region
END
```

So now here is an insert statement that inserts the procedure name and the current time (GETDATE () is a function to return the current time), but what happens if this insert fails? Time for some error checking

Error Handling

In Sybase IQ you should check the variable SQLCODE and not @@error as in other T-SQL systems. An example of this is given in Fig 8.7

Fig 8.7

```
ALTER PROCEDURE sp_sales_people @sales_region varchar(20) = 'EUROPE'
AS
BEGIN
        DECLARE @ERR INT
        INSERT  my_auditing_table
        (       procedure_name,
                        execution_time
        )
        SELECT 'sp_sales_people', GETDATE()


        SELECT @ERR = SQLCODE
        IF (@ERR < 0)
        BEGIN
                RETURN 1
        END


        SELECT DISTINCT sales_person, sales_region
        FROM sales
        WHERE sales_region = @sales_region


        RETURN 0
END
```

In Fig 8.7 we declare a local variable called @ERR then immediately after the **SELECT** statement we set this to be the value of **SQLCODE**. Setting a variable to equal **SQLCODE** is good practise as you may require the value later either in an error message or using it as a return code.

In this example I have just returned a 1 for an error and explicitly returned a zero upon success. Sprocs will always return a zero for success by default but again it is good practise to explicitly return it to make code clearer.

Now if we want to specify an owner of the procedure or a schema for it to reside in. all you need to do is qualify the procedure when you create it. You cannot add a qualifier in an **ALTER** statement as the **ALTER** statement will try to **ALTER** the already qualified procedure not add a qualifier.

So in our example we would have to create a script to drop and recreate the procedure with a qualifier as in Fig 8.8. Notice the use of the semi colon after the **END** and before the **CREATE** statement to signify the end of the IF statement. IQ can be strict about this kind of error, but it lets you get away with blue murder in other circumstances.

Fig 8.8

```
IF EXISTS (SELECT 1
             FROM    sysobjects so,
                     sysusers su
             WHERE
                     so.NAME = 'sp_sales_people'
             AND     su.uid = so.uid
             AND     su.name = 'DBA')
BEGIN
    DROP PROCEDURE SALES_USER.sp_sales_people
END;


CREATE PROCEDURE SALES_USER.sp_sales_people
        @sales_region varchar(20) = 'EUROPE'
AS
BEGIN
        DECLARE @sql_code INT

        INSERT my_auditing_table
        (       procedure_name,
                execution_time
        )
        SELECT 'sp_sales_people', GETDATE()

        SELECT @sql_code = SQLCODE
        IF (@sql_code < 0)
        BEGIN
                    RETURN 1
        END

        SELECT DISTINCT sales_person, sales_region
        FROM sales
        WHERE sales_region = @sales_region

        RETURN 0
END
```

No in order for us to return our error we have to check the database option "On_tsql_error"

Fig 8.9

```
SELECT *
FROM SYSOPTIONS
WHERE "option" = 'On_T-SQL_error'
```

This option has three values

* **"CONDITIONAL"** – If the sproc declares the **ON EXCEPTION RESUME** Clause, and the statement following the error handles the error then it will continue onto the error handling otherwise it will exit. As the **ON EXCEPTION RESUME** clause can only be used in Watcom SQL Procedures I suggest for T-SQL based systems you go with one of the other options.

* **"STOP"**– Stops the execution immediately and returns the error code (use this option if you don't have any error trapping in your code.

* **"CONTINUE"** – Continue execution, regardless of the following statement. If there are multiple errors, the first error encountered in the stored procedure is returned. This option most closely mirrors Adaptive Server Enterprise behaviour but IQ doesn't do it properly. If your sproc has a lot of processing IQ will continue happily trying to run the other statements in the procedure and wait until the whole thing finished before returning and error.

Try experimenting with each of the options to see what you prefer, I have used all three options on different project depending on the project managers own preference to error trapping. My personal favourite is STOP, as I know it will exit and give me the error code. Our example relies on the CONTINUE option being set.

In our example so far we return a 1 from the procedure when it fails. Of course this approach means the calling program should check the return value of the procedure. Say however we want to make things a bit more generic and return an error back to the calling program like it would without any error checking. We also want to raise our own error codes and messages and return these back to the program calling the procedure, to do this we can call the **RAISERROR** statement. For example:-

Fig 8.10

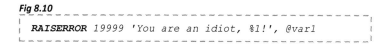

```
RAISERROR 19999 'You are an idiot, %1!', @var1
```

If in this example the variable @var1 was set to 'gbush' then we return the error code 19999 and the message 'You are an idiot, gbush'.

Returning errors in this way also means we can raise our own errors dependant on variable entered, results returned etc. when using RAISERROR the error code can be an integer over 17,000. The error code is stored in the global variable @@error when the **RAISEERROR** is run. IF you do not supply a message then the code is looked up in the SYS.SYSUSERMESSAGES table for codes over 20,000 and will be blank for values 17,000 to 19000. If the error string is provided then the message can up to 255 characters long.

In example Fig 8.11 our procedure will return an error if the region supplied is not in the list 'USA', 'EUROPE' or 'ASIA', if it is not the error code 21000 is returned to the calling program.

Fig 8.11

```
IF EXISTS (SELECT 1
                FROM     sysobjects so,
                         sysusers su
                WHERE
                         so.NAME = 'sp_sales_people'
                AND      su.uid = so.uid
                AND      su.name = 'DBA')
BEGIN
    DROP PROCEDURE SALES_USER.sp_sales_people
END;


CREATE PROCEDURE SALES_USER.sp_sales_people
        @sales_region varchar(20) = 'EUROPE'
AS
BEGIN

        IF (@sales_region not in ('EUROPE','USA','ASIA') )
        BEGIN
                RAISERROR 21000,'Sales region %1! is invalid',@sales_region
        END


        DECLARE @sql_code INT


        INSERT my_auditing_table
        (       procedure_name,
                    execution_time
        )
        SELECT 'sp_sales_people', GETDATE()


        SELECT @sql_code = SQLCODE
        IF (@sql_code < 0)
        BEGIN
                    RETURN 1
        END


        SELECT DISTINCT sales_person, sales_region
        FROM sales
        WHERE sales_region = @sales_region


        RETURN 0
END
```

Now we have a clearly written procedure with error trapping we may want to grant other users permissions to execute our procedure. To grant permissions for other users or groups we can just run a grant statement as in Fig 8.12.

Fig 8.12

```
GRANT EXECUTE ON SALES_USER.sp_sales_people TO ACCOUNTING_USER
```

This example shows us granting permission to the ACCOUNTING_USER to execute the procedure sp_sales_people owned by the user SALES_USER. You can put **GRANT** statements in the same script as your procedure creation or keep your **GRANT** statements separately. What ever your choice is I suggest source controlling both your procedure and **GRANT** statements on a regular basis to enable them to be restored quickly.

The final step in our basic procedure is to add some comments. Comments are useful not only for debugging purposes but also for adding headers and reminding you what the procedure is for.

In Sybase IQ you may use the following comments.

Fig 8.13

```
/*
This is a block comment
and can be used to span several lines
*/


-- This is a single line comment


// This is a single line comment
```

The percent sign (%) can also be used for comments and has the same meaning as the double hyphen/slash (single line comments), if the **PERCENT_AS_COMMENT** option is set to ON. However I don't recommend this as hardly anyone uses it, it depends on a database option and it is just plain ugly.

I do suggest you at the very least add a comment to the top of your procedures in the form of a header. For example Fig 8.14 shows a header for out procedure:-

Fig 8.14

```
/***************************************************************
 *
 * Procedure Name:     sp_sales_people
 * Owner:              SALES_USER
 * Created By:         Trevor Moore
 * Created Date:       1st September 2011
 * Parameters:  @sales_region varchar(20)- Sales Region
 * Returns:            0 - Success, 1 - Failure
 *
 ***************************************************************/
```

User Functions

User functions are a useful way of extending your SQL easily, allowing you to write once any repeatable functions you may use.

If for example we wanted a procedure called "Biggest" that always returned the larger of two integer values we could declare it as in Fig 8.15.

Fig 8.15

```
CREATE FUNCTION Biggest (@firstInt INT, @secondInt INT)
RETURNS INT
AS
BEGIN

    DECLARE @BiggestInt INT

    IF (@firstInt > @secondInt)
    BEGIN
        return (@firstInt)
    END

        return (@secondInt)

END
```

We can use our function to select the higher of two given integers, as in Fig 8.16 which returns the value 55

Fig 8.16

```
SELECT Biggest(22,55)
```

We can use our function to return the highest of two columns per row as in Fig 8.17

Fig 8.17

```
SELECT Biggest(column1,column2)
FROM   myTable
```

Or we may want to use our function to set the value of a function

Fig 8.18

```
DECLARE @myBiggest INT
SELECT  @myBiggest = Biggest(2,199)
```

Remember that all parameters passed into a function are IN parameters and you must declare a single return type and return a value of that type. Also try not to do anything like put **SELECT** statements in your function as they wont return any results anyway!!

Differences in Sprocs with other T-SQL Databases

There are few differences with other T-SQL database (Sybase ASE and MS SQL Server)

1) In Sybase IQ parameters can be given a default value by using the DEFAULT Keyword, other T-SQL databases set the default using the equality symbol (=).

2) You do not have to prefix your variables with an @ sign as long as it is a valid identifier (Although I would suggest you do for clarity and readability for other non IQ aware developers).

3) You can use a RESULT clause to specify the returned result sets. In other databases (and in IQ by default) the column names/aliases of the firth query returned are given to the calling environment. This includes using meta-data objects in Java.

4) Input and Output parameters in IQ are specified as **OUT**, **IN** or **INOUT**, in other databases you specify **INPUT** or **OUTPUT** (**INPUT** being the default). Parameters declared as **INOUT** or **OUT** in IQ would be declared as **OUPUT** in other T-SQL databases.

5) In Sybase IQ the **WITH RECOMPILE** clause does nothing, all procedures are stored as a list of statements and there is no query plan, it will continue regardless.

6) Setting the Isolation Level of a procedure in IQ is also another pointless exercise as IQ is always in isolation level 4 (). However this option does set the isolation level on the catalogue store which in 99% of cases will do nothing (unless you are changing system tables). I recommend not setting the isolation level any way as this is normally just lazy programming on other T-SQL databases.

7) Extended values for the **RAISERROR** statement supported by the SQL Server and Sybase ASE are not supported in Sybase IQ.

Using Cursors

Now I could use this section to explain why I hate cursors, why you shouldn't use them and that if you like them so much go and play on an Oracle database. But I will instead firstly give an example of a cursor in Fig 8.19.

Fig 8.19

```
CREATE PROCEDURE testMyCursor
AS
BEGIN
    // Declare the variables used in this Sproc
    DECLARE @myName varchar(35), @myType char(1)


    // Declare the Cursor
    DECLARE myCursor Cursor
    FOR
    SELECT [name], [type]
    FROM    sysobjects

    // Open the Cursor
    OPEN myCursor

    // Fetch the first row of results into the variables
    FETCH myCursor INTO @myName, @myType

    // Loop through all results while there are results or the
    //cursor is in success


    WHILE (@@FETCH_STATUS = 0)
    BEGIN
                // Check the cursor returned a result
        IF (@@FETCH_STATUS <> -2)
        BEGIN
            IF (@myName = 'SYSFILE')
            BEGIN
                        INSERT myTestTable
                SELECT @myName, @myType, @@FETCH_STATUS
            END
        END
        FETCH  myCursor INTO  @myName, @myType
    END

// Close and deallocate the cursor
CLOSE myCursor
DEALLOCATE myCursor

END
```

In our example we cycle through the cursor until we have a value in the variable @myName called SYSFILE, we then select out a result-set containing the variable values.

Every time the cursor fetches a row it also populates the variable **@@FETCH_STATUS** with one of three values (Fig 8.20), you can use this variable as a control for your while loop.

Fig 8.20

Return Value	Return Description
0	The cursor successfully returned a record.
-1	The cursor failed or the row was beyond the result set.
-2	The row fetched is missing.

Events

Event Overview

An event is just a batch of SQL commands that are triggered to execute when a condition is met. Events that trigger the commands can be anything from backups ending to users connecting to running according to a schedule.
You can see all events in the database by running the code in Fig 8.21

Fig 8.21
```
SELECT *
FROM   sys.sysevent
```

Events can be created and in either an enabled or disabled status, in fact they can be very useful for database maintenance tasks and performance metrics capturing!! To create an event the user MUST have DBA authority, but you can of course till use objects owner by other users by qualifying them. For example the event in Fig 8.22 will populate a table called context data by executing the sp_iqcontext procedure every minute starting at one minute past midnight every day. The event is executing according to a schedule defined by the clause "START TIME '00:01 AM' EVERY 1 MINUTES"

Fig 8.22
```
CREATE EVENT test_event
SCHEDULE
START TIME '00:01 AM' EVERY 1 MINUTES
HANDLER
BEGIN

    INSERT context_date
    SELECT GETDATE(), *
    FROM   sp_iqcontext()

END
```

Event Syntax

The syntax to create an event is given in Fig 8.23 (You may also use ALTER EVENT on pre-existing events).

Fig 8.23

```
CREATE EVENT <event_name>
[
        TYPE <event_type> WHERE <trigger_condition> [AND
<trigger_condition> etc]
        or SCHEDULE <schedule_specification>
]
ENABLE/DISABLE
AT CONSOLIDATED/REMOTE/ALL
HANDLER
BEGIN
        <sql statements>
END
```

Event TYPE or SCHEDULE

Your event can either be an event **TYPE** or a **SCHEDULE** Event **TYPE**

If using the syntax **TYPE** <event_type> **WHERE** <trigger_condition> then you may use the following event_type option. Each event type can only use specific trigger conditions, the event_conditions a type can use are listed in the conditions column in the table below.

name	description	Example Trigger conditions
GrowDB	Triggers an event when a database file is extended	WHERE event_condition('DBSize') > 5000 or WHERE event_condition('Interval') > 120
GrowLog	Triggers an event when the transaction log is extended	WHERE event_condition('LogSize') > 50 or WHERE event_condition('Interval') > 120
GrowTemp	Triggers an event when the temporary file is extended.	WHERE event_condition('TempSize') > 5000 or WHERE event_condition('Interval') > 120
DatabaseStart	Triggers an event when the database is started	WHERE event_condition('Interval') > 120
ServerIdle	Triggers and event when the server is idle for the time specified in the event_condition. The server is checked for activity every 30 seconds.	WHERE event_condition('IdleTime') > 3600 or WHERE event_condition('Interval') > 120
Connect	Triggers and event when a user connects	WHERE event_condition('Interval') > 120
Disconnect	Triggers and event when a user disconnects	WHERE event_condition('Interval') > 120

ConnectFailed	Triggers an event when a user connect fails	WHERE event_condition('Interval') > 120
RAISERROR	Triggers an event when a RAISERROR is issued	WHERE event_condition('ErrorNumber') > -60045 or WHERE event_condition('Interval') > 120
BackupEnd	Triggers an event when a backup completes	WHERE event_condition('Interval') > 120
DBDiskSpace	Triggers an event when the database disk space in the .db file is changed.	WHERE event_condition('DBFreePercent') < 80 or WHERE event_condition('DBFreeSpace') < 2000 or WHERE event_condition('Interval') > 120
LogDiskSpace	Triggers and event when the transaction log disk space changes	WHERE event_condition('LogFreePercent') < 75 or WHERE event_condition('LogFreeSpace') < 1000 or WHERE event_condition('Interval') > 120
TempDiskSpace	Triggers and event when temporary file disk space changes.	WHERE event_condition('TempFreePercent') < 90 or WHERE event_condition('TempFreeSpace') < 1000 or WHERE event_condition('Interval') > 120
GlobalAutoincrement	Triggers an event when the global autoincrement default value for a table is within one percent of the end of its range. You can specify further checking with the event_condition.	WHERE event_condition('RemainingValues') < 1000 or WHERE event_condition('Interval') > 120
MirrorServerDisconnect	Trigger and event when a connection to a mirror server fails	WHERE event_condition('Interval') > 120
MirrorFailover	Triggers an event when failover to a mirror server occurs.	WHERE event_condition('Interval') > 120
Deadlock	deadlock occurred	WHERE event_condition('Interval') > 120

For the event conditions listed above this is what there values mean (The syntax for event condition comparison is **"event_condition (<condition name>) = or < or >or != or <= or >= <value>"**. The event_condition('Interval') represents the last time since the event was triggered and can be used for all event types.

Event Condition	Comparison Value
event_condition('DBFreePercent')	Number representing the percentage
event_condition('DBFreeSpace')	Number representing Megabytes
event_condition('DBSize')	Megabytes
event_condition('ErrorNumber')	Number representing the error number of a RAISEERROR
event_condition('IdleTime')	Number representing Seconds
event_condition('Interval')	Number representing Seconds
event_condition('LogFreePercent')	Number representing the percentage
event_condition('LogFreeSpace')	Number representing Megabytes
event_condition('LogSize')	Number representing Megabytes
event_condition('RemainingValues')	Number representing values remaining
event_condition('TempFreePercent')	Number representing the percentage
event_condition('TempFreeSpace')	Number representing Megabytes
event_condition('TempSize')	Number representing Megabytes

Event SCHEDULE

If you choose to schedule your event to run at specific times then you must specify this in the event creation statement as in Fig 8.24

Fig 8.24

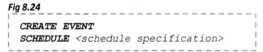

```
CREATE EVENT
SCHEDULE <schedule specification>
```

A schedule specification can have the following clauses.

Fig 8.25

```
<schedule name>

START TIME <start time> or BETWEEN <start time> AND <end time> }

EVERY <period>    HOURS/MINUTES/SECONDS

 ON   ( <day of week>,<day of week>, etc )   or ( <day of month>,<day
of month>, etc )

START DATE <start-date>
```

The parameter values passed are:-

Parameter	Description
<start time>	A time defined in a single quoted string as 'HH:MM(AM/PM)' e.g. '02:45AM'
<end time>	A time defined in a single quoted string as 'HH:MM(AM/PM)' e.g. '02:45AM'
<period>	If the postfix of the parameter is HOURS then it can be any value between 1 and 24, MINUTES 1-60 and SECONDS 1-60
<day of week>	This may be any of the following single quoted values 'Monday','Tuesday','Wednesday','Thursday','Friday','Saturday','Sunday','Mon','Tue','Wed','Thur','Fri','Sat' or 'Sun'.
<day of month>	This can be any value from 0-31 where a 0 specifies to run on the last day of the month.
<start date>	The date when the event is scheduled to start executing, the default is the current date.

ENABLE/DISABLE

Specifying this is used to tell IQ if the event is **ENABLED** (and will execute) or is **DISABLED** and will not Execute even when scheduling times or event conditions are met.

AT CONSOLIDATED/REMOTE/ALL

This is used to execute events at remote or consolidated databases. If your system is part of a SQL Remote setup then this clause can be used to restrict the databases at which the event is handled. The default is to execute the event on ALL databases.

HANDLER

Every event has a **HANDLER** (Only one). A Handler is akin to the body of a procedure or function and holds a compound statement. You can call procedures, execute functions and run a batch of commands within the body of the handler but not return result sets.

Event Examples

Automated Backup

The event in Fig 8.26 will run a full backup every day at 1 minute past midnight

Fig 8.25

```
CREATE EVENT full_backup
SCHEDULE
START TIME '00:01AM' EVERY 24 HOURS
HANDLER
BEGIN
    BACKUP DATABASE FULL
    TO '/home/my_area/backups/full_db_backup.dat'
END
```

Capture user connections

The event in Fig 8.26 inserts the resultset returned from the sp_iqconnection procedure into the user_connections table very time a user connects.

Fig 8.26

```
CREATE EVENT user_connects
TYPE CONNECT
HANDLER
BEGIN
    INSERT user_connections
    SELECT GETDATE(),* FROM sp_iqconnection()
END
```

Triggers

The statement below is from the Sybase IQ 15.1 documentation:-

> *Support for triggers differs as follows:*
>
> *SQL Anywhere supports both row-level and statement-level triggers.*
>
> *Adaptive Server Enterprise supports only statement-level triggers.*
>
> *Sybase IQ does not support triggers.*

So you may be thinking why is there a section on triggers, well they may not be supported but they are available in a limited capacity!

As Sybase have said that IQ does not "officially" support this functionality there is little documentation to be found anywhere (official or otherwise) about triggers in IQ. So that said I have written this section to cover functionality I have tried and tested regarding triggers in IQ.

Triggers Overview

Triggers in IQ can be thought of stored procedures that execute AFTER an INSERT statement, although you can create DELETE and UPDATE triggers I have not been able to get these to work. You can use them to check data, write auditing logging or enforce data integrity. Another limitation in IQ appears to be that you cannot use the inserted or deleted tables that you can use with other T-SQL databases such as SQL Server. As such IQ seems to have only basic insert trigger capability.

Let's look at an example in Fig 8.27

Fig 8.27

```
-- TABLE USED TO HOLD DATA
CREATE TABLE test
(
        col_1 NUMERIC(22,0)   IDENTITY,
        col_2 VARCHAR(40)     NULL
)

-- TABLE USED TO AUDIT CHANGES
CREATE TABLE test_audit
(
        audit_time      DATETIME       NOT NULL,
        audit_message VARCHAR(255)     NULL,
        col_1           NUMERIC(20,0) NULL,
        col_2           VARCHAR(40)    NULL
)
GO

-- THIS IS A TRIGGER
CREATE TRIGGER my_test_trigger
ON test
FOR INSERT
AS
BEGIN

    INSERT test_audit
    SELECT GETDATE(), 'insert trigger worked', col_1, col_2
    FROM test

END
```

Now execute an insert statement as in Fig 8.28

Fig 8.28

```
INSERT test (col_2)
VALUES ('TEST_1')
```

The insert will cause the insert trigger on the test table to execute as we can see in the results of Fig 8.30.

Fig 8.29

```
SELECT *
FROM test
```

Results of Fig 8.29

col_1	col_2
1	TEST_1

Fig 8.30

```
SELECT *
FROM test_audit
```

Results

audit_time	audit_message	col_1	col_2
20/07/10 12:52	Insert trigger worked	1	TEST_1

I have found triggers most useful when updating data already inserted into the table, for example the code below will ensure that the identity column of a table increments the values by 5 instead of by 1.

Fig 8.31

```
CREATE TABLE testme
(
        col_1 NUMERIC(20,0)  IDENTITY,
        col_2 VARCHAR(20)      NULL
)
go

CREATE TRIGGER test_trigger ON testme
FOR INSERT
AS
BEGIN
    MESSAGE 'trigger fired' TYPE INFO TO CLIENT
    SET TEMPORARY OPTION identity_insert = 'testme'


    UPDATE testme SET col_1 = SELECT MAX(col_1) +5 FROM testme)
    WHERE col_1 = (SELECT MAX(col_1) FROM testme)


    SET TEMPORARY OPTION identity_insert = ''
END
```

In summation, Sybase say triggers do not work so my guess is that they may not support them, so check with them first! Secondly although they are available they are restrictive so be diligent in your application of them and test thoroughly any code you use in them.

Transaction Management

This chapter covers transaction management, how to rollback changes when errors occur and how to use savepoints. We shall also look at ATOMIC transactions in Watcom and how transaction levels are affected by COMMIT statements.

We shall look at the most significant transaction database option available "CHAINED" and how the setting of this option effects your transactions by implicitly starting and committing them.

If you have used other database's you may have preconceived ideas on how you think transactions work. The best thing you can do is forget about them and read this chapter as IQ works differently. For example there is not a concept of isolation levels in IQ and only one connection can have write access to a table at any one time.

The Basics

The CHAINED Option

For T-SQL procedures we have the database option **CHAINED** (See chapter on **OPTIONS**). When this option is OFF then each individual statement executed has an implicit **BEGIN TRANSACTION** statement and is committed individually unless there is an explicit **BEGIN TRANSACTION** statement. When this option is ON then your statements are chained into one transaction and you will have to explicitly commit them.

One thing to be aware of is that the default value is ON except in the case of JDBC and Open Client Connections when IQ "helpfully" switches the default to OFF!!!!

Basic Transactions

The best way to explain transactions is by example, so that said consider the steps below. Consider the code below in Fig 9.1:-

Fig 9.1

```
MESSAGE @@trancount TYPE INFO TO CLIENT
BEGIN TRANSACTION
MESSAGE @@trancount TYPE INFO TO CLIENT
BEGIN TRANSACTION
MESSAGE @@trancount TYPE INFO TO CLIENT
COMMIT TRANSACTION
MESSAGE @@trancount TYPE INFO TO CLIENT
COMMIT TRANSACTION
MESSAGE @@trancount TYPE INFO TO CLIENT
```

The output from Fig 9.1 is...

0
1
2
1
0

So as you can see by explicitly using a **BEGIN TRANSACTION** statement we increment the transaction level by 1 and by executing a **COMMIT TRANSACTION** the transaction level decreases by 1. Ok so far this is what you would expect; now consider the code in Fig 9.2 which has a **ROLLBACK TRANSACTION**.

Fig 9.2

```
MESSAGE @@trancount TYPE INFO TO CLIENT
BEGIN TRANSACTION
MESSAGE @@trancount TYPE INFO TO CLIENT
BEGIN TRANSACTION
MESSAGE @@trancount TYPE INFO TO CLIENT
COMMIT TRANSACTION
ROLLBACK TRANSACTION
MESSAGE @@trancount TYPE INFO TO CLIENT
COMMIT TRANSACTION
MESSAGE @@trancount TYPE INFO TO CLIENT
```

The output from Fig 9.2 is....

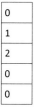

0
1
2
0
0

As you can see the **ROLLBACK** did not just rollback within its own transaction but rolled back everything to the most outer transaction. This is contrary to the documentation provided by Sybase so be careful here. I have raised this as an issue but Sybase have said this is how it is intended to work!!

In IQ a reading session can only read **COMMITTED** data, a transaction can be committed by explicitly running a **COMMIT** statement or by using the database option **CHAINED=OFF**. The **CHAINED** option is at the heart of transaction processing in IQ and can affect every part of your system.

The ROLLBACK Statement

ROLLBACK Basics

Now say we wanted to rollback any changes we have made in a procedure when an error occurs, the example in Fig 9.4 shows has we do this in IQ. Be aware that a **ROLLBACK** will only undo any changes that have been made since the last COMMIT or **ROLLBACK** statement was issued.

I would suggest that when using **ROLLBACKs** in the way described below that you ensure that the **CHAINED** option is set to ON (You can put this in your procedure is required as a temporary option) and that the option **ON_TSQL_ERROR** is set to '**CONDITIONAL**'. Both of these options can be found in the options chapter, but basically you want **CHAINED ON** as you do not want to issue implicit **COMMIT**s and you want the **ON_TSQL_ERROR** equal to **CONDITIONAL** so that you can decide on how to handle errors in your code (But still error out of the procedure if you do not).

In order to provide an example of a **ROLLBACK** we first create a table and insert a value as in Fig 9.3

Fig 9.3

```
CREATE TABLE test1
(col_1 INT NULL)

INSERT test1
VALUES (99)
```

So we now have a table called *test1* that has one column called *col_1* with one row of data containing the value 99.

Now we can create a procedure as in Fig 9.4 that will first delete all data from our *test1* table and attempt to insert the value 'AA' which of course will error as *col_1* is an INT datatype.

Fig 9.4

```
CREATE PROCEDURE level1
AS
BEGIN
        -- Ensure that error trapping can occur to do the rollback
        SET TEMPORARY OPTION ON_T-SQL_ERROR = 'CONDITIONAL'

        DECLARE @sql_code INT

        BEGIN TRANSACTION

            DELETE FROM test1

            SELECT @sql_code = SQLCODE
                    IF (@sql_code < 0)
            BEGIN
                ROLLBACK
                MESSAGE 'ERROR DELETING DATE' TYPE INFO TO CLIENT
            END

            ----- THIS WILL ERROR -----
            INSERT test1
            VALUES ('AA')
            --------------------------

            SELECT @sql_code = SQLCODE

            IF (@sql_code < 0)
            BEGIN
                ROLLBACK
                MESSAGE 'ERROR INSERTING DATE' TYPE INFO TO CLIENT
            END

        COMMIT

        RETURN 0
END
```

If we execute the procedure in Fig 9.4 it will return a message 'ERROR INSERTING DATA' and rollback the delete and leave the table *test1* with the value 99 that we originally inserted as if the procedure never ran!

Now if we change the procedure in Fig 9.4 as below in Fig 9.5

Fig 9.5

```
CHANGE THIS
----- THIS WILL ERROR -----
INSERT test1
VALUES('AA')
-------------------------

TO THIS
----- THIS WILL WORK -----
INSERT test1
VALUES (22)
```

Now when the procedure is executed it will run successfully and we will be left with one row of data in *test1* with the value 22.

A rollback only rolls back to the last commit, regardless of if you started another begin transaction. Certain statements cause a commit including executing a sub procedure, hence the code in Fig 9.6 would not rollback the delete and you would be left with an empty table

Fig 9.6

```
BEGIN TRANSACTION

        DELETE FROM test1

        SELECT @sql_code = SQLCODE
        IF (@sql_code < 0)
        BEGIN
            ROLLBACK
            MESSAGE 'ERROR DELETING DATA' TYPE INFO TO CLIENT
        END

        EXEC child_procedure 'value'

        ----- THIS WILL ERROR -----
        INSERT test1
        VALUES ('AA')
        -------------------------
        SELECT @sql_code = SQLCODE
        IF (@sql_code < 0)
        BEGIN
            ROLLBACK
            MESSAGE 'ERROR INSERTING DATA' TYPE INFO TO CLIENT
        END

    COMMIT
```

At best IQ offers very simplistic transaction handling as such you when writing T-SQL procedures you cannot name your transactions or nest them.

Using SAVEPOINT's with ROLLBACK's

A **SAVEPOINT** is used when you only want to roll back certain operations within your batch of commands. They enable you to commit operations within your procedure and save the progress of your transaction.

To demonstrate **SAVEPOINT**'s lets first construct a table and insert one value into it as in Fig 9.7

Fig 9.7

```
CREATE TABLE test1
(col_1 INT NULL)
go

INSERT test1 VALUES (99)
go
```

Now lets first demonstrate how not to use a savepoint in Fig 9.8, in this example the underlying table test1 will remain unchanged.

Fig 9.8

```
CREATE PROCEDURE level1
AS
BEGIN
    -- Ensure that error trapping can occur to do the roll-back
    SET TEMPORARY OPTION ON_T-SQL_ERROR = 'CONDITIONAL'
    DECLARE @sql_code INT

    BEGIN TRANSACTION

        DELETE FROM test1

        SELECT @sql_code = SQLCODE
        IF (@sql_code < 0)
        BEGIN
            ROLLBACK
            MESSAGE 'ERROR DELETING DATA' TYPE INFO TO CLIENT
        END

        INSERT test1
        VALUES (33)

        SELECT @sql_code = SQLCODE
        IF (@sql_code < 0)
        BEGIN
            ROLLBACK
            MESSAGE 'ERROR INSERTING DATA' TYPE INFO TO CLIENT
        END

        -------- SAVEPOINT ------------
        SAVE TRANSACTION my_savepoint_1
        ------------------------------
        DELETE FROM test1

        SELECT @sql_code = SQLCODE
        IF (@sql_code < 0)
        BEGIN
            ROLLBACK TRANSACTION my_savepoint_1
            MESSAGE 'ERROR DELETING DATA' TYPE INFO TO CLIENT
        END

        ----- THIS WILL ERROR -----
        INSERT test1
        VALUES ('AA')
        --------------------------
        SELECT @sql_code = SQLCODE
        IF (@sql_code < 0)
        BEGIN
            ROLLBACK
            MESSAGE 'ERROR INSERTING DATA' TYPE INFO TO CLIENT
        END

    COMMIT
    RETURN 0
END
```

If we execute the code in Fig 9.9 to execute the procedure and then select the results from the test1 table, we can see the values in test1 are unchanged.

Fig 9.9

```
EXEC level1
go
SELECT * FROM test1
go
```

The out put is:-

```
99
```

The value of test1 after the execution of the procedure level1 is 99 because the code that errors is performing a **ROLLBACK** and not a **ROLLBACK TRANSACTION** <savepoint>. To demonstrate this if we change the code for the incorrect statement in Fig 9.10 to the code in Fig 9.11

Fig 9.10

```
----- THIS WILL ERROR -----
INSERT test1
VALUES ('AA')
---------------------------
SELECT @sql_code = SQLCODE
IF (@sql_code < 0)
BEGIN
      ROLLBACK
      MESSAGE 'ERROR INSERTING DATA' TYPE INFO TO CLIENT
END
```

Fig 9.11

```
----- THIS WILL ERROR -----
INSERT test1
VALUES ('AA')
---------------------------
SELECT @sql_code = SQLCODE
IF (@sql_code < 0)
BEGIN
      ROLLBACK   TRANSACTION my_savepoint_1
      MESSAGE 'ERROR INSERTING DATA' TYPE INFO TO CLIENT
END
```

If we make the change to our procedure, re-create it and execute the code in Fig 9.12 the output has now changed to include all the changes made in the stored procedure up to the **SAVEPOINT**.

Fig 9.12

```
EXEC level1
go
SELECT * FROM test1
go
```

The out put is:-

```
33
```

Atomic Transactions

Watcom SQL has a useful **ATOMIC** clause that can be used in a **BEGIN-END** block to group together a group of statements, if any one of the statements fails then everything within the ATOMIC block fails. The example in Fig 9.13 shows how this works.

Fig 9.13

```
CREATE PROCEDURE test_atomic ()
BEGIN
    INSERT test
    SELECT 'VALUE BEFORE ATOMIC', 1;

    COMMIT;

    BEGIN ATOMIC
        -- THIS WILL WORK
        DELETE test;

        -- THIS WILL WORK
        INSERT test
        SELECT 'FIRST INSERT IN ATOMIC', 2;

        -- THIS WILL WORK
        DELETE test;

        -- THIS WILL FAIL (IT ATTEMPTS TO INSERT A CHAR INTO AN
INT)
        INSERT test
        SELECT 'SECOND INSERT IN ATOMIC', 'XXXXX';
    END;
    COMMIT;
END
```

Now we create the test table, execute the procedure and output the results of the test table in Fig 9.14 (which also used Watcom SQL syntax).

Fig 9.14

```
CREATE TABLE test
    (
        col_1    VARCHAR(50) NULL,
        col_2    INT          NULL
    );

CALL test_atomic();

SELECT * FROM test;
```

Result of Fig 9.14

col_1	col_2
VALUE BEFORE ATOMIC	1

The result of the execution of the *test_atomic* stored procedure is to leave the test table with the values from the first insert, even though the procedure returned an errorm-157. This shows that because of the failure within the **ATOMIC** block, the values remain as they did before the **ATOMIC** block executed. Statements within a **BEGIN ATOMIC** block must execute completely are not at all!!!! You cannot use a **COMMIT** or a **ROLLBACK** statement within an **ATOMIC** block. Of course it can be argued that depending on the **CHAINED** options setting that all operations are **ATOMIC** within IQ, however the **ATOMIC** clause of the **BEGIN** statement allows you to explicitly declare this for easier reading and to force other developer who update your code to think atomically about the operations the need to perform.

TABLE LOCKING

Overview of Table Locking in IQ

IQ does not perform locking as in traditional OLTP databases such as ASE and SQL Server. For example if you try and insert into a table that another user is inserting into your code will return an error instead of waiting for the table to be available.

We can get round this by using the Watcom SQL statement **LOCK TABLE**; this enables you to issue a command that will wait until a table has a **WRITE LOCK** available. A **WRITE LOCK** is required in order to **INSERT**, **UPDATE** or **DELETE** from a table (Including **TRUNCATES**).

If you want to change the DDL of a table then there can be NO USER LOCKS on that table.

To see what locks are on tables used the *sp_iqlocks* system procedure.

Using LOCK TABLE

Please find below a proof of concept for using a generic table lock. I tested by running several MY_TEST_1 and MY_TEST_2 procs at the same time (Set the option in DBISQL to run a commit after every statement or it will hold the locks).

First we create a Watcom SQL stored procedure in Fig 9.15 that waits for a lock on a supplied table_name for 1 minute before it will return with a SQLCODE error -1175 "Unable to acquire table locks in specified time".

The reason we put this in a procedure is that we can call a Watcom SQL procedure from a T-SQL procedure and thus make use of Watcom functionality in T-SQL procedures!!!

Fig 9.15

```
CREATE PROCEDURE lock_table
(@table_name VARCHAR(50))

ON EXCEPTION RESUME
BEGIN

EXECUTE IMMEDIATE('LOCK TABLE ' + @table_name + ' IN WRITE MODE WAIT
''00:00:10'' ');

END
```

Backups, Restores & DR

Sybase IQ can back up data in both the IQ store and the catalog store (ASA) by running a simple back up process. You may also restore the database via a simple restore process. But as with most things in IQ the options you use can have a dramatic effect on the process.

Overview

This chapter presumes you have am IQ 15.x installation set up, but the process is much the same for 12.x with the differences listed below:-

- In IQ 15.x by using the **READWRITE FILES ONLY** keywords a full, incremental-since-full or incremental backup can be restricted to only the set of read-write files (these files must be IQ DBSpaces) in the database.

- In IQ 15.x a backup can back up a set of read-only DBSpaces and/or read-only files as long as these are IQ DBSpaces.

- A restore of a backup may be used restore only a subset (must be **READONLY** DBSpaces/files) of the files and/or DBSpaces.

- You may use the system views **SYSIQBACKUPHISTORY** and **SYSIQBACKUPHISTORYDETAIL** to look at historical back up information.

I would also suggest reading the section on DBSpaces in the "Creating/Altering a Database" chapter to understand the differences between **READONLY** and **READWRITE** files and DBSpaces.

Other things to note:-

- When a **BACKUP** is executed it overwrites existing archive files unless you move the old files or use a different archive device name or path. If you are backing up using a third party implementation you should remember that although Windows supports tape partitioning, Sybase IQ does not use it, so do not use another application to format tapes for **BACKUP**. A Windows base IQ system only support fixed-length I/O operations to tape devices,

- You cannot restore a backup from a 12.x system to a 15.x system. You must first restore it a 12.x system and then migrate the server to 15.x.

- A **BACKUP** does not support raw devices as archival devices.

- If a **BACKUP** is interrupted it will fail and the database will remain as it was before the **BACKUP** was executed.

- Also worth noting is that IQ treats leading backslashes in a string as an escape character, when the backslash precedes an n, an x, or another backslash. So when you specify the backup tape devices, you must double each backslash required by the Windows naming convention. '\\\\.\\my_tape0'. If you omit the extra backslashes or don't spell a tape device name correctly then IQ thinks you mean the name to be a disk file name!!

- If a non DBA user is doing the backup then they must have **BACKUP** authority.

- When disk striping is used the striped disks are treated as a single device.

- As IQ only rewinds tapes (only on rewinding devices) after using them and both before you need to ensure the tapes used for **BACKUP** or **RESTORE** are at the correct starting point before putting them in the tape device.

If IQ cannot open a device when **BACKUP** or **RESTORE**'s are executed and the **ATTENDED** parameter is ON (**BACKUP** only as **RESTORE**'s must always be attended), then it waits for ten seconds before trying to execute the statement again. It will continue to attempt until the command is interrupted.

When you use **RESTORE** to restore an **INCREMENTAL** back up then IQ ensures that backup media sets are accessed in the proper order. i.e. The last full backup tape set first, then the first incremental backup tape set, then the next most recent set, etc. This means that if you take a **FULL** back up then an **INCREMENTLE** then an **INCREMENTAL SINCE FULL** then the restores must also follow that order!! If you don't IQ will return an error.

When restoring to a raw device, make sure is has enough space to hold the DBSpaces/DBSpaces you are restoring. IQ will check before it attempts the restore and return an error if there is not enough!!

If you are restoring a **FULL** back up followed by an **INCREMENTAL or INCREMENTAL SINCE FULL** back up then you cannot modify the database between the restores.

Before starting a full restore, you must delete the catalog store file (default name *dbname.db)* and the transaction log file (default name *dbname.log)*.

To restore read-only files or DBSpaces from an archive backup, the database may be running and the administrator may connect to the database when issuing the **RESTORE** statement. The read-only file pathname need not match the names in the backup, if they otherwise match the database system table information.

The basics

Back ups on IQ are performed by the DBA or database owner by executing the **BACKUP** statement. A BACKUP can be executed when other database operations are running with only a couple of exceptions:-

No meta-data changes can occur while the catalog store is backed up

No commands that issue checkpoints or DBCC can be executed.

A **BACKUP** will only be able to back up committed data so normally I would advise that they are performed at a time of day when there is minimal activity and if possible ensure that all users' data is committed before executing the **BACKUP** command. A **BACKUP** also issues an implicit **CHECKPOINT** command and will only backup data changes up to the point when the **CHECKPOINT** (**BACKUP** statement) was executed. A check points is normally performed automatically by IQ according to an internal algorithm, but you can run the **CHECKPOINT** statement explicitly as well as implicitly when issuing a **BACKUP**.

In its simplest form you could run the command in Fig 10.1 to back up the entire database.

Fig 10.1

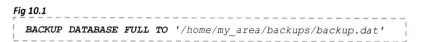

```
BACKUP DATABASE FULL TO '/home/my_area/backups/backup.dat'
```

When running this files called backup.dat.n will be created in the directory /home/my_area/backups/

that stores the backups. "n" is a sequential number that is used to create several files for your back up. For example on Unix/Linux based systems each backup file is a default size of 2Gb (1.5Gb on Windows) when storing to disk, therefore if your backup is 11 Gb in size then the following files will be created.

File Name	File Size
backup.dat.1	2Gb
backup.dat.2	2Gb
backup.dat.3	2Gb
backup.dat.4	2Gb
backup.dat.5	1Gb

Before you run your backup statement ensure you have sufficient space to store the backup files and also note that BACKUP does not support using a raw device as an archival device.
To restore from this back up simply run the RESTORE statement in Fig 10.2.

Fig 10.2
```
RESTORE DATABASE 'my_database'
FROM 'backup.dat.1'
FROM 'backup.dat.2'
FROM 'backup.dat.3'
FROM 'backup.dat.4'
FROM 'backup.dat.5'
FROM 'backup.dat.6';
```

When restoring the database the DBA user requires exclusive database access which is obtained by setting the **–gd** switch to DBA (default). Once the restore is complete then the DBA issues a **START DATABASE** command to allow user access. Before a restore you should ensure that there is sufficient space to restore the files.

You should always check the size of your database prior to back up. The code in Fig 10.3 will tell you the % of the current space used and also the amount of the current space used. I would suggest adding 10% the total amount used to ensure there is enough space (belts and braces approach).

Fig 10.3
```
SELECT *
FROM    sp_iqstatus()
WHERE   Name = ' Main IQ Blocks Used:'
```

The BACKUP Statement

So we have seen how to run a complete (FULL) back up of your database system, however often due to time constraints you may only want to run an incremental back up or only back up specific data. Luckily the **BACKUP** statement has a number of options that will allow you to do this. You may also want to back up to tape rather than disk or specify the size of the back up files. All of this is possible. The basic syntax of a **BACKUP** statement is

Fig 10.4

```
BACKUP DATABASE <backup_options>
TO  <archive_device> <archive_options> [ WITH COMMENT string ]
```

<backup_options>

Backup Option	Description
VIRTUAL DECOUPLED or **VIRTUAL ENCAPSULATED** 'shell_command'	**VIRTUAL DECOUPLED** Specifies a decoupled virtual backup. For the backup to be complete, you must copy the IQ DBSpaces after the decoupled virtual backup finishes, and then perform a non-virtual incremental backup. VIRTUAL ENCAPSULATED 'shell_command' Specifies an encapsulated virtual backup. The *'shell-command'* argument can be a string or variable containing a string that is executed as part of the encapsulated virtual backup. The shell commands execute a system-level backup of the IQ store as part of the backup operation.
READWRITE FILES ONLY or **READONLY** (DBSPACES *identifier-list* or FILES *identifier-list*)	**READWRITE FILES ONLY** The READWRITE FILES ONLY clause is used to restrict the backup to only the set of read-write files in the database. The read-only DBSpaces/files must be IQ DBSpaces. When **READWRITE FILES ONLY** is used with the **INCREMENTAL** or **INCREMENTAL SINCE FULL** options, the backup will not back up data on read-only DBSpaces or DBFiles that has changed since the last FULL backup. **READONLY** When the **READONLY** clause is used then the backup will only back up the **READONLY** DBSpaces or files specified. **READONLY** DBSPACES and FILES must be IQ DBSpaces. A READONLY DBSpaces can only be in the IQ main store and will not allow DML statements on any object within the **READONLY** DBSpaces. You cannot do a **INCREMENTAL** back up on READONLY DBSpaces or files.
ATTENDED (ON/OFF)	When the ON (the default) option is used then this clause is used when backing up to a tape device. The back up will send a message to the application that issued the **BACKUP** statement if the tape drive requires intervention. When this option is OFF and there is a problem with the tape device (e.g. It may require additional tapes) then IQ will return an error and abort the **BACKUP**. However even when the option is OFF a short delay is used to account for any automatic tape switches/operations that you may have in place. Basically when this option is OFF then you are telling IQ that an operator will not be present during the back up and there fore an operator is not required to respond to prompts and that the archive devices may be stacker drives that require no manual intervention. However IQ will try to detect any reasons for failure before the back up by checking if there is enough free space (at the time the command is first executed) for the back up. When backing up to tape you must number of kilobytes in the TO *<archive-device)* clause so that IQ can check the information stored internally to see how much room it needs to back up your database. If it calculates that there is enough space on the tape, the backup will start. If you overestimate the amount of space available on your tape(s) and IQ runs out of space, the backup will fail at that point. If you do not specify the SIZE option for an unattended backup, the entire backup must fit on one tape. A final point to note is that a **RESTORE** cannot be unattended!!

	Example:- **BACKUP DATABASE** **INCREMENTAL SINCE FULL** **TO** '/dev/my_backup/backup1n' **SIZE** 10000000 **TO** '/dev/ my_backup /backup2n' **SIZE** 20000000;
CRC (ON/OFF)	When set ON (the default) then the back up activates 32-bit cyclical redundancy checking on a per block basis. Also when using a RESTORE on the BACKUP the numbers computed on the backup are verified during the **RESTORE**. Like any other clause/option that requires a command to do more work this may affect performance.
BLOCK FACTOR <integer>	Put simply this option is used to specify the number of blocks that the back up can write at any one time. The default is 15 on windows based systems and 25 on Unix/Linux; Sybase recommends these as the lowest values to use on each O/S respectively. If you use this clause to overwrite the value then it must be a value greater than 0. The option is used to control the memory used for buffers during the back up using the calculation below:- **Memory = <BLOCK FACTOR VALUE> * THREADS USED TO EXTRACT DATA**
FULL or INCREMENTAL Or INCREMENTAL SINCE FULL	**FULL (the default)** As you would expect this is used to specify a full backup **INCREMENTAL** (Cannot be used with READONLY files/DBSpaces) Specifies an incremental backup meaning that any data blocks changed since the last backup "of any kind" are saved to the archive devices. **INCREMENTAL SINCE FULL** Specifies an incremental backup that will back up all blocks changed "since the last full backup"
WITH COMMENT <comment_string>	This clause is used to add a comment (with a max length of 32 Kb) that is recorded in the archive file and in the backup history file. If you do not specify a value, a **NULL** string is stored.

TO <archive device> clause

This is used to specify the archive device to be used for the backup. The archive device options can be seen in the section below <archive_options>. If you are using multiple <archive-devices> then they must be specified using separate **TO** clauses. The number of **TO** clauses determines the parallelism that IQ can use in relation to output devices.

On Solaris, the letter *n* after the tape device name specifies the "no rewind on close" feature. You should always specify this feature with **BACKUP** (use the naming convention for your Unix system). This example in Fig 10.5 backs up all changes to the database since the last full backup:

Fig 10.5

```
BACKUP DATABASE
INCREMENTAL SINCE FULL
TO '/dev/my_backup/backup1n' SIZE 10000000
TO '/dev/ my_backup /backup2n' SIZE 20000000;
```

<archive_device>

The *archive_device* is a tape drive or file name to hold the for the archive file/files.

<archive_options>

Archive Option	Description
SIZE <integer>	As seen in the explanation of the **ATTENDED** clause above this clause is used to specify the maximum tape or file capacity in Kb per output device (this applies to tape and disk files but not 3rd party devices). No volumes used on the corresponding device should be shorter than this value. Remember that if multiple devices are specified, **BACKUP** distributes the information across all devices. The value of the **SIZE** parameter is per output device and does not limit the number of bytes per device. It can be used to limit each file size and each output device can have a different size specified. When a **BACKUP** statement is executed and the data reaches the size specified then IQ will do one of the following:- • If the device is a file system device, then the current file is closed and another file is created of the same name, with the next ascending number appended to the file name (see the section on The Basics). • If the device is a tape unit, then the **BACKUP** will close the current tape and you need to mount another tape. For an example see the example in the backup option **ATTENDED**.
STACKER <integer>	The stacker clause is used to specify the device that is automatically loaded and the number of tapes it is loaded with. This value is the number of stacker devices and is used along with the Size clause to determine if there is enough space for a **BACKUP**.

The RESTORE Statement

We have seen (in the basics) a **RESTORE** of a full database dump. However there are times when you may want to use more advanced options and only restore parts of your database.
There are two basic syntax's for a **RESTORE** statement (Given in Fig 10.6 and 10.7 below).

Fig 10.6

```
RESTORE DATABASE '<db_file>'
FROM '<archive_device>' [FROM '<archive_device>'] [KEY key_spec]
[RENAME '<DBSpaces_name>'
TO '<new_Dbspace_path>'] [CATALOG ONLY]
```

Fig 10.7

```
RESTORE DATABASE '<database_name> <restore_option>
FROM '<archive_device>'
```

<db_file>

This is the relative or absolute path of the database to be restored. This can be the original location, or a new location for the catalog store file.

<archive_device>

The archive_device is a tape drive or file name which holds the archive file/files used for the restore. You need to supply all relevant archive devices (see section on the basics for an example of restoring a multi device back up).

The **FROM** clause is used to specify the name of the <archive_device> from which you are restoring, delimited with single quotation marks. When multiple archive devices are being restored then you must specify them using separate **FROM** clauses. A comma-separated list is not allowed. Archive devices must be distinct. The number of **FROM** clauses determines the amount of parallelism Sybase IQ attempts with regard to input devices. (much like the TO clause in the backup).

<key_spec>

This is a string of numbers, mixed case letters and special characters that is used as an encryption key by the database. You may require this when dropping the database as in the example in Fig 10.8 (Obviously you wouldn't normally restore a database and then drop it).

Fig 10.8

```
RESTORE DATABASE 'my_database'
FROM 'backup _file1'
FROM 'backup_file2'
KEY '123456abcdef';

DROP DATABASE 'my_database.db' KEY '123456abcdef';
```

For more information on encryption keys see the chapter on "Creating/Altering a database".

<database_name>

The name of the database to restore

<restore-option>

You can use the **READONLY** <DBSpaces or file>, **KEY** key_spec or **RENAME** file-name **TO** new-file-path as restore options.

RENAME '<DBSpaces_name>' TO '<new_Dbspace_path>'

The **RENAME** clause is used to restore one or more IQ database files to a new location. Each <DBSpaces_name> you are moving must have the same name it had in the SYSFILE table on the database you backed up. The value of the< new_DBSpacepath> can be a new raw partition or a new (full or relative) path name.
If a database was created using relative paths then the restored files will be restored relative to the catalog store file and a rename is not required. If absolute paths were used and you are restoring a different database (fro example restoring a test environment from a production back up) then you will want to **RENAME** the file otherwise it will be restored to its original location.
One exception is don't use the **RENAME** clause to move the **SYSTEM** DBSpaces (catalog store). To

move the catalog store, and any files created relative to it and not specified in a **RENAME** clause, specify a new location in the db_file parameter.

CATALOG ONLY

This clause restores only the backup header record from the archive.

Restores of READONLY Backups

Given the following **BACKUP** statement in Fig 10.9

Fig 10.9

```
BACKUP DATABASE READONLY DBSPACES iq_main
TO '/system1/IQ15/IQ-15_1/demo/backup/iqmain'
```

The DBSpace *iq_main* can be restored using either of the **RESTORE** statements in Fig 10.10 or Fig 10.11:

Fig 10.10

```
RESTORE DATABASE 'iqdemo' READONLY DBSPACES iq_main
FROM '/system1/IQ15/IQ-15_0/demo/backup/iqmain'
```

Fig 10.11

```
RESTORE DATABASE 'iqdemo'
FROM '/system1/IQ15/IQ-
15_0/demo/backup/iqmain'
```

A selective backup backs up either all **READWRITE** DBSpaces or specific read-only DBSpaces or DBFiles.

Notes:

- You can take a **READONLY** selective backup and restore all objects from this backup (as in the second example above).

- You can take an all-inclusive backup and restore read-only files and DBSpaces selectively.

- You can take a **READONLY** selective backup of multiple read-only files and DBSpaces and restore a sub-set of real-only files and DBSpaces selectively.

- You can restore the read-only backup, only if the read-only files have not changed since the backup. Once the DBSpace is made read-write again, the read-only backup is invalid, unless you restore the entire read-write portion of the database back to the point at which the read-only DBSpace was read-only.

Check the database

What is the point of backing up your database if it is internally inconsistent???

Before commencing any backups (and generally at least once a week) it is recommended that you run DBCC checks. The easiest way to do this is to run the command in Fig 10.12

Fig 10.12

```
sp_iqcheckdb 'check database'
```

Executing this (if your have the right server switches) will run the IQ DBCC (Database Consistency Checker)
DBCC has three ways/modes to check the database, of you specify 'check database' then every database object is checked. You may also specify individual tables and indexes to check, however when checking a table the IQ DBCC also checks its indexes. The DBCC does not check or repair referential integrity violations. For multiplex you may run **sp_iqcheckdb** on any node, but on a secondary/child node the DBCC checks can't access the freelist, hence no freelist checks are performed.

DBCC has different verification modes that perform increasing amounts of consistency checking. There are three modes for checking database consistency and one for resetting allocation maps. Each mode checks all database objects, if you specify 'database' as the target in the **sp_iqcheckdb** command string. Individual tables and indexes can also be specified in the command string. If you specify individual table names, all indexes within those tables are also checked.

Some examples of running this procedure are given in Fig 10.13 and Fig 10.14

Fig 10.12

```
sp_iqcheckdb 'check  table sales.sales_orders'
```

Fig 10.13

```
sp_iqcheckdb 'check  index HG_sales_orders_id'
```

Instead of using the check options you can also specify allocation, verify or drop leaks modes, for example

Fig 10.14

```
sp_iqcheckdb 'allocation database'
```

Fig 10.15

```
sp_iqcheckdb 'verify database'
```

Fig 10.16

```
sp_iqcheckdb 'dropleaks database'
```

Each of these modes plus the check option executes checks described in the table below.

Mode	Description	Error checking and output	Speed (per sybase stats)
check	Every database object is checked.	Will detect allocation and most	60GB an Hour

		index errors and output all available statistics	
allocation	Checks allocation with blockmap information for the entire database, a specific index, a specific index type, a specific partition, specific table, or a specific DBSpace. Does not check index consistency.	Will detect allocation errors and output allocation statistics only	4TB an Hour
verify	Verifies that all database pages can be read for the entire database, specific index, specific index type, specific table, specific partition, or specific DBSpace. If the table is partitioned, then check mode will check the table's partition allocation bitmaps.	Will detect allocation and all index errors and output all available statistics	15GB an Hour
dropleaks	When running in a single node set up you can execute the dropleaks DBCC for either a DBSpace or the database to reset the allocation map. When using on a DBSpaces then no write operations can be performed on the DBSpaces. When running on multiplex coordinator node (You cannot execute dropleaks on secondary/child nodes), dropleaks will also detect duplicate blocks, leaked blocks or extra blocks across the multiplex system.	Will detect allocation errors and output allocation statistics only	4TB an hour

SP_IQCHECKDB Output

The output of the sp_iqcheckdb procedure is dependant on the mode/parameters you have executed it with. The output may include errors, information, stats and repair stats and may contain up to three different resultsets (In one report). Errors are displayed with asterisks and will only be displayed if an error has been detected. Errors are indicated by asterisks (*****), and appear only if errors are detected. Output is also placed in the IQ message log/file and if the **DBCC_LOG_PROCESS** option is ON then progress messages are also placed in the IQ message log/file as the procedure executes. Below is an example of a the output generated by running the command in Fig 10.17

Fig 10.17

```
sp_iqcheckdb 'check table sales.sales_order'
```

Stat	Value	Flags
====================	==================================	======
DBCC Check Mode Report		
====================	==================================	======
DBCC Status	No Errors Detected	
====================	==================================	======
Index Summary		
====================	==================================	======
Verified Index Count	13	
====================	==================================	======
Allocation Summary		
====================	==================================	======
Blocks Total	234881012	
Blocks in Use	20326455	
====================	==================================	======
Allocation Statistics		

====================	==============================	======
Marked Logical Blocks	10368	
Marked Physical Blocks	3758	
Marked Pages	648	
Blocks in Freelist	26014402	
Highest PBN in Use	21418543	
1 Block Page Count	12	
3 Block Page Count	40	
4 Block Page Count	345	
5 Block Page Count	28	
6 Block Page Count	2	
7 Block Page Count	110	
8 Block Page Count	33	
9 Block Page Count	23	
10 Block Page Count	2	
11 Block Page Count	3	
16 Block Page Count	50	
====================	==============================	======
Partition Summary		
====================	==============================	======
====================	==============================	======
Index Statistics		
====================	==============================	======
Verified Index	sales.sales_order.ASIQ_IDX_T1684_C2_FP	
Verified Index	sales.sales_order.sales_order_load_id_LF	
Verified Index	sales.sales_order.ASIQ_IDX_T1684_C6_FP	
Verified Index	sales.sales_order.sales_order_valid_to_LF	
Verified Index	sales.sales_order.ASIQ_IDX_T1684_C1_FP	
Verified Index	sales.sales_order.ASIQ_IDX_T1684_C4_FP	
Verified Index	sales.sales_order.ASIQ_IDX_T1684_C5_FP	
Verified Index	sales.sales_order.ASIQ_IDX_T1684_C7_FP	
Verified Index	sales.sales_order.ASIQ_IDX_T1684_I8_HG	
Verified Index	sales.sales_order.ASIQ_IDX_T1684_C3_FP	
Verified Index	sales.sales_order.sales_order_valid_from_LF	
Verified Index	sales.sales_order.sales_order_account_number_HG	
Verified Index	sales.sales_order.sales_order_account_shortform_HG	
FP Indexes Checked	7	
LF Indexes Checked	3	
HG Indexes Checked	3	
====================	==============================	======
Container Statistics		
====================	==============================	======
Database Objects Checked	70	
B-Array Count	17	
B-Array Physical Block Count	3840	
B-Arrays with Data	15	
Blockmap Page Count	512	
Blockmaps with Mapped Pages	32	
Blockmap Identity Count	272	
Blockmap Max Links	1	
Bitmap Count	22	
Bitmaps with Data	12	
Bitmap Physical Block Count	12	
Bitmap L1 Root Pages	12	
Bitmap Leaf Pages	10	
Bitmap Range Slice Count	160	
B-Tree Count	4	

B-Tree Pages	6032	
B-Tree Leaf Pages	5984	
B-Tree Segment Pages	48	
B-Tree Total Height	371	
B-Tree Max Depth	1	
B-Trees with Data	1	
G-Array Count	4	
G-Array Singletons	850696	
G-Array List Groups	84193	
VDO Count	1	
VDO Mapped Blocks	1	
VDOs with data	1	
==================	==============================	======
Buffer Manager Statistics		
==================	==============================	======
==================	==============================	======
Catalog Statistics		
==================	==============================	======
Tables Checked	1	
Fields Checked	7	
Indexes Checked	13	
==================	==============================	======
Connection Statistics		
==================	==============================	======
InsertIters	2	
Insert Count	2	
Insert Fields	8	
Insert Indexes	8	
Sort Records	1564458	
Sort Sets	7	
==================	==============================	======
Compression Statistics		
==================	==============================	======
Non-compressed Pages [BARRAY]	18	
LZW Pages [BT]	282	
LZW Pages [BT_FIXED]	95	
LZW Pages [VDO]	1	
LZW Pages [GARRAY]	115	
LZW Pages [BARRAY]	93	
LZW Physical Blocks [BT]	1148	
LZW Physical Blocks [BT_FIXED]	381	
LZW Physical Blocks [VDO]	3	
LZW Physical Blocks [GARRAY]	826	
LZW Physical Blocks [BARRAY]	588	
LZW Logical Blocks [BT]	4512	
LZW Logical Blocks [BT_FIXED]	1520	
LZW Logical Blocks [VDO]	16	
LZW Logical Blocks [GARRAY]	1840	
LZW Logical Blocks [BARRAY]	1488	
==================	==============================	======
DBCC Info		
==================	==============================	======
DBCC Work units Dispatched	21	
DBCC Work units Completed	21	
DBCC Buffer Quota	16300	
DBCC Per-Thread Buffer Quota	4075	
Max Blockmap ID found	508375	

Max Transaction ID found	6838856	

Scheduling routine backups

Make a full backup of each database just after you create it, to provide a base point, and perform full and incremental backups on a fixed schedule thereafter. It is especially important to back up your database after any large number of changes.
Your backup plan depends on:

- The load on your system

- The size of your database

- The number of changes made to the data

- The relative importance of faster backups and faster recovery

The overall time it takes to complete a backup or restore a database depends largely on the strategy you choose for mixing full and incremental restores. Several other factors also affect the speed of backup and restore operations: the number of archive devices, data verification, the memory available for the backup, and size of the IQ and catalog stores. Most implementations I have worked on over the years have gone for a weekend **FULL BACKUP** with **INCREMENTAL BACK UP**s taken on weekdays. This approach is good for an overnight batch based system but you may need to consider intra-day backup on more volatile data/systems.

Disaster Recovery

DR should be considered on mission critical applications, of course in a book such as this and without knowing your system it is impossible to make recommendations. When considering DR on IQ below are some of the considerations you may want to make

- Do you go for SRDF storage and use a storage based DR solution?

- How often does a back up need to be taken?

- Can data feeds be used to restore data faster than a DB restore?

- Do you need a mixture of DB restore and file backups to restore your system?

- Will a multiplex system give you more resilience?

- Cost vs Risk – Does the cost of the DR solution outweigh the risk of losing data?

Multiplex

This chapter gives an overview of the basic architecture and the differences between 12.x and 15.x versions of IQ multiplex systems.

In Sybase IQ a multiplex is a hybrid cluster of IQ servers that share Main (Permanent) IQ data but have an independent catalog store, temporary store and transaction logs.

The advantage of this is you can load balance your server queries, CPU costs and offer a higher availability of your system.

It also means that objects can be queried by many users across "nodes" while a single writer transaction handles the loading and manipulation of data.

Multiplex Overview

A multiplex system is a collection of IQ servers (nodes) that share an IQ store but can use local temporary space and system resources to execute queries.

From IQ 15 onwards nodes can be readers or writers (in 12.x all nodes were read-only) with the synchronisation of DDL operations communicated via a table version log handled by a primary server (sometimes referred to as the co-ordinator or co-ordinating server). You can also use the architecture combined with security and views to logically partition user access by using views to ensure users of a particular node only see a certain set of data and therefore load balance your resources even better. There is also inter-node communication that the primary server can use to propagate changes out to other nodes.

The diagram in Fig 11.1 gives is a diagrammatic view of the architecture used in multiplex systems.

Fig 11.1

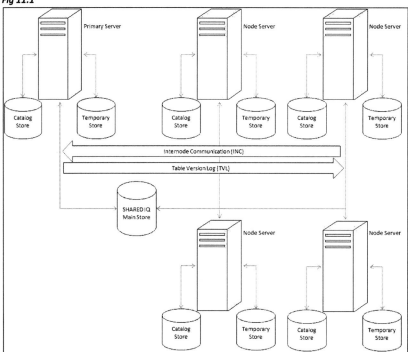

When setting up your multiplex it is recommended that you place the IQ main store on a shared disk array and you MUST ensure that the primary server and all nodes in the multiplex are running the same versions of IQ.

This means that when you need to upgrade a version of install an EBF you may have to bring down your entire cluster (In the event of a version upgrade then you definitely will) it is recommended you contact your Sybase rep to ask about the impact of EBF's on your multiplex.

It is also recommended for reasons of compatibility (and the sanity of the developer/DBA) that you use Sybase Central to handle all you multiplex administration tasks. As the layout and functionality of Sybase central is likely to change (and indeed has between versions12-15) then it is worth checking you have the correct version for your multiplex environment before commencing any tasks.

Apart from the fact that you may be executing code on a **NODE** (or the **PRIMARY SERVER**) you should not experience many differences than if you were running on single node IQ architecture. The only obvious difference is that your local stores (catalog/temp) and local system resources (cpu/memory) will be used for running your code and therefore the only external bound you have is when I/O is performed to the shared main IQ store.

The chapters on system procedures, system tables and options all give the required information on their repective multiplex objects. Teh sections below cover in some more detail the various common tasks and features of multiplex.

Multiplex Infrastructure

The **PRIMARY SERVER** (co-ordinator) and the **NODES** must all be on the same O/S and have the same release version of IQ. It is recommended that the storage for the main IQ store is location on a shared disk array and for nodes you must set up the paths to the main store identically to the primary server. For each node they can have their own local path to their respective catalog and temporary stores. Each server in the multiples requires the following files.

File Name	File Description
dbname.db	This file is used to contain the local catalog store. Like simplex systems this cannot be a raw device.
dbname.iqmsg	This file is the server's local Sybase IQ message log file.
dbname.iqtmp	This file is the local IQ temp store, but this file only exists if the IQ temp store is added as a O/S file. However it is recommened you use RAW devices for your IQ temp store.
dbname.log	This is the local IQ Transaction Log.
dbname.lmp	This is the local IQ licence, this file remains even when a database is dropped.
params.cfg	This is your local parameter configuration file; much like in simplex you can populate this with your own customized options.
start_server	This is the local script used to start the server; it is generated by Sybase Central.

Creating and Altering a Multiplex Server

Creating a Multiplex Server

To create a Multiplex server you use the command **CREATE MULTIPLEX SERVER** as per the syntax in Fig 11.2.

Fig 11.2

```
CREATE MULTIPLEX SERVER <server name> DATABASE '<db file>'
HOST  '<server hostname>'  PORT <server port number>
ROLE  (READER or  WRITER)
STATUS (INCLUDED or EXCLUDED)
```

When you execute the **CREATE MULTIPLEX SERVER** statement then a row for the **PRIMARY SERVER** and **NODE** are added to the SYS.ISYSIQMPXSERVER system table which is used to store the server host and port numbers. Although you can execute a **CREATE MULTIPLEX SERVER** statement from any server in a multiplex system the **PRIMARY SERVER** must be running.The following options are allowed in the **CREATE MULTIPLEX SERVER** statement.

Property
SERVER <server name>
DATABASE '<db file>'
HOST '<server hostname>'
PORT <server port number>
ROLE (READER or WRITER)
STATUS (INCLUDED or EXCLUDED)

Altering a Multiplex Server

You may use the **ALTER MULTIPLEX SERVER** statement to change any (except the server name) attributes of your server. For example Fig 11.3 changes the server called my_multiplex_1 to a **WRITER**.

Fig 11.3

```
ALTER MULTIPLEX SERVER my_mutiplex_1 ROLE WRITER
```

Dropping multiplex servers

To drop a Multiplex server first shut the target down, you can only drop the FAILOVER server if it is the last NODE server remaining. When you drop the last remaining NODE then your **PRIMARY SERVER** will be shut down and when restarted it will be back to running an IQ Simplex system.
To drop a server simply execute the DROP MULTIPLEX SERVER statement as in Fig 11.4

Fig 11.4

```
DROP MULTIPLEX SERVER <my server name>
```

Primary Server (Co-Ordinator) Failover

Every Multiplex system must specify a **FAILOVER NODE** that can be used as the **PRIMARY SERVER** if the **PRIMARY SERVER** is unavailable. You can set this in Sybase Central or by executing an **ALTER MULTIPLEX SERVER** statement as in Fig 11.5

Fig 11.5

```
ALTER MULTIPLEX SERVER <server name> ASSIGN AS FAILOVER SERVER
```

If you ever need to failover it is recommended you refer to your IQ release versions current failover procedures (available from Sybase) as the recommendations on doing so seem to change on a regular basis. However one consistant message is that you **MUST** ensure that your **PRIMARY SERVER** is not running before attempting the failover.

Backups and Restores

A last point to note is that you can only execute the **BACKUP** and **RESTORE** commands on the **PRIMARY SERVER** in a multiplex system. Please refer to the chapter on Back ups and Restore for futher info.

Java in the Database

There are occasions where SQL can prove an inefficient language for manipulating your data. Examples can include complex methodical calculations, pivoting of resultsets and XML manipulation. Luckily Sybase IQ allows you to write both functions and stored procedures in Java that can be used to return resulsets and values to underlying SQL.

Another advantage of this is that to the user the functions and stored procedures are used in exactly the same way as you would use their SQL counterparts.

This section covers how we import java classes for use in the database, how they are run and how you can call them in your code. You should have an understanding of Java (as programming Java is outside the scope of this book) and how java is executed via the Java Virtual Machine from Byte code within a class.

The Basics

Sybase IQ enables you to write your own User defined functions and procedures in Java; it enables this by leveraging off the JAVA functionality in the catalog (ASA) database, therefore if you require further reading or have questions that are not answered in this chapter then please refer to the ASA/SQL Anywhere documentation on the Sybase website.

As all java functions run in the catalog store there can be a performance hit when moving small amounts of data many times between the stores. However you can write much more complicated algorithms in Java and in some cases the speed of the calculations in Java will negate any negative effects from the data movement in the IQ architecture.

Some things to note about Java support in IQ are:-

- You cannot use any GUI components such as applets, swing, AWT etc
- All Java code must be 100% java and cannot call any native methods.
- The Java program cannot have any user input (except from passing in parameters) for example you cannot prompt a user to enter a name or age from within the java.

Apart from that you should be able to do most functionality you require including JDBC calls, manipulating and returning resultsets.

Any output from the java program that is sent to standard out will be captured and placed into the message log.

For example the Java code in Fig 12.1 will output the string "I am going to standard out" to the message log (rather like using the MESSAGE statement in SQL).

Fig 12.1

```
System.out.println(
```

The Java Virtual Machine

When Java code is compiled into a class it is converted to byte-code, this byte code requires and interpreter to run. The interpreter is called the JVM (Java Virtual Machine). The catalog store (ASA/SQL Anywhere) database starts a JVM automatically when required.

The SQL processor in the ASA database can call the JVM, process requests from the JVM and enable data access. You can unload the JVM by calling the **STOP JAVA** SQL statement and re-start it with the **START JAVA** SQL statement. You can tell the database to use a specific JVM on the server (this is useful if you want to use a later version of the JVM than the one supplied with IQ/ASA).

To change the JVM you can run the **ALTER EXTERNAL ENVIRONMENT** statement as in Fig 12.2

Fig 12.2

```
ALTER EXTERNAL ENVIRONMENT JAVA
LOCATION
```

You can see all external environments in the SYSEXTERNENV system table (You can also use C, Perl, php etc (But Java is easier).

The CLASSPATH

When the JVM is executed it uses the environment variable, CLASSPATH. The CLASSPATH variable tells the JVM where it should look to find classes or **JAR** files that are referenced in the java code. The CLASSPATH variable on your host must include references to the java directories you need to use.

When you install a new class or **JAR** file on your database using the "INSTALL JAVA" statement the class or **JAR** file is added to the CLASSPATH.

For example Fig 12.3 will add the file /home/myarea/java/testIQProg.class to the CLASSPATH. This means that the JVM will now have access to the class testIQProg and its methods.

Fig 12.3

```
INSTALL JAVA NEW
FROM FILE
```

Install a CLASS or JAR file

To install a new Java Class or **JAR** file simply use the syntax given in Fig 12.4

Fig 12.4

```
INSTALL JAVA NEW
FROM FILE '<Path and file name of .class or .jar file
```

To see all the classes installed you can select from the SYSJAVACLASS table.

Update a CLASS or JAR file

If you have made alterations to a class you will need to update it in the database in order to pick up the changes. To do this you run an **INSTALL JAVA UPDATE** statement as in Fig 12.5

Fig 12.5

```
INSTALL JAVA UPDATE
FROM FILE '<Path and file name of .class or .jar file
```

Remove a CLASS or JAR file

To remove a class or **JAR** file simply run a REMOVE JAVA statement using the syntax in Fig 12.6

Fig 12.6

```
REMOVE JAVA
CLASS <jave class name> or JAR <jar name>
```

Creating a Function from a Java Method

To create a function you first need to install the class, and then you create a function on it.
If we for example have a class as in Fig 12.7 which has a method to double a number.

Fig 12.7

```
public class testIQProg
{
        public static double multiplyMyNumber(double balance)
        {
            double doubled_number;

            // Instantiate a new object
            doubled_number = (balance * 2);

            return doubled_number;
        }
}
```

We first install our class as in Fig 12.8

Fig 12.8

```
INSTALL JAVA NEW
CLASS '//home//myarea//java/testIQProg.class'
```

We now create our function in Fig 12.9

Fig 12.9

```
CREATE FUNCTION multiply_number(
RETURNS DOUBLE
EXTERNAL NAME 'testIQProg.multiplyMyNumber(
```

We can now run the SQL in Fig 12.10 to produce a result set containing the value 480.

Fig 12.10

```
SELECT multiply_number(
```

Let's take another look at our function declaration in Fig 12.9.

* The first line is "**CREATE FUNCTION** testProg(IN arg1 double)", this tells the SQL processor that the function takes one argument of type DOUBLE.

* The next line "**RETURNS DOUBLE**" tells the SQL processor that a value of data type DOUBLE will be returned.

* The next line "**EXTERNAL NAME** 'testIQProg.doubleMyNumber(D)D'". This tells the processor that the function uses an external call to the testIQProg class using the method doubleMyNumber. The (D) tells the compiler that the external program expects a type **DOUBLE** passed to it and the D after the brackets informs the processor that it will return a **DOUBLE**. Other types than can be specified are given in Fig 12.11.

* Finally the last line "**LANGUAGE JAVA**" tells the processor that the external function is written in JAVA and to use the JVM to execute the function.

Fig 12.11

Parameter type	Data Type
[	A square bracket is used to indicate each dimension of an array.
B	This is the Java byte data type
C	This is the Java char datatype
D	This is the Java double datatype
F	This is the Java float datatype
I	This is the Java int datatype
J	This is the Java long datatype
Lclass-name;	We prefix a java class instance with an L as in "Ljava/lang/String". The class names must be fully qualified and use backslashes instead of dot notation!
S	This is the Java short datatype
V	This indicates a VOID return type
Z	This is the Java boolean datatype

Creating a Stored Procedure from a Java Method

Now say we wish to use static class variables in our code. For example we wish to call the main or the init method of a class to set up some variables and let subsequent calls to functions use those static class variable values.

Firstly let's change the testIQProg class from the functions example to the one in Fig 12.12

Fig 12.12

```
import java.io.*;

public class testIQProg
{
        public static double MULTIPLIER=2;

        public static void init(double arg_multiplier)
        {
                MULTIPLIER = arg_multiplier;
        }

        public static double multiplyMyNumber(double balance)
        {
                double doubled_number;

                // Instantiate a new object
                doubled_number = (balance * MULTIPLIER);

                return doubled_number;
        }

        public static void main( String[] args )
        {
          System.out.print( "Main Method Called In testIQProg" );

        }
}
```

The next step is to update the java class (or install it as in Fig 12.8 if you did not use the Function example). To update the class we run the code in Fig 12.13

Fig 12.13

```
INSTALL JAVA UPDATE
CLASS '//home//myarea//java/testIQProg.class'
```

Now we create a procedure to call the init method and a function that calls the multiplyMyNumber method as in Fig 12.14. (If you already created the function in the Functions example then execute a **DROP FUNCTION** multiply_number to drop it first).

Fig 12.14

```
CREATE PROCEDURE init_testIQProg(
            'testIQProg.init(
LANGUAGE JAVA;

CREATE FUNCTION multiply_number(
RETURNS DOUBLE
EXTERNAL NAME   'testIQProg.multiplyMyNumber(
LANGUAGE JAVA
```

Now if we call the init_test stored procedure we can set the value of the class's static variable MULTIPLIER.

For example the SELECT statement in Fig 12.15 returns a value of 150, whereas the SELECT statement in Fig 12.16 returns 250.

Fig 12.15

```
EXEC init_testIQProg (  ;
SELECT multiply_number (    ;
```

Fig 12.16

```
EXEC init_testIQProg (5 ;
SELECT multiply_number (    ;
```

Java Methods and JDBC

You can also use java JDBC functionality to interact with the database, this gives you the flexibility to use you procedure to transform data or return resultsets.

Returning resultsets

We can use java methods to connect to databases and return resultsets as you would in a SQL stored procedure. We will demonstrate this using the class in Fig 12.17. This class has three methods:-

- **getConnection** – This obtains the default connection for the database, the default is to connect to the database you are running the code on.

- **getObjects** – This selects all columns and rows from the system table SYSOBJECTS using the connection from the **getConnection** method.

- **getOptions** – This selects all columns and rows from the system table SYSOPTIONS using the connection from the **getConnection** method.

For this class we will create two SQL procedures that reference the java methods **getObjects** and **getOptions**.

Fig 12.17

```
public class mySysTables

  public static void getObjects(

    Connection conn = getConnection(
    Statement stmt = conn.createStatement(
    ResultSet sysobjectsResults = stmt.executeQuery (

    sysobjects[0] =

  public static void getOptions(

      Connection conn = getConnection(
      Statement stmt = conn.createStatement(
      ResultSet sysoptionsResults = stmt.executeQuery (



  public static Connection getConnection (


    try

      conn = DriverManager.getConnection(
    catch (

      System.out.println (
      System.exit(-
```

Now we have our class the first step is to install it into the database as in Fig 12.18.

Fig 12.18

```
INSTALL JAVA NEW
FROM FILE '//home//myarea//java//mySysTables.class'
```

The next step is to create two stored procedures that each reference one of the java methods as in Fig 12.19. You will notice two things here, one that the java methods has an input variable of type Ljava/sql/ResultSet, the second is that the java methods retun VOID. The CREATE PROCEDURE knows that we want to return a result set using the DYNAMIC RESULT SETS options, the 1 means we are only returning the first resultset the method creates (i.e. the First Entry in the ResultSet[] object defined as an input to the method).

The processor implicitly knows that by including the resultset as an input we wish to return it. Later in this chapter we will see a similar method for returning out variables from a procedure.

Fig 12.19

```
CREATE PROCEDURE get_sysobjects()
  DYNAMIC RESULT SETS 1
    EXTERNAL NAME
      'mySysTables.getObjects([Ljava/sql/ResultSet;)V'
    LANGUAGE JAVA

CREATE PROCEDURE get_sysoptions()
  DYNAMIC RESULT SETS 1
    EXTERNAL NAME
      'mySysTables.getOptions([Ljava/sql/ResultSet;)V'
    LANGUAGE JAVA
```

Now our procedures are created we can execute them as we would a normal stored procedure. Each procedure will output the results from the relevant java method.

Fig 12.20

```
/* This returns the contents of the SYSOBJECTS table */

EXEC get_sysobjects

/* This returns the contents of the SYSOPTIONS table */

EXEC get_sysoption
```

Returning Multiple Resultsets

We can now look at how we can return multiple resultsets using the DYNAMIC RESULTSETS OPTION. If we had a java class as in Fig 12.21

Fig 12.21

```
public class getTwoResultsets

  public static void getResults(
      throws

    Connection conn = getConnection(

    /* GET THE FIRST RESULTSET */
    Statement stmt_1 = conn.createStatement(

    ResultSet sysobjectsResults = stmt_1.executeQuery (



    /* GET THE SECOND RESULTSET */
    Statement stmt_2 = conn.createStatement(

    ResultSet sysoptionsResults = stmt_2.executeQuery (


    resultsets [1] = sysop


  public static Connection getConnection (


        try

           conn = DriverManager.getConnection(

        catch (

           System.out.println (
           System.exit(-
```

First we install the java class as in Fig12.21

Fig 12.21

```
INSTALL JAVA UPDATE
FROM FILE '//home//my_area//java/getTwoResultsets.class'
```

We now create two stored procedures from our class (Fig 12.22), the first one returns only the first result set using the DYNAMIC RESULT SETS 1 option and the second returns both result sets using DYNAMIC RESULT SETS 2. You could of course return more than two and change your class and DYNAMIC RESULT SETS option accordingly. Be aware that if you set you DYNAMIC RESULT SETS option to more results than the java method returns then you will get a run time error when executing your procedure.

Fig 12.22

```
-- This will only return the frist resultset
CREATE PROCEDURE get_first_resultset()
DYNAMIC RESULT SETS 1
EXTERNAL NAME 'getTwoResultsets.getResults([Ljava/sql/ResultSet;)V'
LANGUAGE JAVA

-- This will return both resultsets
CREATE PROCEDURE get_both_resultsets()
DYNAMIC RESULT SETS 2
EXTERNAL NAME 'getTwoResultsets.getResults([Ljava/sql/ResultSet;)V'
LANGUAGE JAVA
```

Now we have the procedures we can execute them as we would a normal SQL stored procedure as in Fig 12.23

Fig 12.23

```
--This only returns the first resultset
EXEC get_first_resultset

--This returns both resultsets
EXEC get_both_resultsets
```

Returning values from Java via stored procedures

You may wish to write a stored procedure to use **OUT** or **INOUT** parameters as you would in a T-SQL procedure or function.

As Java does not have the concept of **INOUT** or **OUT** you use an array of parameters like in the multiple resultsets section above.

If for example you wanted a java method to return a single integer value as an **OUT** parameter you would do this by creating a parameters of type array of integers in your java method to use an integer **OUT** parameter, create an array of exactly one integer as in Fig 12.24:

Fig 12.21

```
public class returnValues
{
        public static boolean returnAnInteger( int[] param )
        {
            param[0] = 99;
            return true;
        }
}
```

We now install the java class as in Fig 12.25

Fig 12.25

```
INSTALL JAVA NEW
FROM FILE '//home//myarea//java//returnValues.class'
```

And finally create a procedure as in Fig 12.26, we use the "(I) Z" signature to indicate that the method has a single parameter that is an array or integers

Fig 12.26

```
CREATE PROCEDURE return_an_integer( OUT p
INTEGER )
EXTERNAL NAME
'returnValues.returnAnInteger([I)Z'
LANGUAGE JAVA
```

We can now call the procedure as in Fig 12.27, the variable @myint is set to the value 99 in the procedure.

Fig 12.27

```
DELCARE @myint INT
EXEC return_an_integer(@myint)
SELECT @myint
```

Other Languages in the Database (VB.Net, C#, Perl, PHP etc...)

The reason I have used java is because it not only supports resultsets but it is platform independent. However it is not the only language you can use in IQ to write external functions. You can see a complete list by querying the SYSEXTERNENV system table as in Fig 12.28

Fig 12.28

object id	name	scope	supports result sets	location	options
496	java	D	Y		[ARG][VERBATIM]-cp [ARG][QUOTE] [QUALFY]sajvm.jar

					[PATH_SEP][QUALIFY]jodbc.jar[PATH_SEP][Q UALIFY]cis.zip [PATH_SEP][QUALIFY]Jconn3.jar[PATH_SEP] [QUALIFY]sajvminclude.jar[QUOTE] [ARG][VERBATIM] ianywhere.sa.jvm.SAJvmMain [PARM1] [PARM2] [PARM3] [PARM4]
497	perl	C	N	/usr/bin/perl	[ARG][QUOTE][QUALIFY]perlenv.pl[QUOTE] [PARM1] [PARM2] [PARM3] [ARG][VERBATIM]2638 [PARM4]
498	clr	D	Y	dbextclr11	[PARM1] [PARM2] [PARM3] [PARM4]
499	php	C	N	php	[ARG][QUOTE][QUALIFY]phpenv.php[QUOTE] [PARM1] [PARM2] [PARM3] [PARM4]
500	c_esql32	C	Y	bin32[SLASH]dbextern c11	[ARG][VERBATIM]ESQL [PARM1] [PARM2] [PARM3] [PARM4]
501	c_odbc32	C	Y	bin32[SLASH]dbextern c11	[ARG][VERBATIM]ODBC [PARM1] [PARM2] [PARM3] [PARM4]
502	c_esql64	C	Y	bin64[SLASH]dbextern c11	[ARG][VERBATIM]ESQL [PARM1] [PARM2] [PARM3] [PARM4]
503	c_odbc64	C	Y	bin64[SLASH]dbextern c11	[ARG][VERBATIM]ODBC [PARM1] [PARM2] [PARM3] [PARM4]

This table shows you the name of the other languages/platforms supported, for example the entry for CLR refers to a DLL written in a CLR language such as VB.NET or C#. Other languages supported (as at V15.1) are perl, php and a variety of c. Some of these languages support the return of resultsets and others such as perl and php do not. Before you come to install and use your functions it is best to check with Sybase on which features are supported for the language you wish to use.

For Sybase documentation on the external language/environment functionality you should refer to the Sybase ASA documentation which gives a more comprehensive overview.

Remote Objects & Application/Language Connectivity

Remote Objects and CIS

Overview

Sybase IQ uses CIS (Component Integration Services) to allow you to share tables and procedure across servers. You can use this functionality to define a proxy table on your IQ database that is a pointer to a table on a remote server, or a proxy table on the remote server database that points to IQ. You can also create remote procedures that will execute a stored procedure on a remote server, and finally you can execute code from your database that is passed through to a remote database server.

The functionality works "out of the box" with other Sybase databases, but for oracle and Microsoft you may have to use a connectivity bridge such as Sybase repserver or Sybase RAX.

All CIS services on IQ run through the ASA catalog store so for a more in-depth technical explanation you may want to check the Sybase ASA documentation. The documentation also refers to using Excel and text files as remote tables but I have not tested this functionality and it is not explained in the sections below.

IS/Remote Tables

One way to bring data in to your IQ database from a remote database is to use proxy table.

You can create a proxy table on your database that points to a table on another database, or you can create a table on another database that points to a table on your database. Both of the syntaxes for doing this are very similar.

The CREATE table statement is used in both of these scenarios (with a different syntax for each). Columns in remote tables are defined as ASA datatypes any columns not in ASA datatype format will be converted on your local table to an ASA datatype. Other things to note are

- Tables created as proxies must be named in less that 31 characters
- Primary keys will work on the remote table if the remote databases supports them
- Foreign Key definitions are ignored on the remote table as are local foreign keys that point to remote table columns.
- You cannot create a proxy table that refers to a local table or table within a multiplex!
- Triggers will not work on proxy tables
- You cannot use backwards scrolling cursors or any position functions on the proxy table
- If any column/columns on the remote table has a name that is also a keyword on the remote server then you cannot access the data in that column/columns.
- You cannot use an ALTER TABLE against a remote table
- calls to functions that contain an expression that references a proxy table

In order to use any remote server functionality you first have to ensure that the remote server has been set up on your system and an external login to that server has also been set up (Fig 13.1). You should also ensure that any server you are connecting to is in your interfaces/sql.ini file.

Create a remote server and login

Fig 13.1

```
CREATE SERVER <remote database server name>
CLASS 'ASAJDBC'
USING '<remote host name> : <remote port name>'

CREATE EXTERNLOGIN <local login>TO <remote database server name>
REMOTE LOGIN <remote login name> IDENTIFIED BY <remote password>
```

For example

Fig 13.2

```
CREATE SERVER REMOTEIQ
CLASS 'ASAJDBC'
USING 'remotehost :2643 '

CREATE EXTERNLOGIN sales TO REMOTEIQ
REMOTE LOGIN sales IDENTIFIED BY pa55word
```

Your remote server needs to be in the same case sensitivity mode as your local database as otherwise you may get unexpected/strange results.

Create a proxy table on your database to point to a remote table

To set up a proxy table we simply use the EXISTING and AT clauses in the CREATE TABLE statement as in Fig 13.3

Fig 13.3

```
CREATE EXISTING TABLE
my_proxy_sales_figures
AT 'REMOTEIQ..sales.sales_figures'
```

The AT clause is of the form

'<remote server>.<remote database>.<remote owner>.<remote table/view>'

In our example I am assuming I am connecting to another IQ database and therefore have omitted the database name as the server name is sufficient. You may also use a semicolon instead of a period as the delimiter for the string given to the AT clause.

Anyway back to out example, we can now select from our proxy table as in Fig 13.4. This will cause our database to connect to the remote server and run the select on the remote table.

Fig 13.4

```
SELECT * FROM my_proxy_sales_figures
```

Some things to remember are that if the table def of the remote table changes your proxy table will need to be dropped and re-created to pick up the changes. If for example a column is dropped called sales_region and your proxy table was created before this column was dropped on the remote server you will get an error like Fig 13.5.

Fig 13.5

```
Server 'REMOTEIQ': SQL Anywhere Error -143: Column 'sales_region' not
found
SQLCODE=-660, ODBC 3 State="HY000"
```

When you drop a local proxy table the remote table still exists.

If you want to see the columns on a remote table before you create your proxy you can execute the sp_remote_columns stored procedure as in Fig 13.6

Fig 13.6

```
/**********************************************************
*Syntaxt is:-
*sp_remote_columns <remote server>,<remote table>
* -- optionally ,<remote table owner>, <remote database name>
*
**********************************************************/

EXEC sp_remote_columns 'REMOTEIQ','sales_figures','owner'
```

This will return a resultset of all columns including there datatypes, widths, scales and if they are nullable for the table provided.

Create a proxy table on a remote database to point to a table on your IQ database

To create a table on a remote server the external login you have set up must have create table privileges on the remote server. Once this is confirmed you can create the table on the remote server using code like the example in Fig 13.7

Fig 13.7

```
CREATE TABLE accounts
(
account_number        INTEGER          NOT NULL,
account_name     VARCHAR(255) NULL
)
AT 'REMOTEIQ..sales.test1'
```

The code in Fig 13.7 has the effect of creating a local table called accounts and a proxy table on the server REMOTEIQ called test1 and owner by the sales user. The sales user on the remote database can now use your table. When you drop a table created with this syntax then both the local table and the remote proxy table are dropped!! For a definition of the AT clause see the previous section.

Remote Procedures

If you are a Java programmer you may have used RMI for invoking remote methods, or if you are from an ASE background you may have used rpc's across databases in a server. The concept of a remote procedure call in IQ is very similar. You can create a procedure thats only function is to call a procedure on a remote server and return the results from that remote procedure (i.e. operate as if the remote procedure was running locally. Fig 13.8 gives an example where we execute the sp_iqcontext procedure on our remote server REMOTEIQ as our local procedure called remotecontext

Fig 13.8

```
CREATE PROCEDURE
AT 'REMOTEIQ
```

So we can execute the procedure as in Fig 13.8 and it will send the procedure call over to REMOTEIQ and return the results back to our session.

This example is ok if all we want is return a result from a procedure, but what if we also want to pass parameters in. To do this we can declare them as we would normally. For example if I create the procedure in Fig 13.9 on our remote server REMOTEIQ as the user sales.

Fig 13.9

```
CREATE PROCEDURE get_column_names(@table_name VARCHAR(200) = NULL
AS
BEGIN
        SELECT cname
        FROM   sys.syscolumns
        WHERE  tname = @table_name
END
```

We can now create a local procedure on our IQ database that performs an RPC to the remote procedure as in Fig 13.10.

Fig 13.10

```
CREATE PROCEDURE get_remote_columns ( @table_name CHAR(200))
AT 'REMOTEIQ..sales.get_column_names'
```

We can now get_remote_columns the procedure as in Fig 13.11(get_coumn_names to get the results from the remote procedure get_column_names.

Fig 13.11

```
EXEC get_remote_columns @table_name = 'SYSUSER'
```

You may have noticed in our local declaration of get_remote_columns the variable @table_name is declared as a CHAR not a VARCHAR, this is because a VARCHAR is not in supported datatypes for RPC calls. A list of supported datatypes for RPC is given below in Fig 13.12.

Fig 13.12

Datatype	In/Out Parameters
BIGINT (INCLUDING **UNSIGNED**)	Both
BIT	Both
CHAR	Both
DECIMAL	IN Only (not INOUT or OUT)
DOUBLE	Both
INT (INCLUDING UNSIGNED)	Both
NUMERIC	IN Only (not INOUT or OUT)
REAL	Both
SMALLINT (INCLUDING UNSIGNED)	Both
TINYINT	Both

Send native statements to remote servers

The FORWAR TO statement can be used to run a batch of statements into a remote server via your local IQ database. It does this by placing the ASA catalog database into pass-through mode where commands are sent to the remote server instead of executed locally.
The example in Fig 13.13 forwards three **SELECT** statements to the server REMOTEIQ from the local IQ database.

Fig 13.13

```
FORWARD TO REMOTEIQ
    SELECT * FROM sales
    SELECT * FROM accounts
    SELECT * FROM products
FORWARD TO
```

You use the FORWARD TO without a server name to stop all the redirection, alternatively another syntax you can use is to place the commands in braces as in Fig 13.14

Fig 13.14

```
FORWARD TO REMOTEIQ
{
        SELECT @@SERVERNAME
        SELECT @@VERSION
}
```

As the FORWARD TO statement operates in a very basic way for connectivity executing code as in Fig 13.14 can prove useful when testing if a remote server is available for requests. When a connection cannot be made then an error is returned.

Remote transaction management overview

There are some things you need to be aware of with regards to using transactions with remote objects. Remote objects are accessed using a 2 phase commit protocol, and in most scenarios this will work. But if you use more than a single remote server within a transaction then IQ can become confused and data may not be committed correctly. SQL Anywhere prefaces work to a remote server with a BEGIN TRANSACTION notification.

The steps that are followed when remote objects are used within a transaction are, first the ASA database will issue a PREPARE TRANSACTION statement to the remote servers used in the transaction when the transaction is ready to be committed. Second if the PREPARE STATEMENT statement request fails then ALL remote servers are sent an instruction to ROLLBACK the transaction.

Things to be aware of are:-

- If the transaction has nested transactions then only the outermost transaction is processed.

- Any SAVEPOINT's will not apply to remote objects

In summary, remote objects are useful but they can be slow to retrieve data, difficult to manage/source control and are reliant on the connectivity behaving as you expect it to....my advice is to use sparingly!!

Language Connectivity

C#

There are several ways to connect to IQ, for example you could use ODBC, ADO or as in our example below OLEDB.

You can use an OLEDB connection as you would to any other database; the example in Fig 13.15 opens a connection to the database called MY_IQDB.

Fig 13.15

```
String CONN_STRING="Provider=SAOLEDB;ENG= MY_IQDB;DBN= MY_IQDB;Integrated
Security=false;LINKS=tcpip(host=mydbhostmachine;port=2643)"

OleDbConnection conn = null;
bool bSuccessfulConnection = false;

try
{
        // Make connection.
        conn = new OleDbConnection(CONN_STRING);
        conn.Open();
}
catch (Exception e)
{
        System.out.println("Connection Failed");
}
```

DBISQL

Dbisql is a Sybase provided client that has both Java and Classic Versions. I would always suggest using the Java version as it has more functionality (such as multiple resultsets) and allows you more configuration options.

Depending on the version of Sybase IQ you are using will depend on the client you should use, below is a list from 12.5 upwards

Sybase IQ Version	dbisql Version
12.5	7.0.4
12.6	9.0.1
12.7	9.0.2
15.1	11.0.1

Dbisql can be used in both GUI and NOGUI (Command Line) modes and is available on Windows, Linux and Unix operating Systems. An example of its use is given below (This will work on all OS versions).

Fig 13.16

```
dbisql -nogui -onerror exit -c "UID=DBA;PWD=sql;DBN:MY_IQ_DB"
-host myhostmachine -port 2643 "select @@VERSION"
```

Dbisql is a useful tool for replacing isql in dos batch files, Unix scripts and even called from other languages such as perl.

For example if you had a Unix script that you wanted to use to create a file from the results you could simple redirect the output to the file as in Fig 13.17

Fig 13.17

```
dbisql -nogui -onerror exit -c "UID=DBA;PWD=sql;DBN:MY_IQ_DB"
-host myhostmachine -port 2643 "select * from sysobjects" >
myfile.txt
```

Apart from being able to pass in SQL Options for out put (see the Loading and Extracting Data chapter), dbisql also has several command line switches/options you can use to control login and behaviour, these are given below:-

dbisql option	dbisql option description
-c "key-word=value;keyword=value; etc...."	The -c options is used to declare a list of connection parameters contained in double quotes. Appendix III gives a list of the connection parameters you may use with ASA (And thus IQ).
-codepage <codepage number>	This is used to specify the codepage that is used when reading or writing files. The default is the codepage for your platform. A list of codepages is given in Appendix IV.

–d <delimiter> or "<delimiter>	This is used to specify a command delimiter. You may optionally put quotes around the delimiter you are specifying
–d1	This is a switch that will echo all statements to the command window.
–datasource <dsn name>	This is used to specify an ODBC datasource.
–f <filename> or <file location/filename>	This is used to specify a file that is opened (not run). You may optionally put the filename/location in quotes. If the file does not exist then dbisql returns an error. If no location is given then the file is assumed to be relative to the directory executing dbisql
–host <hostname> or <host ip address>	This is used to specify the host of the database server.
–JConnect	This is a switch used to specify that you wish to connect using the JDBC JConnect Driver.
–nogui	This switch is used at the command line to say you that dbisql should be run without a windowed client. When this is specified then you can capture the status of dbisql, it will return one of the following status's. 0: Success 1: General Failure 5: The user terminated the dbisql session. 255: Bad command or option supplied to dbisql.
–ODBC	This is used to specify that the connection should be made using the Ianywhere JDBC driver. This is the default connection method.
–onerror CONTINUE or STOP or PROMPT or CONTINUE or EXIT or NOTIFY_CONTINUE or NOTIFY_STOP or NOTIFY_EXIT	This parameter is use to specify what happens when an error is encountered, allowable values are:- **STOP**: Stops Executing statements. **PROMPT:** Prompts the user to see if the user wishes to continue. **CONTINUE:** Ignore the error and continues executing the SQL. **EXIT:** Terminate the dbisql session. **NOTIFY_CONTINUE:** The error is reported and the user is prompted to continue. **NOTIFY_STOP:** The error is reported, and the user is prompted to stop executing statements. **NOTIFY_EXITL** The error is reported and the user is prompted to terminate the dbisql session. When running a file then the STOP and EXIT values operate in the same way
–port <db server port number>	This is used to specify the port that the database server is running on (The IQ default is 2638).
–q	This is used to suppress all output messages except errors
–x	This is a switch that will check the syntax of your command but will not execute them.

You may also redirect output an error messages to separate files by numbering the out put

For example in Fig 13.18 the file declared after the "1>" will contain the results of the statement and the file declared after the "2>" will contain a log of any errors.

Fig 13.18

```
dbisql -nogui -onerror exit -c "UID=DBA;PWD=sql;DBN:MY_IQ_DB"
-host myhostmachine -port 2643 "select * from
sys.XXXsyscolumns" 1>"c:\results.txt" 2>"c:\errorlog.log"
```

There is a deliberate typo (no table called XXXsyscolumns) in the above example in Fig 13.19 so that the contents of the file "C:\errorlog.log" are:-

Fig 13.19

```
Could not execute statement.
  Table 'XXXsyscolumns' not found
  SQLCODE=-141, ODBC 3 State="42S02"
  File: "my_sql.sql" on line 1, column 1
  select cname from sys.XXXsyscolumns where tname= ''
```

DOS Batch Scripts

Create DOS Script test_iq_dos.bat

Fig 13.20

```
@echo=off
echo select cname from sys.syscolumns where tname= '%1' > c:\my_sql.sql
echo go >> script.sql

set ResultsFile="c:\results.txt"
set ErrorLog="c:\sqllog.log"

"C:\SybaseClientTools\dbisql" -nogui -onerror exit -c
"UID=DBA;PWD=sql;DBN:MY_TESTDB" -host myhostmachine -port 2643
"h:\my_sql.sql" 1> %ResultsFile% 2> %ErrorLog%


del c:\my_sql.sql
```

Run the file

Fig 13.21

```
test_iq_dos.bat SYSUSER
```

You will get the results below:-

Fig 13.22

```
cname
-----------------------------------------------------
user_id
object_id
user_name
password
login_policy_id
expire_password_on_login
password_creation_time
failed_login_attempts
last_login_time
```

The error file "c:\sqllog.log" is empty as the command ran successfully.

Java

Java Overview

Java works really well with IQ. The first thing you will need to do is download JConnect from the Sybase website as this contains the **JAR** files you will require to connect to IQ.
I have used several versions of JConnect and the JConn<n>.jar file used for connectivity, the <n> refers to the JConn number. Below is a table of JConnect versions, JConn<n>.jar files and Sybase IQ versions I have run tests on. This is not to say that other combinations of IQ will not work with different JConn files but these are the ones I have tested.

JConnect Version	JConn JAR File	Sybase IQ Versions
5.x	JConn2.jar	Sybase IQ 12.4
6.x	Jconn3.jar	Sybase IQ 12.5,12.6,12.7,15.1 and 15.2
7.x	JConn4.jar	Unable to download at the time of writing but it should work with Sybase IQ 15.x

For differences in the JCONNECT releases you should refer to the Sybase website. I normally try to use the latest version as upgrading at a later stage can prove a pain.

Java Basic Connectivity Test

Once we have JConnect downloaded and extracted to a directory, find and locate the JConn<n>.jar file. Our examples below use JCONNECT 6 which contains the **JAR** file Jconn3.jar which you may move to any directory you can access from your programs command line. The examples below are running on a windows environment.

Step 1
We set the classpath variable to point to the location of the Jconn3.jar file.

Fig 13.23

```
set classpath=.;c:\jconn3.jar
```

Step 2
In your class ensure that you import the Sybase code/drivers.

Fig 13.24

```
import com.sybase.jdbcx.*;
```

Step 3
In your class ensure that you use the Class.forName functionality to load the driver before you use it.

Fig 13.25

```
try{
        Class.forName("com.sybase.jdbc3.jdbc.SybDriver");
}
catch (ClassNotFoundException e){
        System.err.println("Error loading the Sybase Driver " + e.getMessage() );
}
```

Now we can look at an example as in Fig 13.26.

Fig 13.26

```java
import java.io.*;
import java.sql.*;
import com.sybase.jdbcx.*;

public class testIQProg{

        public static void main(String args[]){
            Connection iqConn = getConnection();
            String iqProductName = getDBProduct( iqConn );
            System.out.println("Database Product Is: " + iqProductName );
        }

        private static Connection getConnection(){
            // Load the Sybase JDBC Driver
            try{
                Class.forName("com.sybase.jdbc3.jdbc.SybDriver");
            }
            catch (ClassNotFoundException e){
                System.err.println("Error loading Driver" + e.getMessage() );
            }

            //set the connection variables
            String host = "mylocalmachine";
            int port =2643;
            String userName = "DBA";
            String password = "sql";
            String sybaseIQURL = "jdbc:sybase:Tds:" + host + ":" + port;
            Connection localConnection = null;

            try{
                localConnection =
                  DriverManager.getConnection(sybaseIQURL, userName, password);
            }
            catch (SQLException e) {
                System.err.println("Error obtaining conn " + e.getMessage() );
                }

             return localConnection;

        }

        private static String getDBProduct(Connection localConn){

            try{
                DatabaseMetaData dbmd = localConn.getMetaData();
                String dbProduct =  dbmd.getDatabaseProductName();
                return dbProduct;
            }
            catch (SQLException e){
                return "NO PRODUCT FOUND";
            }
        }
}
```

We can now compile and execute our Java program

Fig 13.27

```
--Compile the Program
C:\ Javac testIQProg.java

--Execute the Program
C:\ Java testIQProg

--The programs output
 "Database Product Is: Sybase IQ"
```

Java Basic ResultSet

So we now have an example that shows how to connect to a Sybase IQ database and execute a basic connectivity test.
Now we can look at obtaining resultsets, to do this we use the Java resultset object as we would with any other database. An example is given in Fig 13.28

Fig 13.28

```java
import java.io.*;
import java.sql.*;
import com.sybase.jdbcx.*;

public class testIQProg{

        public static void main(String args[])      {
            Connection iqConn = getConnection();
            printResults( iqConn  );
        }

        private static Connection getConnection(){

                // Load the Sybase JDBC Driver
                try{
                    Class.forName("com.sybase.jdbc3.jdbc.SybDriver");
                }
                catch (ClassNotFoundException e) {
                    System.err.println("Error loading Driver "+e.getMessage());
                }

                String host = "mylocalhost";
                int port = 2643;
                String userName = "DBA";
                String password = "sql";
                String sybaseIQURL = "jdbc:sybase:Tds:" + host + ":" + port;
                Connection localConnection = null;

                try{
                localConnection =
                  DriverManager.getConnection(sybaseIQURL, userName, password);
                }
                catch (SQLException e){
                    System.err.println("Error obtaining conn "+e.getMessage());

                }

                return localConnection;
          }

        private static void printResults (Connection myconn){

                try{
                    Statement stmt = myconn.createStatement();
                    ResultSet rs =
                        stmt.executeQuery("Select top 5 name from sysobjects");

                    while (rs.next()){
                        String value = rs.getString(1);
                        System.out.println("Value:=" + value);
                    }

                    rs.close();
                    stmt.close();
                }
                catch (SQLException e){
                    System.out.println("SQl Exception : " +  e.getMessage());
                }

        }

}
```

Fig 13.29

```
--Compile the Program
C:\ javac testIQProg.java

--Execute the Program
C:\ java testIQProg

--The programs output
Value:=ISYSTAB
Value:=ISYSTABCOL
Value:=ISYSOBJECT
Value:=ISYSIDX
Value:=ISYSPHYSIDX
```

IsqlApp

When you extract the JConnect files you will also obtain some useful pre-built classes you can use.
One such class is called IsqlApp.class.
In order to use this just place it in your CLASSPATH and run it with java as in Fig 13.30

Fig 13.30

```
java IsqlApp -U DBA -P SQL -S jdbc:sybase:Tds:mydbhost:2643 -c go
```

You will then be presented with a command prompt where you can run your sql. This operates just like
isql as in Fig 13.31

Fig 13.31

```
Enter a query:
1 > select top 5 cname from sys.syscolumns
2 > go

----------------- Result set 1 ----------------------

Columns:          cname
[ 1]     table_id
[ 2]     Dbspace_id
[ 3]     count
[ 4]     creator
[ 5]     table_page_count
```

You can pass switches to the IsqlApp Class as listed below:-

IsqlApp Switch	IsqlApp Switch Description
-U <user>	The user Id to connect with
-P <password>	The password to connect with
-S <server>	The name of the server to connect with (this is the jdbc server. "jdbc:Sybase:Tds:<servername>:<port number>"
-G <gateway>	This is used to specify the gateway address, for HTTP protocol, the URL is: given

	in the format of "http://<host>:<port>", but for HTTPS the URL is in the format "https://<host>:<port>/<servlet alias>
-p	Specifies whether you want to use the HTTP protocol or the HTTPS protocol that supports encryption.
-D <ALL or Class List>	This is used to switch on debugging, you may specify the word ALL to debug all classes or a class list e.g. **-D** ALL of **-D** class2, class1
-v	This is used to switch on verbose output for display or printing.
-I <input file>	You may use this switch to specify a file that contains the SQL you wish to run rather than use the command line. The file must contain terminators between statements, the default terminator is "go" but you can override this with the –c switch.
-c <terminator>	This switch is used to specify a keyword that will be used to terminate commands. The default is a newline; I suggest using the work "go" to operate like regular isql.
-C <character set>	This is used to specify the character set for strings that are passed through the Tds connection. The default is the database server's character set.
-L <language>	This is used to specify the language in which to display JConnect and server error messages.
-K <principal name>	This is used to pass in the principal name that you wish to use for a Kerberos login. The example below is used to indicate that you wish to use a Kerberos login with a principal name mySalesuser. **-K** mySalesUser
-F <JASS cfg file path>	This is used to specify a file and path of a JASS config file; you must set this when also using the –K switch.
-T <session id>	This switch is used to inform JConnect that you wish to resume a connection on an existing TDS session in the TDS tunnelling gateway. The session id provided will be used for the connection and login parameters are ignored. wards all
-V <JConnect Version>	You may use this switch to specify the version of JConnect you wish your connection to use.

Perl

The first thing you need to do is to download and install a database connectivity package from CPAN. For my example below I am using the DBD ODBC package but you can use DBLib, CTLib,DBD:Sybase or many others. You can use the package in your code by using the USE statement as in Fig 13.32

Fig 13.32

```
use DBD::ODBC;
```

We can use the functionality within the ODBC package Create a new perl module called Sybclass.pm which we can use to connect to the database and execute some SQL. The example for this is given in Fig 13.33.

Fig 13.33

```perl
package SybClass;
use DBD::ODBC;

sub new{
  my $reference = shift;
  my $class = ref($reference) || $reference;
  my $self ={};
  $self->{_dbh} =undef;
  $self->{_sth} =undef;
  $self->{_driver} = 'dbi:ODBC:Adaptive Server IQ Demo';
  $self->{_user} = 'DBA';
  $self->{_password} = 'SQL';
  bless $self, $class;
  return $self;
}

sub dbConnect{
  $self = shift;
  $dbh = DBI->connect($self->{_driver},$self->{user}, $self->{password});
  $self->{_dbh} = $dbh;
}

sub runSQL{
        $self = shift;
        $sql =  $_[0];
        $sth = $self->{_dbh}->prepare($sql);
        $sth->execute();
        $self->{_sth} = $sth;
}

sub printResults{
  $self = shift;
  $sth = $self->{_sth};
  print join (",", @{$sth->{NAME}} ) . "\n";

        do {
                my @row;

                while (@row = $sth->fetchrow_array) {
                        print join (",", @row). "\n"
                }
        } while ($sth->{odbc_more_results});
}
1;
```

We can now create a perl program to call the perl class that uses our SybClass to output the results of the passed SQL to standard out.

Fig 13.34

```perl
use SybClass;

my $syb = SybClass->new();

$syb->dbConnect();
$syb->runSQL("select * from sys.syscolumns");
$syb->printResults();
```

Unix/Linux

It doesn't matter which scripting language you are using. I would suggest building generic database connectivity and utility function that you can use to retrieve results, parse error messages, obtain login credentials etc.

By doing this you only need to change one piece of code for your scripts instead of many.
In the example in Fig 13.35 I have again (like the dos example) used the dbisql utility on Unix to handle my requests. The function in Fig 13.35 is in a file called dbisql_utlity.ksh

Fig 13.35

```ksh
function execute_sql
{
        # SET INPUT PARAMTERS
        USER_ID=$1
        USER_PWD=$2
        DATABASE=$3
        HOST=$4
        PORT=$5
        SQL_COMMANDS=$6
        MESSAGE_FILE=$7
        ERROR_FILE=$7

        # EXECUTE DBISQL
        dbisql -nogui -onerror exit -c
"UID=${USER_ID};PWD=${USER_PWD};DBN:${DATABASE}" -host ${HOST} -port ${PORT}
${SQL_COMMANDS} 2> ${MESSAGE_FILE} 1> ${ERROR_FILE}

        #CHECK OUTPUT
        dbisql_status=$?

        if [ $dbisql_status -ne 0 ]
        then
            echo "Error running SQL in $0"
            cat ${SQL_COMMAND_FILE}
            cat ${ERROR_FILE}
        fi

        return $dbisql_status
}
```

To use out function we can call it from other scripts as in Fig 13.36

Fig 13.36

```
#!/bin/ksh

# impot the function for use
. $HOME/scripts/dbisql_utlity.ksh

#execute the function
exec_sql DBA SQL MY_DB myhostmachine 2643 "EXEC sp_iqstatus"
"/home/logs/sql_message.log" "/home/logs/sql_error.log"
```

Application/3rd Party Tools

Below is a list of applications I have tested with Sybase IQ.

Business Objects and Crystal Reports

At the time of writing SAP AG has just purchased Sybase Inc and therefore I see a greater convergence of these produce in the future. That said they work fine now. You can connection from Crystal reports using ODBC and from Business Objects creating a connection based on the generic ODBC driver or the ASIQ driver. IQ is fully compliant with the Business Objects ANSI SQL implementation so feel free to use this option if you wish.

Embarcadero Rapid SQL and DB Artisan

You cannot use DBArtisan with Sybase IQ as DBArtisan attempts to use some system details when connecting to Sybase database that do not exist on IQ. You also cannot use RapidSQl using the native Embarcadero connection methods. You can however use ODBC to connect via Rapid SQL.

WebLogic

All you need to do to build you Sybase IQ connection pools is unsure that the JConn<n>.jar file from the Sybase JConnect package is included in your class path. You can then set up the connection string, user name and password and thus use weblogic to control connection pooling to Sybase IQ.

SAS

IQ will work fine with SAS, but you must remember that SAS can try to be a bit too clever for its own good. Let me explain.
If you create a SAS table and join it to an IQ table the SAS processor will bring ALL the data from the IQ table into SAS and then perform the join...yuck!!!! It is therefore best to make you SAS code pass-through queries to the IQ server and not to join large tables or view with SAS tables.

Tibco Business Works

Business Works can be used to connect to IQ allowing you to create processes that insert, delete, update and transform Tibco messages and update that message into IQ.

Tips and Tricks

This chapter is here to help you find solutions for problems, questions and issues that you WILL encounter when using Sybase IQ.

For example you may wonder how you can get an objects creation date as it's not in the sysobjects view. Or you may wonder why when you run a **SELECT** statement you get a set of values but the miraculously change when you insert them into a table.

As such I have tried to cover several issues I have encountered and the simple solution to them. Some of this information is covered in more detail in other sections but hopefully this chapter gives you a first point of call.

How do I get an objects creation date/time?

As Sybase seem to have forgotten to populate the crdate column in the sysobjects view, you can instead use the SQL in Fig 14.1 to get this information.

Fig 14.1

```
SELECT a.*, b.*
FROM    sys.sysobject a,
        sysobjects b
WHERE a.object_id = b.id
AND b.name = 'my_object'
```

Why when I select some values do I not get the same result if I insert data into a table?

Datatypes, datatypes and datatypes (did I forget to mention datatypes????). The main cause of this issue is the use of the float datatype

For example we can see from Fig 14.2 that if we divided by a **FLOAT** we get a different result than when we use a precise datatype such as a numeric.

Fig 14.2

```
DECLARE @myfloat       FLOAT
DECLARE @mynumeric1    NUMERIC (38,20)
DECLARE @mynumeric2    NUMERIC (22,2)

SELECT   @myfloat      = 1.1,
         @mynumeric1   = 1.1,
         @mynumeric2   = 1.1

SELECT  @mynumeric2 / @myfloat  AS result_with_float,
    @mynumeric2 / @mynumeric1 AS result_with_numeric,
    convert(NUMERIC(38,25),@mynumeric2) / convert(NUMERIC(38,25),@myfloat) AS
        result_with_float_2,
    convert(NUMERIC(38,25),@mynumeric2) / convert(NUMERIC(38,25),@mynumeric1) AS
        result_with_numeric_2
```

The results produced from Fig 14.2 are:-

Result with float	Result with numeric	result_with_float_2	Result with numeric_2
0.9999999783255843	1	0.99999997832558228796221151993206150126 6	1

As you can see the results are different, the examples using the **FLOAT**'s are wrong (As a number divided by itself should always be 1). As such you should always try to use the correct precision and scale when defining your datatypes to ensure consistent and correct results. Also when calculations are performed the precision of the result is directly correlated to the datatypes used as we can see in the example above where we explicitly convert the values to a high precision/scale before we calculate the result.

Why when I use the TOP statement with a variable to select into a temp table is the table empty?

This is another cross store issue. For example the code in Fig 14.3 below will work because it is selecting from a table in the catalog store.

Fig 14.3

```
DECLARE          @inte int
SELECT  @inte = 10

SELECT top @inte *
INTO    #my_temp
FROM sysobjects
```

However if you try this from a table in the IQ store as in Fig 14.4 the resulting temp table will be empty (but no error is raised).

Fig 14.4

```
DECLARE          @inte int
SELECT           @inte = 10

SELECT top @inte *
INTO    #my_temp
FROM my_table
```

The way round this is to send the command via a dynamic SQL statement as in Fig 14.5, in fact this often resolves other problems as well.

Fig 14.5

```
DECLARE          @inte int
SELECT  @inte = 10

EXECUTE ('SELECT TOP ' + convert(varchar(10),@inte) + ' * into
#trev_temp from trev_test')
```

I have set an option but it doesn't appear to have worked, why?

Option values can be set with the wrong case, but in some circumstances they should be in the recommended case. For example setting a value to 'On' may not work but setting it to 'ON' or 'on' may work. It is worth checking the chapter on options and also referring to Sybase IQ and ASA documentation to get the correct case. You can also check the sysoptiondefaults table to see the default values case and mimic it!!

How do I get the rowcount from a result-set produced by a stored procedure?

The value of @@rowcount in Fig 14.6 will be zero as the last command executed is the actual execution (exec) not the final select of the sub procedure.

Fig 14.6

```
EXEC sp_iqstatus()
SELECT  @@rowcount
```

To get round this create another local variable and assign it to the count value of the output of the procedure as in Fig 14.7

Fig 14.7

```
DECLARE @proc_rowcount int
SELECT @proc_rowcount = count(*) FROM sp_iqstatus()
SELECT @proc_rowcount
```

The value of **@proc_rowcount** is the actual number of rows returned in the result-set from the **sp_iqstatus** procedure. One thing to bear in mind is that IQ will first have to run the procedure and then it will perform the count so this can be slow. When running procedures in **SELECT** statements the results are processed in the catalog store so you need to ensure that your catalog store has enough space allocated to its temporary file area to handle the result set.
Another workaround is if the procedure is a user one you can simply declare an output variable and set the value of from **@@rowcount** in the procedure.

How can I strip a time from a TIME?

Sometimes you may want to strip the time value from a date, this often occurs in banking applications where you may want to strip a Trade Date from a Trade Date/Time field. To do this simply convert your DATETIME value to a DATE as in Fig 14.8

Fig 14.8

```
SELECT CONVERT(DATE,GETDATE())      AS The_DATE,
       GETDATE()                    AS The_DATETIME
```

This will yield the results in Fig 14.9

Fig 14.9

The_DATE	The_DATETIME

2010-01-26	2010-01-26 10:42:38.074

This is very useful when different developers have implemented DATES in different ways.

Why has my variable that was passed to a stored procedure has changed?

In Sybase IQ there is no concept of an out variable, all out variables are actual in out. The example below demonstrates how this works.

First we create a procedure with an in/out variable

Fig 14.10

```
CREATE PROCEDURE test2 ( @myvar_2 VARCHAR(9) OUT)
AS
BEGIN

        SELECT @myvar_2 = @myvar_2 + 'A'

END
```

Now execute the procedure and output the result

Fig 14.11

```
DECLARE @my_1  VARCHAR(9)
SELECT @my_1 = '12345678'
EXEC    test2 @myvar_2 = @my_1
SELECT  @my_1
```

The output of the variable @my_1 at the end is given in Fig 14.12

Fig 14.12

12345678A

How can I clear the cache to get consistent timings for my procedures and SQL scripts?

Execute the system procedure sa_flush_cache before every execution of your code. This will clear the cache and you should then get consistent timings.

How can I see which tables are locked in IQ and the catalog/system store?

For the tables that are locked (including shared read locks) in IQ execute the system procedure sp_iqlocks to see the locks in the AS/catalog store use the system procedure sa_locks.

How can I increment an IDENTITY column by more than one on each insert?

This is an example where we can use a trigger, although Sybase say they aren't available in IQ, they are and here is an example on how to use one. One thing to note though is that triggers are not fired on bulk operations like **LOAD TABLE**.

First let's create a test table and trigger.

Fig 14.13

```
CREATE TABLE test
(
        col1    NUMERIC(20,0)   IDENTITY,
        col2    VARCHAR(20)     NULL
)
GO

CREATE TRIGGER test_trigger ON test
FOR INSERT
AS
BEGIN
    MESSAGE 'In the Trigger' TYPE INFO TO CLIENT

    SET TEMPORARY OPTION IDENTITY_INSERT = 'test'

    UPDATE    test
    SET col1 = (SELECT MAX(col1) +1  FROM   test)
    WHERE col1 = (SELECT MAX (col1)    FROM test)

    SET TEMPORARY OPTION IDENTITY_INSERT = ''

END
```

And now we can run a test

Fig 14.14

```
INSERT test(col2)
SELECT 'testing'

SELECT *
FROM    test
```

The results of Fig 14.14 are:-

col1	col2
2	testing

How can I obtain a query plan locally?

A simple way to get a local query plan is to use the **HTML_PLAN** function, however be aware that this will only work on simple statements (not Stored Procedures etc). The example in Fig 14.15 creates a query plan called c:\hplan.html with the query plan from the supplied **SELECT** statement.

Fig 14.15

```
SET TEMPORARY OPTION QUERY_PLAN_TEXT_ACCESS = ON;

SELECT HTML_PLAN ('SELECT TOP 10 * FROM sales WHERE sales_id =10');
OUTPUT TO 'c:\hplan.html' HEXADECIMAL ASIS QUOTE '';
```

How can I pad out a fixed width string to be right aligned?

Sometimes you need to create a fixed width field containing a numeric, to right align this you can use code as in Fig 14.16

Fig 14.16

```
DECLARE @number NUMERIC(20,2)

SELECT @number = 199.22

SELECT CONVERT(VARCHAR(20), REPEAT(' ',20 -(CHAR_LENGTH(CONVERT(VARCHAR
(20),@number)) ))) +
CONVERT(VARCHAR(20),@number) as done_deal
```

How can I obtain some DBA functionality without having DBA authority

There is some functionality in IQ that can only be performed by a user with DBA authority for example changing another user's password.

To leverage off DBA only functionality create a procedure as the user with DBA authority and **GRANT** other permission to execute it. The procedure will execute as if the user has DBA authority.
The example in Fig 14.17 allows a non DBA user to change another user's password

Fig 14.17

```
CREATE PROCEDURE DBA.change_a_password
(   @userid     VARCHAR(30) = NULL,
    @new_pw     VARCHAR(30) = NULL
 )
AS
BEGIN

DECLARE @SQL_ALTER VARCHAR(255)
SELECT @SQL_ALTER = 'ALTER USER' + @userid + ' IDENTIFIED BY  ' + @new_pw
EXECUTE (@SQL_ALTER)

END
GO

GRANT EXECUTE ON DBA.change_a_password TO another_user
```

My server crashed, any ideas?

It could be the ASA Temporary Space!

ASA temporary space is held in a file that will grow as the database requires more temporary processing space. This ASA temporary space may cause the server to run into performance issues and even crash if it is not large enough to handle the queries being passed through the catalog database.

The default location of the ASA temporary file is set from the environment variable ASTMP. If this variable is not set on Windows then the server traverses the environment variables TMP, TMPDIR and finally TEMP until it finds a location t can use to store the temporary file. On Unix if the variable is not set then the /tmp directory is used and
creates the temporary file/files in the location below:-

/tmp/.SQLAnywhere/<database name> /tmp

Situations can occur when the database appears to be frozen (allowing no logins or activity) or reports an error indicating that all available temporary space has been used. Before you recycle your IQ server check the size of this file and the space available for it to grow (**df -k** on Unix). You may find that the ASA temporary file is the cause of your server crash. To stop this happening either changes the **ASTMP** environment variable to a location with more space or add more space to the existing location.

It is also worth noting that any files used for shared memory access form part of the ASA temporary files on Unix/Linux.

It could be the ASA database size

Like the ASA temporary space the main ASA/Catalog store can only grow and it never shrinks back no matter how much data you delete. As such when you create your database the directory that contains your .db file must be large enough to enable growth. It is worth creating a monitoring script to keep an eye on this space to ensure you always have enough available. You should also consider migrating any data you have in the catalog store into the main IQ store on a periodic basis.

It could be CIS/ Remote services

All remote connections and CIS services go through the ASA catalog store. I have witnessed occasions where a simple **SELECT** statement is used to bring down an entire server. You should never allow users to select or manipulate data on remote tables directly and if possible use replication server to bring your data into IQ as remote table have a large processing overhead.

I am selecting data but cannot see any results (I know the table is populated)?

Check that you have not left any of the **TEMP_EXTRACT** options set, your **SELECT** statement could be having the results re-directed to a file (Although the columns will still be displayed on your client).

How do I relocate data from one DB space to another?

The answer to this depends on your version of IQ.

For IQ12.x you should use the following steps:-

* Step 1: You need to execute an "**ALTER DBSPACE** <logical DBSpaces name> **RELOCATE**" command to let IQ know you wish to relocate the data.

* Step 2: You can execute the "sp_iqrelocate 'database'" system procedure, using the 'database ' option will have the effect of relocating all data from DBSpaces marked as **RELOCATE** to DBSpaces that are in **READWRITE** mode. This procedure will output a report on the blocks that have been relocated.

* Execute a **COMMIT** statement as sp_iqrelocate does not automatically commit changes.

For IQ 15.x you should do the following

* Step 1: You need to execute an "**ALTER DBSPACE** <logical DBSpace name> **READONLY**" this will put the DBSpaces into read-only mode and stop any writes going there

* Step 2: You need to execute a "**sp_iqemptyfile** '<DBSpace name>", this will have the effect of moving the data to the available read-write spaces on the database. (Note that this can only be run on the co-ordinator in multiplex systems). If there is not a read-write space available then this procedure will return an error.

My code used to execute, now it gives an error about a missing column?

The order of a **WHERE** clause depends on the parallelism used by the query processor.
For example if we had a query as in Fig 14.18

Fig 14.18

```
SELECT 1
FROM table_1
WHERE col1 = 10
AND col2 = 100
```

If the query processor uses parallelism then both columns (col1 and col2) in the **WHERE** clause will have there SARGs checked. However if the query processor runs in a singular mode then and the first condition (col1= 10) is NOT met then it will not check col2.
This means that if col2 does not exist on the table table_1 then it is possible for the SQL to still execute as col2 is never checked. However as soon as the query executes in parallel then it tries to check the SARG (col2 = 100) and fails with an error because col2 does not exist.

Parallelism of queries are determined by server and database options so it is worth remembering this when you get errors after changing any options (By default 15.2 has parallelism options set that IQ 15.1 does not so this can also cause the problem).

I am getting an error saying a table is locked, but no other users are on the system and sp_iqlocks returns nothing?

One thing to bear in mind is that a procedure can LOCK a table from itself!!
This can be done when executing code as in Fig 14.19

Fig 14.19

```
DECLARE @sql_statement VARCHAR(100)

UPDATE table_1
SET col1 = 1

SET @sql_statement = 'INSERT table_2 LOCATION 'MYSERVER.MYSERVER' {SELECT
col1 FROM table_1'}

EXECUTE (@sql_statement)
```

The problem occurs because there is not a **COMMIT** after the **UPDATE** statement and the **EXECUTE** as spawned in another thread meaning that the table is still locked by the main thread calling the code. To ensure this does not happen insert a **COMMIT** statement before the **EXECUTE**. This issue can also occur when calling sub procedures so it is worth putting **COMMIT** statements in your code frequently. Unfortunately this issue is not consistent and depends on the parallelism used by the query processor. As such I recommend always using **COMMIT**s.

I am getting an error SAYING Large Objects Management is not licensed?

This could be because of a Sybase bug. It appears that some functions when used to select data into a temp table do not work as expected. This is due to system functions returning large datatypes where they are not required.

For example one such error occurs in the **USER_NAME** function. Fig 14.20 works fine but Fig 14.21 returns an error "Large Objects Management is not licensed"

Fig 14.20

```
SELECT name,
       USER_NAME() AS user_name
FROM   sysobjects
```

Fig 14.21

```
SELECT name,
       USER_NAME() AS user_name
INTO   #test
FROM   sysobjects
```

As a workaround we can substring the user_name function to the first 32,000 characters (a user name "should" never be 32,000 characters and who ever programmed this function really should have looked at there data types)

Fig 14.21

```
SELECT name,
       SUBSTRING (USER_NAME(),1,32000) AS user_name
INTO   #test
FROM   sysobjects
```

System Tables and Views

This section could just be called system views as from a user point of view all you will use are views built on top of the system tables (except for the DUMMY table). System tables are stored in the ASA catalog store and are row locked. They are used to hold meta-data about the database and to hold user information and messages used. Users cannot perform deletes, inserts, updates or any DDL operations on system tables.

There are two main types of ways user obtain system table data, there are System Table Views which are views built directly onto the underlying system tables and consolidated vies which are used to provide a view that is more often required by users. Consolidated views provide joins across tables to provide more useful information. The consolidated view may for example display a user name in a column where the system view would display the user id. So consolidated views will give you useful names instead of id numbers.

The DUMMY system table

The DUMMY table is provided as a table that always has exactly one row. This can be useful for extracting information from the database, as in Fig 15.1 example that gets the current user ID and the current date from the database. This is also the only system table that you have direct access to and not just a view.

Fig 15.1

```
SELECT USER, today(*) FROM SYS.DUMMY
```

The create statement for the DUMMY table is given in Fig 15.2

Fig 15.2

```
CREATE TABLE SYS.DUMMY
(
        dummy_col INT NOT NULL
)
```

For Oracle users you can think of the DUMMY table as akin to the use of DUAL.
The use of the **DUMMY** system table is implied for any queries that do not have a **FROM** clause.

These queries are run by the ASA catalog database, rather than by Sybase IQ. You can create a dummy table in the Sybase IQ database, as in Fig 15.3.

Fig15.3

```
CREATE TABLE iq_dummy
(
        dummy_col INT NOT NULL
)
```

You can now use this table explicitly as in Fig 15.4

Fig 15.4

```
SELECT GETDATE() FROM iq_dummy
```

The reason for doing this is if you execute a piece of code that has no table (selecting constants) it will sometimes run through the ASA database. When you then **UNION** this with code from an IQ table then the system moves all the IQ data into the ASA database to process. In short, try to use a dummy table of some kind when selecting out constants.

SYSTEM TABLE DIRECT VIEWS

Below is a list of system table views, these are views on underlying system tables and unlike the compatibility views are not in a user friendly structure.

IQ_MPX_INFO

This table has one row for each server in a multiplex installation. Sybase Central uses this table to manage the multiplex.

Column Name	Data Type	Nullable	Primary Key	Description
id	NUMERIC(8,0)	N	Y	The IQ server Id number
server_name	VARCHAR(30)	N		The IQ server name
host_name	VARCHAR(30)	N		The host the IQ server resides on
port_number	VARCHAR(40)	N		The port number of the IQ server
db_path	VARCHAR(1024)	N		The full path of the catalog store for this server.
role	CHAR(1)	N		R for a READ server and W for a write server.
node_status	VARCHAR(10)	N		Active or Inactive
remote_user	VARCHAR(40)	N		The remote user ID used by SQL Remote replication.

IQ_MPX_STATUS

This table is used to store dynamic data in relation to the management of old table versions in a multiplex environment. The data in this table changes as transactions are began or committed on multiplex servers. Each server updates its own data and SQL remote replicates the changes across the other servers in the multiplex.

Column Name	Data Type	Nullable	Primary Key	Description
server_name	VARCHAR(30)	N		The name of the server.
oldest_version	UNSIGNED BIGINT	N		The version number of the oldest active transaction on the server.
current_version	VARCHAR(10)	N		The current transactions number on the server.
catalog_version	UNSIGNED BIGINT	N		Every time the write server changes the table schema the catalog version changes to the current version. The catalog version changes the write server's version, but it remains static until the next multiplex synchronisation. You can check this value across servers to see if they are in synch!

IQ_MPX_VERSIONLIST

This table contains data about each query server in the multiplex, including inactive servers.

Column Name	Data Type	Nullable	Primary Key	Description
id	integer	N		The Server Id
active_versions	LONG VARCHAR	N		The set of Active Versions.

IQ_SYSTEM_LOGIN_INFO_TABLE

Each row in this table holds the default values for IQ Login Management. When a new user is added the default values that are used come from this table.

Column Name	Data Type	Nullable	Primary Key	Description
user_admin_enabled	CHAR(1)	N		Used to indicate if IQ Login Management is enabled.
number_connects	INT	N		Maximum number of concurrent connections the user can have, The default is 0 meaning no maximum.
number_db_connects	INT	N		The number of connections allowed to the database.
password_days	INT	N		The number in days until a password expires, 0 means no expiration.
password_warning_days	INT	N		The number of days before password expiration that IQ sends a warning to the users.

IQ_USER_LOGIN_INFO_TABLE

This table holds IQ login management values for each user in the system.

Column Name	Data Type	Nullable	Primary Key	Description
userid	VARCHAR(128)	N		The user id
login_locked	CHAR(1)	N		Y/N Flag to indicate if the user is locked out
number_connects	INT	N		Maximum number of concurrent connections for the userid.
password_created	TIMESTAMP	N		The date the users password was created
password_days	INT	N		The number of days until password expiration.

SYSARTICLE

Each row of SYSARTICLE describes an article in a SQL Remote publication.

Column Name	Data Type	Nullable	Primary Key	Description
publication_id	UNSIGNED INT	N	Y	The publication ID of which the article is part

				of.
table_id	UNSIGNED INT	N	Y	The table id which the article is associated with.
where_expr	LONG VARCHAR	Y		Any where clause associated with the article
subscribe_by_expr	LONG VARCHAR	Y		For articles that contain a subset of rows from a table defined by a **SUBSCRIBE BY**. This column contains the subscribe by expression.
query	CHAR(1)	N		Used internally to hold the article type.

SYSARTICLECOL

Each row identifies a column in an article, identifying the column, the table it is in, and the publication it is part of.

Column Name	Data Type	Nullable	Primary Key	Description
publication_id	UNSIGNED INT	N	Y	The publication ID of which the column is part of.
table_id	UNSIGNED INT	N	Y	The table id which the column belongs to.
column_id	UNSIGNED INT	N	Y	Column Id (references **SYSCOLUMN** system view)

SYSCAPABILITY

Each row in this table refers to a capability of a remote server.

Column Name	Data Type	Nullable	Primary Key	Description
capid	INT	N		The capability id
capvalue	CHAR(128)	N		The value of the capability
svrid	INT	N	Y	The server id, references the **SYSSERVERS** system view.

SYSCAPABILITYNAME

Each row on this table names a capability.

Column Name	Data Type	Nullable	Primary Key	Description
capid	INT	N	Y	Tha capability id
capname	CHAR(128)	N		The capability name

SYSCHECK

Each row refers to a check constraint on a table

Column Name	Data Type	Nullable	Primary Key	Description
check_id	UNSIGNED INTEGER	N	Y	The id of the constraint
check_defn	LONG VARCHAR	N		The **CHECK** definition.

SYSCOLLATION

This table is used internally by Sybase IQ to store the collation sequences available to it.

Column Name	Data Type	Nullable	Primary Key	Description
collation_id	SMALLINT	N	Y	The unique id for the collation sequence
collation_table	CHAR(10)	N		A string identifying the collation sequences available.
collation_name	CHAR(128)	N		The name of the sequence
collation_order	BINARY(1280)	N		An array of how each of the codes is used in comparisons. All string comparisons translate each character in the string to the collation order table when comparing characters.

SYSCOLLATIONMAPPINGS

This table contains the collation mappings available in Sybase IQ. There is no way to modify the contents of this table. For newly-created databases, this table contains only one row with the database collation mapping. For databases created with version 12.5 or earlier, this table includes collation mappings for all built-in collations.

Column Name	Data Type	Nullable	Primary Key	Description
collation_label	CHAR	N	Y	The collation sequence to be used is selected when the database is created by specifying the collation label with the COLLATION option of the **CREATE DATABASE** command.
collation_name	CHAR	N		The collation name used to describe the character set encoding.
cs_label	CHAR	Y		The GPG character set mapping label.
so_case_label	CHAR	Y		The collation sort order for case-sensitive GPG character set mapping.
so_caseless_label	CHAR	Y		The collation sort order for case-insensitive GPG character set mapping.
jdk_label	CHAR	Y		The JDK character set label.

SYSCOLPERM

The **GRANT** command can give **UPDATE** permission to individual columns in a table. Each column with **UPDATE** permission is recorded in one row of **SYSCOLPERM**.

Column Name	Data Type	Nullable	Primary Key	Description
table_id	INT	N	Y	The table number for the table containing the column.
grantee	INT	N	Y	The user number of the user ID given UPDATE permission on the column. If the grantee is the user number for the special PUBLIC user ID, the UPDATE permission is given to all user IDs.
grantor	INT	N	Y	The user number of the user ID granting the permission.
column_id	INT	N	Y	This column number, together with the *table_id*, identifies the column for which **UPDATE** permission has been granted.
priviledge_type	SMALLINT	N	Y	The number in this column indicates the kind of column permission (**REFERENCES**, **SELECT** or **UPDATE**).
is_grantable	CHAR	N		Indicates if the permission on the column was granted by the grantor to the grantee **WITH GRANT OPTION**. (Y/N).

SYSCOLUMN

This table holds data about each column of every table.

Column Name	Data Type	Nullable	Primary Key	Description
table_id	UNSIGNED INT	N	Y	The table number uniquely identifies the table or view to which this column belongs.
column_id	UNSIGNED INT	N	Y	Each table starts numbering columns at 1. The order of column numbers determines the order that columns are displayed in the command SELECT * FROM table.
pkey	CHAR	N		Indicates whether this column is part of the primary key for the table (Y/N).
domain	SMALLINT	N		Identifies the data type for the column by the data type number listed in the SYSDOMAIN table.
nulls	CHAR	N		Indicates whether the **NULL** value is allowed in this column (Y/N).

width	SMALLINT	N		This column contains the length of string columns, the precision of numeric columns, and the number of bytes of storage for all other data types.
scale	SMALLINT	N		The number of digits after the decimal point for numeric data type columns, and zero for all other data types.
estimate	INT	N		A self-tuning parameter for the optimizer. Sybase IQ "learns" from previous queries by adjusting guesses that are made by the optimizer.
max_identity	BIGINT	N		The largest value of the column, if it is an **AUTOINCREMENT**, **IDENTITY**, or **GLOBAL AUTOINCREMENT** column. Sybase IQ does not support **IDENTITY** columns.
column_name	CHAR	N		The name of the column.
remarks	LONG VARCHAR			A comment String about the column
default	LONG VARCHAR			The default value for the column. This value is only used when an **INSERT** statement does not specify a value for the column.
check	LONG VARCHAR			Any **CHECK** condition defined on the column.
user_type	SMALLINT			If the column is defined on a user-defined data type, the data type is held here.
format_str	CHAR			NOT USED
column_type	CHAR	N		The column type
remote_name	VARCHAR			The name of the remote column
remote_type	UNSIGNED INT			The type of remote column, this is defined by either the remote server or the interface.

SYSCONSTRAINT

This table holds the list of constraints by column and table.

Column Name	Data Type	Nullable	Primary Key	Description
constraint_id	INT	N	Y	The unique constraint ID
table_id	INT	N		The table ID of the table to which the constraint applies.
column_id	INT	Y		The column ID of the column to which the constraint applies. The column is **NULL** for any constraints that are not column constraints.

index_id	INT	Y		The index ID for a unique constraint. The column is **NULL** for all constraints that are not unique constraints.
fkey_id	INT	Y		The foreign key ID for a foreign-key constraint. The column is NULL for all constraints that are not foreign-key constraints.
constraint_type	CHAR	N		Set to one of the following values: • C is the constraint is a column check constraint. • T if the constraint is a table constraint. • P if the constraint is a primary key. • F if the constraint is a foreign key. • U if the constraint is a unique constraint.
constraint_name	CHAR	N		The name of the constraint.

SYSDOMAIN

Each of the predefined data types (also called domains) in Sybase IQ is assigned a unique number. The **SYSDOMAIN** table is provided for informational purposes to show the association between these numbers and the appropriate data type. This table is never changed by Sybase IQ.

Column Name	Data Type	Nullable	Primary Key	Description
domain_id	SMALLINT	N	Y	The unique number assigned to each data type. You cannot change these numbers.
domain_name	CHAR	N		A string containing the data type normally found in the **CREATE TABLE** command, such as char or integer.
type_id	SMALLINT	Y		The ODBC data type. This corresponds to "data_type" in the **TransactSQL**-compatible DBO.SYSTYPES table.
precision	SMALLINT	Y		The number of significant digits that can be stored using this data type. The column value is **NULL** for nonnumeric data types.

SYSEVENT

This table holds the list of events created in the database. Each row in **SYSEVENT** describes an event created with **CREATE EVENT**.

Column Name	Data Type	Nullable	Primary Key	Description
event_id	INT	N	Y	The unique number assigned to each event.

creator	INT	N		The user number of the owner of the event. The name of the user can be found by looking in SYSUSERPERM.
event_name	CHAR	N		The name of the event.
enabled	CHAR	N		Indicates whether or not the event is allowed to fire.
location	CHAR	N		The location where the event is allowed to fire: • C = consolidated • R = remote • A = all
event_type_id	INT	Y		For system events, the event type as listed in **SYSEVENTTYPE**.
action	CHAR	Y		The event handler definition.
external_action	CHAR	Y		Not Used
condition	CHAR	Y		The **WHERE** condition used to control firing of the event handler.
remarks	CHAR	Y		Comments about the event
source	CHAR	Y		This column contains the original source for the event handler if the **PRESERVE_SOURCE_FORMAT** option is ON. It is used to maintain the appearance of the original text

SYSEVENTTYPE

Each row in the **SYSEVENTTYPE** table describes a system event type which can be referenced by **CREATE EVENT**.

Column Name	Data Type	Nullable	Primary Key	Description
event_type_id	INT	N	Y	The unique number assigned to each event type.
name	CHAR	N		The name of the system event type.
description	CHAR	Y		The description of the system event type

SYSEXTERNLOGINS

Each row describes an external login for remote data access.

Column Name	Data Type	Nullable	Primary Key	Description
user_id	INT	N	Y	The user ID on the local database.
srvid	INT	N	Y	The remote server, as listed in SYSSERVERS.
remote_login	CHAR	Y		The login name for this user, for the remote server.

remote_password	BINARY	Y		The password for this user, for the remote server.

SYSFILE

Every database consists of one or more operating system files. Each file is recorded in **SYSFILE**.

Column Name	Data Type	Nullable	Primary Key	Description
file_id	SMALLINT	N	Y	Each file in a database is assigned a unique number. This file identifier is the primary key for **SYSFILE**. All system tables are stored in file_id 0.
file_name	CHAR	N		The database name is stored when a database is created. This name is for informational purposes only. For the **SYSTEM** DBSpace, the file name always reflects the name when the data base was created. Changes to the file name are not reflected here.
Dbspace_name	CHAR	N		Every file has a DBSpace name that is unique. It is used in the **CREATE TABLE** command.
store_type	CHAR	N		Defines the file as belonging to either the Catalog Store (SA) or the IQ STORE.

SYSFKCOL

Each row of SYSFKCOL describes the association between a foreign column in the foreign table of a relationship and the primary column in the primary table.

Column Name	Data Type	Nullable	Primary Key	Description
foreign_table_id	INT	N	Y	The table number of the foreign table.
foreign_key_id	SMALLINT	N	Y	The key number of the **FOREIGN KEY** for the foreign table. Together, *foreign_table_id* and *foreign_key_id* uniquely identify one row in **SYSFOREIGNKEY**, and the table number for the primary table can be obtained from that row.
foreign_column_id	INT	N	Y	This column number, together with the *foreign_table_id*, identify the foreign column description in **SYSCOLUMN**.
primary_column_id	INT	N		This column number, together with the *primary_table_id* obtained from **SYSFOREIGNKEY**, identify the primary column description in **SYSCOLUMN**.

SYSFOREIGNKEY

Every foreign key is defined by one row in **SYSFOREIGNKEY** and one or more rows in **SYSFKCOL**.

SYSFOREIGNKEY contains general information about the foreign key, while **SYSFKCOL** identifies the columns in the foreign key and associates each column in the foreign key with a column in the primary key of the primary table.

Column Name	Data Type	Nullable	Primary Key	Description
foreign_table_id	INT	N	Y	The table number of the foreign table.
foreign_key_id	SMALLINT	N	Y	Each foreign key has a foreign key number that is unique with respect to: ◉ The key number of all other foreign keys for the foreign table ◉ The key number of all foreign keys for the primary table ◉ The index number of all indexes for the foreign table
primary_table_id	INT	N		The table number of the primary table.
root	INT	N		Foreign keys are stored in the database as B-trees. The root identifies the location of the root of the B-tree in the database file.
check_on_commit	CHAR	N		Indicates whether **INSERT** and **UPDATE** commands should wait until the next **COMMIT** command to check if foreign keys are valid. A foreign key is valid if, for each row in the foreign table, the values in the columns of the foreign key either contain the **NULL** value or match the primary key values in some row of the primary table. (Y/N).
nulls	CHAR	N		Indicates whether the columns in the foreign key are allowed to contain the **NULL** value. This setting is independent of the nulls setting in the columns contained in the foreign key. (Y/N).
role	CHAR	N		The name of the relationship between the foreign table and the primary table. Unless otherwise specified, the role name is the same as the name of the primary table. The foreign table cannot have two foreign keys with the same role name.
remarks	CHAR			Comments about the foreign key
primary_index_id	INT	N		The *index_id* of the primary key, or root if the primary key is part of a combined index.
fk_not_enforced	CHAR			Is N if one of the tables is remote.
hash_limit	SMALLINT			Contains information about physical index representation.

SYSGROUP

There is one row in **SYSGROUP** for every member of every group. This table describes a many-to-many relationship between groups and members. A group may have many members and a user may be a member of many groups.

Column Name	Data Type	Nullable	Primary Key	Description
group_id	INT	N	Y	The user number of the group
group_member	INT	N	Y	The user number of the group member

SYSINDEX

Each and every index in the database has one row in the **SYSINDEX** table.

Column Name	Data Type	Nullable	Primary Key	Description
table_id	INT	N	Y	The table number uniquely identifies the table to which this index applies.
index_id	INT	N	Y	Each index for one particular table is assigned a unique index number.
root	INT	N		Indexes are stored in the database as B-trees. The root identifies the location of the root of the B-tree in the database file.
file_id	SMALLINT	N		The index is completely contained in the file with this *file_id* (see "**SYSFILE** system table"
unique		N		Holds a Y/N to determine if the index is unique.
creator		N		The user number of the creator of the index.
index_name		N		The name of the index. A user ID cannot have two indexes with the same name.
remarks		Y		Comments about the index
index_type		N		The type of index: **FP**, **HG**, **HNG**, **LF**, **DATE**, **TIME**, **DTTM**, **CMP**, **WD**, **LD**, or **SA** (for a non-IQ index created in the Catalog Store).
index_owner		N		The name of the index owner: **USER**, **IQ**, **SA**, **AUTO**.
hash_limit		N		Used internally by IQ to hold the hash limit of the index.

SYSINFO

This table indicates the database characteristics as defined when the database was created using **CREATE DATABASE**. It always contains only one row.

Column Name	Data Type	Nullable	Primary	Description

			Key	
page_size	INT	N		The catalog page size specified to **CREATE DATABASE**. The default value is 1024.
encryption	CHAR	N		Whether encryption was specified with **CREATE DATABASE**.
blank_padding	CHAR	N		Whether the database was created to use blank padding for string comparisons in the database.
case_sensitivity	CHAR	N		Whether case sensitivity was specified with **CREATE DATABASE**. Case sensitivity affects value comparisons, but not table and column name comparisons. For example, if case sensitivity is enabled, the system catalog names such as SYSCATALOG must be specified in uppercase since that is how the name was spelled when it was created.
default_collation	CHAR	N		A string corresponding to the *collation_label* in **SYSCOLLATE** corresponding to the collation sequence specified with **CREATE DATABASE**. The collation sequence is used for all string comparisons, including searches for character strings as well as column and table name comparison.
database_version	SMALLINT	N		A small integer value indicating the database format. As newer versions of Sybase IQ become available, new features might require the format of the database file to change. The version number allows Sybase IQ Software to determine if this database was created with a newer version of the software and thus cannot be understood by the software in use.
classes_version	CHAR	Y		A small string describing the current version of the **SYS.JAVA.CLASSES** library that is currently installed on your computer.

SYSIQCOLUMN

Each column in every table is described by one row in **SYSIQCOLUMN**, which corresponds to a same row in **SYSCOLUMN** based on the primary key.

Column Name	Data Type	Nullable	Primary Key	Description
table_id	INT	N	Y	The table number uniquely identifies the table to which this column belongs. It corresponds to the table_id column of **SYSTABLE**.
column_id	INT	N	Y	Each table starts numbering columns at 1. The order of column numbers determines the order that columns are displayed in the command select

				* from table.
link_table_id	INT	Y		Used Internally by IQ
link_column_id	INT	Y		Used Internally by IQ
max_length	INT	N		Indicates the maximum length allowed by the column.
approx_unique_count	INT	N		Approximate number of unique values (cardinality) of this column.
cardninality	INT	N		The actual number of unique values (cardinality) of this column.
has_data	CHAR	N		Indicates that the column contains data
has_original	CHAR	N		Indicates the join index has the original data
original_not_null	CHAR	N		Indicates the join index column with the original data was **NOT NULL**
original_unique	CHAR	N		Indicates the join index column with the original data was **UNIQUE**
info_location	INT	N		Not used. Always zero.
info_recid	INT	N		Not used. Always zero.
info_location	INT	N		Not used. Always zero.

SYSIQFILE

Every database uses operating system files for different reasons e.g. DBSpaces, message logs etc. Each file used by an IQ database is stored in this table.

Column Name	Data Type	Nullable	Primary Key	Description
file_id	INT	Y	Y	Each file in a database is assigned a unique number. This file identifier is the primary key for SYSIQFILE, and it is linked to a same value in SYSFILE.
start_block	INT	Y		Number of the first block
block_count	INT	Y		Number of blocks for this file
create_time	DATETIME	Y		Time stamp the file was created
segment_type	CHAR	Y		Defines the type of segment: Main, Temp, or Msg.
allocated	CHAR	Y		Defines whether the segment is preallocated (T) or autoallocated (F).
server_name	CHAR	Y		For nonmultiplex databases and write servers, always blank. For multiplex query servers, always contains the query server's name.
file_name	CHAR	Y		For nonmultiplex databases, always equal to

					SYS.SYSFILE *file_name* entry. For multiplex, the IQ DBSpace name used by the multiplex server to open the IQ DBSpace.
data_offset	INT	Y			Used only for mixed-platform multiplex. Identifies the byte location of where the Sybase IQ data starts, relative to the beginning of the raw partition. Sybase IQ does not use the disk header block on a raw device. Because the disk header block is used by entities such as volume managers, Sybase IQ skips the first 65536 bytes of a raw device. Block numbers within Sybase IQ always start at 1. The first block would start at offset 65536.

SYSIQINDEX

Each index in the database is described by one row in SYSIQINDEX, which corresponds to an index in SYSINDEX.

Column Name	Data Type	Nullable	Primary Key	Description
table_id	INT	N	Y	The table number uniquely identifies the table to which this index applies. It corresponds to the table_id column of SYSTABLE.
index_id	INT	N	Y	Each index for one particular table is assigned a unique index number.
max_key	INT	N		Used internally by IQ
identity_location	BINARY	N		Used internally by IQ
identity_size	INT	N		Used internally by IQ
identity_location_siz e	INT	N		Used internally by IQ
link_table_id	INT	N		Used internally by IQ
link_index_id	INT	N		Used internally by IQ
delimited_by	CHAR			(**WD** indexes only.) List of separators used to parse a column's string into the words to be stored in that column's **WD** index.
limit	INT			(**WD** indexes only.) Maximum word length for WD index (between 1 and 255 bytes).

SYSIQINFO

This table holds the database information that is defined when the IQ database was created using the **CREATE DATABASE** statement. It only contains only one row.

Column Name	Data Type	Nullable	Primary Key	Description
last_full_backup	TIMESTAMP	Y		Date and Time the last backup completed
last_incr_backup	TIMESTAMP	Y		Date and Time the last incremental back up completed
create_time	TIMESTAMP	N	Y	Date and Time the database was created
update_time	TIMESTAMP	N		Date and Time of the last updated
file_format_version	UNSIGNED INTEGER	N		File format number of files for this database
cat_format_version	UNSIGNED INTEGER	N		Catalog format number for this database
sp_format_version	UNSIGNED INTEGER	N		Stored procedure format number for this database.
block_size	UNSIGNED INTEGER	N		Block size specified for the database
chunk_size	UNSIGNED INTEGER	N		Number of blocks per chunk as determined by the block size and page size specified for the database.
file_format_date	CHAR(10)	N		Date when file format number was last changed.
dbsig	BINARY(136)	N		Internal binary used by the catalog store

SYSIQJOININDEX

Each row of SYSIQJOININDEX describes one IQ join index in the database.

Column Name	Data Type	Nullable	Primary Key	Description
joinindex_id	UNSIGNED INT	N	Y	Each join index is assigned a unique number that is the primary key for SYSIQJOININDEX.
jvt_id		N		Used internally by IQ
joinindex_name	CHAR(128)	N		Defines the name of the join index.
joinindex_type	CHAR(12)	N		Used internally by IQ
creator	UNSIGNED INTEGER	N		The number of the user that created the join index. The name of the user can be found by looking in **SYSUSERPERM**.
join_info_location	BINARY(16)	N		Used internally by IQ.
join_info_loc_size	UNSIGNED INTEGER	N		Used internally by IQ.
join_info_size	UNSIGNED INTEGER	N		Used internally by IQ.

block_map	BINARY(32)	N		Used internally by IQ.
block_map_size	UNSIGNED INTEGER	N		Used internally by IQ.
vdo	BINARY(256)	N		Used internally by IQ.
vdo_size	UNSIGNED INTEGER	N		Used internally by IQ.
commit_txn_id	XACT_ID	N		Used internally by IQ.
txn_id	XACT_ID	N		Used internally by IQ.
valid	CHAR(1)	N		The displays wether this join index has been to be synchronized.
remarks	LONG VARCHAR	Y		Used internally by IQ.

SYSIQJOINIXCOLUMN

This table's data describes the columns that are used in each join index.

Column Name	Data Type	Nullable	Primary Key	Description
joinindex_id	UNSIGNED INTEGER	N	Y	Corresponds to a join index value in the table SYSIQJOININDEX.
left_table_id	UNSIGNED INTEGER	N	Y	Corresponds to a table value in the table SYSTABLE that forms the left side of the join operation.
left_column_id	UNSIGNED INTEGER	N	Y	Corresponds to a column value in the SYSCOLUMN table that is part of the left side of the join.
join_type	CHAR(4)	N		Only value currently supported is "=".
right_table_id	UNSIGNED INTEGER	N	Y	Corresponds to a table value in SYSTABLE that forms the right side of the join.
right_column_id	UNSIGNED INTEGER	N	Y	Corresponds to a column value in the table SYSCOLUMN that is part of the right side of the join.
order_num	UNSIGNED INTEGER	N		Used internally by IQ.
left_order_num	UNSIGNED INTEGER	N		Used internally by IQ.
right_order_num	UNSIGNED INTEGER	N		Used internally by IQ.
key_type	CHAR(8)	N		Defines the type of join on the keys. 'NATURAL' is a natural join, 'KEY' is a key join, 'ON' is a left outer/right outer/full join.
coalesce	CHAR(1)	N		Not Used

SYSIQJOINIXTABLE

The rows of **SYSIQJOINIXTABLE** describe the tables that explicitly participate in a join index.

Column Name	Data Type	Nullable	Primary Key	Description
table_id	UNSIGNED INTEGER	N	Y	Corresponds to a table value in the table **SYSTABLE** that is included in a join operation.
joinindex_id	UNSIGNED INTEGER	N	Y	Corresponds to a join index value in table **SYSIQJOININDEX**.
active	UNSIGNED INTEGER	N		Defines the number of times the table is used in the join index.

SYSIQTABLE

Each row of **SYSIQTABLE** describes one IQ table in the database, which has a corresponding entry in the table **SYSTABLE**.

Column Name	Data Type	Nullable	Primary Key	Description
table_id	UNSIGNED INTEGER	N	Y	Each table is assigned a unique number (the table number) that is the primary key for **SYSIQTABLE**.
block_map	BINARY(32)	N		Used internally by IQ.
block_map_size	UNSIGNED INTEGER	N		Used internally by IQ.
vdo	BINARY(265)	N		Used internally by IQ.
vdoid_size	UNSIGNED INTEGER	N		Used internally by IQ.
info_location	HS_VDORECID	N		Always Zero
info_recid_size	UNSIGNED INTEGER	N		Always Zero
info_location_size	UNSIGNED INTEGER	N		Always Zero
commit_txn_id	UNSIGNED INTEGER	N		Used internally by IQ.
txn_id	UNSIGNED INTEGER	N		Used internally by IQ.
join_id	UNSIGNED INTEGER	N		Used internally by IQ.
create_time	TIMESTAMP	N		Date and time the IQ table was created
update_time	TIMESTAMP	N		Last Date and Time the table was modified

SYSIXCOL

This table list the columns used in an index (one row per column).

Column Name	Data Type	Nullable	Primary Key	Description
table_id	UNSIGNED INTEGER	N	Y	Each table is assigned a unique number (the table number) that is the primary key for **SYSIQTABLE**.
index_id	UNSIGNED INTEGER	N	Y	Identifier for the index where the column is used
sequence	SMALLINT	N	Y	In an index, each column used is given a unique sequence number.
column_id	UNSIGNED INTEGER	N		The column id of the column that is indexed (use SYCOLUMN table to lookup)
order	CHAR(1)	N		A or D for ascending or descending index.

SYSJAR

Each row in the **SYSJAR** view relates to a **JAR** file stored in the database.

Column Name	Data Type	Nullable	Primary Key	Description
jar_id	INTEGER	N	Y	The ID of the **JAR** file
creator	UNSIGNED INTEGER	N		The Id number from **SYSUSERPERM** of the **JAR** files owner
jar_name	LONG VARCHAR	N		Name of the **JAR** file
jar_file	LONG VARCHAR	Y		The file name of the **JAR** file
create_time	TIMESTAMP	N		The time the **JAR** file was created
update_time	TIMESTAMP	N		The time the **JAR** file was last updated
remarks	LONG VARCHAR	Y		Comments about the **JAR** file

SYSJARCOMPONENT

Each row in this view defines a **JAR** file component.

Column Name	Data Type	Nullable	Primary Key	Description
component_id	INT	N	Y	Id of the component
jar_id	INT	N		The **JAR** Id (used to join to the **SYSJAR** view)
component_name	LONG VARCHAR	N		Name of the component.

component_type	CHAR(1)	N		The type of the component.
create_time	TIMESTAMP	N		The time the component was created
contents	LONG BINARY	N		The Byte code of the **JAR** file.
remarks	LONG VARCHAR	Y		Comment about the component.

SYSJAVACLASS

This table holds all data relating to java classes held in the database.

Column Name	Data Type	Nullable	Primary Key	Description
class_id	INT	N	Y	The java class Id
replaced_by	INT	Y		Used to reference the class_id field
creator	UNSIGNED INTEGER	N		The user_id of the creator of the class (can be looked up in **SYSUSERPERM**)
jar_id	INT	Y		The **JAR** ID (see SYSJAR)
type_id	UNSIGNED INTEGER	Y		The user type (see **SYSUSERTYPE**)
class_name	LONG VARCHAR	Y		The name of the java class
public	CHAR(1)	Y		Indicates if the class is public or private
component_id	INT	Y		Used to reference the **SYSJARCOMPONENT** table.
create_time	TIMESTAMP	N		The time the component was created
update_time	TIMESTAMP	N		The time the component was last updated
class_descriptor	LONG BINARY	Y		The Byte code for the **JAR** file
remarks	LONG VARCHAR	Y		Comments about the class

SYSLOGIN

This table holds a list of user profile names that can be used to connect to the database using an integrated login. This table can only be viewed by DBA's.

Column Name	Data Type	Nullable	Primary Key	Description
integrated_login_id	CHAR(128)	N	Y	The user profile that maps to the database user Id.
login_uid	UNSIGNED INTEGER	N		Used to reference the **SYSUSERPERM** table
remarks	LONG VARCHAR	Y		A comment about the integrated login Id.

SYSOPTION

This is used to hold all database options. Options are normally set using the **SET** command, and all option names are case sensitive.

Column Name	Data Type	Nullable	Primary Key	Description
user_id	UNSIGNED INTEGER	N	Y	The owner of the option can be public or depending on the option user id specific.
option	CHAR(128)	N	Y	The name of the option (case sensitive and can be miss typed so be careful)
setting	LONG VARCHAR	N		The setting of the option e.g. ON, OFF etc

SYSOPTIONDEFAULTS

This table is used to store the default settings; you can use this table to reset options if you want to know the default values.

Column Name	Data Type	Nullable	Primary Key	Description
option_name	varchar(128)	N		The option name.
default_value	varchar(40)	N		The default setting of the option.

SYSPROCEDURE

Every stored procedure in the database has one row in this table.

Column Name	Data Type	Nullable	Primary Key	Description
proc_id	UNSIGNED INTEGER	N	Y	The procedure Id.
creator	UNSIGNED INTEGER	N		The user Id of the creator can be used to reference the **SYSUSERPERM** table.
proc_name	CHAR(128)	Y		The name of the stored procedure.
proc_defn	LONG VARCHAR	Y		The command used to create the procedure.
remarks	CHAR(1)	Y		A comment about the stored procedure.
replicate	INT	N		This is a Y if the procedure is a primary source used in a rep server otherwise it is an N
srvid	LONG VARCHAR	N		If the procedure is on a remote database this is the remote server.
source	LONG VARCHAR	Y		Contains the original source for the procedure if the option **PRESERVE_SOURCE_FORMAT** is set to ON

avg_num_rows	FLOAT	Y		This data is used to aid the query planner when the procedure is used in a FROM clause.
avg_costs	FLOAT	Y		This data is used to aid the query planner when the procedure is used in a FROM clause.
stats	LONG BINARY	Y		This data is used to aid the query planner when the procedure is used in a FROM clause.

SYSPROCPARM

Every parameter used by a stored procedure in the database has a row in this table.

Column Name	Data Type	Nullable	Primary Key	Description
proc_id	UNSIGNED INTEGER	N	Y	The procedure ID number
parm_id	SMALLINT	N	Y	The parameter ID, starting at 1 and continuing in the order the parameters were defined.
parm_type	SMALLINT	N		The type of parameter is one of the following: 1) Normal parameter 2) An **SQLSTATE** error value 3) An **SQLCODE** error value 4) A Result variable, if the procedure returns a result sets
parm_mode_in	CHAR(1)	N		Is this an **IN** or an **INOUT** parameter
parm_mode_out	CHAR(1)	N		Is the an **OUT** or an **INOUT** parameter
domain_id	SMALLINT	N		The domain id (type) of the parameter in from the **SYSDOMAIN** table
width	SMALLINT	N		The length of the parameter if a char, the precision if numeric or the number of bytes for other types
scale	SMALLINT	N		The scale for numeric types (zero for others)
parm_name	CHAR(128)	N		The parameter name
remarks	LONG VARCHAR	Y		Comments about the parameter
default	LONG VARCHAR	Y		The default value of the parameter, always a char but you can cast this.
user_type	INTEGER	Y		The user type id of the parameter

SYSPROCPERM

This table hold the permissions of users who can call procedures the grantee is the user Id who can call the procedure identified by the proc_id.

Column Name	Data Type	Nullable	Primary	Description

			Key		
proc_id	UNSIGNED INTEGER	N	Y		The stored procedure Id
grantee	UNSIGNED INTEGER	N	Y		The user Id of the grantee who can call the procedure.

SYSPUBLICATION

Each row in this table describes an SQL remote publication.

Column Name	Data Type	Nullable	Primary Key	Description
publication_id	UNSIGNED INTEGER	Y	Y	The unique publication Id
creator	UNSIGNED INTEGER	Y		The user id who owns the publication
publication_name	CHAR(128)	Y		The name of the publication
remarks	LONG VARCHAR	N		Comments about the publication

SYSREMOTEOPTION

Each row describes an **SQL REMOTE** message link parameter.

Column Name	Data Type	Nullable	Primary Key	Description
option_id	UNSIGNED INTEGER	N	Y	The id of the link parameter
user_id	UNSIGNED INTEGER	N	Y	The user id that the parameter is set for
setting	VARCHAR(255)	N		The link parameters message value

SYSREMOTEOPTIONTYPE

Each row describes an **SQL REMOTE** message link parameters.

Column Name	Data Type	Nullable	Primary Key	Description
option_id	UNSIGNED INTEGER	N	Y	The Id of the link parameter
type_id	SMALLINT	N		Id of the message type
option	VARCHAR(128)	N		The name of the message link parameter

SYSREMOTETYPE

This table contains information about **SQL REMOTE** types.

Column Name	Data Type	Nullable	Primary Key	Description
type_id	SMALLINT	N	Y	The id which identifies the message systems supported by SQL remote.
type_name	CHAR(128)	N		The name of the message system supported by the **SQL REMOTE**
publisher_address	LONG VARCHAR	N		The address of the remote db published
remarks	LONG VARCHAR	Y		Comments about the SQL remote type

SYSREMOTEUSER

Each row relates to a user ID (a subscriber) with **REMOTE** permissions and the remote messages sent to and from that user.

Column Name	Data Type	Nullable	Primary Key	Description
user_id	UNISGNED INTEGER	N	Y	The user id of the remote user
consolidate	CHAR(1)	N		Holds a Y for **CONSOLIDATE** permissions or an N for a user with remote permissions.
type_id	SMALLINT	N		The type of messages to be sent to the user
address	LONG VARCHAR	N		The address to send the messages to
frequency	CHAR(1)	N		How often the messages should be sent
send_time	TIME	Y		The next time messages will be sent to the user.
log_send	NUMERIC(20,0)	N		Messages are sent only to subscribers for whom log_send is greater than log_sent.
time_sent	TIMESTAMP	Y		Time that the last message was sent to the user.
log_sent	NUMERIC(20,0)	N		Offset for the most recent sent operation.
confirm_sent	NUMERIC(20,0)	N		Offset for the most recent confirmed operation.
send_count	INTEGER	N		The number of messages that have been sent.
resend_count	INTEGER	N		Used to ensure messages are only applied once to the subscriber database.
time_received	TIMESTAMP	Y		The time the last message was received from

				the user.
log_received	NUMERIC(20,0)	N		Offset for the most recently received message from the user.
confirm_received	NUMERIC(20,0)	Y		Offset for the most recently confirmed message from the user.
receive_count	INTEGER	N		The number of messages received from the user.
rereceive_count	INTEGER	N		Used to ensure messages received are only applied once.

SYSSCHEDULE

Each row in **SYSSCHEDULE** describes the times at which an event is to fire.

Column Name	Data Type	Nullable	Primary Key	Description
event_id	INTEGER	N	Y	The unique event identifier
sched_name	VARCHAR(12)	N	Y	The scheduled name.
recurring	TINYINT	N		Used to indicate if the event is recurring.
start_time	TIME	N		The scheduled start time
stop_time	TIME	Y		The scheduled stop time if the **BETWEEN** clause was used.
start_date	DATE	Y		The first date the event is scheduled to run.
days_of_week	TINYINT	Y		Bit mask relating to the day of the week the event is scheduled for:- **x02** – Monday. **x04** – Tuesday. **x08** – Wednesday. **x10** – Thursday. **x20** – Friday. **x40** – Saturday. **x01** – Sunday.
days_of_month	UNSIGNED INTEGER	Y		Bit mask relating to the days of the month on which the event is scheduled. **x01** – first day of the month. **x02** – second day of the month. **x40000000** – 31st day of the month. **x80000000** – last day of the month.
interval_units	CHAR(10)	Y		The interval unit specified in the scheduled. **HH** – hours. **NN** – minutes.

				SS – seconds.
interval_amt	INTEGER	Y		The specified period for every run.

SYSSERVERS

Each row in this table describes a remote server.

Column Name	Data Type	Nullable	Primary Key	Description
srvid	INTEGER	N	Y	The id number of the remote server
srvname	VARCHAR(128)	N		The name of the remote server.
srvclass	LONG VARCHAR	N		The class of the server specified when the **CREATE SERVER** statement was run.
srvinfo	LONG VARCHAR	Y		Information about the remote server
srvreadonly	CHAR(1)	N		Y/N flag pertaining to if the server is readonly (Y=Readonly, N read/write)

SYSSQLSERVERTYPE

This table contains information relating to compatibility with Adaptive Server Enterprise.

Column Name	Data Type	Nullable	Primary Key	Description
ss_user_type	SMALLINT	N	Y	The ASE user type
ss_domain_id	SMALLINT	N		The ASE domain id
ss_type_name	VARCHAR(30)	N		The ASE type name
primary_sa_domain_id	SMALLINT	N		The id of the primary domain
primary_sa_user_type	SMALLINT	Y		The type of the primary user

SYSSUBSCRIPTION

Each row holds a subscription from one user ID which has REMOTE permissions to one publication.

Column Name	Data Type	Nullable	Primary Key	Description
publication_id	UNSIGNED INTEGER	N	Y	The Id for the publication that the user_id is subscribed to
user_id	UNSIGNED INTEGER	N	Y	The user id that is subscribed to the publication
subscribe_by	CHAR(128)	N		If the publication has a **SUBSCRIBE BY** expression then this holds the matching value for the subscription.
created	NUMERIC(20,0)	N		The offset in the tran log when the subscription was created

| started | NUMERIC(20,0) | Y | | The offset in the tran log when the subscription was started |

SYSTABLE

Each row in this table describes either a view or a table in the database.

Column Name	Data Type	Nullable	Primary Key	Description
table_id	UNSIGNED INTEGER	N	Y	The unique identifier relating to the view/table.
file_id	SMALLINT	N		The *file_id* is a **FOREIGN KEY** for **SYSFILE**. It is used to hold which file holds the database table.
count	UNSIGNED BIGINT	N		The count is always 0 for a view or an IQ table.
first_page	INTEGER	N		This value identifies the first page containing information for this table, and is used internally to find the start of this table. The *first_page* is always 0 for a view. Each table in IQ is divided into fixed size data pages.
last_page	INTEGER	N		Last page containing information for this table. The *last_page* is always 0 for a view.
primary_root	INTEGER	N		The *primary_root* locates the root of the B-tree for the primary key for the table. It is 0 for a view and also zero for a table with no primary key.
creator	UNSIGNED INTEGER	N		This is the user id of the table/view owner; The name of the user can be looked up in the **SYSUSERPERM** table.
first_ext_page	INTEGER	N		This is used internally by Sybase IQ.
last_ext_page	INTEGER	N		This is used internally by Sybase IQ.
table_page_count	INTEGER	N		This is used internally by Sybase IQ.
ext_page_count	INTEGER	N		This is used internally by Sybase IQ.
table_name	CHAR(128)	N		This is the name of the table/view. One user/schema cannot have more than one table or view with the same name.
table_type	CHAR(10)	N		This column is **BASE** for base tables, **VIEW** for views, **GBL TEMP** for global temp tables and **JVT** for join indexes.
view_def	LONG VARCHAR	Y		For a view, this column contains the **CREATE VIEW** command used to create the view. For tables it contains any **CHECK** constraints for the table.
remarks	LONG VARCHAR	Y		Comments about the view/table.

replicate	CHAR(1)	N		Holds a Y if the table is a primary data source in a Replication Server installation, or an N if not.
existing_obj	CHAR(1)	Y		This is a Y/N flag that indicates if the table previously existed or not.
remote_location	LONG VARCHAR	Y		Indicates the storage location of the remote object.
remote_objtype	CHAR(1)	Y		Indicates the type of remote object: **'T'** for a table; **'V'** for a view; **'R'** for an RPC and **'B'** for a Javabean.
srvid	INTEGER	Y		The unique ID for the server.
server_type	CHAR(4)	N		Used to show if the table was created in the Catalog Store (SA) or IQ Store.
primary_hash_limit	SMALLINT	N		This is used internally by Sybase IQ.

SYSTABLEPERM

This table holds the permissions on tables that have been given by using a **GRANT** statement.
The values in the <type>auth columns of this table can have one of 3 values

- **N** – No Permission granted
- **Y** – Permission granted
- **G** – Permission granted along with permission to grant to other users.

Column Name	Data Type	Nullable	Primary Key	Description
stable_id	UNSIGNED INTEGER	N	Y	The table id
grantee	UNSIGNED INTEGER	N	Y	The user id of the grantee
grantor	UNSIGNED INTEGER	N	Y	The user id of the grantor
table_id	UNSIGNED INTEGER	N		The table id (same as the value in stable_id)
selectauth	CHAR(1)	N		Does the grantee have select permissions?
insertauth	CHAR(1)	N		Does the grantee have insert permissions?
deleteauth	CHAR(1)	N		Does the grantee have delete permissions?
updateauth	CHAR(1)	N		Does the grantee have update permissions?
alterauth	CHAR(1)	N		Does the grantee have alter table permissions.
referenceauth	CHAR(1)	N		Does the grantee have reference permissions?

SYSTYPEMAP

This table contains the compatibility mappings for the **SYSSQLSERVERTYPE** system table.

Column Name	Data Type	Nullable	Primary Key	Description
ss_user_type	UNSIGNED INTEGER	N		The Sybase ASE user type.
sa_domain_id	UNSIGNED INTEGER	N		The Domain Id
sa_user_type	UNSIGNED INTEGER	N		The User Type
nullable	char(1)	N		Can the type be null
primary_sa_user_type	UNSIGNED INTEGER	N		The primary user type

SYSUSERMESSAGES

Each row hold a user defined message relating to an error id that can be used in a **RAISEERROR** statement.

Column Name	Data Type	Nullable	Primary Key	Description
error	VARCHAR(1024)	N		The error id (relates to the error in the **RAISEERROR** statement)
uid	INTEGER	N		The User Id who created the message
description	VARCHAR(1024)	N		The message description
langid	SMALLINT	Y		This is reserved

SYSUSERPERM

Each row in this table holds a users information and there permissions/authorisations .

Column Name	Data Type	Nullable	Primary Key	Description
user_id	UNSIGNED INTEGER	N	Y	The unique user id
user_name	CHAR(128)	N		The unique user name
password	BINARY(36)			The user's password.
resourceauth	CHAR(1)	N		Does the user have resource authority?
dbaauth	CHAR(1)	N		Is the user a DBA
scheduleauth	CHAR(1)	N		Does the user have schedule authority
publishauth	CHAR(1)	N		Does the user have SQL remote publisher authority
remoteauth	CHAR(1)	N		Does the user have SQL **REMOTE** DBA

				authority
user_group	CHAR(1)	N		Is this user a Group
remarks	LONG VARCHAR	Y		Comments about the user

SYSUSERTYPE

Each row contains data on a user defined datatype (domain).

Column Name	Data Type	Nullable	Primary Key	Description
type_id	SMALLINT	N	Y	The unique type identifier
creator	UNSIGNED INTEGER	N		The creator of the type
domain_id	UNSIGNED INTEGR	N		The underlying domain (datatype) from the **SYSDOMAIN** table.
nulls	CHAR(1)	N		Does the type allow nulls (Y for nulls, N for no nulls allowed)
width	SMALLINT	N		The precision for numeric based types and the number of bytes for others.
scale	SMALLINT	N		The scale for numerics (numbers after the decimal point) and zero for all others
type_name	CHAR(128)	N		The name of the data type.
default	LONG VARCHAR	N		Not used
check	LONG VARCHAR	N		Not Used
format_str	CHAR(128)	Y		Not used
super_type_id	SMALLINT	N		Not used

SYSWEBSERVICE

Each row contains data about a web service.

Column Name	Data Type	Nullable	Primary Key	Description
service_id	UNSIGNED INTEGER	N	Y	The Id number of the service id
service_name	CHAR(128)	N		The name of the web service
service_type	VARCHAR(40)			The type of web service (**SOAP,HTTP,SOAP** etc)
auth_required	CHAR(1)			Is authorisation required to call the service
secure_required	CHAR(1)			Does the service require a secure connection (**https**)

url_path	CHAR(1)			Used to control url interpretation
user_id	UNSIGNED INTEGER			The user id who created the service
parameter	VARCHAR(250)			A prefix that identifies the **SOAP** services to be included in a **DISH** service.
statement	LONG VARCHAR			The SQL statement that is executed in response to a request.
remarks	LONG VARCHAR			Comments about the web service.
super_type_id	SMALLINT			

System Consolidated Views

System consolidated views offer a user perspective of data translating id numbers for real values for example in the sysoptions consolidated view offers the same information as the sysoptions view but translates user id numbers for user names which saves you looking it up yourself.
Below is a list of the consolidated views and the descriptions of the system tables they are based on.

SYSARTICLECOLS

This is a user friendly view of the system table **SYSARTICLECOL**.

SYSARTICLES

This is a user friendly view of the system table **SYSARTICLE**.

SYSCAPABILITIES

This is a user friendly view of the system table **SYSCAPABILITY**.

SYSCATALOG

This is a user friendly view of the system table **SYSTABLE**.

SYSCOLAUTH

This is a user friendly view of the system table **SYSCOLPERM**.

SYSCOLUMNS

This is a user friendly view of the system table **SYSCOLUMN**.

SYSFOREIGNKEYS

This is a user friendly view of foreign key data from the **SYSFORIEGNKEY** and **SYSFKCOL** system tables.

SYSGROUPS

This is a user friendly view of the system table **SYSGROUP**.

SYSINDEXES

This is a user friendly view of index data from the system tables **SYSINDEX** and **SYSIXCOL**.

SYSOPTIONS

This is a user friendly view of the system table **SYSOPTION**.

SYSPROCAUTH

This is a user friendly view of the system table **SYSUSERPERM**.

SYSPROCPARMS

This is a user friendly view of the system table **SYSPROCPARM**.

SYSPUBLICATIONS

This is a user friendly view of the system table **SYSPUBLICATION**.

SYSREMOTEOPTIONS

This is a user friendly view of the system tables **SYSREMOTEOPTION** and **SYSREMOTEOPTIONTYPE**.

SYSREMOTETYPES

This is a user friendly view of the system table **SYSREMOTETYPE**.

SYSREMOTEUSERS

This is a user friendly view of the system table **SYSREMOTEUSER**.

SYSSUBSCRIPTIONS

This is a user friendly view of the system table **SYSPUBLICATION**.

SYSTABAUTH

This is a user friendly view of the system table **SYSTABLEPERM**.

SYSUSERAUTH

This is a user friendly view of the system table **SYSUSERPERM**. Because the underlying system table shows passwords this view does not have public **SELECT** permissions like the other consolidated views.

SYSUSERLIST

This is a user friendly view of the system table **SYSUSERPERM** but does not display passwords.

SYSUSEROPTIONS

This is a user friendly view of the other views **SYSOPTIONS** and **SYSUSERAUTH** and is used to display permanent option settings for each user (or the **PUBLIC** setting if no value is available for a user).

SYSUSERPERMS

This is a user friendly view of the system table **SYSUSERPERM** (but does not display passwords).

SYSVIEWS

This is a user friendly view of the system table **SYSTABLE**, but only displays data on **VIEWS**.

Sybase ASE (T-SQL) compatibility views

Because IQ and Sybase ASE (and therefore Microsoft SQL Server) have different tables to hold meta-data these views are provided. These views may be used by applications that require meta-data in the same format as ASE/SQL Server.

As system tables in ASE/SQL Server are owned by the user dbo and in IQ are owned by SYS, these compatibility views are also owned by the IQ user dbo to ensure compatibility. The dbo user is used solely to hold ASE compatibility objects. As such when accessing these objects you will need to qualify them as in Fig 15.5

Fig 15.5

```
SELECT *
  FROM dbo.SYSCOLUMNS
```

SYSALTERNATES

This holds one row for each user that is mapped to a database user.

SYSCOLUMNS

This holds one row for each column in a table/view, and one for each parameter in a stored procedure

SYSCOMMENTS

This table has one or more rows for every view/rule/default/procedure, giving the SQL definition statement

SYSCONSTRAINTS

This table has one row for each check/ referential constraint linked with a table or column

SYSDEPENDS

This table has one row for each table/view/procedure that is referenced by a stored procedure or view

SYSINDEXES

This has one row for every clustered/nonclustered index, and one row for each table with no Indexes it also has an additional row for each table containing text or image data

SYSKEYS

This has one row for each primary, foreign, or common key.

SYSLOGS

This holds information about the Transaction log.

SYSOBJECTS

One row for each table, view, procedure, rule, default, log, and (in tempdb only) temporary object. Contains compatible data only sysprocedures One row for each view, rule, default, and procedure, giving internal definition

SYSPROTECTS

This is used to display user permission information.

SYSREFERENCES

This is used to hold a row for each referential integrity constraint declared on a either a table or a column

SYSROLES

This is used to maps server roles to local database groups

SYSSEGMENTS

This is used for data about each segment.

SYSTHRESHOLDS

This has one row for each threshold defined for the database

SYSTYPES

This is used to store data on data types, both system and user defined.

SYSUSERMESSAGES

This has information on the user messages.

SYSUSERS

This holds data on each user in the database.

SYSCHARSETS

This holds data on character sets.

SYSCONFIGURES

This holds data about configuration parameters that that have been/can be set by a user

SYSCURCONFIGS

This has data about the configuration parameters currently being used by the server

SYSDATABASES

A bit superfluous for IQ as it has one row for each database on the server

SYSDEVICES

This has one row for each tape dump /disk dump device, disk for databases and disk partition for databases

SYSENGINES

This shows one row for each server currently on-line

SYSLANGUAGES

This holds one row for each language known to the server (Except US English)

SYSLOCKS

This holds data about active locks

SYSLOGINROLES

This has one row for each server login that possesses a system-defined role

SYSLOGINS

This has one row for each valid user account in the database.

SYSMESSAGES

This stores data about system messages.

SYSPROCESSES

This has data about server processess.

SYSREMOTELOGINS

This is used to hold data about remote users.

SYSSRVROLES

This has data about server-wide roles.

SYSSERVERS

This holds data about remote servers

System Procedures

This chapter looks at some of the most common Sybase IQ System procedures. Like most RDMS, Sybase IQ comes with a set of utility procedures owned by the database owner. The database owner can issue grants to execute the procedures (see the chapter on security). Some procedures report information on running processes or meta-data, some are used to alter security and other make changes to objects.
This chapter gives a quick reference of the functionality and syntax of the common system procedures allowing you to investigate further if required (Some System Procedures could have chapters or indeed whole books written about them). But in most cases what is written is all you need to know. Some of the procedures listed may also be discussed more in depth in other chapters pertaining to the subject the functionality relates to.

There are four main types of system procedures, these are:-

IQ System Procedures:- These are system functions that are implemented as system stored procedures.

Catalog Procedures:- These are used to display in tabular form system information.

Multiplex Procedures:- These are used to perform functions in a multiplex environment

IQ Implementations of ASE Procedures:- These Sybase IQ implementations of Sybase ASE system procedures.

Enterprise Procedures:- These are used to perform common functionality on the whole system.

IQ System Procedures

SP_IQADDLOGIN

Use	Adds a new Sybase IQ user account.
Syntax	sp_iqaddlogin ('userid', 'password', [number_of_connections] [,password_expiration])
Input Parameters	**userid** = The user's login name. **password** = The user's password. **number_of_connections** = Maximum number of concurrent database connections for the user. The default is 0 meaning no Maximum **password_expiration** = Password expiration interval, in days. Must be between from 0 through 32767. The Default is 0 meaning the password does not expire.
Comments	The DBA user cannot have expiration for its password. Passwords set to one day will expire the day after tomorrow (tomorrow being the one day). By default, you can add users with sp_iqaddlogin only on multiplex write servers, If you need to enable sp_iqaddlogin on query servers, you must set the option MPX_LOCAL_SPEC_PRIV.

SP_IQCHECKDB

Use	Checks the Database and (optionally) will repair indexes/allocation issues.
Syntax	sp_iqcheckdb 'mode target [...] [resources resource-percent]'
Input Parameters	**mode** = allocation or check or verify or repair **target** = main or local or indextype <index_type> or table <table_name> or index <index_name> or database or database resetclocks
Comments	This stored procedure reads and checks storage in the database. When is successfully completes the "database free list" (an internal allocation map) is updated to reflect the true storage allocation for the database, if the -iqdroplks server switch is used. sp_iqcheckdb then generates a report listing the actions it has performed. If an error is found, sp_iqcheckdb reports the name of the object and the type of error. sp_iqcheckdb does not update the free list, if any errors are detected. The sp_iqcheckdb stored procedure also allows you to check the consistency of, and optionally repair, a specified table, index, index type, or the entire database. sp_iqcheckdb is the user interface to the Sybase IQ Database Consistency Checker and sometimes referred to as DBCC.

SP_IQCHECKOPTIONS

Use	Displays the permanent and temporary options for the user running the procedure
Syntax	sp_iqcheckoptions
Input Parameters	No Parameters
Comments	For the connected user, the sp_iqcheckoptions stored procedure displays a list

	of the current value and the default value of database and server start up options that have been changed from the default for the user.

SP_IQCOLUMN

Use	Displays information about all table columns in a database or for a specific table, owner or both if specified.
Syntax	**sp_iqcolumn** table_name='*tablename*' , table_owner='*tableowner*'
Input Parameters	*table_name* = The name of the table containing the columns. *table_owner* = The name of the table owner
Comments	Specifying no parameters to the procedure returns all columns for all the non system tables in the database.

SP_IQCONNECTION

Use	Displays information about database connections. This includes which connections/users are using system resources such as version use, temporary DBSpace etc.
Syntax	sp_iqconnection [connhandle]
Input Parameters	Connhandle = The connection Id
Comments	Specifying no parameters to the procedure returns information on all connections.

SP_IQCONSTRAINT

Use	Lists referential integrity constraints defined using **CREATE/ALTER TABLE** DDL for a specific table, column or owner.
Syntax	**sp_iqconstraint** table-name or column-name or table-owner
Input Parameters	**table name** = Name of the table to list information on **column name** = Name of column to list information on **table owner** = Name of owner of the table constraints to list
Comments	If table name, column name and table owner are omitted, reports all referential integrity constraints for all tables including temporary ones in the current connected database.

SP_IQCONTEXT

Use	Displays, by connection, information about statements currently executing on the database.
Syntax	**sp_iqcontext** [connhandle]
Input Parameters	*Connhandle* = Connection Id
Comments	If no parameter is specified then information on all connections are displayed.

SP_IQCUSORINFO

Use	Displays detailed information about cursors currently open on the server.
Syntax	sp_iqcursorinfo [cursor-name] [, conn-handle]
Input Parameters	cursor-name = The name of the cursor. conn-handle = The connection ID using the cursor
Comments	DBA owner privileges are required to run this procedure. The sp_iqcursorinfo procedure can be invoked without any parameters. If no parameters are specified, sp_iqcursorinfo returns information about all cursors open on the server. If you do not specify the first parameter, but specify the second parameter, you must substitute NULL for the omitted parameter. e.g. sp_iqcursorinfo NULL, 99

SP_IQDATATYPE

Use	Displays information about system and user defined data types.
Syntax	sp_iqdatatype [type-name], [type-owner], [type-type]
Input Parameters	type-name The name of the data type. type-owner The name of the creator of the data type. type-type The type of data type. Allowed values are SYSTEM (just types owned by SYS or dbo) or ALL
Comments	If no parameters are specified, only information about user-defined data types (data types not owned by dbo or SYS) is displayed by default. If you do not specify parameters, but specify the next parameter in the sequence, you must use a NULL for the omitted parameter/parameters. e.g. sp_iqdatatype NULL, NULL, ALL

SP_IQDBSIZE

Use	Displays the size metrics of the Database.
Syntax	sp_iqdbsize main	local --Only use parameters in multiplex
Input Parameters	main = Displays the size metrics of the main database in multiplex mode. local = displays size metrics about the local store owned by the query server in multiplex mode.
Comments	Returns the size metrics such as the number of pages required and the amount of blocks used by the database.

SP_IQDBSPACEINFO

Use	Displays the number of blocks used per index per main or local DBSpace for one or all DBSpaces.
Syntax	sp_iqDBSpaceinfo ['DBSpace-name-pattern'] [,'local']
Input Parameters	DBSpace-name-pattern = If specified, sp_iqDBSpaceinfo displays output only for DBSpaces that match LIKE pattern. local = The local keyword is specified to enable the display of objects in the multiplex local IQ

	store. By default on a query server, sp_iqDBSpaceinfo displays information about the shared main IQ store on a query server.
Comments	DBA permissions are required to run. The sp_iqDBSpaceinfo stored procedure shows the DBA which objects reside on each DBSpace. The DBA can use this information to determine which objects must be moved or deleted before a DBSpace can be dropped. The following output displays information about a specific DBSpace in the database: sp_iqDBSpaceinfo IQ_SYSTEM_MAIN_2; If no parameters are specified then all DB spaces are displayed.

SP_IQDBSTATISTICS

Use	Displays the results of the most recent sp_iqcheckdb.
Syntax	sp_iqdbstatistics
Input Parameters	None
Comments	Displays the stats and metrics that were collected by the most recent execution of sp_iqcheckdb (DBCC)

SP_IQDROPLOGIN

Use	This procedure is used to drop an account/login.
Syntax	sp_iqdroplogin 'userid'
Input Parameters	userid = The user id of the account/login to drop
Comments	This procedure will also drop the user from the IQ_USER_LOGIN_INFO_TABLE.

SP_IQESTSPACE

Use	Estimates the amount of space needed to create an index based on the number of rows in the table.
Syntax	sp_iqestspace (table_name, #_of_rows, iq_page_size)
Input Parameters	table_name = table name #_of_rows = Number of rows in the table iq_page_size = Page size if not using the default
Comments	Displays the amount of space that a database requires based on the number of rows in the underlying database tables and on the database IQ page size.

SP_IQINDEXINFO

Use	For each main or local DBSpace this displays the number of blocks used for a given object.

Syntax	sp_iqindexinfo '{ database	local| [table table-name	index index-name] [...] }
Input Parameters	**Target =** Can be table table-name or index index-name
Comments	You may display information at a table or index level. e.g. dbo.sp_iqindexfragmentation ('index mytable.myhgindex') or dbo.sp_iqindexfragmentation ('table mytable')

SP_IQEVENT

Use	Displays information about system and user-defined events
Syntax	**sp_iqevent** [event-name], [event-owner], [event-type]
Input Parameters	**event-name** = The name of the event. **event-owner** = The owner of the event. **event-type** = The type of event ("SYSTEM" or "ALL" or any other vlaue for user events)
Comments	If no parameters are specified, only information about user events are displayed by default.

SP_IQHELP

Use	Displays information about system and user-defined objects and data types.
Syntax	**sp_iqhelp** [obj-name] ,[obj-owner], [obj-category] ,[obj-type]
Input Parameters	**obj-name** = The name of the object. **obj-owner** = The owner of the object. **obj-category** = An optional parameter that specifies the category of the object. **obj-type** = Type of Object ("SYSTEM" or "ALL")
Comments	Columns, constraints, and indexes are associated with tables and cannot be queried directly. When a table is queried, the information about columns, indexes, and constraints associated with that table are displayed. By default, only information about non-system objects is displayed.

SP_IQINDEX

Use	Displays information about indexes.
Syntax	**sp_iqindex** ([table_name],[column_name],[table_owner])
Input Parameters	**table_name** = Name of Table to display index information on **column_name** = Name of Table Column to display index information on **table_owner** = Name of Table Owner to display index information on
Comments	The **sp_iqindex** format always produces one line per index You may substitute parameters with a **NULL** value

SP_IQINDEX_ALT

Use	Displays information about indexes.
Syntax	**sp_iqindex_alt** ([table_name],[column_name],[table_owner])
Input Parameters	**table_name** = Name of Table to display index information on **column_name** = Name of Table Column to display index information on **table_owner** = Name of Table Owner to display index information on
Comments	The **sp_iqindex_alt** format produces one line per index per column if there is a multicolumn index. You may substitute parameters with a **NULL** value

SP_IQINDEXADVICE

Use	Displays index advice messages and/or can clear down advice that is stored.
Syntax	sp_iqindexadvice ([resetflag])
Input Parameters	**resetflag** = Use any non zero number to clear advice held in the store
Comments	Allows users to query aggregated index advisor messages using SQL. Information can be used to help decide which indexes or schema changes will affect the most queries. The index advice option must be set to on to collect this information in the store.

SP_IQINDEXFRAGMENTATION

Use	Displays how fragmented indexes are showing the amount of empty space within the btrees, garrays, and bitmaps in Sybase IQ indexes.
Syntax	dbo.sp_iqindexfragmentation ('target ')
Input Parameters	**Target** = Can be table table-name or index index-name
Comments	You may display information at a table or index level. e.g. dbo.sp_iqindexfragmentation ('index mytable.myhgindex') or dbo.sp_iqindexfragmentation ('table mytable')

SP_IQINDEXmeta-data

Use	Displays meta-data in a given index or indexes for a specific table or owner
Syntax	**dbo.sp_iqindexmeta-data** {'index-name'[, 'table-name' [, 'owner-name']] }
Input Parameters	**index-name** = Name of index to display meta-data about. **table-name** = Name of table containing indexes to display meta-data about. **owner-name** = Name of index owner to display meta-data about.

Comments	Specifying a table name limits output to those indexes belonging to that table. Specifying an owner name limits output to indexes owned by that owner. You may omit parameters by specifying **NULL** in there place.

SP_IQINDEXSIZE

Use	Displays the size of the specified index
Syntax	**sp_iqindexsize** [[owner.] table.] index_name
Input Parameters	**index_name** = The name of the index
Comments	An example of the use of this procedure is e.g. *sp_iqindexsize owner.mytable.myindex*

SP_IQLISTEXPIREDPASSWORDS

Use	Lists users with expired passwords, or if a userid is specified will return if that user's password has expired.
Syntax	sp_iqlistexpiredpasswords ['userid']
Input Parameters	**userid** = returns 1 row if the users password has expired or nothing if it is ok.
Comments	DBA Permission (initialy) required to execute this procedure. With no parameters will display all users whos passwords have expired.

SP_IQLISTLOCKEDUSERS

Use	Lists users with locked accounts, or if a userid is specified will return if that users account is locked
Syntax	**sp_iqlistlockedusers** ['userid'] ['server-name	all servers']
Input Parameters	**userid** = returns the lock status for the user, **server-name/all servers** = Only specify in a multiplex environment, the server or all servers..
Comments	DBA Permission (initialy) required to execute this procedure. With no parameters will display all users whos passwords have expired.

SP_IQLISTLOCKEDUSERS

Use	Returns users with locked accounts, or if a userid is specified will return if that users account is locked
Syntax	**sp_iqlistlockedusers** ['userid'] ['server-name	all servers']
Input Parameters	**userid** = returns the lock status for the user, **server-name/all servers** = Only specify in a multiplex environment, the server or all servers..
Comments	DBA Permission (initialy) required to execute this procedure. With no parameters will display all

	users whos passwords have expired.

SP_IQLISTPASSWORDEXPIRATIONS

Use	Displays users (or single user if one is specified), their password creation dates, and how many days the password is valid from the creation date.
Syntax	sp_iqlistpasswordexpirations ['userid']
Input Parameters	**userid** = returns the lexpiration data for the specified user
Comments	Requires DBA permission. A value of 0 for Days_till_Expiration indicates that the password does not

SP_IQLOCKLOGIN

Use	Locks an IQ user account so that the user cannot log in.
Syntax	**sp_iqlocklogin** '*userid*'[, '*server-name*' | 'all servers'] '[lock | unlock]'
Input Parameters	**userid** = Name of the account to be locked or unlocked. **server-name /all servers** = Optional parameter, Name of server to lock/unlock the account on in a multiplex environment **lock/unlock** = lock or unlock the userid specified.
Comments	You cannot lock the DBA account or your own account. Connected users can be locked, but they remain connected. A locked account can still own objects and can even be the database owner.

SP_IQLOCKS

Use	Shows information about locks in the database, (IQ store and ASA)
Syntax	**sp_iqlocks** ([connectionId,] [[owner.]table_name] max_locks,] [sort_order])
Input Parameters	**ConnectionId** = The connectionId you require lock information about **owner.table_name** = Display any locks on the table specified *max_locks* = The maximum number of locks to display information about *sort_order* = ('C' sorts by connection (default), 'T' sorts by table_name)
Comments	Displays information about current locks in the database. Depending on the options you specify (they are all optional), you can restrict results to show locks for a single connection, a single table, or a specified number of locks.

SP_IQMODIFYADMIN

Use	Enables Sybase IQ Login Management for servers and modifies Sybase IQ user account information in the IQ_SYSTEM_LOGIN_INFO_TABLE system table.
Syntax	**sp_iqmodifyadmin** '{enable | disable}'

	or **sp_iqmodifyadmin** 'option ' , [value] [, 'server-name']
Input Parameters	**enable | disable** = Enables or disables Sybase IQ Login Management. (This cannot be used with the server-name parameter). **Option/Value** = Name of the option to change, a list is given below:- user connections Sets the maximum number of connections per user for new users. 0 means no limit is enforced. Cannot be specified with the server-name argument. db_connections Sets the maximum number of connections to the database allowed on a server. Can be specified with the server-name argument. This serves as the default value for new users, but does not affect existing users' settings. 0 means no limit is enforced. password_expiration Sets the default number of days a password is valid. 0 means the password does not expire. Can only be set globally, not per server. Cannot be specified with the server-name argument. password_warning Sets the number of days before a password expires that a warning is sent to the user console. Can only be set globally, not per server. Cannot be specified with the server-name argument. **Server-name** = This Parameter is only allowed only when specifying db_connections. (Server Name or 'All Servers')
Comments	Enabling login management through sp_iqmodifylogin automatically adds existing users to the Sybase IQ Login Management tables. New users added after executions are not added until the procedure is run again.

SP_IQMODIFYLOGIN

Use	Modifies the maximum number of connections or the password expiration interval for a given user.
Syntax	**sp_iqmodifylogin** '{userid | all users}', 'option', value [,'servername'])
Input Parameters	**Userid** = UserId to modify **all users** = If all users keyword is specified, the option and its value apply to all users (except DBA). **Option/Value** = Name of the option to change, a list is given below:- password_expiration Password expiration in days, from 0 to 32767 inclusive. 0 means the password does not expire. You cannot set this option on a per-server basis. number_of_connections Maximum number of concurrent database connections permitted for a given user. 0 is unlimited connections.

	servername = The name of the server to apply the options to
Comments	Requires DBA permissions. Changes take effect when Sybase IQ Login Management is enabled with sp_iqmodifyadmin, or immediately if Sybase IQ Login Management is already enabled.

SP_IQPASSWORD

Use	Adds or changes a password for a Sybase IQ user account.
Syntax	**sp_iqpassword** 'caller_password', 'new_password' [, 'userid']
Input Parameters	**caller_password** = Your password. When you are changing your own password, this is your old password. When the DBA is changing another user's password, caller_password is the DBA's password. **new_password** = New password for the user, or for *loginname*. **Userid** = (if specified) Login name of the user whose password is being changed by the *DBA*.
Comments	Changes take effect when Sybase IQ Login Management is enabled with sp_iqmodifyadmin, or immediately if IQ Login Management is already enabled.

SP_IQPKEYS

Use	Displays information about primary keys and primary key constraints by table, column, table owner, or for all IQ tables in the database.
Syntax	**sp_iqpkeys** { [table-name], [column-name], [table-owner] }
Input Parameters	**Table-name** = The name of a base or global temporary table. If specified, the procedure returns information about only about the table specified. **Column-name** = The name of a column. If specified, the procedure only returns information about the specified column. **Table-owner** = The owner of a table. If specified, the procedure returns information only on tables owned by the specified owner.
Comments	f you do not specify either of the first two parameters, but specify the next , you must substitute **NULL** for the omitted parameters. If no of the parameters are specified, a description of all primary keys on all tables in the database is displayed. If any of the specified parameters is invalid, no rows are displayed in the output.

SP_IQPROCEDURE

Use	Displays information about stored procedures.
Syntax	**sp_iqprocedure** [proc-name], [proc-owner], [proc-type]
Input Parameters	**proc-name** = The name of the procedure. **proc-owner** = The owner of the procedure. **proc-type** = The type of procedure (SYSTEM or ALL)

Comments	The sp_iqprocedure procedure can be invoked without any parameters. If no parameters are specified, only information about user-defined procedures are displayed. If you do not specify either of the first two parameters, but specify the next parameter in the sequence, you must substitute **NULL** for the omitted parameters.

SP_IQPROCPARM

Use	Displays information about stored procedure parameters, including result set variables and SQLSTATE/SQLCODE error values.
Syntax	**sp_iqprocparm** [proc-name], [proc-owner], [proc-type]
Input Parameters	**proc-name** = The name of the procedure. **proc-owner** = The owner of the procedure. **proc-type** = The type of procedure (SYSTEM or ALL)
Comments	Beware that when a procedure has multiple result sets including ones in if conditions then the result set information may not be correct. The sp_iqprocparm procedure can be invoked without any parameters. If no parameters are specified, input/output and result parameters of all the user defined procedures are displayed. If you do not specify either of the first two parameters, but specify the next parameter in the sequence, you must substitute **NULL** for the omitted parameters.

SP_IQ_PROCESS_LOGIN

Use	Checks that a user is permitted to connect to the database.
Syntax	sp_iq_process_login
Input Parameters	None
Comments	Beware that when a procedure has multiple result sets including ones in if conditions then the result set information may not be correct. The sp_iqprocparm procedure can be invoked without any parameters. If no parameters are specified, input/output and result parameters of the entire user defined procedures are displayed. If you do not specify either of the first two parameters, but specify the next parameter in the sequence, you must substitute **NULL** for the omitted parameters. When a user logs in, Sybase IQ calls the stored procedure specified by the database option LOGIN_PROCEDURE. The default setting of the LOGIN_PROCEDURE option is the sp_iq_process_login procedure. When Sybase IQ Login Management is enabled, sp_iq_process_login checks that the user is not locked out, that the maximum number of connections for the user and database is not exceeded, and that the user's password has not expired, and then either allows user login to proceed or sends an error message. When Sybase IQ Login Management is disabled, user login proceeds without any checking. When user login is allowed to proceed, sp_iq_process_login calls the sp_login_environment system procedure for additional processing. This procedure is called automatically. You do not need to call it directly, unless you are creating your own login procedures. If you set LOGIN_PROCEDURE to call a different procedure, no login checking occurs.

SP_IQREBUILDINDEX

Use	Rebuilds one or more indexes on a table with the original IQ UNIQUE value specified in the CREATE TABLE statement, or a new IQ UNIQUE value to change storage required and/or query performance. To rebuild an index other than the default index, specify the index name.
Syntax	sp_iqrebuildindex (table_name, index_clause)
Input Parameters	**table_name** = Partial or fully qualified table name on which you require the index rebuild process to happen. If the user both owns the table and executes the procedure, a partially qualified name may be used; otherwise, the table name must be fully qualified. **index_clause** = One or more of the following strings, separated by spaces: column column_name [count (IQ Unique Value)] index index_name Each *column_name* or *index_name* must refer to a column or index on the specified table. The IQ unique value is an approximation of the cardinality of the specified column. The cardinality (number of distinct values) affects query speed and storage requirements.
Comments	You must have INSERT permission on a table to rebuild an index.

SP_IQRELOCATE

Use	Relocates specified tables and indexes on main DBSpaces with relocate mode to main DBSpaces with read write mode.
Syntax	sp_iqrelocate 'target [maxsize nMB] [resources resource-percent]'
Input Parameters	**target** = database name or| {table table-name} or (index index-name} **nMB** = Specifies the maximum number of megabytes of data to relocate. **resource-percent** = Must be an integer greater than 0. The resources percentage allows you to limit the CPU utilization of the sp_iqrelocate procedure by specifying the percent of total CPU's to use.
Comments	This procedure relocates tables and indexes on main DBSpaces with relocate mode to main DBSpaces with read write mode. If the database keyword is specified, then all objects found in relocate DBSpaces are relocated. If one or more tables or indexes are specified, only the specified tables and indexes are relocated. Data that belongs to the specified tables or indexes that does not reside on relocate DBSpaces is not relocated.

SP_IQRENAME

Use	Renames user-created tables, columns, indexes, constraints (unique, primary key, foreign key, and check), stored procedures, and functions.
Syntax	sp_iqrename object-name, new-name [, object-type"]
Input Parameters	**object-name** = The original name of the object. **new-name** = The new name of the object. **object-type** = An optional parameter that specifies the type of the user-created object being renamed.
Comments	You Must be the owner of the object or have DBA permissions or alter permission on the object. When changing the object you will require exclusive access to the object.

SP_IQ_RESET_IDENTITY

Use	Sets the seed of the Identity/Autoincrement column associated with the specified table to the specified value.
Syntax	sp_iq_reset_identity (*table_name, table_owner, value*)
Input Parameters	**table_name** = Name of the table to set the identity seed value on **table_owner** = The owner of the table **value** = The seed value for the identity column of the table specified.
Comments	The Identity/Autoincrement column stores a number that is automatically generated and increased. These values generated are unique identifiers for incoming data. The values are sequential, generated automatically, and are never reused, even when rows are deleted from the table. The seed value specified replaces the default seed value and persists across database shutdowns and failures.

SP_IQROWDENSITY

Use	Reports information about the internal row fragmentation for a table at the FP index level.
Syntax	dbo.sp_iqrowdensity ('*target*')
Input Parameters	**target** = (table <table-name>	(column <column-name/column-names>)
Comments	This procedure is owned by dbo. This procedure measures row fragmentation at the default index level. Density is the ratio of the minimum number of pages required by an index for existing table rows to the number of pages actually used by the index. This procedure returns density as a number such that 0 < *density* < 1. For example, if an index that requires 8 pages minimum storage occupies 10 pages, its density is .8. The density reported does not indicate the number of disk pages that could be reclaimed by recreating or reorganizing the default index. This procedure displays information about the row density of a column, but does not recommend further action. You must determine whether or not to recreate, reorganize, or rebuild an index.

SP_IQSHOWPSEXE

Use	Displays information about the settings of database options that control the priority of tasks and resource usage for connections.
Syntax	sp_iqshowpsexe [*connection-id*]
Input Parameters	**connection-id** = The connection ID Number
Comments	If *connection-id* is specified, the procedure displays information on the connection. If *connection-id* is not specified, it displays information about all connections. If the specified *connection-id* does not exist, sp_iqshowpsexe returns no rows.

SP_IQSPACEINFO

Use	Displays the number of blocks used by each object (or listed objects) in the current database and the name of the DBSpace in which the object is located.
Syntax	sp_iqspaceinfo ['main	local	[table *table-name*	index *index-name*] [...] ']
Input Parameters	**main	local** = In multiples mode specify which db to display information on. **table-name** = Table to display information about. **index-name** = Index to display information about.
Comments	sp_iqspaceinfo requires no parameters. If the database is a multiplex database, the default is main, the size of the shared IQ main store. The optional parameter local specifies only information about the local IQ store owned by the query server.

SP_IQSPACEUSED

Use	Shows information about space available and space used in the IQ main and temporary stores.
Syntax	**sp_iqspaceused**(out mainKB unsigned bigint, out mainKBUsed unsigned bigint, out tempKB unsigned bigint, out tempKBUsed unsigned bigint)
Output Parameters	**MainKb** = Main store space in Kb **MainKb Used** = Main store space used in Kb **tempKb** = Temp store space in Kb **tempKbUsed** = Temp store space used in Kb
Comments	This procedure returns four values as unsigned bigint out parameters. It can be called by user-defined stored procedures to determine the amount of Main and Temporary IQ Store space in use. In a multiplex environment, this procedure applies to the server on which it executes. If a query server has no IQ Local Store, it returns 0 in the first two out parameters.

SP_IQSTATUS

Use	Displays a variety of status information about the current database. Including space used and other versions.
Syntax	sp_iqstatus
Input Parameters	None
Comments	Shows status information about the current database, including the database name, creation date, other versions, page size, number of DBSpace segments, block usage, buffer usage, I/O, backup information etc. If this is run in multiplex on a query server then is displays information about the IQ Local Store as well as the shared IQ Main and Temporary Stores.

SP_IQSYSMON

Use	Monitors multiple components of Sybase IQ, including the management of buffer cache, memory, threads, locks, I/O functions, and CPU utilization.

Syntax	sp_iqsysmon start_monitor sp_iqsysmon stop_monitor [, "section(s)"] sp_iqsysmon "time-period" [, "section(s)"] sp_iqsysmon start_monitor, 'filemode' [, "monitor-options"] sp_iqsysmon stop_monitor
Input Parameters	**start_monitor** = Starts monitoring. **stop_monitor** = Stops monitoring and displays the report. **time-period** = The time period for monitoring. Must be in the form HH:MM:SS. **section(s)** = The abbreviation for one or more sections to be displayed by sp_iqsysmon. When more than one section is specified, the section abbreviations must be separated by spaces and the list must be enclosed in single or double quotes. The default is to display all sections.
Comments	For the sections related to IQ Store, you can specify Main or Temporary Store by prefixing the section abbreviation with "m" or "t"

SP_IQTABLE

Use	Displays information about tables in the database.
Syntax	**sp_iqtable** [table_name='*tablename*'],[table_owner='*tableowner*'],[table_type='*tabletype*']
Input Parameters	**tablename** = Name of table to display information on **tableowner** = Owner of the table to display information on tabletype = 'SYSTEM' (system tables),'TEMP ' (Global temporary tables), VIEW (Views),'ALL' (IQ tables, system tables, and views),any other value IQ tables
Comments	Specifying one parameter returns only the tables that match that parameter. Specifying more than one parameter filters the results by all of the parameters specified. Specifying no parameters returns all Sybase IQ tables in the database.

SP_IQTABLESIZE

Use	Returns the size of the specified table
Syntax	**sp_iqtablesize** (table_owner.table_name)
Input Parameters	**table_owner** = Owner of the table to display information on. table_name = Name of table to display information on.
Comments	Returns the total size of the table in KBytes and NBlocks (IQ blocks). Also returns the number of pages required to hold the table in memory, and the number of IQ pages that are compressed when the table is compressed (on disk). You must specify the *table_name* parameter with this procedure. If you are the owner of *table_name*, then you do not have to specify the *table_owner* parameter.

SP_IQTRANSACTION

Use	Displays version usage for the IQ Main store.
Syntax	sp_iqversionuse

Input Parameters	None
Comments	The sp_iqtransaction output does not contain rows for connections that do not have a transaction started. To see all connections, use sp_iqconnection.

SP_IQVERSIONUSE

Use	Shows information about transactions and versions.
Syntax	sp_iqtransaction
Input Parameters	None
Comments	The sp_iqversionuse system stored procedure helps investigate problems/issues where the database uses excessive storage space due to multiple table versions.

SP_IQVIEW

Use	Displays information about views in a database.
Syntax	sp_iqview [view_name='viewname'], [view_owner='viewowner'],[view_type='viewtype']
Input Parameters	viewname = Name of the view to display information about. viewowner = Name of the view owner to display information about. viewtype = 'ALL' or 'SYSTEM'
Comments	Specifying one of the parameters returns only the views with the specified view name or views that are owned by the specified user. Specifying more than one parameter filters the results by all of the parameters specified. Specifying no parameters returns all user views in a database.

SP_IQWHO

Use	Displays information about all current users and connections, or about a particular user or connection.
Syntax	sp_iqwho [{ connhandle	user-name } [, arg-type]]
Input Parameters	Connhandle = connection ID. To display information about. user-name = A user login name to display information about. arg-type = The arg-type parameter is optional and can be specified only when the first parameter has been specified. The only value for arg-type is "user". If the arg-type value is specified as "user", sp_iqwho interprets the first parameter as a user name, even if the first parameter is numeric. If any value other than "user" is specified for arg-type, sp_iqwho returns the error "Invalid parameter."
Comments	This is the IQ equivalent of the Sybase ASE and MS SQL Server sp_who procedure.

Catalog stored procedures

The following Catalog Store stored procedures return result sets displaying database server, database, and connection properties in tabular form. These procedures are owned by the dbo user but the PUBLIC group has EXECUTE permission on them.

SA_AUDIT_STRING

Use	Adds a string onto the transaction log
Syntax	**sa_audit_string** (*'string'*)
Input Parameters	**String** = String to add to the log
Comments	DBA Permissions Required. If auditing is turned on, this system procedure adds a comment into the audit log. The string must <= 200 bytes long.

SA_CHECKPOINT_EXECUTE

Use	Allows the execution of shell commands during a checkpoint.
Syntax	**sa_checkpoint_execute** *'shell_commands'*
Input Parameters	**shell_commands** One or more user commands to be executed in a system shell. The shell commands are specific to the system shell. Commands are **separated by a semicolon (;).**
Comments	sa_checkpoint_execute allows users to execute shell commands to copy a running database from the middle of a checkpoint operation, when the server is quiescent.

SA_CONN_ACTIVITY

Use	Returns the most recently prepared SQL statement for each connection on the database.
Syntax	**sa_conn_activity**
Input Parameters	None
Comments	The sa_conn_activity procedure returns a result set consisting of the most recently prepared SQL statement for each connection if the server has been told to collect the information. To obtain the result set, specify the -zl option when starting the database server or execute: **sa_server_option**('Remember_last_statement','ON')

SA_CONN_INFO

Use	Displays information about one or all database connections.
Syntax	sa_conn_info ([*connection-id*])
Input Parameters	**connection-id** = Connection id to display information about.
Comments	If no *connection-id* is supplied, information for all current connections to databases on the server is returned.

SA_CONN_PROPERTIES

Use	Displays properties about one or all database connections.
Syntax	**sa_conn_properties**([*connection-id*])
Input Parameters	**connection-id** = Connection id to display information about.
Comments	If no *connection-id* is supplied, information for all current connections to databases on the server is returned.

SA_CONN_PROPERTIES_BY_CONN

Use	Displays properties about one or all database connections.
Syntax	**sa_conn_properties_by_conn** ([*property-name*])
Input Parameters	**property-name** = Property Name to display
Comments	This is a variant on the sa_conn_properties system procedure. It returns results only for connection properties that match the *property-name* string. You can use wildcards in *property-name*, as the comparison uses a LIKE operator.

SA_CONN_PROPERTIES_BY_NAME

Use	Displays properties about one or all database connections.
Syntax	**sa_conn_properties_by_name** ([*connection-id*])
Input Parameters	**connection-id** = Connection id to display information about.
Comments	This is a variant on the sa_conn_properties system procedure. It returns the same result columns. The information is sorted by property name and connection number.

SA_DB_INFO

Use	Reports database property information.
Syntax	**sa_db_info** ([*database-id*])
Input Parameters	**database-id** = Use in multiplex mode.
Comments	You only require the db id if you execute in multiplex mode and require another database.

SA_DB_PROPERTIES

Use	Reports database property information.
Syntax	**sa_db_properties** ([database-id])
Input Parameters	**database-id** = Use in multiplex mode.
Comments	Returns the database ID number and the Number, PropNum, PropName, PropDescription, and Value, for each property returned by the sa_db_info system procedure.

SA_ENABLE_AUDITING_TYPE

Use	Enables auditing and specifies which events to audit.
Syntax	**sa_enable_auditing_type**(['string])
Input Parameters	**string** = comma-delimited string containing one or more options.
Comments	sa_enable_auditing_type works in conjunction with the PUBLIC.AUDITING option to enable auditing of specific types of information. If you set the **PUBLIC.AUDITING** option to ON, and do not specify which type of information to audit, the default setting (all) takes effect. In this case, all types of auditing information are recorded.

SA_ENG_PROPERTIES

Use	Executes database server property information.
Syntax	**sa_eng_properties**
Input Parameters	None
Comments	Returns property information including name and value for each server property.

SA_TABLE_PAGE_USAGE

Use	Displays information about database table usage.
Syntax	**sa_table_page_usage**
Input Parameters	None
Comments	The results include the same information provided by the Information utility.

SA_DISABLE_AUDITING_TYPE

Use	Disables auditing of specific events
Syntax	**sa_disable_auditing_type**(['string'])
Input Parameters	**string** = comma-delimited string containing one or more options.
Comments	You can use the sa_disable_auditing_type system procedure to disable auditing of one or more categories of information. Setting this option to all disables all auditing. You can also disable auditing by setting the public.auditing option to OFF.

SA_FLUSH_CACHE

Use	Clears the database server cache.
Syntax	**sa_flush_cache**
Input Parameters	None
Comments	Database administrators can use this procedure to empty the contents of the database server cache. This procedure affects the Catalog Store. It is of used to ensure repeatable results when doing performance testing.

SA_MAKE_OBJECT

Use	Used in a SQL script, ensures that a skeletal instance of an object exists before executing an ALTER statement that provides the actual definition.
Syntax	**sa_make_object** (objtype, objname [, owner [, tabname])
Input Parameters	**objtype** = The type of object being created. The parameter must be one of 'procedure', 'function', 'view', 'service' or 'trigger'. **objname** = The name of the object to be created. **owner** = The owner of the object to be created. The default value is CURRENT USER. **tabname** = Required only if objtype is 'trigger', in which case it specifies the name of the table on which the trigger is to be created.

Comments	This procedure is particularly useful in scripts or command files that are run repeatedly to create or modify a database schema. A common problem in such scripts is that the first time they are run, a **CREATE** statement must be executed, but subsequent times an ALTER statement must be executed. This procedure avoids the necessity of querying the system tables to find out whether the object exists. To use the procedure, follow it by an **ALTER** statement that contains the entire object definition.affects the Catalog Store. It is of used to ensure repeatable results when doing performance testing.

SA_ROW_GENERATOR

Use	Returns a result set with rows between a specified start and end value.
Syntax	**sa_rowgenerator** ([*rstart* [, *rend* [, *rstep*]]])
Input Parameters	*rstart* This optional integer parameter specifies the starting value. The default value is 0. • *rend* This optional integer parameter specifies the ending value. The default value is 100. • *rstep* This optional integer parameter specifies the increment by which the sequence values are increased. The default value is 1.
Comments	The sa_rowgenerator procedure can be used in the FROM clause of a query to generate a sequence of numbers. e.g. **SELECT dateadd**(day,row_num-1,ymd(datepart(year,CURRENT DATE), datepart(month,CURRENTDATE), 1)) **AS** day_of_month **FROM** sa_RowGenerator(1,31,1) **WHERE** datepart(month,day_of_month) = datepart(month,CURRENT DATE) **ORDER BY** row_num

SA_SERVER_OPTION

Use	Overrides a database server command line option while the database server is running.
Syntax	sa_server_option (option_name, option_value)
Input Parameters	**option_name** = The name of the option to change **option_value** = The value to change for the option specified Examples:- Disable_connections ON or OFF **Liveness_timeout** Integer, in seconds **Procedure_profiling** ON, OFF, RESET, CLEAR **Profile_filter_conn** connection-id **Profile_filter_user** user-id **Quitting_time** Valid date and time

Comments	Database administrators can use this procedure to override some database server options without restarting the database server.

SA_SET_HTTP_HEADER

Use	Permits a Web service to set an HTTP header in the result.
Syntax	**sa_set_http_header** (*field-name, value*)
Input Parameters	**field-name** = field name to set **value** = value to set
Comments	Setting the special header field @HttpStatus sets the status code returned with the request. The following example sets the status code to 403 Forbidden. dbo.sa_set_http_header('@HttpStatus', '403') The body of the error message is inserted automatically. Only valid HTTP error codes can be used. Setting the status to an invalid code causes an SQL error.

SA_SET_HTTP_OPTION

Use	Permits a Web service to set an HTTP option in the result.
Syntax	**sa_set_http_option** (*option-name, value*)
Input Parameters	**option-name** = Only one is currently supported 'CharsetConversion' **value** = The only supported values are ON and OFF.
Comments	Use this procedure within statements or procedures that handle Web services to set options within an HTTP result set.

SA_VALIDATE

Use	Validates all tables in the Catalog Store (ASA Database)
Syntax	**sa_validate** ['tbl_name',] ['owner_name',] ['check_type']
Input Parameters	**tbl_name** = Name of table to validate **owner_name** = Owner of tables to validate **check_type** = Type of validation check to perform (data, express, full, index, or checksum)
Comments	Validate a table or the entire Catalog Store while no connections are making changes to the database; otherwise, spurious errors might be reported, indicating some form of database corruption even though no corruption actually exists. The procedure returns a single column, named Messages. If all tables are valid, the message displayed is "No errors detected"

SA_VERIFY_PASSWORD

Use	Validates the password of the current user

Syntax	sa_verify_password (*string*)
Input Parameters	*String* = Password of current user
Comments	This procedure is used by sp_password. If the password matches, the procedure simply returns. If it does not match, the error string returned by the procedure is returned.

SP_LOGIN_ENVIRONMENT

Use	Sets connection options when users log into the database.
Syntax	sp_login_environment
Input Parameters	None
Comments	At start-up, sp_login_environment is called by the system procedure DBA.sp_iq_process_login, the default procedure called by the LOGIN_PROCEDURE database option. It is recommended that you *not* change this procedure. Instead the database option LOGIN_PROCEDURE option to point to a different procedure.

SP_REMOTE_COLUMNS

Use	Displays a list of the columns on a remote table, and a description of those columns. For each column, the procedure returns its database, owner, table, column, domain ID, width, scale, and nullability.
Syntax	sp_remote_columns servername [, tablename] [, owner] [, database]
Input Parameters	servername = Name of the Server that the remote table is on. tablename = Table name of the remote table. owner = Owner of the remote table. database = Name of the database the remote table is on..
Comments	If you are entering a CREATE EXISTING statement and you are specifying a column list, it might be helpful to get a list of the columns that are available on a remote table

SP_REMOTE_EXPORTED_KEYS

Use	Provides information about tables with foreign keys on a specified primary key table.
Syntax	sp_remote_exported_keys @server_name , @table_name [, @table_owner] [, @table_qualifier]
Input Parameters	server_name = Name of the Server that the remote table is on. table_name = Table name of the remote table. table_owner = Owner of the remote table. table_qualifier = type of remote table e.g. 'production'
Comments	The sp_remote_exported_keys result set includes the database, owner, table,column, and name for both the primary and the foreign key, as well as the foreign-key sequence for the foreign-key column. The result set might vary because of the underlying ODBC and JDBC calls, but

	information about the table and column for a foreign key is always returned.

SP_REMOTE_IMPORTED_KEYS

Use	Provides information about remote tables with primary keys that correspond to a specified foreign key.
Syntax	**sp_remote_imported_keys** @server_name , @table_name [,@table_owner] [, @table_qualifier]
Input Parameters	**server_name** = Name of the Server that the remote table is on. **table_name** = Table name of the remote table. **table_owner** = Owner of the remote table. **table_qualifier** = type of remote table e.g. 'production'
Comments	The server must be defined with the CREATE SERVER statement to use this system procedure. Foreign keys reference a row in a separate table that contains the corresponding primary key. This procedure allows you to obtain a list of the remote tables with primary keys that correspond to a particular foreign key table.

SP_REMOTE_PRIMARY_KEYS

Use	Provides primary key information about remote tables using remote data access.
Syntax	**sp_remote_primary_keys** @server_name [, @table_name][, @table_owner] [, @table_qualifier]
Input Parameters	**server_name** = Name of the Server that the remote table is on. **table_name** = Table name of the remote table. **table_owner** = Owner of the remote table. **table_qualifier** = Database containing the foreign key table
Comments	Differences in the underlying ODBC/JDBC calls, may cause the information returned to differ slightly in terms of the catalog/database value, depending upon the remote data access class that is specified for the server. However, the important information (for example, column name) is as expected.

SP_REMOTE_TABLES

Use	Returns a list of the tables on a server.
Syntax	**sp_remote_tables** servername [, tablename] [, owner][, table_qualifier] [, with_table_type]
Input Parameters	**server_name** = Name of the Server that the remote table is on. **table_name** = Table name of the remote table. **table_owner** = Owner of the remote table. **table_qualifier** = Database containing the foreign key table **with_table_type** = Selects the type of remote table. This parameter is a bit type and accepts two values, 0 (the default) and 1. You must enter the value 1 if you want the result set to include a column that lists table types.
Comments	This displays a list of the remote tables available on a particular server. sp_remote_tables

	returns a list of the tables on a server.

SP_SERVERCAPS

Use	Displays information about a remote server's capabilities.
Syntax	**sp_servercaps** *servername*
Input Parameters	**servername** = Name of the Remote Server.
Comments	The *servername* specified must be the same server name used in a CREATE SERVER statement.The system tables that contain server capabilities are not populated until after Sybase IQ connects to the remote server.

SP_TSQL_ENVIRONMENT

Use	To set connection options when users connect from JConnect or Open Client applications.
Syntax	**sp_tsql_environment**
Input Parameters	None
Comments	At startup, sp_login_environment is called by DBA.sp_iq_process_login, the default procedure called by the LOGIN_PROCEDURE database option. If the connection uses the TDS communication protocol (that is, if it is an Open Client or JConnect connection), sp_login_environment calls sp_T-SQL_environment. This procedure sets database options so that they are compatible with default Sybase ASE behavior. To change the default behavior, create new procedures and alter your LOGIN_PROCEDURE option to point to these new procedures.

Multiplex system procedures

The procedures in this section affect multiplex databases and servers. These system procedures shoul only be executed via a program. Do not execute them from ISQL.

Mostly, these procedures are intended for to be executed within the server, from Sybase Central or b administration scripts. Most of these procedures require DBA privileges.

SP_IQMPXCOUNTDBREMOTE

Use	Returns a count of dbremote connections for a multiplex database. This is a function implemented as a stored procedure.
Syntax	**dbo.sp_iqmpxcountdbremote ( )**
Input Parameters	None
Comments	Examples of Use:

	1)	**SELECT** dbo.sp_iqmpxcountdbremote()
	2)	**DECLARE** dbcount int; **SET** dbcount = dbo.sp_iqmpxcountdbremote(); **SELECT** dbcount;

SP_IQMPXGETCONNVERSION

Use	Displays the version number for a specified connection.
Syntax	**sp_iqmpxgetconnversion ( )**
Input Parameters	None
Comments	On a multiplex query server, returns in an UNSIGNED BIGINT the version number that the current connection uses for the current transaction. On a write server, always returns 0. The version number is a database-wide monotonically-increasing integer that increases any time the write server commits new data in the IQ Main store.

SP_IQMPXREPLACEWRITESERVER

Use	Converts the query server on which it runs into the new write server for the multiplex. Must be called on the query server. (This is not the complete way to move multiplex write servers and the latest advice for your version of IQ should be sought from Sybase.
Syntax	**sp_iqmpxreplacewriteserver('servername')**
Input Parameters	**servername** = Name of the new write server.
Comments	Drops and recreates main IQ Store definitions for the new write server to match those of the query server. Drops any IQ Temporary Store definitions for the former write server.

SP_IQMPXVALIDATE

Use	Checks multiplex configuration for inconsistencies.
Syntax	**dbo.sp_iqmpxvalidate(' show_msgs')**
Input Parameters	**show_msgs** = 'Y' to show messages
Comments	Multiple checks on tables SYS.SYSIQFILE and DBA.IQ_MPX_INFO, and SQL Remote configuration. May execute on any server.

SP_IQMPXVERSIONINFO

Use	Shows the current version information for this server.
Syntax	**sp_iqmpxversioninfo( )**

Input Parameters	None
Comments	Information includes server type (write server, query server, single-node mode) and synchronization status.

SP_IQMPXCFG_<SERVERNAME>

Use	Sets up query server named *servername* for SQL Remote replication.
Syntax	**DBA.sp_mpxcfg_<servername>**
Input Parameters	None
Comments	Sybase IQ calls this procedure when synchronizing query servers. This procedure in turn runs specified procedure or procedures on the named query server. When finished, this procedure returns the following message in the server log: Query server auto-configuration complete.

IQ Implementations of Sybase ASE System/Catalog Procedures

Sybase ASE provides system and catalog procedures to perform admin tasks and for displaying information about the system.

Sybase IQ has implemented some of these procedures. The system procedures are used to update and report on system tables and catalog procedures retrieve data from the system tables in a tabular form.

While these procedures perform the same functions as they do in Sybase ASE in Sybase IQ Version 11.X of before they are not the same as in Sybase IQ 12.x and above. If you are migrating from 11.X to a newer version you may want to check the implementation by running sp_helptext 'owner.procedure_name'

All IQ implementations of ASE system stored procedures in IQ are owned by dbo.

The following Sybase ASE catalog procedures are not supported in Sybase IQ:

- sp_column_privileges
- sp_databases
- sp_datatype_info
- sp_server_info

SP_ADDGROUP

Use	Adds a group to a database
Syntax	**sp_addgroup** group-name

Input Parameters	group-name = Name of the new group to add
Comments	This is used to add a user group.

SP_ADDLOGIN

Use	Adds a new user account to the server/database.
Syntax	sp_addlogin userid, password[, defdb [,deflanguage [, fullname]]]
Input Parameters	user_id = Name of user to add password = Password for the new user defdb = Default database deflanguage = Default Language fullname = Full Name of the user e.g. 'John Smith'
Comments	This is used to add a new user to the database.

SP_ADDMESSAGE

Use	Adds user-defined messages to SYSUSERMESSAGES
Syntax	sp_addmessage messagenum,message_text
Input Parameters	messagenum = Message number message_text = Message text to add
	Adds user-defined messages to SYSUSERMESSAGES which can be used in RAISE ERROR and PRINT statements inside stored procedures.

SP_ADDTYPE

Use	Creates a user-defined data type.
Syntax	sp_addtype typename, datatype
Input Parameters	typename = Name of the User defined type datatype = Datatype definition to base the user defined type on
Comments	Creates a user defined data type

SP_ADDUSER

Use	Adds a new user to the database
Syntax	sp_adduser userid [,name_in_db [, grpname]]
Input Parameters	userid = user's name in the database name_in_db = is a new name for the user in the current database. grpname = adds the user to an existing group in the database.

Comments	Adds a new user to the database,

SP_CHANGEGROUP

Use	Changes a user's group or adds a user to a group
Syntax	**sp_changegroup** new-groupname,userid
Input Parameters	**new-groupname** = Name of the new group to add the user to. **userid** = The user id to add to the group
Comments	Changes a user's group or adds a user to a group

SP_DROPGROUP

Use	Drops a group from a database
Syntax	**sp_dropegroup** groupname
Input Parameters	**group-name** = Name of the group to add the user to drop
Comments	Drops a group from a database

SP_DROPLOGIN

Use	Drops a user from a database
Syntax	**sp_droplogin** *userid*
Input Parameters	**userid**= User Id to drop
Comments	Drops a user from a database

SP_DROPMESSAGE

Use	Drops user-defined messages
Syntax	sp_dropmessage messagenumber
Input Parameters	**messagenumber** = Message Number to drop
Comments	Drops user-defined messages

SP_DROPMESSAGE

Use	Drops a user-defined data type

Syntax	**sp_droptype** messagenumber
Input Parameters	**typename** = Name of the user defined type to drop
Comments	Drops a user-defined data type

SP_DROPUSER

Use	Drops a user from a database
Syntax	**sp_dropuser** userid
Input Parameters	**userid** = User Id to drop
Comments	Drops a user from a database

SP_GETMESSAGE

Use	Retrieves stored message strings from SYSMESSAGES and SYSUSERMESSAGES for PRINT and RAISERROR statements.
Syntax	**sp_getmessage** message-num,@msg-var output [, language]
Input/output Parameters	Input **message-num** = Message number to retrieve output **@msg-var** = The message output
Comments	Retrieves stored message strings from SYSMESSAGES and SYSUSERMESSAGES for PRINT and RAISERROR statements.

SP_HELPTEXT

Use	Displays the text of a procedure or view
Syntax	**sp_helptext** 'owner.objectname'
Input Parameters	**owner** = Owner of the object **objectname** = Name of the object to display information about
Comments	Displays the text of a procedure or view

SP_PASSWORD

Use	Adds or changes a password for a user ID
Syntax	**sp_password** caller_passwd, new_passwd [, userid]
Input	**caller_passwd** = is the password os the user calling the procedure. When you are changing your

Parameters	own password, this is your old password. When a System Security Officer is using sp_password to change another user's password, caller_passwd is the System Security Officer's password. **new_passwd** = The password to set/change the users password. **userid** = The User Id of the password to change (if changing your own then you dont need to specify this).
Comments	Displays the text of a procedure or view

SP_COLUMNS

Use	Returns the data types of the specified column
Syntax	**sp_columns** table-name [, table-owner] [, tablequalifier][, column-name]
Input Parameters	**table-name** = Table to display column information on. **table-owner** = Owner of the Table **tablequalifier** = Database Name **column-name** = .Name of column
Comments	Returns the data types of the specified column. If no parameters are entered it will return data on all columns for all tables in the database.

SP_FKEYS

Use	Returns foreign-key information about the specified table
Syntax	**sp_fkeys** pktable_name [, pktable-owner][,pktable-qualifier] [, fktable-name] [,fktable_owner] [, fktable-qualifier]
Input Parameters	**pktable_name** = Name of the primary key table. The use of wildcard characters in pattern matching is not supported. You must specify either the pktable_name or the fktable_name, or both. **pktable_owner** = Name of the primary key table owner. The use of wildcard characters in pattern matching is not supported. If you do not specify the table owner, sp_fkeys looks for a table owned by the current user and then for a table owned by the Database Owner. **pktable_qualifier** = Name of the database that contains the primary key table. This can be either the current database or NULL. **fktable_name** = Name of the foreign key table. The use of wildcard characters in pattern matching is not supported. Either the fktable_name or the pktable_name, or both, must be given. **fktable_owner** = Name of the foreign key table owner. The use of wildcard characters in pattern matching is not supported. If an fktable_owner is not specified, sp_fkeys looks for a table owned by the current user and then for a table owned by the Database Owner. **fktable_qualifier** = Name of the database that contains the foreign key table. This can be either the current database or null.
Comments	sp_fkeys returns information about foreign key constraints created with the create table or alter table command in the current database. A foreign key is a key column in a table that logically depends on a **primary key** column in another table.

SP_PKEYS

Use	Returns primary-key information for a single table
Syntax	**sp_pkeys** table-name [, table_owner] [,table_qualifier]
Input Parameters	**table_name** = Name of the table. **table_owner** = Name of the table owner. **table_qualifier** = Name of the database that contains the table. The current database or NULL.
Comments	You may also use **sp_iqpkeys**

SP_SPECIAL_COLUMNS

Use	Returns the optimal set of columns that uniquely identify a row in a table
Syntax	**sp_special_columns** table_name [, table-owner][, table-qualifier] [, col-type]
Input Parameters	**table_name** = Name of the table. **table_owner** = Name of the table owner. **table_qualifier** = Name of the database that contains the table. The current database or NULL. **col_type** = "R" to return information about columns with values that uniquely identify any row in the table, or "V" to return information about timestamp columns, whose values are generated by ASE each time a row is inserted or updated.
Comments	Returns the optimal set of columns that uniquely identify a row in a table

SP_SPROC_COLUMNS

Use	Returns information about the input and return parameters of a stored procedure
Syntax	**sp_sproc_columns** proc-name [, proc_owner] [,proc-qualifier] [, column-name]
Input Parameters	**procedure_name** = The Name of the stored procedure. **procedure_owner**= The owner of the stored procedure. **procedure_qualifier** = The name of the database **column_name** = The parameter about which you require information If you do not supply a parameter name, it displays information about all input and return parameters for the stored procedure.
Comments	sp_sproc_columns reports the type_name as float, and data_type as 6 for parameters defined as double precision.

SP_STORED_PROCEDURES

Use	Returns information about one or more stored procedures
Syntax	**sp_stored_procedures** [sp-name] [, sp-owner][, sp-qualifier]
Input	**sp-name** = The Name of the stored procedure.

Parameters	sp-owner= The owner of the stored procedure. sp-qualifier = The name of the database
Comments	Returns information about one or more stored procedures, on IQ you may use sp_iqprocedure.

SP_TABLES

Use	Returns information about one or more stored procedures
Syntax	sp_tables table_name [, table_owner] [, table_qualifier] [, table_type]
Input Parameters	table_name = Name of the table. table_owner = Name of the table owner. table_qualifier = Name of the database that contains the table. The current database or NULL. table_type = List of values, separated by commas, giving information about all tables of the table type(s) specified, including "'TABLE', 'SYSTEM TABLE', 'VIEW'"
Comments	Returns a list of views and tables

Options

IQ offers many on-line configurable options that can effect at a server, database, connection, user or group level. This chapter covers all the options you should require in order to configure your database.

Under the covers there are also some Sybase controlled options, but for a user book these are out of scope. However ask Sybase about them as they can affect the performance of your system and are subject to change with different versions of IQ.

Overview

There are 3 main types of options in Sybase IQ:-

- **General Options** that effect the general database behaviour
- **T-SQL Compatibility Options** used to make IQ behave like Sybase ASE (ISO SQL92).
- **DBISQL Options** used to set working options for the Sybase DBISQL tool.

In reality you will probably only use about 20 of these options and sometimes you will set them once when you start up your database and then never use them again.
However it is worth knowing what is out there in case you come across some strange behaviour.
Options can be set as temporary or permanent and can also be set for specific user ids or for PUBLIC.

To further complicate matters not all options can be set temporarily. Also to further complicate matters some options are set depending on how you are connecting to the database.

To set options the general syntax for setting options is given in Fig 17.1

Fig 17.1

```
SET [ EXISTING ] [ TEMPORARY ] OPTION [ userid. <OR PUBLIC.]
<option_name> = <option_value>
```

To Unset an option (revert it to its default setting just set the value to an empty value) as in the example in Fig 17.2.

Fig 17.2

```
SET OPTION  ON_T-SQL_ERROR  =;
```

The sections below firstly highlight the most commonly used options to give you a first point of reference; the section following that lists other database options by there category. These category's are based on where I think an option should/will be mostly used in my experience. Some of the options cross boundary's (A query optimising option may also be a database option) so it's best to check other areas if you cannot find what you are looking for.

Another thing to note is that Sybase IQ will allow you to set option values to an incorrect case. For example the code in Fig 17.3 will work with no error returned and set the option value to 'CoNtiNuE' instead of 'Continue'.

Fig 17.3

```
SET OPTION ON_T-SQL_ERROR ='CoNtNuE';
```

For some options this is fine and for others it stops them working correctly, as such I recommend using the values suggested and sticking to the correct case.

You can see all options by selecting from the system views **SYSOPTION** or **SYSOPTIONS**(The only difference being one gives you a user id for the option and the other gives you the user_name, I suggest reading the chapter on system views and tables to see why this is the case). You may also check if options have been changed from the Sybase IQ default setting by running the system procedure **sp_iqcheckoptions**.

To check connection level options you can run the procedure sa_connn_properties which lists all the properties associated with a given connection, or run the function connection_property(<<connection value>), the example in Fig 17.4 will give you your current connections value of the On_tsql_error property.

Fig 17.4

```
SELECT connection_property('on_T-SQL_error');
```

The maximum length of an option value is 127 bytes. Also note that if the option value is expected to be an integer and you enter a decimal value then the value is truncated not rounded.

TEMPORARY Options

A **TEMPORARY** option will only effect the current connection and will only last while the connection is open as long as the option is not set for PUBLIC. If the option is set **TEMPORARY** for **PUBLIC** then all connections are effected and the option will last until the database is recycled/shut down. When the database is brought back up the option will revert back to its permanent setting , or if no permanent option has been set it will revert back to its default setting. **TEMPORARY** options are a great way of finding out if an option change will work for the entire system and aids in negating the risk if you forget to change it back. On the inverse side of this your temporary option may work fine and you may forget to set it permanent and then recycle the server. Another good use of **TEMPORARY** options is to set them at the beginning of a stored procedure and then set them back at the end, for example if your permanent setting for the option DATE_ORDER is set to 'DMY' and your procedure uses tables where the order is 'MDY' you can set this DATE_ORDER option temporary at the beginning of your procedure.

The procedure sp_T-SQL_environment is executed whenever a block/procedure of T-SQL code is executed, this procedure sets **TEMPORARY** options pertaining to what it believes you T-SQL environment should be. It is worth familiarising yourself with this procedure in Sybase Central so you know what is being set.

Commonly Used Options

DATE_FORMAT

This option sets the format of dates retrieved from the database, it is a string value option with a default of 'YYYY-MM-DD'. This option can be set for a **TEMPORARY** and for the **PUBLIC** group. Changing this option takes effect immediately. There is also a **TIME_FORMAT** option, but it will be very rare that you want to change the format of a TIME (The option is included in the next section).

DATE_ORDER

This option controls the interpretation of date formats that are used. The allowed values are 'MDY', 'YMD', or 'DMY' (The default is 'YMD').
If your option is set to the incorrect setting then you will not be able to use dates in other formats even if it is explicit (naming of the month etc) on what the date is.

Fig 17.5

```
-- THIS WILL FAIL --
SET TEMPORARY OPTION DATE_ORDER='DMY';
DECLARE @mydate datetime
SELECT @mydate = 'MAR 1 2010'

-- THIS WILL WORK --
SET TEMPORARY OPTION DATE_ORDER='MDY';
DECLARE @mydate datetime
SELECT @mydate = 'MAR 1 2010'
```

This can be useful when you are receiving feeds from different locations and aid in solving cross regional issues where different date formats are required.

ALLOW_NULLS_BY_DEFAULT – T-SQL Compatibility Option

This option controls whether new columns created without specifying either **NULL** or **NOT NULL** are allowed to contain **NULL** values. This options is one of those strange ones where depending on how you connect to the database will effect the option setting, the default is OFF for Open Client and JDBC connections but ON for all others. This means that if you run a create table that does not explicitly say if a column is **NULL** or **NOT NULL** then it will set the default differently depending on how you connect. To solve this ALWAYS be explicit and declare a column as **NULL** or NOT NULL.

CHAINED - T-SQL Compatibility Option

This function controls the transaction mode in where an explicit **BEGIN TRANSACTION** command has not been used
The default for this option in Open Client and JDBC connections is OFF and ON for other connections. When this option is set to OFF (unchained mode) every statement is committed individually unless an explicit **BEGIN TRANSACTION** statement is used to begin a transaction this is the same as Sybase ASE/SQL Server. When it is set to ON (chained mode), then transactions are implicitly started before any data retrieval or modification statement.

FORCE_NO_SCROLL_CURSORS

When this option is set to ON it forces ALL cursors (cursors are used to retrieve result sets) in IQ to be non-scrolling. When cursors are scrolling then IQ creates a Buffer to store the temporary results (every row) that may be scrolled. Hence when this option is ON then no buffer needs to be created and therefore memory usage and query time is improved. Some applications require this option to be set to OFF in order to scroll through the result sets but in general it is best to set it to ON unless you explicitly require scrolling.

IDENTITY_INSERT

This option enables users to insert or update an **IDENTITY** or **AUTOINCREMENT** column. The option can only be set as **TEMPORARY** (for non DBA's), and you may set it for a user or for PUBLIC

If for example you have an identity column on a table called "SALES" and you wish to insert values into the identity column, you would set the option as below.

Fig 17.6
```
SET TEMPORARY OPTION IDENTITY_INSERT = 'SALES';
```

As you can only insert/update one table containing identity values at any one time you should always clear this option down afterwards by setting the table name to blank.

Fig 17.7
```
SET TEMPORARY OPTION IDENTITY_INSERT = '';
```

If you are logged on as DBA and set this option without specifying **TEMPORARY**, then all other users connected as DBA will also be able to insert/update the same **IDENTITY** column.

This is a very useful option if used wisely, but also very dangerous is abused/misused. A general use for this option can be seeding identity values.

ISOLATION_LEVEL

This option controls the locking isolation level for catalog store tables, the reason I include it here is that it is one of the most commonly misunderstood options in IQ. Sybase IQ **ALWAYS** enforces level 3 for tables in the IQ store. This option only affects the catalog/system store so for most everyday purposes is useless.
You may set this option to 0,1,2 or 3 (The default is 0) , as with Sybase ASE/SQL Server the catalog store (Being Sybase ASA) allows the following values:-

Isolation level	Description
0	Allow dirty reads, non-repeatable reads, and phantom rows.
1	Prevent dirty reads. Allow non-repeatable reads and phantom rows.
2	Prevent dirty reads and guarantee repeatable reads. Allow phantom rows.
3	Serializable. Do not allow dirty reads, guarantee repeatable reads, and do not allow phantom rows.

INDEX_ADVISOR and INDEX_ADVISOR_MAX_ROWS

The **INDEX_ADVISOR** option generates messages suggesting indexes that may improve performance of one or more queries. The number of messages stored can be set using the **INDEX_ADVISOR_MAX_ROWS** option default 0).

This option can be set **TEMPORARY** and as such is a very useful tool for optimising procedures and queries, an example is given in Fig 17.8.

Fig 17.8

```
-- SET THE OPTIONS --
SET TEMPORARY OPTION INDEX_ADVISOR='ON';
SET TEMPORARY OPTION INDEX_ADVISOR_MAX_ROWS= 200;


-- RUN YOUR CODE TO THAT YOU WANT TO ANALYSE --
EXEC MY_procedure


-- GET THE ADVICE --
sp_indexadvice


-- CLEAR THE ADVICE --
sp_indexadvice 1 - add any non zero value to clear the advice


-- SET THE OPTION OFF --
SET TEMPORARY OPTION INDEX_ADVISOR='OFF';
```

See also the chapter on indexes in this book for more information on using the index advice. Also remember that advice obtained from sp_indexadvice will contain advice provided to any other user using the option (and clearing the advice clears other user's advice).

MINIMIZE_STORAGE

This option is used to minimize use of disk space for newly created columns. By default it is set to OFF, why anyone would want to use more disk space is beyond common sense and I have always recommended switching this option on. There is minimal overhead when a table is first loaded in deciding on the correct indexing options, but if your tables maintain cardinality across chars or the volatility is low-medium then I suggest using it. I am yet to find a system where it should not be set to ON.

In Sybase IQ 12.7 and below the option will create the best fit 1 or 2 byte FP index and in 15+ it will expand to a 3 byte before creating an FP.

More information on FP indexes and minimize storage can be found in the indexes chapter. An example to set it is given in Fig 17.9

Fig 17.9

```
SET OPTION PUBLIC.Minimize_Storage = 'ON';
```

NOEXEC

This option generates query plans instead of executing the plan which can be useful in optimizing a procedure if you don't want it to execute. The default for this option is OFF and it can be set **TEMPORARY**. When the option is set to ON the optimizer sends a query plan to the IQ message log/file. Any operations that do not use a query plan such as **LOAD** statements, **INSERT..VALUES** etc are not affected by this option (So be careful when using it with procedures).

Fig 17.10

```
SET OPTION noexec = 'ON';
```

For more information on query plans see the chapter on SQL.

QUERY_TEMP_SPACE_LIMIT

This option estimates the amount of temp space before a query is rejected. The default is '0' which means no limit.

DO NOT USE THIS OPTION IT, LEAVE SET TO ZERO.

The reason for the above statement is that IQ's estimator is way off and this stops perfectly reasonable queries from running by generating the error "Query rejected because it exceeds total space resource Limit"
I would suggest using the option **MAX_TEMP_SPACE_PER_CONNECTION** instead (see below) which monitors and limits **ACTUAL** temporary store usage for all DML statements, not just queries.

MAX_TEMP_SPACE_PER_CONNECTION

This option limits the actual temporary storage used by a connection. The default value is 0, meaning no limit is applied. If the connection uses all the space allocated with this option then the current stamen is rolled back and a message is returned to the client or IQ message log/file "The current operation has been cancelled:
Max_Temp_Space_Per_Connection exceeded". This is normally triggered by bad queries or a lack of space on the server to meet requirements. It is very useful for limiting resources on a connection by connection basis.
Example of use are given in Fig 17.11

Fig 17.11

```
-- SET THE LIMIT TO 2GB FOR ALL CONNECTIONS --
SET OPTION PUBLIC.MAX_TEMP_SPACE_PER_CONNECTION = 2048;

-- SET THE LIMIT TO 512MD FOR THE USER SALES --
SET OPTION sales.MAX_TEMP_SPACE_PER_CONNECTION = 512;
```

You my want to instead consider using the **MAX_QUERY_TIME** option to limit query run times!

ROW_COUNT

This option limits the rows effected by a query, be aware that unlike ASE that if you set this option in a procedure and carry on using the connection then the limit remains so always set it back to zero (no limit) when you are finished with it.

If you are just doing a simple select you may want to use the **TOP** command instead but for inserts/updates/deletes then stick to the **ROW_COUNT** option. An example of use is given in Fig 17.12

Fig 17.12

```
-- SET THE OPTION --
SET ROWCOUNT 100


-- THIS WILL NOW ONLY RETURN A MAXIMUM OF 100 ROWS --
SELECT * FROM SALES


-- SET THE OPTION BACK (TURN THE LIMIT OFF) --
SET ROWCOUNT 0
```

STRING_RTRUNCATION - T-SQL Compatibility Option

This option determines if an error is raised when an **INSERT** or **UPDATE** truncates a **CHAR** or **VARCHAR** string.
From version 15+ the default is ON prior to this it was set to OFF. If your system truncates a lot of strings then set it to OFF. Many legacy systems and ones that are upgrading from 12.x to 15.x should consider looking at this option.
You could consider using the **SUBSTR** function on a field instead of truncating it as in Fig 17.12.

Fig 17.12

```
DECLARE @account_number char(12)
DECLARE @account_prefix char(3)

SELECT @account_number = '123456789ABC'

-- DON'T DO THIS --
SELECT @account_prefix = @account_number
SELECT @account_prefix = CONVERT(CHAR(3),@account_number)

-- DO THIS INSTEAD --
SELECT @account_prefix = SUBSTR(@account_number,1,3)
```

T-SQL_VARIABLES - T-SQL Compatibility Option

This option controls whether the "**@**" sign can be used as a prefix for Embedded SQL host variable names. The default is ON for Open Client and JDBC connections and OFF for others. If you are using a non JDBC or Open Client approach then you may want to consider switching this option on to make code more readable and consistent across your applications code base.

ON_TSQL_ERROR - T-SQL Compatibility Option

This option is used to determine how errors inside stored procedures should be handled, it may be set as either a permanent or temporary option.

This option has three possible values

Option Value	Description
STOP	This causes the SQL to stop the execution of the statement and return an error immediately upon the error occurring ignoring any error trapping that may have been programmatically put in place.
CONDITIONAL	If the procedure used the **ON_EXCEPTION_RESUME** clause this will check if there is any error handling following the SQL that caused the error. Sybase IQ determines this by checking if one of the following statements immediately follows the code that caused the error:- ● SELECT @variable = ● LEAVE ● IF ● RESIGNAL ● DECLARE ● SET VARIABLE ● CASE ● CONTINUE ● LOOP

	⊛ **SIGNAL**
	⊛ **EXECUTE** or **CALL**
	Of course sometimes these statements may not be actually trapping an error and unfortunately the query processor will not know this. So if using the **CONDITIONAL OPTION** then do to wisely.
CONTINUE	This allows execution of the stored procedure to continue until it ends, once it completes the first error that was encountered is returned. This option closely follows the default Sybase ASE/SQL server settings.
	If you set the option to **CONDITIONAL** then when a **RAISERROR** statement occurs the value of the option **CONTIUE_AFTER_RAISERROR** is checked (ON or OFF) to determine if the procedure can continue after the **RAISEERROR**.
	When set to **STOP** or **CONTINUE** then no check of the **CONTINUE_AFTER_RAISERROR** option occurs. My recommended setting for this option is either to set it to STOP if your code has little or no error checking and to **CONDITIONAL** (The default) if you wish to handle errors programmatically. I have found very little use for **CONTINUE** as when an error occurs you would normally want to be informed of the occurrence as quickly as possible and to stop any further processing of the procedure. If you have a mixture of code then set the global setting of the option to **STOP** and place a temporary set option to **CONDITIONAL** in each procedure that with error handling. Also refer to the chapter on stored procedures to see error handling in use.

ALLOW_CLIENT_READ_FILE and ALLOW_CLIENT_WRITE_FILE

You will want to set these options to On (The default value if Off) if you are going to be reading any client side. You will also need to **GRANT READCLIENTFILE** permissions to the user/group reading the client side files. The reading of client side files is performed when using the **"LOAD TABLE USING CLIENT FILE"** statement.

ANSINULL – T-SQL Compatibility Option

Query Optimisation Options

The options below may be used for query optimisation; I would suggest setting them as temporary and seeing how it goes!! You should also check the other sections as some of the other options can also effect your query optimisation. Also by the term query I mean updates, deletes and inserts as well as selects.

AGGREGATION_PREFERENCE

This option is used to override the query processors decisions on how it will process a query containing aggregation functions such as **DISTINCTS** and **GROUP BY**. Normally this is only set by experienced users who are investigating performance and tuning options. It accepts the values -3 through to 3 (the default is 0) with each value representing a different internal preference for calculating the best aggregation algorithm.

The values represent the actions below:-

Value	Description

-1	Avoid aggregation with a sort
-2	Avoid aggregation using IQ indexes
-3	Avoid aggregation with a hash
0	Let the optimizer choose
1	Prefer aggregation with a sort
2	Prefer aggregation using IQ indexes
3	Prefer aggregation with a hash

BT_PREFETCH_MAX_MISS

This is another of those options that I would not recommend changing; it is used to control the pre-fetching of data in queries using **HG** indexes. IQ internally determines when it should no longer pre-fetch results increasing the value increases the likelihood of IQ continuing to pre-fetch results past its default limits. Generally I would suggest speaking with Sybase before changing this option as it may have knock on effects to the rest of your application. (The default value is 2, but it allows values 0-1000).

BT_PREFETCH_SIZE

This option is used to control the pre-fetch buffer of queries using HG indexes. The default is 10, but it allows values 0-100. It can **ONLY** be set for individual users, but in my experience I have never found just cause to change this value.

BTREE_PAGE_SPLIT_PAD_PERCENT

This option is used to aid in the incremental inserts by setting the page fill factor for **HG,LF,DATE,TIME** and **DTTM** Indexes (As they are all B-Tree based Indexes). The more space that is reserved equals more space is required to hold the data but also means that inserts are faster. The default value is 50 but it will accept the values 0-90, the lower the value the less storage is reserved, but inserts will be quicker. I would suggest only changing this option if your inserts are running slowly and you have investigated other reasons for the issue. You need DBA privileges to set this option.

CACHE_PARTITIONS

This option is used to control the number of partitions that are used for the main and temporary buffer caches (0, 1, 2, 4, 8, 16, 32 or 64). When set to 0 (the default) then IQ will calculate the number of partitions. IQ is very good at computing the partitions required based on the number of CPU's on the host. However if your system is running slower for queries/loads than you would expect then you can try changing the value of this option. This option can only be set for **PUBLIC** though so be careful about adverse effects on other parts of your system that are running OK.

CURSOR_WINDOW_ROWS

This option is used to determine how many rows of data are held in the buffer that is used to scroll result sets.. It is a **FIFO** buffer that will hold the latest rows returned (i.e. the last 200 for the default setting). The default for this option is 200 but it accepts values from 20-100000. Fro example if your query returns 600 rows (the whole result set) then the buffer will hold rows 401 to 600. If your application requests rows before 401 then the query is restarted. This would normally only be the case if you have allowed SCOLLING cursors (See the option **FORCE_NO_SCROLL_CURSORS** in the Common use section).

DEFAULT_HAVING_SELECTIVITY_PPM

This option is used to determine the selectivity estimates when the optimizer parses a HAVING clause, the allowed values are 0 – to 1,000,000 (The default is 0).
When this is set to the default value 0 then the optimizer estimates the amount of rows filtered by a **HAVING** clause, unfortunately the optimizer does not always have the required information to accurately estimate this value and a default of 40% is used. When this option is set then the user/DBA has more control on how the optimizer with estimate the selectivity.

DEFAULT_LIKE_MATCH_SELECTIVITY_PPM

This option is used by the optimizer to define selectivity estimates when parsing **LIKE** predicates. The allowed values are 0 to 1000,000 (Default 150,000).
The optimizer uses this value when the match string does not begin with a set of constant characters followed by a wildcard (%) and there is no other selectivity information available. If the column has an **LF** or **FP** index then this value is not required.

DEFAULT_LIKE_RANGE_SELECTIVITY_PPM

This option is used by the optimizer to define selectivity estimates when passing **LIKE** ranges.
The allowed values are 0 to 1000,000 (Default 150,000).
If the column has an **LF** or **FP** index then this value is not required.
This value is used when the optimizer is parsing a like clause where there is a constant followed by a wildcard (%) for example " **LIKE** '<string>%' ".

EARLY_PREDICATE_EXECUTION

This option decides whether a simple local predicate is executed before query optimization (The default is ON).
When set to ON then the optimizer finds, prepares and executes predicates that only contain local constraints and columns prior to query optimisation. Also when the option is On the execution is done prior to the generation of a query plan.
When this option is OFF then the optimizer will find and prepares local predicates but does not execute them.

HG_DELETE_METHOD

This option is used to set a value 0-3 that relates to the algorithm used to calculate database cost when deleting date contained in a HG index. The database cost takes into account CPU, I/O, data cardinality, data width, threads, referential integrity, data to delete and data size when calculating the cost. The default value is 0, the values corresponding to the algorithm types are given below:-

Option Value	Description
1	IQ will decide the best algorithm.
2	Use the small method algorithm.
3	Use the medium method algorithm.
4	Use the large method algorithm.

I have never found just cause to change this value, but as it can be set temporary you can test your changes before making permanent and public.

INDEX_PREFERENCE

This option is used to set the value of the index choice optimiser makes when choosing the best index for a query.
You can set this option temporary and it can be set for values -10 to 10 (the default is 0) each relating to an optimizer preference. A list of these is given below:-

Option Value	Description
10	Prefer **DTTM** Indexes
9	Prefer **TIME** indexes
8	Prefer **DATE** indexes
6	Prefer **WD** indexes
5	Prefer the default indexes
4	Prefer the **CMP** indexes
3	Prefer **HNG** indexes
2	Prefer **HG** indexes
1	Prefer **LF** indexes
0	Let the optimizer decide on the correct index
-1	Avoid **LF** indexes
-2	Avoid **HG** indexes
-3	Avoid **HNG** indexes
-4	Avoid **CMP** indexes
-5	Avoid the default indexes
-6	Avoid **WD** indexes
-8	Avoid **DATE** indexes
-9	Avoid **TIME** indexes
-10	Avoid **DTTM** indexes

IN_SUBQUERY_PREFERENCE

This option is used to override the default optimizer choices when materialising queries from "IN" sub-queries.

Normally you can get better performance by adding correct indexes and data types but if you want to test it out the values relating to this option are given below (The default is 0).

Option Value	Description
3	Prefer hash-based IN sub-query
2	Prefer vertical IN sub-query (where a sub-query is a child of a leaf node in the query plan)
1	Prefer sort based IN sub-query
0	Let the optimizer choose
-1	Avoid sort based IN sub-query
-2	Avoid vertical IN sub-query
-3	Avoid hash-based IN sub-query

JOIN_EXPANSION_FACTOR

This option is used by the query optimizer to decide how conservative it should by when result-sets resulting from joins in complex queries. The smaller the value (The default is 30, but it can be 0-100) the less conservative the optimizer is. This option is used when optimizer has estimated a result-set that has already passed through an intermediate join that can result in multiple copies of a row. If this option was set to 0 (The lowest value) then the optimizer would use the same estimation when estimating result-sets for further joins. When set to 100 (the highest value) then IQ is more conservative and estimates larger result-sets.

JOIN_OPTIMIZATION

This option can be ON (default) or OFF, when it is ON then the optimizer chooses a join order that will reduce the size of intermediate (temporary) results and sorts and thus balance system load. When it is set to OFF then the optimizer uses the join order set out in the FROM clause. I recommend only changing the temporary value of this operation for joins that you want to perform in a specific way. On the whole though, for this option the IQ optimizer generally knows best!!

JOIN_PREFERENCE

The best way to perform joins in IQ is handled by the optimizer whether is be a hash join or a sort-merge. This option allows you to set a value that specifies how to or not to join. The default value is 0 with the other values listed below:-

Option Value	Description
7	Prefer sort-merge push-down

6	Prefer pre-join
5	Prefer hash push-down
4	Prefer hash
3	Prefer a nested-loop push-down
2	Prefer a nested-loop
1	Prefer a sort-merge
0	Let the optimiser choose
-1	Avoid a sort-merge
-2	Avoid a nested-loop
-3	Avoid a nested-loop push-down
-4	Avoid hash
-5	Avoid hash push-down
-6	Avoid pre-join
-7	Avoid sort-merge push-down

PREFETCH

When this option is set to ON (default) then catalog store data is fetched into the client side before being made available to the calling client application. This fetches several rows in one call even when the client only request one row. However this option is not used requests to the IQ store or by Open Client or JDBC applications.

QUERY_ROWS_RETURNED_LIMIT

Another option where IQ tries to estimate how many rows will be returned from a query and will reject it if it thinks it will return more rows than the value of this option. The value default is 0 which means no limit (it can be any integer) and I suggest leaving it as it is and using other means to limit rows from a result-set (**SET ROWCOUNT, TOP** etc)

SCALE

This option only affects the catalog store and is used to specify the number of digits after a decimal point that an arithmetic calculation will truncate on. The default is 38 and values may be from 0-126.

SIGNIFICANTDIGITSFORDOUBLEEQUALITY

This option is used to specify the number of significant digits after the decimal point in exponential notation that can be used in equality tests between two arithmetic expressions. If set to 0 (the default) then all digits are used). (This is also the most ridiculously long option name I have seen!!!).

SORT_COLLATION

This option is used to allow implicit use of the **SORTKEY** function when executing ORDER BY statements. The Allowed values are Internal (default), a collation name or a collation_id.
 When set to the default then order bys remain unchanged. However by setting to a collation name or id then the SQL is implicitly run with a **SORTKEY** function.

Fig 17.13

```
SET TEMPORARY OPTION sort_collation='binary';

SELECT sales_person, sales_id
FROM sales
ORDER BY 1,2;
```

When the SQL in Fig 17.13 is executed then the SQL is run as if it was entered as in Fig 17.14.

Fig 17.14

```
SELECT sales_person, sales_id
FROM sales
ORDER BY SORTKEY(sales_person, 'binary'), sales_id
```

SUBQUERY_CACHING_PREFERENCE

This option is used to control how sub-query predicates are processed and which type of caching occurs when the optimizer parses them. The default value is 0 which means that the optimizer decides, but the allowed values are between -3 to 3.

Option Value	Description
3	Cache one previous sub-query result. Does not use SORT and HASH.
2	Use the hash table to cache results for all sub-query predicates when it is legal. If available temp cache cannot accommodate all of the sub-query results, performance may be poor.
1	Use sort-based processing for the first sub-query predicate. Other sub-query predicates that do not have the same ordering key are processed using a hash table to cache sub-query results.
0	Let the optimizer choose.
-1	Avoid using SORT. The IQ optimizer chooses HASH if it is legal.
-2	Avoid using HASH. The IQ optimizer chooses SORT or cache-one value if it is legal.
-3	Avoid using cache-one value. The IQ optimizer chooses either HASH or SORT if it is legal.

SUBQUERY_FLATTENING_PERCENT

When the optimizer encounters a correlated scalar sub query it can convert it into an equivalent join operation effectively flattening the sub query. The option is used to determine a percentage of the estimated inner distinct values used to estimate the outer distinct values in a sub query. The higher percentage the cost of optimizing the sub query as a join is smaller than individual index probes. The allowable values for this option are 0 to 4,294,967,296 and the default is 100. If you are thinking "How can a percentage value be higher than 100?" then let me explain a little further. The estimated inner distinct values may be more that the estimated outers meaning that there may be 1000's of percent more distinct inner values than the distinct value in the sub query.

Remember though that when you set this option it will affect all sub-queries so if you have a query that has several sub-queries then they all will use this value!!!

SUBQUERY_FLATTENING_PREFERENCE

This option is used to override the way the optimizer decides how to flatten out scalar of **EXISTS** sub-queries into joins. The default value 0 mean the optimizer will decide, other values are:-

Option Value	Description
3	Ignore cost of both EXISTS and scalar sub-query
2	Ignore cost flattening scalar, if possible
1	Ignore cost flattening EXIST, if possible
0	Allow the IQ optimizer to decide to flatten sub-queries
-1	Avoid flattening an EXISTS sub-query to a join operation
-2	Avoid flattening a scalar sub-query to a join operation
-3	Avoid flattening both EXISTS and scalar sub-queries to a join operation

SUBQUERY_PLACEMENT_PREFERENCE

There may be several places that a correlated sub-query can be placed in a query plan. The default value of 0 (allowed -1,0 and 1) means that the optimizer will decide the best place. If set to 1 then the optimizer places the sub query as high as possible in the plan meaning that the sub-query will be executed as late as possible within the query. When set to -1 then the sub query is placed at its lowest possible location and therefore executed as early as possible.

T-SQL, DBISQL and ASNSI SQL Options

These options are used for obtaining behaviour akin to ASE (T-SQL Options), effecting functionality of the DBISQL client software or ensuring ANSI compliant behaviour.

ANSI_CLOSE_CURSORS_ON_rollback (T-SQL)

This option is used to determine if cursors that where opened with a "WITH HOLD" are subsequently closed when a rollback operation is executed.

The only allowed value for this and hence also the default is ON. However the option CLOSE_ON_ENDTRANS (default ON) does override this option.

ANSI_PERMISSIONS (T-SQL)

This option is used to control if permissions are checked prior to UPDATE and DELETE statements executing. As you would expect the default value is ON, but surprisingly the default in ASE is OFF. No individual user or group settings can be set for this option, it is set only for PUBLIC.

ANSI_UPDATE_CONSTRAINTS (ANSI)

This option is used to constrain the SQL extensions that IQ provides to update statements such as joins. You would set this to "STRICT" is you wanted to make users only use correct ASNI updates/deletes, set it to OFF to allow them to do anything and set to CURSORS (The default) to only apply ANSI constraints to cursor updates. I would suggest leaving this as CURSORS or changing to OFF to allow developers to make the choice.

ASE_BINARY_DISPLAY (T-SQL)

When set to ON this option is used to display binary columns from the IQ store in readable ASCII format, when set to OFF they are displayed as binary output.

ASE_FUNCTION_BEHAVIOR (T-SQL)

This option is used to ensure that the outputs of IQ functions are consistent with the output of ASE functions. The default is OFF. As IQ uses unsigned 64 bit in the conversion functions INTTOHEX and HEXTOINT and ASE uses a signed 32 bit conversion you can set this option ON if you need your functions to behave the same as there ASE counterparts. The default value for this function is OFF.

CLOSE_ON_ENDTRANS (T-SQL)

This option would be used to control if cursors are closed or left open at the end of a transaction. As the only allowed value for this option and hence also the default value is ON, then this option is currently superfluous.

CONTINUE_AFTER_RAISERROR (T-SQL)

I suggest you read about the option **On_tsql_error** in the section above on common use options before progressing. This option is used to control what happens after a **RAISERROR** statement occurs (and also based on the value of the **On_tsql_error** option).

When set to ON (the default) then a **RAISERROR** statement does not signal an executing ending error, but instead continues until the procedure completes and then raises the first error it encounters. This means that sub-procedure calls that fail do not cause the calling procedure to fail.

When this option is switched to OFF then procedures are ended immediately with the error. I would also suggest reading the chapter on stored procedures to see how this can be used in error handling.

DEFAULT_ISQL_ENCODING (DBISQL)

This option is used to specify the code page that is used by **READ** and **OUTPUT** statements. The defaul is an empty string that means that the system code page is used.

EXTENDED_JOIN_SYNTAX (ANSI)

This option is used to control if queries with an ambiguous syntax used in multi table joins are allowed or reported as an error. The default value is ON meaning that they are allowed.
An example is given below

Fig 17.15

```
(<Table 1> RIGHT OUTER JOIN <Table 2>,
 <Table 2> JOIN <Table 3> ON (<Join Condition>)
```

When the option is OFF the code in Fig 17.15 will be reported as an error, but when the option is ON then this is interpreted by the optimizer as:-

Fig 17.16

```
(<Table 1> RIGHT OUTER JOIN <Table 2> ON (<Join Condition>))
JOIN <Table 3> ON (<Join Condition>)
```

NON_KEYWORDS (T-SQL)

This option allows you to effectively turn off keywords, and as such you can then use them as identifiers for variables, columns, tables etc. If for example we wanted to turn off the keyword **TRUNCATE** we could set the value of this option to '**TRUNCATE**', we could add more keywords by separating the value with a comma

Fig 17.17

```
SET OPTION NON_KEYWORDS = '<keyword>, <keyword>,<keyword>,...'
```

I would not suggest using this option and would instead recommend changing your identifiers to more reasonable names. The reason is that once a keyword is "turned off" then operations that use it will fail. For example imagine not being able to truncate a table!!

SQL_FLAGGER_ERROR_LEVEL (T-SQL)

This option specifies ho w IQ should flag errors when SQL code that is not part of SQL92 is executed (or an attempt is made to execute it. The allowed values are W(default),E,I and F.

Option Value	Description
W (default)	Allow all supported syntax
E	Flag Syntax that is not entry level SQL92 syntax
I	Flag syntax that is not intermediate-level SQL92 syntax
F	Flag syntax that is not full-SQL92 syntax

SQL_FLAGGER_WARNING_LEVEL (T-SQL)

This option specifies how IQ should flag warnings when SQL code that is not part of SQL92 is executed (or an attempt is made to execute it. The allowed values are W(default),E,I and F.

Option Value	Description
W (default)	Allow all supported syntax
E	Flag Syntax that is not entry level SQL92 syntax
I	Flag syntax that is not intermediate-level SQL92 syntax
F	Flag syntax that is not full-SQL92 syntax

Query Plan Options

The option listed below are used to produce and affect the output of Query Plans.

QUERY_DETAIL

When this option is set ON (the default is OFF) then additional information is placed in Query Plans (if switched on via either the **QUERY_PLAN** or **QUERY_PLAN_AS_HTML** options).

QUERY_NAME

Used to name an executed query in a query plan. This name can be an 80 byte character string. BY setting this name before each query in a batch statement the query plan becomes easier to use by identifying the query by the name given. In HTML plans the **QUERY_NAME** is also appended to the HTML file name.

QUERY_PLAN

This option is used to specify if query plans are generated, the default is ON, I suggest setting this to OFF until you require a query plan. As this option can be set temporary I would also suggest doing that as plans are written to the IQ message log. In fact I prefer using the **QUERY_PLAN_AS_HTML** option as they are sent to separate files and are much more readable (and can be read via a browser).

QUERY_PLAN_AFTER_RUN

When the option **QUERY_PLAN** or **QUERY_PLAN_AS_HTML** are ON then this option can be used to print the entire plan after execution is complete. The default for this option is OFF. By setting it ON you can gather a more complete picture of your execution as the query plan can display attributes such as the actual number of rows.

QUERY_PLAN_AS_HTML

This option is used to generate query plans as HTML files, the default value for this is OFF, but when it is ON you can use it as the SQL chapter to produce a query plan in a html file. As by default the HTML files are saved in the same directory as the message log (in the format <user id>_<query name>_YYYYMMDD_HHMMSS_<query number<.html) ensure your disk space is sufficient!

QUERY_PLAN_AS_HTML_DIRECTORY

This option is used t override the default location where IQ puts HTML query plans. As the default location is in the same directory as the IQ message file you run the risk of filling system space (though the html should be small enough not to) and also you may want to save plans to a specific directory. The value of this option is a string containing a directory location. However please note that if this option is set to a directory that does not exists then no error is reported when IQ tries to generate and save the query plan. See the SQL chapter for more detail on producing a query plan.

QUERY_PLAN_TEXT_ACCESS

If this option is set to ON (default is OFF) then users can view, save and print query plans from the dbisql client. When set to OFF then no query plans are displayed/cached and no query plan options have any effect on the dbisql client.

QUERY_PLAN_TEXT_CACHING

This option is used to control whether a query plan is cached for display purposes e.g. the dbisql client. The default value for this option is OFF (meaning no caching).

QUERY_TIMING

When this option is set to ON (default OFF) then timing statistics are gathered and displayed in query plans. As calculating the query time can take time it self and slow the query down it should be used sparingly.

Data Conversion and Formatting Options

These options are used to format and convert data from one format/data type to another.

CONVERSION_ERROR (T-SQL)

This option is used to determine if data type conversion errors are reported to the IQ message log/file. When it is set to OFF then errors are reported as warnings (the **SQLE_CANNOT_CONVERT** is written). When set to ON (the default) then an **SQLE_CONVERSION_ERROR** is generated.

CONVERSION_MODE

This is used to control the implicit conversion between non-binary and binary datatypes. The default value is 0 (it can only be 0 or 1), which means implicit is allowed. Setting the value to 1 will restrict the implicit conversion. This option can be set as temporary or permanent, it will stop the implicit conversion on inserts, updates, load tables as well as comparisons across datatypes e.g.

DATE_FIRST_DAY_OF_WEEK

The value for this option holds the integer value for what is determined to be the first day of the week. The default value is 0 (Sunday) allowed values are

Option Value	Description
0	Sunday
1	Monday
2	Tuesday
3	Wednesday
4	Thursday
5	Friday
6	Saturday

The value of this option effects the **DOW** and **DATEPART** functions so for system with a lot of date processing the effect can be dramatic (particularly financial systems that have month and year end cut off's).

LARGE_DOUBLES_ACCUMULATOR

As seen in the Tips chapter IQ can bring back results you do not agree with due to truncation, rounding and implicit data type conversion. The option affects the way that **AVG**, **SUM** and floating point numbers are accumulated. This option can be ON or OFF (Default), when it is set to OFF the optimizer will choose a faster hash to accumulate results but you may lose some accuracy if the number range is outside the magnitude range
1e-20 to 1e20. When the option is set to on then the accumulation retains a higher degree of accuracy but the optimization of the accumulation suffers.

MAX_CLIENT_NUMERIC_PRECISION

As mentioned in other chapters IQ attempts to implicitly convert value to a value it thinks maintain accuracy. This option allows you to set the maximum numeric precision that is returned to the client. can be any value between 0 and 126 (0 is the default and means no maximum). When a client requests data that is over this options value (if non zero) and IQ cannot cast it to a data type within the value then an error or SQL code -1001006 is returned. Option is useful if you want to truncate numeric values (stop trailing zeros) in client applications. You should use this option in conjunction with the **MAX_CLIENT_NUMERIC_SCALE** option. This

MAX_CLIENT_NUMERIC_SCALE

Like the option above (**MAX_CLIENT_NUMERIC_PRECISION**) this option controls the maximum scale of numeric data returned to clients. The values can be 0 to 126 (o is the default and means no maximum). If for example the option **MAX_CLIENT_NUMERIC_PRECISION** was set to 25 and **MAX_CLIENT_NUMERIC_SCALE** is 4 then numerics are returned as **DECIMAL** (25, 4).

NEAREST_CENTURY (T-SQL)

Well it looks like all that work on Y2K still didn't sort out 2 character dates. This option tells IQ which century to allocate to dates that are given with only a 2 character year. If the year is less than the number in this option then it sets them to 20YY otherwise it sets it to 19YY. The default value is 50 but as we progress through the century you may want to change this limit, or do the sensible thing and only use 4 character years!!

NON_ANSI_NULL_VARCHAR

If this option is set to ON (default OFF) then zero length varchars are stored as **NULL** of **LOAD**'s, **INSERT**'s and **UPDATE**'s. When it is set to OFF (default) then they are treated as zero length varchars (''). This option can be set temporary to allow you to control individual operations differently.

ODBC_DISTINGUISH_CHAR_AND_VARCHAR

This option is used to describe how **CHAR** and **VARCHAR** columns are describe via the IQ and SQL Anywhere ODBC drives. If this value is set to OFF (the default) then **CHAR** columns are described as **SQL_VARCHAR**, if it is set to ON they are described as **SQL_CHAR**. varchar's are always described as **SQL_VARCHAR**.

ON_CHARSET_CONVERSION_FAILURE

This option has three values **IGNORE** (default), **WARNING** and **ERROR** and it is used to control the behaviour when a character conversion fails.

Option Value	Description
IGNORE	Errors and warnings do not appear.
WARNING	Reports substitutions and illegal characters as warnings. Illegal characters are not translated.
ERROR	Reports substitutions and illegal characters as errors.

Single-byte to single-byte converters are not able to report substitutions and illegal characters, and must be set to **IGNORE**.

PRECISION

This option is only applicable to the catalog database, and is used to limit the maximum number of digits in the result of arithmetic performed on tables from the catalog database.
This only has one allowed value ad hence it is also the default – 126. A similar option is available for the IQ store called **MAX_CLIENT_NUMERIC_PRECISION**, which you can change the value of!!!

PRESERVE_SOURCE_FORMAT

This option when switched ON (default) saves the source definition for procedures, views and events preserving the formatted source data. Unformatted versions are stored in proc_defn and view_defn and are not very readable. By switching/leaving this option ON then the formatted code is stored in the **SYSTABLE**, **SYSPROCEDURE** and **SYSEVENT** system tables and is used by Sybase central to present readable DDL.

QUOTED_IDENTIFIER (T-SQL)

This option when switched ON (the default) will interpret anything inside double quotes as an identifier. This is useful when wanting to put spaces in column names or when a column identifier is the same as a keyword.
For example in Fig 17.18 below, the column option can be returned as it is enclosed in double quotes, if it was not then IQ returns a "Syntax Error near 'option' on line 1, SQLCODE=-131" error.

Fig 17.18

    SELECT "option" FROM SYSOPTIONS

RETURN_DATE_TIME_AS_STRING

When set to ON (The default is OFF) then dates, datetimes, timestamps and time are converted to a string before sending to a client. It will format the string of the date, timestamp or time in line with the settings for the options **TIMESTAMP_FORMAT, DATE_FORMAT, or TIME_FORMAT**.

TDS_EMPTY_STRING_IS_NULL

When this option is set to OFF (default) then a string containing one blank character in will be returned as one blank character to TDS connections. However when this is option is switched to ON then strings with one blank character are returned to TDS connections as **NULL** strings.

TIME_FORMAT

This options value is the format that times are retrieved from the database in. The default is 'HH:NN:SS.SSS' for Open Client and JDBC connections (TDS), often the T-SQL settings are overwritten using the Login Procedures (See commonly used options section). Time Formats are comprised of the symbols HH, NN, MM and SS where SS is seconds and Microseconds. See the chapter on SQL for the TIME_FORMAT function.

TIMESTAMP_FORMAT

This option sets the format for **TIMESTAMP** retrieval from the database. the default is 'YYYY-MM-DD HH:NN:SS.SSS'. See the section in the chapter on SQL for the **DATE** formatting function and also the section on **DATE** data types in the Tables, Data Types and Views Chapters.

Extract and Loads

The options below are used when loading and extracting data to/from the database. Please refer to the chapter on loading and extracting data for examples on how these options can be used.

APPEND_LOAD

This option can be set temporary and for individuals and groups. When this option is set to ON it means that any LOAD to INSERT statements will append rows to the table and not re-use space created when rows have been deleted from a table. The default for this option is OFF and space will be re-used.

LOAD_MEMORY_MB

This option sets the amount of heap memory in Mb that loads can use, the default is 0 (no limit) but it can be set from 0 to 2000. For IQ 15.x the load process does not require as much heap memory as in previous releases and this option in 15.x is mostly for fixed width loads. If you run out of memory when running a **LOAD TABLE** then set this value initially to the upper bound of 2000 and then decrease the value until your **LOAD TABLE** no longer returns an error. Of course the trade off is that if you set the value to low for the data you are trying to load then this may also cause a failure. You may also want to set the **BLOCK FACTOR** or **BLOCK SIZE LOAD** options that control the virtual memory used for block sizes during loads.

LOAD_ZEROLENGTH_ASNULL

Put simply this option if ON (default is OFF) will set any zero-length values to **NULL** from a **LOAD** statement.
The **NULL(ZEROS)** or **NULL(BLANKS)** options must also be set in the **LOAD TABLE** and this will only work for data types of **CHAR**, **VARCHAR**, **BINARY** and **VARBINARY** (and **LONG VARCHAR** and **LONG VARBINARY** is applicable)

TEMP EXTRACT OPTIONS

The options below are used when extracting data via the **TEMP EXTRACT** Process, see the chapter on Loading and Extracting Data for examples.

TEMP_EXTRACT_APPEND

When set to ON (default OFF) then any extracted data will be appended to the end of an output file. This option cannot be used in conjunction with **TEMP_EXTRACT_SIZEn** option.

TEMP_EXTRACT_BINARY

When set to ON (default is OFF) then the extract is defined to be of type **BINARY** when set to OFF it is ASCII (if the option **TEMP_EXTRACT_SWAP** is also set to OFF).

TEMP_EXTRACT_COLUMN_DELIMITER

This option accepts any 4 character string value (default ',') to specify how columns should be delimited (not separated) in the data extract.

TEMP_EXTRACT_DIRECTORY

This option is used to control the directory where the data extraction will be saved to. The default is an empty string but you can set it to the extract directory. If you set it to the string "**FORBIDDEN**" then an error will be reported informing the user they do not have permissions. The value of this option will override a directory path specified in the **TEMP_EXTRACT_NAMEn** option. It will also report back an error at the extraction execution if the directory does not exist. If this value is left blank and there is also no directory specified in the **TEMP_EXTRACT_NAMEn** option then the extracted file will be saved in the sever start up directory.

TEMP_EXTRACT_ESCAPE_QUOTES

This option when set to ON (default OFF) will escape quotes in your extraction. This option only comes into effect when **TEMP_EXTRACT_QUOTE** is set to double quotes, **TEMP_EXTRACT_BINARY** is OFF and either of the following two options is set to ON
TEMP_EXTRACT_QUOTES/TEMP_EXTRACT_QUOTES_ALL.

TEMP_EXTRACT_NAMEn

This option is used to name the extract file (and directory if the option **TEMP_EXTRACT_DIRECTORY** is an empty string). The format of the option is **TEMP_EXTRACT_NAMEn** where n is the number of the extract file. Up to 8 extract files can be named but the must be named sequentially so if for example you wish to use **TEMP_EXTRACT_NAME2** you must have already named **TEMP_EXTRACT_NAME1**. It is recommended you set the option as temporary.
You may append to a file for several **SELECT** statements or you may wish to specify maximum file sizes for the files by using the **TEMP_EXTRACT_SIZEn** option. When specifying file sizes, IQ will progress onto the next file that has been declared until there are no more files to use when it return a file full error (i.e. It will fill the file in **TEMP_EXTRACT_NAME1** before progressing to the file in **TEMP_EXTRACT_NAME2**).
When **TEMP_EXTRACT_NAME1** is set, you cannot execute **LOAD, DELETE, INSERT,** or **INSERT LOCATION,** or **SYNCHRONIZE JOIN INDEX** Statements. I recommend only issuing **SELECT** statements and then setting the **TEMP_EXTRACT_NAME1** option back to an empty string.
It is also worth noting that your select cannot use user defined functions and the select can only be from tables in the IQ store.

TEMP_EXTRACT_NULL_AS_EMPTY

When data extraction is in ASCII format and this value is set to ON (default OFF) then **NULL** values are extracted as an empty string. When this is set to OFF then the string 'NULL' is extracted to represent a **NULL** value.

TEMP_EXTRACT_NULL_AS_ZERO

When data extraction is in ASCII format and this value is set to ON (default OFF) then **NULL** values are extracted as below.

- '0' for arithmetic type

- ⊛ '' (the empty string) for the CHAR and VARCHAR character types
- ⊛ '' (the empty string) for dates
- ⊛ '' (the empty string) for times
- ⊛ '' (the empty string) for timestamps

When this is set to OFF then the string 'NULL' is extracted to represent a **NULL** string value and any columns extracted will have a minimum width of 4 bytes which can cause spacing issues!.

TEMP_EXTRACT_QUOTE

This option is used to specify the string that is used to quote fields in the data extraction (when in ASCII format). The options **TEMP_EXTRACT_QUOTES** or **TEMP_EXTRACT_QUOTES_ALL** must also be set to ON. The default value is an empty string, but which IQ converts to a single quotation mark. The allowed values can be from a 1 to a 4 byte string.

TEMP_EXTRACT_QUOTES

When set to ON (default OFF) then all character fields are output quoted (By the option value from **TEMP_EXTRACT_QUOTE** if the default cannot be used).

TEMP_EXTRACT_QUOTES_ALL

When set to ON (default OFF) then all fields are output quoted (By the option value from **TEMP_EXTRACT_QUOTE** if the default cannot be used).

TEMP_EXTRACT_ROW_DELIMITER

This is used to define the delimiter of rows in the data extract (when output in ASCII format). The default value of the option is an empty string which IQ interprets as a new line character on Unix systems and a carriage return on Windows. Allowed values can be any 4 byte string (that is valid in the collation order of your system).

TEMP_EXTRACT_SIZEn

This option is used to specify the maximum size of a file in Kb. The "n" corresponds to the file number and relates directly to the file in **TEMP_EXTRACT_NAMEn**. For example if **TEMP_EXTRACT_SIZE2** is set to 1024 then the file named in **TEMP_EXTRACT_NAME2** will be a maximum size of 1024Kb.
The default value is zero which depending on the operating system will be interpreted as below:-

Device Type	Size
Disk file AIX and HP-UX	0-64GB
Sun Solaris & Linux	0-512GB
Windows	0-128GB
Other	8192 PetaBytes!!!!

If your file system supports larger sizes than those set out in the defaults then you can change the value of the TEMP_EXTRACT_SIZEn to the relevant size.

You cannot use the TEMP_EXTRACT_APPEND option set to ON when restricting file sizes with this option.

TEMP_EXTRACT_SWAP

This option when set to ON this option specifies the extraction as a **BINARY SWAP** extraction. Leave this set to OFF in conjunction with **TEMP_EXTRACT_BINARY** to obtain ASCII extractions.

Database and Server Options

The options below can be used to control the database and server behaviour, I have also used this section to place all those other options that did not fit into the other categories.

AUDITING

This option is used to enable and disable database auditing the default is OFF. If you want to switch auditing on then set this option to ON and specify the types of auditing information you require using the system procedure sa_enable_auditing_type (See the system procedures chapter). Because this option affects the whole database you will require DBA permissions to set it.

BIT_VECTOR_PINNABLE_CACHE_PERCENT

This option is used to control memory allocation and should not generally be changed. Basically it is used to hold the percentage (as an integer and the default is 40) of memory that a single bit-vector object can use. Before you think about changing it may be worth contacting your Sybase Technical support contact to see what they recommend. I personally have never had to change this option.

BLOCKING

This function controls the behaviour in response to locking conflicts, it can only be set to OFF which means you get an error when trying to obtain a write lock on a table already in use. Like some other options and configurations in IQ this option may change in the future to allow other values.

CHECKPOINT_TIME

This is used to control the maximum time in minutes that an IQ server can run for before it runs a checkpoint. As you require DBA privileges to changes this value and the server requires a reboot for it to take affect it is rarely changed. The default value is 60 minutes but in high volatility systems you may want to reduce this to fit your requirements.

CIS_ROWSET_SIZE

When connecting to remote servers (using CIS over ODBC) then this option is used to determine the number of rows that are retrieved in a single fetch (by setting the ODBC FetchArraySize value). The default value is 50, but if your proxy tables, insert locations etc are running slow you may want to loc at your network settings and result row size and configure this option to be more optimal. If for example your network is a very fats and your result set row size is low you may want to increase this value.

CONVERT_VARCHAR_TO_1242

This option is used to compress data from databases from versions 12.4.2 that have been upgraded to newer versions. The default is 'OFF', when set to ON it will take effect when a **sp_iqcheckdb** is run. It should only be used when converting **VARCHAR** data during the conversion process. As 12.4.2 is now becoming rarer I doubt you will ever have to use it (but it's there for the time being if you do need it).

COOPERATIVE_COMMIT_TIMEOUT

This option is used to control the time in milliseconds that a **COMMIT** from the Tran log is written to disk. The default is 250 milliseconds. The option is only used when the option **COOPERATIVE_COMMITS** has a value ON. The wait time in milliseconds is used to allow other connections to fill a page on the log before writing to disk. IQ is generally good at handling this type of process and I doubt you would have to change the value. Increasing the time means less I/O to disk but that individual connections have to wait longer for the write.

COOPERATIVE_COMMITS

This option dictates whether IQ should wait for the time defined in the **COOPERATIVE_COMMIT_TIMEOUT** option before writing a **COMMIT** to disk. ON (the default) means wait OFF means write immediately.

DBCC_LOG_PROGRESS

When running the sp_iqcheckdb procedure (see the chapter on System Procedures) this option if set to ON (the default is OFF) will force the procedure to send progress messages to the IQ Message Log/File.

DBCC_PINNABLE_CACHE_PERCENT

The value of this option (0-100) hold the percentage of the cache that can be used by the sp_iqcheckdb procedure, the default is 50.

DEBUG_MESSAGES

This option is used to control if **MESSAGE** statements that include the **DEBUG ONLY** clause are executed (The default is OFF). If this option is set to ON then debug messages in stored procedures can be enabled.

DEDICATED_TASK

This option is generally used by DBA's and can be set as temporary only. If set to ON (The default is OFF) then a handling task is dedicated for the duration of the connection ensuring that if the server becomes unresponsive then the DBA still has a dedicated handler for their requests. Please remember that you need to have a pre-existing connection with the option enabled otherwise you will not have a dedicated handler.

DEFAULT_DBSPACE

This option can be set to give a default DBSpace for join indexes and tables to be stored. The default value is an empty string meaning the IQ_SYSTEM_MAIN DBSpace is used.

DEFAULT_DISK_STRIPING

This option is used to determine if disk stripping is ON or OFF (The default is ON). If a new DBSpace is created and you have not specified the stripping option then the DEFAULT_DISK_STRIPPING option is used to determine the default.

DEFAULT_KB_PER_STRIPE

This option is used to set the default size (In KB) for DBSpaces in the IQ Main Store.
It is used by the **CREAT DBSPACE** statement to define the stripping size for all DBSpaces (Unless specified in the **CREATE DBSPACE** statement).

DELAYED_COMMIT_TIMEOUT

This option holds a value in milliseconds that IQ would use to decide then a server returns control to an app following a **COMMIT**. Its pointless because it is designed to work in conjunction with the **DELAYED_COMMITS** option that can only be set to OFF.

DELAYED_COMMITS

This option can only be set to OFF. If it was allowed to be on it would use the value from the **DELAYED_COMMIT_TIMEOUT** option to decide when an application resumes control following it issuing a **COMMIT**.

DISABLE_RI_CHECK

This option can be used to bypass referential integrity checking. When set to ON (The default is OFF) then this option means that referential integrity is not checked when loading, updating, inserting and deleting data.

FORCE_DROP

This option should only be used by DBA's (and only after consulting Sybase tech support) as it means that disk space is leaked rather than reclaimed during a DROP statement. (The default value for this is OFF)
This option should be set temporary (but it can be set PUBLIC). In order to drop a corrupt object (index, table etc) you can set this option to ON, this prevents the free list being incorrectly changed when the object is dropped. Once the corrupt objects have been dropped the DBA can reclaim the space by using the –iqdroplks and –iqfeq server switches.
Once the force drop has been run the server must be immediately restarted.

FORCE_UPDATABLE_CURSORS

When this option is set to ON (The default is OFF) then cursors that have not been explicitly declared as updateable can be updated. It is used to allow lazy programming in applications that require updateable cursors that do not explicitly declare them using the **FOR UPDATE** clause in the **DECLARE CURSOR** statement.

FP_LOOKUP_SIZE

This option is used define the cache size used in the creation of lookup FP indexes. The default is 16 (Mb) but the allowed values are 1-4096 (Mb). This option must be set PUBLC.

FP_LOOKUP_SIZE_PPM

This option is used to set the number of lookup pages size that IQ uses when creating FP indexes. The allowed values are 1 to 1,000,000 and the default is 2500. IQ uses the value of this to restrict the pages based on the value of this option in the calculation in Fig 17.19.

Fig 17.19

$$FP\_LOOKUP\_SIZE\_PPM * size\ of\ main\ memory / 1,000,000$$

Size of main memory is specific by the -iqmc server switch.

FP_PREDICATE_WORKUNIT_PAGES

This option is used to specify the degree of the parallelism that IQ can use in a default index (default 200). The default index will parallelise some predicates (**SUM, RANGE, MAX, COUNT, MIN** etc). This option is used to specify the number of pages worked on by each thread during the parallel processing. The higher the value of this option the less parallel processing will take place (As more pages are used by less threads), and as it is set lower the inverse is true (more parallel processing working on a smaller number of pages).

FPL_EXPRESSION_MEMORY_KB

This option is used when the optimizer processes functional expressions on columns that have enumerated storage. The default value is 1024(Kb) and it can be set between 0 and 20,000(Kb). As it can be set temporary you can test this functionality without affecting other parts of the system. If you set the value to zero then no memory optimisation happens and IQ uses what it needs.

G-ARRAY_FILL_FACTOR_PERCENT

This option is used to decide the percentage of space each **HG** g-array page that should be reserved for future inserts (incremental) this space is used to add values to existing groups only. The default is 25 (allowed 0-100). If you expect your system to do incremental inserts in the future into **HG** indexes with data that already have values in the **HG** index then setting this to a higher value may increase the inserts performance, But remember reserving space mean using more space hence more cost!!!

G-ARRAY_INSERT_PREFETCH_SIZE

This option is used to specify how many pages of data should be pre-fetched (read) when inserting into a column with a **HG** index. The default is 3 (allowed 0-100). I have never had to change or even test this option and Sybase advise not to without first contacting there technical support team!

G-ARRAY_PAGE_SPLIT_PAD_PERCENT

This option will determine the per-page fill factor used during page splits on g-arrays, it is used to specify the percentage of space each **HG** g-array should reserve for future inserts (incremental). When a split occurs the optimiser attempts to leave the percentage specified in this option (default 25) free. My advice is don't change!

G-ARRAY_RO_PREFETCH_SIZE

This option is used to specify how many pages of data should be pre-fetched (read) when querying a column with a HG index. The default is 10, but you can set the value from 0 to 100. My advice is don't change!

HASH_PINNABLE_CACHE_PERCENT

This option determines the maximum percentage of a user's temporary memory that the optimizer can use to pin a hash object to. The default value is 20 (Allowed 0 to100). If you are running lots of large simple queries then you may want to consider increasing this value (I'd suggest never going over 50%). However if you run lots of small complex queries then you may find is beneficial to reduce the value of this option. As this has system wide implications then a complete testing strategy should be used to enable the widest possible number of different queries as possible.

HASH_THRASHING_PERCENT

This option is used to specify the percentage of disk I/O allowed when executing a statement that includes hash algorithms before reporting an error and rolling back. (The default is 10, but allowed values are 0-100).

HG_SEARCH_RANGE

This option is used to specify the amount of b-tree pages that are used when the optimizer evaluates as range predicate using a **HG** index. Any integer value can be used (The default is 10). Basically this option sets the amount of time that is spent by the optimizer on deciding the best index to use for a range predicate. Setting the value higher means that the optimizer spends more time on deciding the best index to use, but may improve the choice and thus the query time, the inverse is true when setting it lower.

IDENTITY_ENFORCE_UNIQUENESS

This option if set to ON (the default is OFF) will create a HG index on any Identity (or AutoIncrement) column defined on a table (If it is not already a primary key).

INFER_SUBQUERY_PREDICATES

This option is used if you want to override by setting the value to OFF (default is ON) the optimizers choice of inferring sub-query predicates from other sub-queries already used in the query. My advice is don't change this!

IQGOVERN_MAX_PRIORITY

This option is used to **LIMIT** the setting of **IQGOVERN_PRIORITY** which is used to control the order in which users queries are queued for execution (run sp_iqcontext to see your currently running queries value). The allowed values are 1-3 (default 2), these values related to the descriptions below:-

Option Value	Description
1	Indicates High Priority
2	Indicates Medium Priority
3	Indicates Low Priority

IQGOVERN_PRIORITY

This option is used to assign a priority to each query waiting to be executed in the –iqgovern queue. This option can be set temporary if required for testing purposes. The default value is 2 and the value is limited by the value of the **IQGOVERN_MAX_PRIORITY** option.

Option Value	Description
1	Indicates High Priority
2	Indicates Medium Priority
3	Indicates Low Priority

IQGOVERN_PRIORITY_TIME

This option sets the time (in seconds) that a high priority (**IQGOVERN_PRIORITY** = 1) query will wait before executing. Once the time limit is reached it will execute regardless if it means the number of queries exceeds the –iqgovern server switch setting. The range is 1 to 1,000,000 seconds the default is zero which effectively switches this option off. This option must be set public so be careful is you must change it.

LF_BITMAP_CACHE_KB option

This option sets the amount of cache in Kb that IQ uses as a cache when loading LF indexes (The default is 4, but can be between 0 and 8). The higher the cardinality of the value being loaded then the more cache is required and if set to low it will impact load performance. The formula for calculating the heap memory that will be used in a load is given below the cache required for a load into an LF index is given below in Fig 17.20.

Fig 17.20

```
(lf_bitmap_cache_kb * 1024)* < The cardinality of the column>
```

LOG_CONNECT

When this option is set to ON (the default) then a message is written to the IQ message log whenever a user connects to or disconnects from the database.

LOG_CURSOR_OPERATIONS

When this option is set to ON (default is OFF) then a message is written to the IQ message log whenever a cursor is opened or closed.

LOGIN_MODE

This option has three allowed values "Standard" (the default), "Mixed" or "Integrated". It is used to control is integrated logins are allowed if the user has been granted an integrated login, DBA level users are not effected by the value of this option.

Option Value	Description
Standard	The default setting, this does not permit integrated logins. An error occurs if an integrated login connection is attempted.
Mixed	Both integrated and standard logins are allowed.
Integrated	All logins to the database must be integrated logins.

LOGIN_PROCEDURE

This option defines the name of the stored procedure that is run whenever a user logs in to the database, the default procedure is sp_login_environment. The procedure is used to set compatibility options that may override your public or user permanent options for certain types of connection protocol.

In stead of changing the code in this procedure you should instead create a new procedure and set the value of this option to reflect the new procedure. (also see the option **POST_LOGIN_PROCEDURE**)

MAIN_RESERVED_DBSPACE_MB

This controls the amount of space in Mb that is reserved in the IQ Main Store. It allows any value greater than or equal to 200 (the default). IQ needs a certain amount of space to store critical data structures that are used when **COMMITs**, **SAVEPOINT** releases and checkpoints are executed. The more concurrent connections you have and the larger the page size the more reserved space you will require. IQ actually reserves a minimum of 1% of the most recent read-write file in the IQ_SYSTEM_MAIN space to a maximum of 50%.

MAX_CARTESIAN_RESULT

This option attempts to limit the number of rows that can be returned from a query with a Cartesian product. The problem is that if IQ cannot find a query plan that ESTIMATES the results to be under this limit then it does not allow you to run the query. I have found IQ is not very good at this estimation and stops completely reasonable queries with small results from being executed. The default value for this is 100,000,000, but I suggest turning it off by setting it to zero and using monitoring and other options to limit bas queries.

MAX_CUBE_RESULT

This is another option where IQ tries to estimate results, as such I would suggest setting the value to 0 to turn it off (allowed values are between 0 and 4,294,967,295). It is used to stop queries executing where it believes the number of rows in a cube will exceed the value of this option. Unfortunately until the optimizers estimation algorithms become more accurate using this type of option to limit data causes more problems than it fixes (in my experience).

MAX_CURSOR_COUNT

This option is used to limit the number of cursors a connection can use at any one time. The default is 50 (0 is no limit) and it requires DBA permissions to change it for any connection. I have never found cause to change this option!

MAX_DAYS_SINCE_LOGIN

This is used to hold the value (in days) that can elapse between user logins from the same user id before the user is locked out.

MAX_FAILED_LOGIN_ATTEMPTS

This is used to set a value of the number of failed attempts a user can try (since the last successful attempt) to login before their account is locked.

MAX_HASH_ROWS

This is another option where the IQ optimizer tries to estimate values. It allows values 0 to 4,294,967,295 (default 2,500,000) which relate to how many rows are produced when running a hash join algorithm. If the number of estimated hash rows exceeds the value of this option then IQ will not consider the hash join. I have always set this to at least 10,000,000 on any system over a 100Gb (And over 50Mb of temp buffer cache)

MAX_IQ_THREADS_PER_CONNECTION

This value controls the number of threads a connection can use at any given time. It can be an integer between 3 and 10,000 (default 144). I have never had to change the default value and I believe 144 should be adequate for most systems and processes.

MAX_IQ_THREADS_PER_TEAM

This option limits the number of threads that a single operation (e.g. a single LIKE statement) can use when executing within a transaction (default 144, but can be between 3 and 10,000). The total threads that a connection can use are limited by the MAX_IQ_THREADS_PER_CONNECTION option.

MAX_JOIN_ENUMERATION

This option is used to limit the join order of table. When the optimizer has optimized the join order of tables by using lookup tables and Cartesian products it then optimizes the remaining tables up to the limit set by this option (default 15, but can be 1-64). I have never had to change this option, but if you want to it is recommended that you set it temporary.

MAX_QUERY_PARALLELISM

This option limits the parallelism of **GROUP BY, UNION, ORDEY BY** and Join operations. For databases with more than 24 CPU cores it is recommended that this value is set high, up to the number of cores. But if your system has les than 24 cores then the default value of 24 should be ok (but you can try lowering it if your CPU's are not performing as expected).

MAX_QUERY_TIME

This is the option I recommend using for controlling DML queries (outside of specific monitoring if available) it is the maximum number of minutes a query can run before returning and error. The default value is 0 (no limit) but can be set up to 4,294,967,295 (Although I would not suggest allowing a query to run this long as it equates to over 8 thousand years). It can also be set temporary so you put it in user applications and limit it to specific operations.

MAX_STATEMENT_COUNT

This is used to limit the number of prepared statements that a single connection can hold at one time. The default it 100 but it can be any integer value. Unless you have a complicated application that needs to prepare over a 100 statements before executing them I suggest you leave the option at its default setting.

MAX_WARNINGS

This limits the number of warnings (the default is 18,446,744,073,709,599,999) are allowed about a DDL commands. It can be set to any integer.

MIN_PASSWORD_LENGTH

This sets the minimum length in characters that a password must be set to (the default is 0 meaning no minimum). It only takes effect for passwords created after the value is set.

MONITOR_OUTPUT_DIRECTORY

The value of this option is the directory location used to store monitor output files.

NOTIFY_MODULUS

This option is used control the frequency of notify messages that are issues by certain commands e.g. **LOAD TABLE**. (the default is 100,000, but can be any integer). When the NOTIFY clause is used e.g. on a **LOAD TABLE** then the value of the NOTIFY clause overrides the value of this option.

OS_FILE_CACHE_BUFFERING

This option when set to OFF (default) prevents files in the IQ store from doing any file system buffering. This saves on copying data from the cache into the IQ store buffer cache and thus reduces memory issues caused by the file system and IQ store buffer cache competing for memory. But if the IQ page size is less than the file systems block size then performance may decrease.
When set to ON the file system will perform buffer caching.

POST_LOGIN_PROCEDURE

This options value is the name of the stored procedure that is run once a user has successfully logged on. The default procedure is dbo.sa_login_procedure, and if you need to change the code this procedure runs then I recommend you create a new procedure and rename the value of this option to the new procedure. The post login procedure supports the client applications dbisql, dbisqlc, and the IQ plug-in for Sybase Central. (also see the **LOGIN_PROCEDURE** option).

PREFETCH_BUFFER_LIMIT

When pre-fetching data this option can be used to control the limit on memory by defining the number of cache pages available. Do not set this option without first speaking to Sybase technical support.

PREFETCH_BUFFER_PERCENT

This option has a value 0 to 100 (default is 40) that specifies the percentage of memory that can be used for pre-fetching of data. Do not set this option without first speaking to Sybase technical support.

PREFETCH_G-ARRAY_PERCENT

This option has a value 0 to 100 (default is 60) that specifies the percentage of memory that can be used for pre-fetching of data when building g-arrays for HG indexes. Do not set this option without first speaking to Sybase technical support.

PREFETCH_SORT_PERCENT

This option has a value 0 to 100 (default is 20) that specifies the percentage of memory that can be used for pre-fetching of data when sorting. Do not set this option without first speaking to Sybase technical support.

RECOVERY_TIME

This option is used to set the maximum amount of time in minutes that a server takes to recover from a system failure. The default is 2 minutes but it can be set to any integer. This option should be used in conjunction with the CHECKPOINT_TIME option which sets the maximum time a server can run before doing a checkpoint.

SORT_PINNABLE_CACHE_PERCENT

This option is used to set the maximum percentage (default 20, allowed 0-100) of available buffers that a sort object can attempt to pin. The larger the sort then a higher value of this option may help as it reduces the number of merges the sort has to perform. However Sybase do not recommend changing this option without first contacting Sybase Technical support.

SUPPRESS_TDS_DEBUGGING

If this option is set to ON (the default is OFF) then TDS debugging does not appear in the server window. When set to OFF it does appear. In order for any TDS debugging to be appear, the server must be started with the –z option.

SWEEPER_THREADS_PERCENT

This option is used to specify the percentage of threads that IQ will use to sweep and therefore clean out dirty pages from the main and temp buffer caches. The default value is 10 (allowed 1 to 40) Function Specifies the percentage of Sybase IQ threads used to sweep out buffer caches

TEMP_RESERVED_DBSPACE_MB

Certain IQ operations (commits, release savepoint etc) require a small amount of space in the temp store; this option is used to specify how much space is reserved (In Mb). The default is 200 and it can be set to any integer value greater than 200 (Although try not to be stupid!!). IQ reserves automatically a maximum of 50% and a minimum of 1% of the last read-write file in the IQ_SYSTEM_TEMP DBSpace. As a rule, the larger your page size, the larger temp space (and thus reserve space) you will require.

TEMP_SPACE_LIMIT_CHECK

This option when set to ON (default) checks the temporary space in the CATALOG store that connection requests. If the connection request more that its quota the connections current query fails. This option should always be left ON as when OFF a fatal error can occur if the temporary space fills its disk. To check its quota IQ first checks is the temporary file has gown to 80% of its maximum size. If it has then any connection that is using more than the maximum size divided by the total number of server connections fails.

TOP_NSORT_CUTOFF_PAGES

When executing a SELECT TOP n with an ORDER BY this option is used to set the threshold (in pages) that is evaluated when running the sort based processing for the ORDER BY. The TOP n process is optimized for when n is less than the number of result rows (without a TOP). In some situations increasing the value of this option may improve query performance by avoiding sort based processing.

TRIM_PARTIAL_MBC

When this option is set to ON (default OFF) then a partial multi-byte character is replaced with a blank when loading into a CHAR column and is truncated when loading into a VARCHAR column. When the option is OFF then the normal errors conversion errors are reported (As set by the CONVERSION_ERRORS option).

USER_RESOURCE_RESERVATION

This option adjusts memory use according to the total number of current users. When IQ allocates memory it is done by tracking the number of currently open cursors. This option can be used to set the minimum number of cursors that IQ "Thinks" it is currently using and there fore allocate less memory across user connections. It is recommended you contact Sybase Tech Support if you believe this option may aid in your query optimisation.

VERIFY_PASSWORD_FUNCTION

You can use this option to set a function to be called when a **GRANT CONNECT** to user **IDENTIFIED BY** password is executed. The option value is set to the form of owner.function_name and it should take two parameters <user_name> and <new_pwd>. When you create your function it is recommended that you also run ALTER FUNCTION *function_ -name* SET HIDDEN to stop users from examining the code contained (if it is sensitive/security restricted). The function should return a string with a message if the password does not verify or **NULL** if it is ok. This option's default value is an empty string which means it has no function to run. Also because the input parameters are in Watcom format (no @ prefix), the function should be written in Watcom SQL.

WASH_AREA_BUFFERS_PERCENT

This option is used to specify the percentage of the buffer caches that are above the wash mark, the default value is 20 (Allowed 1 to 100). The IQ buffer caches are organized in a long MRU/LRU chain. The area in the cache that is above the wash marker is used to write dirty pages to disk. It is recommended you speak with Sybase Technical support before attempting to change this options value.

WAIT_FOR_COMMIT

This option is used to determine when referential integrity is checked after a data in a table is altered/changed. If this option is set to ON (default is OFF) then the database waits until the next **COMMIT** before checking the referential integrity. When set to OFF then any foreign keys that were not created with the **CHECK_ON_COMMIT** option switched ON will be checked as the data is changed.

WD_DELETE_METHOD

This option allows 4 values 0 to 3 (the default is 0) that are used to specify the algorithm used by the optimizer when calculating the cost of a delete on a **WD** index. The values refer to the descriptions below:-

Option Value	Description
0	The delete method is selected by the optimizer; it will select either a medium or large cost based method for deletion.
1	This forces a small cost based method for deletion. This is useful if only deleting a small percentage of the data as it can randomly access the index, causing cache thrashing with large datasets.
2	This forces a large cost based method for deletion. This method scans the entire index searching for rows to delete. This is useful when deleting a large percentage of the data.
3	This forces a medium method for deletion. This is a variation of the small method (option 1) that accesses the index in order and is generally faster than the small method if the data being deleted is in a medium percentage range.

Migration from SQL Server, ASE and Non T-SQL Databases

Many of the implementations of Sybase IQ I have worked on have involved migrating from another database product. This could be Oracle, Sybase ASE or SQL Server, as these are the three main databases currently in the market I will use them in my examples.

Over the past few years I have worked on projects were we have migrated entire legacy systems to IQ from legacy Mainframe systems, Sybase ASE, SQL Server and Oracle. In each of these many of the concepts used in the migration were of a generic nature and can be used if you are migrating from another product.
This section explains the generic processes you can use to migrate both the DDL and DML from another database system.

There are a set of "gotcha's" you need to look for particularly around keywords and code optimisation.

Overview

I have worked on many conversion projects and can safely say there are three main components when migrating to IQ from another database.

- Moving the physical infrastructure, deciding on the best disk layouts, configurations and storage types.
- Moving the DML and data into IQ without losing precision and ensuring data quality with the source.
- Migration of stored procedure and application code.

Each of these steps has its own problems and issues. Hopefully the sections below will aid you in resolving issues and concerns you have.

You may also want to consider purchasing Sybase Power Designer as it allows you to extract the DML from one database and convert to IQ syntax at a click of a button. Although it does have some quirks it is about 80%-90% correct so will allow you to get the bulk of the DML conversion done quickly. You can then also use the DML to create physical data models for your new system.

Physical Infrastructure Migration

Hosts

The type of O/S, the machine specification and the version of IQ you are installing can all have an effect on performance. In general the more power you can throw at IQ the better, but on the other hand you don't want to spend unnecessary money.
It is worth checking with your Sybase representative on what the best O/S and machine specs are for you version of IQ and how you plan to use it.

Storage

RAID levels, disk types and disk layout can have a dramatic effect on the performance of your system. In general IQ prefers concatenated file systems as it stripes the data horizontally across DBSpaces anyway so adding in a vertical stripped can cause a slow down win data reads and writes.
It is worth investing in a contractor, DBA or a consultant Sybase Professional Services who know what they are talking about from this perspective to cover the gap between DBA, sa, network and storage professionals' knowledge. Having experience of another database produce just won't cut it if you want a performant system.

Licenses

The type of license you require will depend on the machine specification you wish to run IQ on, the version of IQ and the data you wish to store. If for example you wish to only use a sub set of the CPU's on your machine then only IQ 15.2 will allow this kind of throttling. Also you may have to pay extra to use large objects such as **BLOBS** and **CLOBS** (See the chapter on data types).

Data Migration

Tables

Keywords

Sybase IQ will only allow you to use Keywords (see Appendix I) as identifiers (table names, column names, index names etc) if you either block bracket them or set the **QUOTED_IDENTIFIERS** option to ON and quote them. For example Fig 18.1 is not allowed but Fig 18.2 and Fig 18.3 are fine.

Fig 18.1

```
CREATE TABLE test_table
(
        DATE DATETIME NULL
)
```

Fig 18.2

```
CREATE TABLE test_table
(
        [DATE] DATETIME NULL
)
```

Fig 18.3

```
SET QUOTED_IDENTIFIER ON

CREATE TABLE test_table
(
        [DATE] DATETIME NULL
)
```

You can also turn identifiers off by setting the option **NON_KEYWORDS** to the keywords you wish to use in your code.

For example, Fig 18.4 will stop the keywords **DROP** and **DELETE** from being recognised as keywords.

Fig 18.4

```
SET OPTION NON_KEYWORDS = 'DROP, DELETE'
```

But using this will mean that if you try to use the keywords in any other code they will not work!!!

To turn this off use the code in Fig 18.5

Fig 18.5

```
SET OPTION NON_KEYWORDS =
```

Overall I would suggest that instead of using the options above you actually change the column names to something more meaningful. For example instead of calling a column "date" you call it "business_date". The choice is yours but using keywords can come back to bite you when migrating code!!!

Global Temporary Tables
Indexes

IQ does not use clustered or non-clustered indexes so you can forget about migrating most of your index code into IQ. You should instead look at your data's cardinality and choose the appropriate IQ indexes. If you define a **PRIMARY KEY** then IQ will implicitly build a **HG** index for you, most of the time you will want to put at least a **HG** index on any columns used in keys (implicit), joins, search arguments, group by statements and order by statements!!

The chapter on Indexes covers this more in depth but your index choices in IQ will be based more on cardinality of the column (number of distinct values) and the datatype rather than the grouping of data!

Moving the Data

Insert Location

If you are moving data from another Sybase database (or via a repserver/repagent) then you can potentially use the **INSERT LOCATION** statement to migrate data. This has the advantage of transferring the data from source with no need for intermediary files. The chapter on moving data gives examples of how to use this statement.

BCP and Load Table

You may find that it is quicker or easier to load your IQ database from files. Particularly if you are migrating from Oracle, SQL Server, a mainframe database or another non Sybase product.
 First you will need to get the files from your source database in a format that can be loaded into IQ. Luckily the **LOAD TABLE** statement can accept data in a variety of formats as explained in the chapter on Loading data.
One thing to note is that some data extraction utilities add "Special Characters" into files, for example on SQL Server 2000 you may find that bcp adds the ACII **NULL** character /x00 to the beginning or end of character fields. As will everything, if you allow rubbish data in you will only get rubbish data out.

Identity columns

If you wish to transfer data into a table with an identity column and you wish to retain the identity values then you need to use the IDENTITY_INSERT option (see the chapter on options).

Code Migration

If you are migrating from a Non T-SQL compliant database such as Oracle you could have your work cut out. For example PSQL cannot be used in IQ so you will have to re-write your processes in IQ from scratch, as this is application specific there's not really much I can add. However any ANSI compliant SQL should transfer over fine.

Things are a lot easier if migrating from another T-SQL compliant database such as Sybase ASA, Sybase ASE or Microsoft SQL Server, but there are still some differences between each platforms versions of TSQL. Below are sections on the most common migration issues you may take and for me they have resolved 80-90% of issues.

Keywords

As in the data migration section above, IQ will not allow you to name columns after keyword but it will allow there use as variables as long as they are prefixed with the @ in T-SQL code (see Appendix I). For example Fig 18.6 is valid

Fig 18.6
```
--VALID
DECLARE @DATE DATETIME
SELECT @DATE = GETDATE()

SELECT @DATE
```

I would suggest changing any variables used in this way to a more meaningful name.

Date Differences

In IQ you can have DATE, DATETIME, TIME and TIMESTAMP types. IQ does allow for some implicit conversions of dates these are given in Fig 18.7

Fig 18.7
```
SELECT CONVERT(DATE,'JAN 1 2010') +1 AS ADD_DAYS,
       CONVERT(DATE,'JAN 1 2010') -1 AS SUBTRACT_DAYS,
       CONVERT(DATE,'JAN 28 2010') - CONVERT(DATE,'JAN 1 2010') AS DIFF_IN_DAYS,
       CONVERT(DATE,'JAN 1 2010') + CONVERT(TIME,'13:40:15.888') AS ADD_DATE_AND_TIME
```

Fig 18.7 gives the results

ADD_DAYS	SUBTRACT_DAYS	DIFF_IN_DAYS	ADD_DATE_AND_TIME
2010-01-02 00:00:00.000	2009-12-31 00:00:00.000	27	2010-01-01 13:40:15.888

However there are some short date expressions you cannot use, for example in SQL Server you can use d as shorthand for date as in Fig 18.8, IQ will not allow this as per the chapter on SQL, IQ requires dd for a short form for day. There are others out there as well which may also return compile or runtime errors.

Fig 18.8
```
SELECT DATEADD(d,1,GETDATE())
```

Sub Query Issues

IQ can be funny with sub queries, for example the TOP statement cannot be used in **UPDATE** statements, and the example in Fig 18.9 is invalid.

Fig 18.9

```
UPDATE sales
SET sales_allowed = 'Y'
WHERE sales_id IN (SELECT TOP 1 sales_id FROM sales_allowed)
```

According to Sybase, IQ will only allow sub queries to be used in compliance with 1989 SQL grammar (whatever that is). However IQ does let you use sub queries in the column specification of a **SELECT** statement as in Fig 18.10

Fig 18.10

```
SELECT sales_person,
            (        SELECT region_name
                     FROM sales_regions
                     WHERE region_id = sales.region_id
            ) AS region_name
FROM sales
```

Column Alteration

IQ does not allow you to alter a columns datatype once it has been defined in a table. However you can **ADD** a column and **DROP** a column, so if you are not worried about the position of the column yc can do the following:-

- ADD a new column in the datatype required
- Transfer over the contents from the old column
- Drop the old column
- ADD the old column back in the new datatype
- Transfer from the column you added in the previous step
- Drop the column from the previous step

An example of this is given in Fig 18.11 which updates col1 to a **VARCHAR** (200) by the way of adding transient column called col3.

Fig 18.11

```
/* THE ORIGINAL TABLE DEF IS AS BELOW
CREATE TABLE test_table
(
        col1 VARCHAR(100)          NULL,
        col2 VARCHAR(100)          NULL
)
*/

ALTER TABLE test_table ADD col3 VARCHAR(200)

UPDATE test_table
SET col3 = col1

ALTER TABLE test_table DROP col1

ALTER TABLE test_table ADD col1 VARCHAR(200)

UPDATE test_table
SET col1 = col3

ALTER TABLE test_table DROP col3
```

However IQ does allow you to change the nullability, defaults etc of a pre-existing column, some valid examples are given in Fig 18.12

Fig 18.12

```
ALTER TABLE test_table ALTER col1 NOT NULL
ALTER TABLE test_table ALTER col1 default 'a'
```

Training

Once aspect I have seen ignored on many migrations is the need for training. Sybase IQ does operate in its own variation of T-SQL that may be mostly familiar to developers, but it is not the same. Developers and DBA's need to be aware of the strengths and weaknesses of IQ and indeed of column based architecture in general. The administration and development on IQ is not a simple port from SQL Server or Sybase ASE. In fact many ASA developers will find the transition easier as will some Oracle developers as things such as Global temporary table operate almost exactly the same.

I would suggest you contact a reputable training organisation such as Sybase Education and get all developers and DBA's up to speed with the version of IQ they will use.

Appendix I – IQ Keywords

Sybase IQ Keywords

ACTIVE	ALTER	AS	BEGIN	BIT
CALIBRATE	CAPABILITY	CERTIFICATE	CHECK	CLOSE
COMMITTED	CONNECT	CONVERT	CURRENT	DATE
DEBUG	DECOUPLED	DELETE	DETERMINISTIC	DOUBLE
ELSE	ENCRYPTED	EXCEPT	EXECUTE	EXPRESS
FIRST	FORCE	FULL	GROUP	HISTORY
IN	INNER	INSERT	INT	INTO
JDK	LATERAL	LOGGING	MATCH	MODIFY
NO	NOTIFY	OFF	OPTION	OTHERS
PAGES	PASSTHROUGH	PRECISION	PRIVILEGES	PUBLICATION
READCOMMITTED	READUNCOMMITTED	REFERENCE	REMOTE	REPEATABLE
RESOURCE	REVOKE	ROOT	SAVE	SECURE
SERVICE	SHARE	SPACE	STOP	SYNTAX_ERROR
TB	TIME	TOP	TRANSFER	TSEQUAL
UNIQUE	UPDATE	USER	VALUES	VARYING
WAITFOR	WHILE	WITH_CUBE	WORD	XLOCK
ADD	AND	ASC	BETWEEN	BOTTOM
CALIBRATION	CASCADE	CHAR	CHECKPOINT	COLUMNS
COMPARISONS	CONSTRAINT	CREATE	CURRENT_TIMESTAMP	DBSPACE
DEC	DECRYPTED	DELETING	DISABLE	DROP
ELSEIF	END	EXCEPTION	EXISTING	EXTERNLOGIN
FLOAT	FOREIGN	GB	GROUPING	HOLDLOCK
INACTIVE	INOUT	INSERTING	INTEGER	IQ
JOIN	LEFT	LOGIN	MEMBERSHIP	NAMESPACE
NOHOLDLOCK	NULL	ON	OPTIONS	OUT
PAGLOCK	PASSWORD	PREPARE	PROC	RAISERROR
READONLY	READWRITE	REFERENCES	REMOVE	REPEATABLEREAD
RESTORE	RIGHT	ROW	SAVEPOINT	SELECT
SESSION	SMALLINT	SQLCODE	SUBTRANS	TABLE
TEMPORARY	TIMESTAMP	TRAN	TRIES	UNBOUNDED
UNIQUEIDENTIFIER	UPDATING	UTC	VARBINARY	VIRTUAL
WEB	WINDOW	WITH_LPAREN	WORK	XML
ALL	ANY	AUTO	BIGINT	BREAK
CALL	CASE	CHAR_CONVERT	CHECKSUM	COMMENT
COMPUTES	CONTAINS	CROSS	CURRENT_USER	DBSPACENAME
DECIMAL	DEFAULT	DENSITY	DISTINCT	DYNAMIC
ENABLE	ENDIF	EXCLUDE	EXISTS	FASTFIRSTROW
FOLLOWING	FORWARD	GOTO	HAVING	IDENTIFIED
INDEX	INPUT	INSTALL	INTEGRATED	IS
KB	LIKE	LONG	MESSAGE	NATURAL

NOLOCK	NUMERIC	OPEN	OR	OUTER
PARTIAL	PLAN	PRIMARY	PROCEDURE	RANGE
READPAST	REAL	RELEASE	RENAME	RESERVE
RESTRICT	ROLLBACK	ROWLOCK	SCHEDULE	SENSITIVE
SET	SOAPACTION	SQLSTATE	SUBTRANSACTION	TABLOCK
THEN	TINYINT	TRANSACTION	TRIGGER	UNCOMMITTED
UNKNOWN	UPDLOCK	USING	VARCHAR	VIEW
WHEN	WITH	WITH_ROLLUP	WRITESERVER	ALGORITHM
APPEND	BACKUP	BINARY	BY	CANCEL
CAST	CHARACTER	CLIENTPORT	COMMIT	CONFLICT
CONTINUE	CUBE	CURSOR	DEALLOCATE	DECLARE
DELAY	DESC	DO	ELEMENTS	ENCAPSULATED
ESCAPE	EXEC	EXPLICIT	FETCH	FOR
FROM	GRANT	HIDDEN	IF	INDEX_LPAREN
INSENSITIVE	INSTEAD	INTERSECT	ISOLATION	KEY
LOCK	MB	MODE	NEW	NOT
OF	OPTIMIZATION	ORDER	OVER	PARTITION
PRECEDING	PRINT	PROXY	RAW	READTEXT
RECURSIVE	RELOCATE	REORGANIZE	RESIZING	RETURN
ROLLUP	ROWS	SCROLL	SERIALIZABLE	SETUSER
SOME	START	SYNCHRONIZE	TABLOCKX	TIES
TO	TRANSACTIONAL	TRUNCATE	UNION	UNSIGNED
URL	VALIDATE	VARIABLE	WAIT	WHERE
WITHAUTO	WITHIN	WRITETEXT		

Appendix II – SQLCODE's

Warnings and Success

SQLCODE	Message
104	Row has been updated since last time read
103	Invalid data conversion
102	Using temporary table
101	Value truncated
100	No data
0	Success

Errors

SQLCODE	Message
-72	No database file specified
-74	The selected database is currently inactive
-75	Request to start/stop database denied
-76	Request denied -- no active databases
-77	Database name not unique
-78	Dynamic memory exhausted!
-79	Invalid local database switch
-80	Unable to start database engine
-81	Invalid database engine command line
-82	Unable to start specified database
-83	Specified database not found
-84	Specified database is invalid
-85	Communication error
-86	Not enough memory to start
-87	Database name required to start engine
-88	Client/server communications protocol mismatch
-89	Database engine not running in multi-user mode
-90	Argument %1 of procedure '%2' cannot be null
-91	Procedure '%1' terminated with unhandled exception '%2'
-92	%1' is not a valid class file
-93	Class '%1' has no public field '%2'
-94	Invalid type for field reference
-95	Invalid parameter

-96	Database engine already running
-97	Database's page size too big
-98	Authentication violation
-99	Connections to database have been disabled
-100	Database engine not running
-101	Not connected to SQL database
-102	Too many connections to database
-103	Invalid userid or password
-104	Invalid userid and password on pre-processed module
-105	Cannot be started -- %1
-106	Cannot open log file %1
-107	Error writing to log file
-108	Connection not found
-109	There are still active database connections
-110	Item '%1' already exists
-111	Index name '%1' not unique
-112	Table already has a primary key
-113	Column %1 in foreign key has a different definition than primary key
-114	Number of columns does not match SELECT
-116	Table must be empty
-118	Table '%1' has no primary key
-119	Primary key column '%1' already defined
-120	User '%1' already has grant permission
-121	Do not have permission to %1
-122	Operation would cause a group cycle
-123	User '%1' is not a user group
-124	More columns are being dropped from table %1 than are defined
-125	ALTER clause conflict
-126	Table cannot have two primary keys
-127	Cannot alter a column in an index
-128	Cannot drop a user that owns tables in runtime engine
-130	Invalid statement
-131	Syntax error near '%1'
-132	SQL statement error
-133	Invalid prepared statement type
-134	Feature '%1' not implemented
-135	Language extension
-136	Table '%1' is in an outer join cycle

-137	Table '%1' requires a unique correlation name
-138	DBSpace '%1' not found
-139	More than one table is identified as '%1'
-140	Userid '%1' does not exist
-141	Table '%1' not found
-142	Correlation name '%1' not found
-143	Column '%1' not found
-144	Column '%1' found in more than one table -- need a correlation name
-145	Foreign key name '%1' not found
-146	There is no way to join '%1' to '%2'
-147	There is more than one way to join '%1' to '%2'
-148	Unknown function '%1'
-149	Function or column reference to '%1' in the select list must also appear in a GROUP BY
-151	Sub query allowed only one select list item
-152	Number in ORDER BY is too large
-153	SELECT lists in UNION do not match in length
-154	Wrong number of parameters to function '%1'
-155	Invalid host variable
-156	Invalid expression near '%1'
-157	Cannot convert %1 to a %2
-158	Value %1 out of range for destination
-159	Invalid column number
-160	Can only describe a SELECT statement
-161	Invalid type on DESCRIBE statement
-162	Cannot outer join a view with a UNION or GROUP BY
-170	Cursor has not been declared
-171	Error opening cursor
-172	Cursor already open
-180	Cursor not open
-181	No indicator variable provided for **NULL** result
-182	Not enough fields allocated in SQLDA
-183	Cannot find index named '%1'
-184	Error inserting into cursor
-185	SELECT returns more than one row
-186	Sub query cannot return more than one result
-187	Invalid operation for this cursor
-188	Not enough values for host variables
-189	Unable to find in index '%1' for table '%2'

-190	Cannot update an expression
-191	Cannot modify column '%1' in table '%2'
-192	Update operation attempted on non-updatable query
-193	Primary key for table '%1' is not unique
-194	No primary key value for foreign key '%1' in table '%2'
-195	Column '%1' in table '%2' cannot be NULL
-196	Index '%1' for table '%2' would not be unique
-197	No current row of cursor
-198	Primary key for row in table '%1' is referenced in another table
-199	INSERT/DELETE on cursor can modify only one table
-200	Invalid option '%1' -- no PUBLIC setting exists
-201	Invalid setting for option '%1'
-202	Only PUBLIC settings are allowed for option '%1'
-203	Cannot set a temporary option for user '%1'
-204	Only the DBA can set the option %1
-205	Integrated logons are not permitted
-206	Standard logons are not permitted
-207	Wrong number of values for INSERT
-209	Invalid value for column '%1' in table '%2'
-210	User '%1' has the row in '%2' locked
-211	Not allowed while %1 is using the database
-212	CHECKPOINT command requires a rollback log
-213	Savepoints require a rollback log
-214	Table in use
-215	Procedure in use
-220	Savepoint '%1' not found
-221	rollback TO SAVEPOINT not allowed
-222	Result set not allowed from within an atomic compound statement
-230	Sqlpp/dblib version mismatch
-231	Dblib/database engine version mismatch
-240	Unknown backup operation
-241	Database backup not started
-242	Incomplete transactions prevent transaction log renaming
-243	Unable to delete database file
-244	Transaction log was truncated
-245	Integrated logon failed
-246	Integrated logons are not supported for this database
-247	The integrated loginid guest can only be mapped to the guest database userid

-248	Cannot map a loginid to the sys or public userid
-249	The loginid '%1' is already mapped to userid '%2'
-250	Identifier '%1' too long
-251	Foreign key '%1' for table '%2' duplicates an existing foreign key
-260	Variable '%1' not found
-261	There is already a variable named '%1'
-262	Label '%1' not found
-263	Invalid absolute or relative offset in FETCH
-264	Wrong number of variables in FETCH
-265	Procedure '%1' not found
-267	COMMIT/rollback not allowed within atomic operation
-270	Cannot drop a user that owns procedures in runtime engine
-274	Procedure calls have nested too deeply
-280	Publication '%1' not found
-281	Table '%1' has publications
-282	Subscription to '%1' for '%2' already exists
-283	Subscription to '%1' for '%2' not found
-284	User '%1' is already the publisher for this database
-285	User '%1' is not a remote user for this database
-286	Remote message type '%1' not found
-287	Passthrough statement inconsistent with current passthrough
-294	Format string argument number %1 is invalid
-295	Cannot uniquely identify rows in cursor
-296	Error number %1 for RAISERROR is less than 17000
-297	User-defined exception signalled
-298	Attempted two active database requests
-299	Statement interrupted by user
-300	Run time SQL error -- %1
-301	Internal database error %1 -- transaction rolled back
-302	Terminated by user -- transaction rolled back
-304	Disk full '%1' -- transaction rolled back
-305	I/O error %1 -- transaction rolled back
-306	Deadlock detected
-307	All threads are blocked
-308	Connection was terminated
-312	User '%1' already has membership in group '%2'
-313	The loginid '%1' has not been mapped to any database userid
-400	Invalid HLI command syntax

-401	Invalid HLI cursor name
-402	Invalid HLI statement name
-403	Invalid HLI host variable name
-404	Invalid HLI host variable value
-405	Invalid HLI callback function
-407	An argument passed to an HLI function was invalid
-610	User message %1 already exists
-611	TransactSQL feature not supported
-612	User message %1 not found
-613	User-defined type %1 not found
-614	Cannot drop a user that owns messages or datatypes
-615	Parameter '%1' not found in procedure '%2'
-616	Too many columns in table
-617	Calling functions outside the database engine is not supported
-618	Mismatch between external function platform specifier and current operating system
-619	Need a dynamic library name
-620	Could not load dynamic library '%1'
-621	Could not find '%1' in dynamic library '%2'
-622	Could not allocate resources to call external function
-623	Data definition statements not allowed in procedures
-624	Expression has unsupported datatype
-625	Too many parameters to this external procedure call
-626	A thread used internally could not be started
-627	Disallowed language extension detected in syntax near '%1'
-628	Division by zero
-629	Invalid escape character '%1'
-630	Invalid escape sequence '%1'
-631	RAISERROR executed: %1
-632	WITH CHECK OPTION violated for view '%1'
-633	Update operation attempted on a read-only cursor
-634	Unterminated C string
-635	GRANT of column permission on view not allowed
-636	Duplicate referencing column
-637	Duplicate insert column
-638	Right truncation of string data
-639	Parameter name missing in call to procedure '%1'
-640	Invalid descriptor index
-641	Error in assignment

-642	Invalid SQL descriptor name
-644	Invalid database page size
-645	Database creation failed
-646	Could not load the store DLL %1
-647	Could not execute store DLL (%1) entry point.
-648	Cannot create item (%1) in the specified DBSpace.
-649	Field '%1' of class '%2' cannot be null
-650	Index type specification of '%1' is invalid.
-651	An attempt to delete database '%1' failed.
-652	Could not decompress class '%1' from Jar.
-653	Cannot remove class '%1': member of Jar
-654	The connection parameters file could not be found.
-655	There was an error parsing the connection parameter string. Please check the string or the connection parameter file.
-656	Unable to connect to server '%1': %2
-658	Remote server %1 is currently configured as read only.
-659	Remote server %1 could not be found. Add the server using CREATE SERVER.
-660	Server %1: %2
-661	Backwards scrolling cursors are not supported for remote objects.
-662	Cannot serialize java object with class %1
-663	Cannot deserialize java object with class %1
-664	Database is active
-665	Database %1 needs recovery
-666	The table '%1' could not be found.
-667	Could not access column information for the table '%1'.
-668	Cursor is restricted to FETCH NEXT operations
-669	Method '%1' cannot be called at this time
-670	Invalid class byte code
-671	Parameter not registered as output parameter
-672	Database upgrade failed
-673	Database upgrade not possible
-674	Statement's size limit is invalid
-675	Java virtual machine could not be started
-676	The specified transaction isolation is invalid
-678	Index name '%1' is ambiguous
-679	Not enough memory is allocated to the java virtual machine for remote access.
-680	Invalid expression in WHERE clause of TransactSQL outer join
-681	Invalid join type used with TransactSQL outer join
-682	1%

-683	The cursor name '%1' already exists
-684	rollback occurred due to deadlock during prefetch
-686	Cannot make a static reference to nonstatic variable '%1' in class '%2'
-687	Syntax error, cannot specify IQ specific options without specifying IQ PATH
-688	Unsupported character set `%1'
-689	Input parameter index out of range
-690	Return value cannot be set
-691	Could not load the backup/restore DLL %1
-692	Could not execute backup/restore DLL (%1) entry point.
-693	JDBC feature '%1' not supported
-761	Server capability name %1 could not be found in the SYSCAPABILITYNAME table.
-1000000	Both QUOTES and ESCAPES options must be off. %1
-1000002	Cannot get index id from the catalog. %1
-1000003	Cross-database joins are not supported. (%2 and %3) %1
-1000004	Index '%2' already exists and has the same join fields as proposed index'%3'. %1
-1000005	Join index '%2' already exists and has same the join fields as proposed index '%3'. %1
-1000007	Index '%2' was not closed properly. %1
-1000008	Unknown error. %1
-1000009	Cannot DISABLE index '%2'. It is open Read/Write and may have updates pending. %1
-1000010	Cannot disable index '%2'. The index is in use. %1
-1000011	Transaction %2 attempted to access an object created by transaction %3. %1
-1000012	Index '%2' cannot be closed because it has %3 users. %1
-1000014	%2 MB is not sufficient for the load, update, or delete. %1
-1000022	Index '%2' has an invalid index type: %3. %1
-1000024	For table pair %2, table '%3' has a datatype mismatch for column %4. %1
-1000026	The join virtual table for table '%2' has duplicate columns in positions %3 and %4. %1
-1000027	The join virtual table '%2' does not have any data. %1
-1000029	Cannot open the requested object for write in the current transaction (%2). Another user has write access in transaction %3. %1
-1000031	Join Index '%1' created from the following join relations:
-1000035	Using views in CREATE JOIN INDEX is not supported. %1
-1000049	%2' is being used in a self join. Self joins are not allowed. %1
-1000051	Cannot retrieve a row from the SYSIQJOINIXTABLE system table. %1
-1000052	Cannot delete a row from the SYSIQJOINIXTABLE system table
-1000053	Cannot commit changes to the SYSIQJOINIXTABLE system table. %1
-1000054	Cannot open %2 in Meta (exclusive) mode. Object is already open. %1
-1000055	Warning: %1
-1000056	Calling functions outside the database engine is not supported
-1000057	Column '%2' has an unknown datatype: '%3'. %1

-1000058	Unable to synchronize join index %1.
-1000060	Column '%2', PRECISION (%3) cannot be greater than %4. %1
-1000061	Column %2 PRECISION (%3) cannot be less than 0. %1
-1000062	Cannot add column with not null constraint on table %2 with data. %1
-1000064	Column %2 cannot be altered because it participates in join %3. %1
-1000065	Table %2 MUST be owned by the creator of the join. %1
-1000066	ALTER on the column would interfere with the natural join to table %2 in join %3. % 1
-1000067	Table '%2' is not defined in the catalog. %1
-1000068	The '%1' join index is in use for table '%2'.
-1000078	IQ PAGE SIZE of '%2' for database '%3' is not valid. %1
-1000079	IQ SIZE of '%2' for database '%3' is not valid. %1
-1000080	Join index %1 already synchronized.
-1000081	The field array for the table '%2' must have at least 1 entry; it has %3 entries. %1
-1000082	The insert must contain all table's '%2' columns because it participates in one or more joins. %1
-1000083	The field array entry must be given a name. %1
-1000084	The %2th join field array entry for table '%3' must have a name. %1
-1000085	The join field array for table '%2' must have at least one entry. %1
-1000095	The join index %1 could not be used in the query because it needs synchronization.
-1000097	DBCC: Parse Error in DBCC command at '%2'. %1
-1000098	Creating a join index on 'varchar' datatype column of size > 255 is not supported. %1
-1000099	The PAGE SIZE divided by the BLOCK SIZE must be equal to 2, 4, 8, or 16. Database: %2 PAGE SIZE: %3 BLOCK SIZE: %4. %1
-1000100	Cannot INSERT to or LOAD a join virtual table. %1
-1000106	Local temporary table, %2, must be committed in order to create an index. %1
-1000113	Field %2 does not have an FP index. %1
-1000115	You cannot DELETE from a join virtual table. (%2) %1
-1000118	Join index %2 was not found in the catalog. %1
-1000120	Join %2 was not found in the catalog. %1
-1000125	Table %2 is not part of join index %3. %1
-1000128	You must delete from join index %2 before you can delete from table %3. %1
-1000132	In table '%2', the START ROW ID value (%3)must be greater than %4. Data has already been inserted at this location. %1
-1000133	When inserting into table '%2', the column count (%3) must be between 1 and %4. %1
-1000134	Column '%2' is being inserted into twice by this insert command. %1
-1000135	Cannot open the existence list for table '%2'. %1
-1000136	A mismatch exists between the existence bitmaps in the insert object. %1
-1000137	While inserting, 'table '%2' already had a Complete started. %1

-1000139	You cannot insert into table '%2' past the original end of the table while there are %3 join virtual tables based on it. %1
-1000140	You cannot change column '%2' because it is a 'link' column. %1
-1000141	Column '%2' must be included in the LOAD since it is used in a join. %1
-1000145	The insert for table '%2' has no insertable columns in the column list. %1
-1000151	NOT **NULL** column '%2' was not included in this insert. Data is needed at row %3. %1
-1000152	The **NOT NULL** column '%2' was not included in this insert. %1
-1000153	Table '%2', pass-x index count mismatch(%3/%4). %1
-1000157	Columns for the index must be in ascending order. %1
-1000158	An Identity size mismatch has occurred. The current transaction will rollback. %1
-1000162	Unable to create the requested object. %1
-1000163	%1 not supported.
-1000164	Only %1 supported.
-1000165	Only a single foreign key constraint can be created on the same foreign key column(s) and same candidate key column(s).
-1000167	Cannot %3 table %2 because of RI concurrency conflict. %1
-1000168	Cannot create %1 HG index because one already exists on the given columns.
-1000169	Cannot create unique HG index because primary key or unique constraint already exists on the given columns.
-1000170	Cannot create a duplicate '%2' index '%3'. %1
-1000185	Cannot drop table %1 because foreign keys still reference it.
-1000186	Cannot create foreign key constraint on a candidate key that is also a foreign key.
-1000187	Unable to implicitly convert column '%2' to datatype (%3) from datatype (%4). %1
-1000189	DDL statements cannot proceed while the %2 is in an out of space condition. %1
-1000223	Cannot SYNCHRONIZE join index %2. %1
-1000226	Location string passed to the attached database insert was invalid. %1
-1000227	Cannot load data with both BINARY and delimited columns. %1
-1000229	Only BINARY [WITH **NULL** BYTE] can be used as a column specification when using UNLOAD FORMAT. %1
-1000230	Columns that allow nulls must use the WITH **NULL** BYTE option. %1
-1000234	Record size of unloaded data: %2, does not match with record size of the load: %3. %1
-1000237	The total number of variable width columns in the unloaded data, %2, does not match the total number of variable width columns in the LOAD command, %3. %1
-1000238	The platform type of the unloaded data, %2, does not match the platform type on the load, %3. %1
-1000239	UNLOAD version number: %2, does not match the LOAD version number: %3. %1
-1000240	Total number of blocks of unloaded data: %2, does not match with total number of blocks loaded: %3. %1

-1000242	Total number of rows of unloaded data: %2, does not match with total number of rows in the load: %3. %1
-1000243	Unload format number: %2, does not match with load format number: %3. %1
-1000244	The BLOCK FACTOR of unloaded data: %2 does not match the BLOCK FACTOR of the LOAD: %3. %1
-1000245	Tape / File already loaded. Block number %2 repeats. %1
-1000246	The number of rows loaded: %3 does not match the number of rows unloaded: %2. %1
-1000247	The number of blocks loaded: %3 does not match number of blocks unloaded: %2. %1
-1000260	ALTER DBSPACE <DBSpace-name> ADD <number> is not supported.
-1000261	An Adaptive Server IQ system DBSpace, '%2', cannot be renamed. %1
-1000264	DBCC: Ambiguous index name '%2'. Please specify owner. %1
-1000265	DBCC: Index '%2' not found. %1
-1000266	DBCC: Table '%2' not found. %1
-1000267	DBCC: Cannot convert '%2' to an integer percent. %1
-1000268	DBCC: The target '%2' overlaps an earlier target. %1
-1000269	DBCC: Multiple modes specified with a write mode. %1
-1000270	DBCC: FP Recreate failed for index '%2'. %1
-1000271	DBCC: Table '%2' is a temporary table, a view, or not an IQ table. %1
-1000272	DBCC: Invalid table name '%2'. %1
-1000273	DBCC: Invalid index name '%2'. %1
-1000274	DBCC: Upgrade options can be used only with CHECK or REPAIR mode. %1
-1000275	DBCC cannot process object '%2' at the current transaction level. %1
-1000276	At least one mode and target must be specified to DBCC. %1
-1000277	allocation database is the only command allowed in drop leaks mode. %1
-1001006	Data exception - data type conversion is not possible. %1
-1001019	Function not supported on varchars longer than 255 %2, %1
-1001030	Feature, %2, is not supported. %1
-1003001	Cannot convert to Adaptive Server IQ datatype: %2 from Client Library datatype %3. %1
-1003002	CtLibrary Error: %2, Severity: %3, Origin: %4, Layer: %5\nError Message: %6\nOS Error: %7, OS Message
-1003003	Adaptive Server Error: %2, Severity: %3, State: %4, Line: %5\nServer Name: %7\nError Messages: %8. %1
-1003004	COMPUTE values may not be used in attached database queries. %1
-1003005	Connectivity libraries cannot be found (check your dynamic library search path). Selects from attached databases are not possible without these libraries. %1
-1003006	A call to ct_con_props failed trying to get the msglist from the connection. %1
-1005017	You cannot DELETE from a join virtual table. (%2) %1

-1005024	Estimate number: %2 exceed the DEFAULT_MAX_CUBE_RESULT of GROUP BY CUBE or ROLLUP %1
-1005025	Query rejected as too complex. After join simplifications there were still %2 tables to be joined, which exceeds the current setting of Max_Join_Enumeration. %1
-1005027	An error occurs during unistring conversion --%2. %1
-1006130	Object not open for file %2 %1
-1008000	Users are not allowed to create FP index. FP indexes are created automatically when the table is created.
-1008001	The user cannot create indexes on a join virtual table.
-1008002	There is a join index using table '%1'. The table cannot be dropped until the join index is dropped or altered.
-1008003	Cannot drop join virtual table '%1'.
-1008004	Cannot DROP index '%1'.
-1008005	Cannot ALTER join virtual table '%1'.
-1008006	You cannot specify a DEFAULT value for a column.
-1008007	The ALTER TABLE option '%1' is not supported by IQ.
-1008008	You cannot TRUNCATE a join virtual table.
-1008009	This statement is not supported by Adaptive Server IQ.
-1008010	A request was made to delete the primary key constraint, but the primary key cannot be found.
-1008012	This single column unique index/constraint must be ENFORCED.
-1008013	This multi-column unique index/constraint must be UNENFORCED
-1008014	This foreign key must be UNENFORCED
-1008015	This check constraint must be UNENFORCED
-1008016	Cannot ALTER DELETE a column that has a unique or primary key constraint.
-1008017	Cannot ALTER DELETE a column that has a multi-column index.
-1008018	Command prohibited on an active multiplex server.
-1008019	Multiplex is currently inactive.
-1008020	Multiplex command or request is unimplemented.
-1008021	The SYSIQFILE table is not configured for this server to run in a multiplex.
-1008022	Cannot find a license for multiplex.
-1008023	Cannot start multiplex query server on a simplex database.
-1008024	Cannot start multiplex write server while another one is running; if the write server did not shutdown correctly, you must restart with the override switch.
-1008025	Cannot run multiplex query server while the write server is running simplex.
-1008026	Multiplex query server out of synchronization with write server.
-1008027	DBSPACES have been added or dropped in simplex without updating multiplex.
-1008029	Cannot create foreign key to an unenforced primary key or unenforced unique constraint.

-1008030	Only IQ index types can be created on IQ tables within a Parallel IQ block.
-1008031	Cannot do Create Index commands on global or local temporary tables or catalog server tables in a Parallel IQ block.
-1009005	Cannot create an HNG index on a column having a floating point datatype. %1
-1009028	Cannot create a WD index with more than 256 separators. %1
-1009094	Cannot use raw partition for MESSAGE LOG or ROW LOG. %1
-1009095	MESSAGE LOG and ROW LOG cannot be the same on-disk file. %1
-1009096	%3 integrity constraint limit (%2) exceeded. %1
-1009097	Cumulative total (%2) for all integrity constraint violations exceeded. %1
-1009098	Invalid MESSAGE LOG or ROW LOG filename. %1
-1009100	Database segment '%2' is not valid. It is of type '%3'. Type BTYPE_DBEXT was expected. This segment cannot be used. %1
-1009101	Database segment '%2' is not valid. PhysicalNBlocks Found: %3 PhysicalNBlocks expected: 1. This segment cannot be used. %1
-1009106	Database segment '%2' is not valid. The catalog file id is incorrect. FileID found: %3 FileID expected: %4. This segment cannot be used. %1
-1009108	Database segment '%2' is not valid. Startblock found in the header: %3 Startblock expected: %4. This segment cannot be used. %1
-1009115	Database segment '%2' is not valid. %3 imaginary freelist blocks were found, but %4 imaginary freelist blocks were expected. This segment cannot be used. %1
-1009118	Database segment '%2' is not valid. %3 freelist blocks were found, but %4 freelist blocks were expected. This segment cannot be used. %1
-1009135	Cannot perform requested command as there is a CREATE DBSPACE command in progress. %1
-1009136	Cannot perform requested command as there is a DROP DBSPACE command in progress. %1
-1009137	Cannot perform DDL command now as a DDL command is already in progress. %1
-1009138	Join index '%2' is in use. %1
-1009139	Cannot perform requested command as there is a CHECKPOINT command in progress. %1
-1009141	Table %2 cannot be found in the IQ store. %1
-1009146	Cannot perform requested command as there is a DBCC command in progress. %1
-1009148	Cannot modify main store on a multiplex query server
-1009149	%2 Internal Inconsistency: %1 (%3, %4, %5)
-1009150	Cannot %3 table %2 because of RI concurrency conflict. %1
-1009151	Cannot %2 CK %3 row %4 because of RI violation. %1
-1009152	Cannot %2 FK %3 row %4 because of RI violation. %1
-1009153	Cannot remove row %3 from CK %2 during LOAD cleanup because of RI violation. %1
-1009412	The INSERT ... LOCATION statement must use a SELECT statement. %1

-1010000	The DBSpace file '%2' already exists. %1
-1010001	Cannot use raw partition for DBSpace file '%2'. %1
-1010002	File format mismatch; database %2; Adaptive Server IQ: %3. %1
-1010003	Catalog format mismatch: database %2; Adaptive Server IQ: %3. %1
-1010004	Stored procedure format mismatch: database %2; Adaptive Server IQ: %3
-1010005	File format date mismatch: database %2; Adaptive Server IQ: %3. %1
-1010006	Maximum blocks for DBSpace '%2' is %3 blocks; %4 blocks were specified. %1
-1010007	The number of blocks (%3) for DBSpace file '%2' must match the number of blocks in the raw partition (%4).
-1010008	For an IQ PAGE SIZE of %2, the DBSpace file '%3' must have at least %4 MB. %1
-1010009	Improper use of cursor - programming error %1
-1010010	An invalid attribute flag was passed to the cursor
-1010011	Not enough server threads available for this query.
-1010012	The cursor is in an invalid state. %1
-1010013	Raw partition %2 is already in use. %1
-1011004	Cannot drop primary key or unique constraint because a foreign key still references it.
-1013017	An internal error occurred while calling a method on a db_sql_*_identifier. Object does not have an IIndex Handle. %1
-1013024	ALTER TABLE MODIFY <column> <datatype> is not supported. %1
-1013025	ALTER TABLE MODIFY <default-value> is not supported. %1
-1013031	An error occurred while calling a method on db_sql_*_identifier. Object does not have an ITable handle. %1
-1013033	An error occurred while calling a method on db_sql_*_identifier. Object does not have an IJoinIndex handle. %1
-1013039	An internal error occurred while constructing a db_sql_*_identifier. The IColumn does not belong to the ITable. %1
-1013042	An error occurred while constructing a db_sql_*_identifier. The IIndex handle does not belong to the ITable. %1
-1013044	An internal error occurred. An invalid table type was encountered. %1
-1013045	An invalid file name ('%2') was specified for a **LOAD TABLE**. The file name has zero length. %1
-1013046	An internal error occurred. An invalid index type was encountered. %1
-1013050	The Temp_Extract_Name1 option is set. The current operation will be rolled back. %1
-1013052	The BLOCK FACTOR for this LOAD cannot be zero. %1
-1013054	Delimiter '%2' must be 1 to 4 characters in length. %1
-1013061	Missing row delimiter detected during a row delimiter insert. %1
-1013063	Expected raw-data column type '%2' on input, but no input data exists.
-1013064	Row delimiter not seen during scan of input file. At least one of the input rows is missing a terminator. %1

-1013091	Column pairs %2=%3 could not be matched. %1
-1013092	MONITOR for this database, connection and buffer cache already exists. %1
-1013094	A matching column cannot be found for the foreign keys in %2. %1
-1013095	CREATE JOIN does not support joining joins. %1
-1013097	Join Index %2 not unique. %1
-1013098	The foreign key %2 participates in join %3 and cannot be ALTERed. %1
-1013099	Join Indexes do not support multipart foreign key found in table %2. %1

Appendix III – Connection Parms

Connection Parameters

Parameter Name	Parameter Short Name	Parameter Description
AppInfo <string>	**APP**	This parameter is used by ADO.NET, ODBC, OLE DB or SQL clients Only (Not Open Client or JConnect) to send a string containing data about the client such as the os the client is on, the name of the os user etc. You can see the property value using the connection_property ('AP-PINFO') system function. The string is sent as a set of semi colon delimited key-value pairs. Possible Key Values are:- **API:**- ADO.NET, DBLIB, ODBC (also returned from ASA JDBC driver connections), or OLEDB. **EXE:**- The name of the client executable. **HOST:**- The host name of the client machine. **IP:**- The IP address of the client machine for NetWare and Unix/Linux client machines. **OS:**- The operating system name and version number. **PID:**- The process ID of the client on the client host. **THREAD:**- The thread ID of the client on the client host. **TIMEZONEADJUSTMENT:**- The number of minutes that must be added to the UTC time to display time local to the connection. **VERSION:**- The version of the connection protocol in use.
AutoStart <YES or NO>	**ASTART**	This parameter is used to stop a local server from being started if no connection is found. The default is YES which means that if no server is founf when the connection attempts to connect and you have also specified a database file then the databasebase is started ont he local machine. I suggest setting this to NO to stop this happening.
AutoStop <YES or NO>	**ASTOP**	If the database/server you are connecting to was started using a connection string then it will by default stop when there are no no more active connections. To switch this behaviour off, you need to set this parameter to NO to allow the database to stay up even when there are no active connections (The default behaviour de-scribed above is YES).
CharSet <string>	**CS**	This parameter is used to specify the character set used for the connection. See the Sybase website for allowable character sets for your specific installation.
CommBufferSize <integer>	**CBSIZE**	This is used to set the maximum size in bytes of com-

		munication packets used in the connection. The allow-able values are between 300 and 16000. The default value is the server's buffer size.
CommLinks <string>	**LINKS**	This is used to specify theclient side communication protocols, you may specify Commlinks=ALL if you do not know which protocols to use. Check the Sybase website for allowable protocols for your installation.
Compress <YES or NO>	**COMP**	This parameter is used to specify if compression is to be used for the connection. The default is NO and com-pression cannot be used with TDS or JCONNECT connec-tions. If you obtain slow network transfers for large datasets you may find setting this parameter to YES will help.
CompressionThreshold <Integer>	**COMPTH**	This parameter is used to increase or decrease the limit in bytes of compression for packets of data sent across the connection. You can use this in combination with the COMP parameter. The default is 120 (Sybase rec-ommends to not set below 80). If for example your data is less than the value set in this parameter then it will not be compressed even if compression is on. You need to trade off the CPU time in compressing packets with the time taken to send the data uncompressed.
ConnectionName <string>	**CON**	This parameter is used to name a connection.
DatabaseFile <string>	**DBF**	This parameter is used to specify a database file you want to load and connect to. If you want to connect to a database that is already running then you should use he DSN parameter instead. This parameter will start the dtabase you wish to connect to if it is not already run-ning. You should not use the DBF paramter in conjunc-tion with the DBN parameter as teh DBF parameter is ignored!!
DatabaseName <string>	**DBN**	This parameter is used to specify the database name that you wish to connect to. You should not use the DBF paramter in conjunction with the DBN parameter as teh DBF parameter is ignored!!
DatabaseSwitches <string>	**DBS**	This parameter is used to specify a list of database switches that are to be used to start the database you wish to connect to if it is not already running.
DataSourceName <string>	**DSN**	This parameter specifies to the ODBC driver manager or the SQL library where to look in the registery or odbc.ini file to find ODBC infromation. In other workds it is used to specify the data source name!
DisableMultiRowFetch <YES or NO>	**DMRF**	This parameter can be used to switch off multi-row fetches (the default is NO, i.e. Not disabled). Setting this value to YES is the same as setting the database option PREFETCH to OFF.
EncryptedPassword <string>	**ENP**	This parameter is used to set an encrypted password to be stored in a datasource. As datasources are stored in files or as regeistry settings if they are not encrypted then that may be able to be read by unauthorised users.
Encryption "none" or "simple"	**ENC**	This parameter can be set to none or simple to specify if you want packets encrypted when sent on this connec-

		tion. The "none" option mean no encryption and simple means it will use a simple ASA encryption algorithm supported on all ASA versions.
EngineName <string>	**ENG**	This parameter is used to specify the database server name.
FileDataSourceName <string>	**FILEDSN**	This parameter specifys an ODBC Data source file that contains the connection information you need to connect. Benefits of this are that the Password you connect with will not show up in a ps (unix/Linux) command unlike the PWD parameter.
ForceStart <YES or NO>	**FORCE**	This parameter specifys that you wish to start a database server bu not connect to it. The default is NO.
Idle <Integer>	**IDLE**	This parameter is used to specify the time in minutes that the connection can be idle before it is dropped (The default is 240). As this can also be set at a server level, the value of this parameter overrides any other settings.
Integrated <YES or NO>	**INT**	This parameter can be used to specify that you wish to use an intergrated login, the default is NO. When set to YES it will attempt an intergrated login and if it fails and the LOGIN_MODE option is set to "Mixed" then it will then attempt a standard login. In order to use integrated logins the datbase option LOGIN_MODE must have a value of either "Intergrated" or "Mixed".
LazyClose <YES or NO>	**LCLOSE**	This parameter is used to keep cursors open until the next database request. By default this option is off (NO). Setting this option on (YES) can improve performance if network latency is bad but will keep resources open on the database when they are not needed, it can also cause clients to think cursors are closed when they are still open on the server.
LivenessTimeout <Integer>	**LTO**	This parameter is used to specify the period between liveness packets sent across the connection to ensure it is still intact. The default is 120 seconds although when there are more than 200 connections the server will up this value. A liveness packet is sent at the specified interval and if the client does not dectect the liveness packet within the interval then the connection is teminated.
Logfile <string>	**LOG**	This parameter is used to specify a log file that is used by the client to send debugging and error messages to a file. The defualt is no log file. This parameter allows you to set different log files on a conncection by connection basis.
Password <string>	**PWD**	This parameter is used to provide a Non Encrypted password (Encrypted passwords use the ENP parameter.
PrefetchBuffer <Integer>	**PBUF**	This parameter is used to specify the maximum memoery that is used for buffering rows in kilobytes. The default is 64 on most platforms (16 on Windows CE). You can increase this value to allow more memory for GET DATA requests.

PrefetchRows <Integer>	PROWS	This parameter sets the maximum rows that the connection can prefetch from queries sent acorss the connection. The default is 10. It is suggested you only increase this value (not decrease). Also when you increase the value then a performance benefit can occur when the connection fetches several hundred rows and the connection is on the same network. An also when the network connection is on a slow network.
StartLine <string>	START	This parameter is used to start a database server that is not already running. The supplied value is a command line string that is used to start the server.
Unconditional <YES or NO>	UNC	This parameter when switched on (YES) then the dbstop ustility is used to stop the database server even if there are active connections. If it is set to off (NO) then the server is only shut down when there are no active connections. The defaul setting is NO (off).
Userid <string>	UID	Ths is used to specify the user Id which you wish to use to connect to the database.

Appendix IV – Code Pages

Supported Code Pages

Code Page	Description
1252	Windows Latin-1
37	USA, Canada (Bilingual, French), Netherlands, Portugal, Brazil, Australia
273	IBM Austria, Germany
277	IBM Denmark, Norway
278	IBM Finland, Sweden
280	IBM Italy
284	IBM Catalan/Spain, Spanish Latin America
285	IBM United Kingdom, Ireland
297	IBM France
420	IBM Arabic
424	IBM Hebrew
437	MS-DOS United States, Australia, New Zealand, South Africa
500	EBCDIC 500V1
737	PC Greek
775	PC Baltic
838	IBM Thailand extended SBCS
850	MS-DOS Latin-1
852	MS-DOS Latin-2
855	IBM Cyrillic
856	IBM Hebrew
857	IBM Turkish
858	Variant of Cp850 with Euro character
860	MS-DOS Portuguese
861	MS-DOS Icelandic
862	PC Hebrew
863	MS-DOS Canadian French
864	PC Arabic
865	MS-DOS Nordic
866	MS-DOS Russian
868	MS-DOS Pakistan
869	IBM Modern Greek
870	IBM Multilingual Latin-2
871	IBM Iceland
874	IBM Thai
875	IBM Greek
918	IBM Pakistan (Urdu)
921	IBM Latvia, Lithuania (AIX, DOS)

922	IBM Estonia (AIX, DOS)
930	Japanese Katakana-Kanji mixed with 4370 UDC, superset of 5026
933	Korean Mixed with 1880 UDC, superset of 5029
935	Simplified Chinese Host mixed with 1880 UDC, superset of 5031
937	Traditional Chinese Host mixed with 6204 UDC, superset of 5033
939	Japanese Latin Kanji mixed with 4370 UDC, superset of 5035
942	IBM OS/2 Japanese, superset of Cp932
942	C Variant of Cp942
943	IBM OS/2 Japanese, superset of Cp932 and Shift-JIS
943	C Variant of Cp943
948	OS/2 Chinese (Taiwan) superset of 938
949	PC Korean
949	C Variant of Cp949
950	PC Chinese (Hong Kong, Taiwan)
964	AIX Chinese (Taiwan)
970	AIX Korean
1006	IBM AIX Pakistan (Urdu)
1025	IBM Multilingual Cyrillic: Bulgaria, Bosnia, Herzegovinia, Macedonia (FYR)
1026	IBM Latin-5, Turkey
1046	IBM Arabic - Windows
1097	IBM Iran (Farsi)/Persian
1098	IBM Iran (Farsi)/Persian (PC)
1112	IBM Latvia, Lithuania
1122	IBM Estonia
1123	IBM Ukraine
1124	IBM AIX Ukraine
1140	Variant of Cp037 with Euro character
1141	Variant of Cp273 with Euro character
1142	Variant of Cp277 with Euro character
1143	Variant of Cp278 with Euro character
1144	Variant of Cp280 with Euro character
1145	Variant of Cp284 with Euro character
1146	Variant of Cp285 with Euro character
1147	Variant of Cp297 with Euro character
1148	Variant of Cp500 with Euro character
1149	Variant of Cp871 with Euro character
1250	Windows Eastern European
1251	Windows Cyrillic
1253	Windows Greek
1254	Windows Turkish
1255	Windows Hebrew
1256	Windows Arabic
1257	Windows Baltic
1258	Windows Vietnamese
1381	IBM OS/2, DOS People's Republic of China (PRC)

1383	IBM AIX People's Republic of China (PRC)
33722	IBM-eucJP - Japanese (superset of 5050)
ASCII	American Standard Code for Information Interchange
ISO8859_1	ISO 8859-1, Latin alphabet No. 1
UnicodeBig	Sixteen-bit Unicode Transformation Format, big-endian byte order, with byte-order
UnicodeBigUnmarked	Sixteen-bit Unicode Transformation Format, big-endian byte order
UnicodeLittle	Sixteen-bit Unicode Transformation Format, little-endian byte order, with byte-order
UnicodeLittleUnmarked	Sixteen-bit Unicode Transformation Format, little-endian byte order
UTF8	Eight-bit Unicode Transformation Format
UTF-16	Sixteen-bit Unicode Transformation Format, byte order specified by a mandatory
Big5	Big5, Traditional Chinese
Big5_HKSCS	Big5 with Hong Kong extensions, Traditional Chinese
Big5_Solaris	Big5 with seven additional Hanzi ideograph character mappings for the Solaris
EUC_CN	GB2312, EUC encoding, Simplified Chinese
EUC_JP	JIS X 0201, 0208, 0212, EUC encoding, Japanese
EUC_KR	KS C 5601, EUC encoding, Korean
EUC_TW	CNS11643 (Plane 1-3), EUC encoding, Traditional Chinese
GB18030	Simplified Chinese, PRC standard
GBK	GBK, Simplified Chinese
ISCII91	ISCII91 encoding of Indic scripts
ISO2022CN	ISO 2022 CN, Chinese (conversion to Unicode only)
ISO2022CN_CNS	CNS 11643 in ISO 2022 CN form, Traditional Chinese (conversion from Unicode only)
ISO2022CN_GB	GB 2312 in ISO 2022 CN form, Simplified Chinese (conversion from Unicode only)
ISO2022JP	JIS X 0201, 0208 in ISO 2022 form, Japanese
ISO2022KR	ISO 2022 KR, Korean
ISO8859_2	ISO 8859-2, Latin alphabet No. 2
ISO8859_3	ISO 8859-3, Latin alphabet No. 3
ISO8859_4	ISO 8859-4, Latin alphabet No. 4
ISO8859_5	ISO 8859-5, Latin/Cyrillic alphabet
ISO8859_6	ISO 8859-6, Latin/Arabic alphabet
ISO8859_7	ISO 8859-7, Latin/Greek alphabet
ISO8859_8	ISO 8859-8, Latin/Hebrew alphabet
ISO8859_9	ISO 8859-9, Latin alphabet No. 5
ISO8859_13	ISO 8859-13, Latin alphabet No. 7
ISO8859_15_FDIS	ISO 8859-15, Latin alphabet No. 9
JIS0201	JIS X 0201, Japanese
JIS0208	JIS X 0208, Japanese
JIS0212	JIS X 0208, Japanese
JISAutoDetect	Detects and converts from Shift-JIS, EUC-JP, ISO 2022 JP (conversion to Unicode only)
Johab	Johab, Korean
KOI8_R	KOI8-R, Russian
MS874	Windows Thai
MS932	Windows Japanese
MS936	Windows Simplified Chinese
MS949	Windows Korean

MS950	Windows Traditional Chinese
MacArabic	Macintosh Arabic
MacCentralEurope	Macintosh Latin-2
MacCroatian	Macintosh Croatian
MacCyrillic	Macintosh Cyrillic
MacDingbat	Macintosh Dingbat
MacGreek	Macintosh Greek
MacHebrew	Macintosh Hebrew
MacIceland	Macintosh Iceland
MacRoman	Macintosh Roman
MacRomania	Macintosh Romania
MacSymbol	Macintosh Symbol
MacThai	Macintosh Thai
MacTurkish	Macintosh Turkish
MacUkraine	Macintosh Ukraine
SJIS	Shift-JIS, Japanese
TIS620	TIS620, Thai

INDEX

CPSIA information can be obtained at www.ICGtesting.com
Printed in the USA
238778LV00002B/70/P

9 781446 657584